The Essential Book of Homesteading

HOMEMADE LIVING

The Essential Book of Homesteading

Ashley English

The Ultimate Guide to Sustainable Living

LARK

New York

New York

An Imprint of Sterling Publishing Co., Inc.
1166 Avenue of the Americas
New York, NY 10036

ISBN 978-1-4547-1020-2

Distributed in Canada by Sterling Publishing Co., Inc.
c/o Canadian Manda Group, 664 Annette Street
Toronto, Ontario, Canada M6S 2C8
Distributed in the United Kingdom by GMC Distribution Services
Castle Place, 166 High Street, Lewes, East Sussex, England BN7 1XU
Distributed in Australia by NewSouth Books
45 Beach Street, Coogee, NSW 2034, Australia

For information about custom editions, special sales, and premium and corporate purchases,
please contact Sterling Special Sales at 800-805-5489 or specialsales@sterlingpublishing.com.

Manufactured in China

2 4 6 8 10 9 7 5 3 1

www.sterlingpublishing.com
www.larkcrafts.com

The pages of this book are richer thanks to the contributed photos. Much gratitude is owed
to the following individuals: Patrick Barber (pages 23, 31, 32), Chris Bryant (page 117, 307, 320),
Laura Carmer (page 63), Cathy Caspersz (page 24), Jean Cobb (page 301, 309), Jen Doumen (page 308),
Deborah Felkel (page 271), Andre Garant (page 158), Sara B. Hodge (page 291), Andrew Langley (page 261),
Robert Masse (page 286), Nicole McConville (pages 12), Ben Melger (page 157), Melissa Mills (page 3),
Rhonda Rolle (page 179), Melinda Seyler (pages 23, 31), Enzie Shahmiri (page 243), Sarah Shevett (page 158),
Krista Theiss (page 261, 284), Mike Tuggle (page 267), Tim vonHolten (page 31), Bob Voors (page 261),
Kenneth Walny (page 290), and Daniel Worrall (page 22).

Contents

Introduction

In barnyards and backyards, on rooftops and in alleyways, a movement is happening. You might've noticed your neighbor installing raised beds in their front yard, appro-priating the grass to make way for tomatoes, basil, and zucchini. Perhaps you've seen flyers for jam-making classes advertised at the local feed and seed store. Maybe you've heard that the nearby public school has added a flock of hens and several beehives to the schoolyard, adjacent to the swings and jungle gym. From coast to coast, continent-to-continent, people are excited about taking back the reins of where their food comes from. They're curious, inspired, and motivated to learn what it takes to trans-form cucumbers into puckery pickles, a gallon of milk into stretchy, pliant mozzarella, and the edible efforts of chickens and honeybees into nutrient-dense eggs and sweet, ambrosial honey.

What all of these efforts have in common is that they're unified under the umbrella of "homesteading." While that word might conjure a sprawling, rambling farmhouse with a wraparound porch, horses in the stable, and a cow in the pasture, modern homesteading is much more open to interpretation. To understand its present use, though, it's helpful to consider the origins of the term. The Homesteading Act of 1862 was the first of several acts created by the

United States federal government that gave a qualifying applicant ownership of public land for little to no cost. Settlers were given 160 acres, called a "homestead," if they were at least twenty-one years old or considered the head of the household, and pledged to live and farm on the land for a minimum of five years, building a home and caring for it during their tenure. Immigrants, women, and freed slaves could all apply. The program formally ended in 1976 under the Federal Land Policy and Management Act.

Though it had its fair share of criticisms, including abuse by corporations posing as individuals in order to obtain land and restrict others' access to it, as well as displacing indigenous Americans, it did serve as a catalyst of inspiration for future movements. During the 1970s, homesteading came to refer to both those leaving city life and returning "back to the land" of their rural ancestors, as well as to an overall lifestyle, one emphasizing self-sufficiency and environmental conscientiousness. In modern parlance, the geographical location of a homesteader matters considerably less than the mindset. Urbanites, suburbanites, and rural dwellers are all on equal footing when it comes to individual definitions of homesteading. It's now nearly as easy to find classes on wild foraging for foods in Central Park as it is in a rural town in the Central Plains states.

This interest in a more hands-on, direct approach to the growing and preparation of one's food is also international in scope. Homesteaders from Brussels to Beijing can be found brewing kombucha in their kitchens, tossing scratch corn to small flocks, and rendering juicy strawberries into jam. Whenever naysayers challenge the time and energy such endeavors might potentially incur, I typically respond (whether verbally or mentally) with the "memory" angle. Do you remember the first time you bought a random carton of eggs from the grocery store? Do you remember the first time you put a jar of shelf-ready dill pickles in your shopping cart? Highly unlikely. But the first time your small flock laid eggs? The first time you pressed grape juice and transformed it into jelly? The first time you pressed curd into homemade feta? Absolutely, you remember. Those activities weren't just satisfying and tasty, they were also deeply empowering.

When we put the herbs and spices of our choosing into a batch of pickles, or pick the blackberries we then boil into jam, or know the farmer whose cow produced the milk we then whip into butter, we put ourselves back into the driver's seat of food production. We not only ensure that we're making food that tastes exactly the way we want it to taste, no longer beholden to and limited by what is offered on the shelves, but also we equip ourselves with a skill set that meets our

most basic human need: to eat. Acquiring the knowledge of, and then actively engaging in food production allows us to outsmart, in a sense, the whims of economic swings, weather patterns, or political volatility. The power to feed our families and ourselves shifts away from the exclusive jurisdiction of grocery stores and large scale food manufacturers, and back into our home kitchens and gardens, providing a profoundly powerful tool in navigating modern life.

Within the pages of *The Essential Book of Homesteading*, you'll find my time-honored tips and suggestions for steering the ship, so to speak, of food production and preservation in your home. Keeping a flock of chickens, canning and preserving shelf-stable foods, crafting homemade dairy products, and keeping a hive of honeybees are all entry points for shifting the origins of the foods that you and your family consume back into your control. I wish I were sitting there with you, reading alongside, offering encouragement and anecdotes as we flip the pages. Absent that, know that I'm cheering you on, silently, from the sidelines. If I can do it, you can do it. We all can do it. From my home to yours, happy homesteading!

Ashley English

ABOUT THE AUTHOR

Years ago, I was hopping into my car each morning, heading off to a job in a medical office. Things changed, though, when a whirlwind romance quickly resulted in marriage, a little homestead at the end of a dirt road, and just the encouragement and support I needed to make some serious life changes. Combining my long-standing interest and education in nutrition, sustainability, and local food, I made the bold decision to leave my stable office job and try my hand at homesteading. It was a huge leap of faith, but I truly believed there was opportunity waiting in a simpler, pared-down life. My goal was to find ways to nourish both body and soul through mindful food practices. And so I jumped in, rubber boots first, completely unaware of what lay ahead.

In my desire to chronicle both the triumphs and lessons of crafting a homemade life, I started up a blog, *Small Measure* (www.smallmeasure.com). In it, I try to convey the same ideals I live every day: there are small, simple measures you can take to enhance your life while also caring for your family, community, and the larger world. It's been a trial-and-error experiment in living, full of a few pitfalls along with the joy.

I've learned so much along the way, and I hope this book serves as continual encouragement for you. If I did it, you certainly can, too.

Book 1
Keeping Chickens

In the world of homesteading, I tend to think of stewarding a flock of chickens as arriving at the intersection of pragmatism and pleasure. Few other occasions provide the opportunity to obtain a nutritious food while being deeply entertained and heartened in the process. Chickens are such magnificent creatures, and spending time getting to know them is equal parts humbling and hilarious. In this section, we'll discuss all the nitty-gritty details and learned-from-experience tips I've gleaned over my years of keeping backyard chickens. From what to consider before you even start your chicken-keeping journey to breed selection, obtaining birds, housing, feeding, hatching eggs, raising chicks, and health and wellness, I'll walk you through everything it takes to successfully get started with what I've lovingly come to refer to as "chicken tendering."

Chapter 1
What to Consider

Welcome to the wonderful world of chickens! Whether you want your own fresh eggs each morning, desire a trusted, wholesome source of meat, or simply wish to add a new pet to your home, chicken raising offers a multitude of rewards. However, before you crack the first catalog or get misty eyed over some antique feeder, you must address several essential preliminaries. Determining if you have adequate time to care for your flock, whether or not you can even keep chickens where you live, and what your neighbors think about having poultry next door are a few of the concerns to address before you get your heart set on that gorgeous Buff Orpington with the adorable pantaloons.

TIME AFTER TIME

Perhaps the first thing to consider when entertaining the idea of backyard animal husbandry is that caring for chickens takes up time. The amount of time will vary based on their ages as well as the size of your flock. If you opt to start out with chicks, be prepared to allocate several hours each day to babysitting them, making sure they haven't harmed themselves or each other, and that all their physical needs are met. Baby chicks need to be checked several times throughout the day.

If your birds are older, they will still need to be fed, cleaned up after, and, depending on their housing situation, let out in the morning and locked up safely away from predators at night. Eggs should also be gathered several times daily.

MONEY MATTERS

In addition to taking up your time, keeping chickens will also take up some of your money. Start-up costs will be the bulk of your chicken-raising expenses. At minimum, you should plan to spend several hundred dollars for purchasing or building a coop, complete with nesting boxes and perches; acquiring feeders, waterers, and feed; and buying the birds themselves. Your setup can be as simple or elaborate as your budget allows. Thrifty, enterprising individuals can craft a coop from a truck cab or a few 2x4s and some chicken wire. Chicken aesthetes might opt for a modern mobile unit or a chicken ark. We'll cover housing in detail in chapter 4, but be mindful for now that it is important to determine if you can afford to develop your chicken infrastructure. Once your chicken compound is all in place, future costs are generally limited to feed, purchasing new birds, and veterinary fees and medications, should either be needed. As you begin thinking about raising chickens, take the time to run the numbers and make sure you can manage the necessary start-up investment and ongoing costs.

WEATHER OR NOT

Selecting chickens suited to your climate and varying weather conditions is another important consideration. One chicken's balmy paradise is another chicken's hothouse of death. Likewise, a fluffy-feathered Brahma will fair well through frosty New England winters, while a Mediterranean breed such as a Leghorn might have a rough go of it if not properly housed.

As you begin toying with the idea of owning and caring for chickens, don't forget to do a little research on their climate needs. Doing so will go a long way toward preventing unnecessary stress for the both of you. A listing of breeds and climate hardiness can be found on page 15.

SPACE IS THE PLACE

While chickens don't need much space, they do need some. I've seen chickens kept in the 8-x-10-foot (2.4-x-3 m) cement backyard of a Scottish bed-and-breakfast, along with rabbits, goats, pigs, and other animals. At my house, the Ladies have an inordinately large coop and run, owning to the coop's previous incarnation as a dog shed for two immense German Shepherds.

Your particular needs will be based on the size of your flock, the size of your breeds, and the amount of outdoor space your chickens will be allocated, if any. In general, chickens need 4 square feet (1.2 m²) per bird if given access to outdoor runs and 10 square feet (3 m²) per bird if they have no outdoor access. That amount will be halved if your birds are bantams. More about space considerations will be discussed in chapter 4 on housing.

It is important to evaluate what space you have available before you begin purchasing birds. Too little space and you can have ornery chickens. Too much and you run the risk of potentially annoying your neighbors and making more cleanup for yourself than necessary.

BEING NEIGHBORLY

After determining if you have the time and space to devote to your feathered friends, your next step should be checking with your neighbors to learn their position on the notion. This is especially important if you live in close proximity to other homes or apartments. Discuss your plans, including the size of your flock, the housing you intend to construct, and the care and maintenance you have in mind. Promises of eggs left on their front stoop (by you, not by the chickens themselves!) may not be enough for some folks. Letting them know there won't be any roosters present as well as your plans for housing and cleanup could assuage the concerns of those not completely bowled over. Doing so in advance of the actual physical appearance of your flock can save headaches and potentially money, should your chickens offend and your neighbors pursue legal action. If you live more than a quarter mile from your closest neighbor, checking in with them may be polite, but most likely unnecessary.

One of my favorite unexpected perks in keeping chickens is the daily lessons they offer in mindfulness. Chickens live in the moment, thrilling at the conquest of a wriggling grub, squawking in triumph at the delivery of an egg, resting contentedly in a dust bath. They don't worry about whether they spent too much time in that dust bath, or if they squawked too loudly about that egg, or if they ought to have squirreled away that grub for another day. They rise with the sun and get to the business of living with a vivaciousness, curiosity, and deliberation we could all learn from. While you may be setting out on your own chicken-raising adventure seeking nourishment for your body, I predict you just might find some for your soul, too.

CRACKING THE CODE

After clearing your plans with your neighbors, the next essential step is to determine whether keeping chickens is permitted where you live. Variations in codes and ordinances exist from state to state, as well as between cities. If you live in a rural area, keeping chickens is almost assuredly legal. However, if you live in a city or suburb, it is imperative to find out what's on the books about raising chickens legally.

This can be done through several routes. Search online or in the phone book for your local county or city commissioner's office. Look for specifics on animal control rules. If an online inquiry fails to locate information on municipal codes for keeping chickens in your area, a direct call to your local municipal animal control office will get you to someone who knows. The local library is also a good place to search for information on local animal ordinances. Some cities will allow a certain number of chickens to be kept without a permit, but flocks in excess of the allotted number require a paper trail. Most permits can be had for a nominal fee and need renewing annually. Keeping the permit is most often conditional upon a lack of complaints from neighbors. Remember, check with the neighbors first! Depending on your local ordinances, it may be necessary to first obtain written consent from your neighbors in order to get a permit or keep chickens at all.

Furthermore, depending on the size of your intended coop, you may need a building permit as well, although more than likely a permit will not be necessary. Check with your local government planning and development office to be sure.

SOMETHING TO CROW ABOUT

Keeping roosters is prohibited in most urban and suburban municipalities. Assuring your neighbors they won't be woken by crowing at the crack of dawn might even be essential to obtaining their consent. While roosters may be majestic to look at, they aren't an essential part of a backyard flock. Hens will lay eggs regardless of whether a rooster is present or not.

Roosters are required for breeding purposes, though. If you live in an area where keeping roosters is not allowed, you will need to replenish your flock another way. Breeding and care for chicks and eggs will be discussed in chapters 6 and 7.

Roosters, while a joy in their own right, may not always be welcome in your neighborhood.

When allowed, keeping a rooster can be a fantastic way to enable breeding chicks at home. Watching a rooster proudly strut his stuff and enliven the airwaves with his crowing can be sheer joy to witness. Roosters also help maintain a pecking order, although one will be established without a rooster around. In my flock, Georgette, the Barred Rock, rules the roost. Even though I live in the country, I've opted not to have a rooster, and the Ladies enjoy a celibate sisterhood in a sort of hen convent. They couldn't be more content.

CAN'T WE ALL JUST GET ALONG?

If you have other animals, it is important to consider how they may interact with your flock. Barnyard cats and adult chickens generally can achieve a peaceful coexistence. Chicks and cats are a lethal combination, though, and caution should always be exercised to keep cats away from chicks until they are of approximately equal size.

Dogs, however, are an entirely different matter. Some dogs will show complete disinterest in your chickens, while others can only be trusted near the chickens with human supervision. My wonderful, kind, gentle, 80-pound (36 kg) German Shepherd, Fly, went nuts with bloodlust when I first brought the chicks home. To curb her behavior, I began a slow, consistent routine of having her come with me to the coop each day, observing as I fed the chickens, stroked them, gathered eggs, and generally socialized with them. Fly is considerably calmer around them these days, but she still likes to jump up on the fence as we approach the coop.

Regardless of where you live, in the country or the city, be aware that allowing chickens to range freely without fencing may make them targets for wandering dogs. I've heard of many folks who lost a hen or two, or 13, to marauding dogs. Gauge your own dog's interest, and note the likelihood of wandering dogs as you consider your chickens' accommodations and fencing.

CHICKENS AND CHILDREN

Some wonderful magic happens between children and chickens. Kids just can't seem to get enough feathery fun. If you have children and are considering raising chickens, a bit of caution is advised, however. Some birds can be aggressive, while others are prone to flighty behavior or nervousness. Select a breed known for a docile, friendly disposition when children will be interacting with them regularly.

Furthermore, proper hygiene will need to be exercised when children handle chickens. Chickens are generally in pretty close contact with their own poop. In order to access their coop, it is often necessary to wade through at least some poop. For these reasons and more, children should wash hands thoroughly after handling chickens.

You might also want to consider shoes reserved just for forays into the chickens' housing. I have a pair of rubber boots whose express purpose is to be worn in the coop. I don my boots, grab the chickens' food, and yell out "Let's go get the chickies!" to the dogs. Once we return from feeding the chickens or gathering up eggs, I remove the boots and park them immediately next to the door. Kids would get a kick out of having "chicken shoes." You would get a kick out of not having chicken poop dispersed throughout your home.

Permaculture

Permaculture is a combination of the words "permanent" and "agriculture," as well as "permanent culture." Australians Bill Mollison and David Holmgren, attempting to describe an approach to creating lasting agricultural systems that mimic nature, coined the word during the 1970s. Permaculture principles borrow greatly from those that govern natural ecology, wherein organisms synergistically complement one another. When applying permaculture tenets to design, the particular needs, properties, and potential output of a physical space are constructed in relation to one another.

Applying permaculture principles to raising chickens involves considering then what a chicken needs, what it produces, and what its inherent properties are. All chickens need water, food, other chickens, and specific climatic conditions. When those needs are met, they produce eggs, meat, fertilizer, and feathers, in addition to breaking up and enriching the soil and eating weeds and unwanted insects.

When incorporating permaculture into a plan for raising chickens, all elements of the design are created in relation to one another, "stacking functions" as it were, so that each design element reinforces, nurtures, and complements the other. Physically, this may manifest as a chicken run that is planted with perennial trees and bushes from which the chickens may forage seeds and fruit themselves. Certain times of the year may necessitate the addition of nutritional supplements, but in a well-designed permaculture setup, the chickens will be able to meet many of their food needs themselves. Set a rain barrel atop the chicken coop, and much of the chickens' water needs can be met with minimal energy expenditure. For housing, a greenhouse could be built along a south-facing wall, providing heat for chickens in the winter and carbon dioxide from the chickens' breath for plants, to help them grow.

Chapter 2
Selecting a Breed

Choosing the right type of chicken is a bit like choosing a mate. Generally, we look for an individual whose interests mesh with our own. Does he like Woody Allen films? Is she fond of Mark Rothko? Can he savor and appreciate a fine smoked Gouda? Of course, questions of marriage, children, career, and such must also be addressed. Chicken selection is not entirely dissimilar. It is important to consider your particular needs and desired characteristics when picking your flock. Careful selection will help to insure a mutually satisfying relationship.

A breed is a group of chickens, most likely distant relations from the same stock, sharing similar characteristics, including size, skin color, and comb and plumage styles. Within their breed, chickens may then be further subdivided into varieties, where distinguishing colors and patterns differentiate, say, a Silver Laced Wyandotte from a Columbian Wyandotte.

There are over 200 breeds of chickens out there, ranging in size from 1 to 12 pounds (.5 to 5.5 kg), and, on rare occasions, larger. Breeds vary in temperament and climate needs, among other distinctions. Take your time, consider your preferences, and choose wisely. As with any good relationship, take into account the needs of both you and your partner; in this case, your partner being a feathered, winged, squawking chicken.

Keep in mind that, no matter your situation, there is a chicken for every scenario, whether the place you hang your hat is a palace or a mere perch. Consider your particular needs, jot them down if needed, and then begin your hunt. Scour catalogs, visit feed stores, and peruse chicken websites with fervor, holding out until you find Mr. or Ms. Right.

THE MAGIC NUMBER

Depending on the size of your property and the size of the human flock that will be consuming what your chickens are offering, you may need few or many. Will you be keeping eggs exclusively for your family, or for market? Will you be keeping chickens for meat or for eggs, or for both? Will your flock be for show or for production? Will your chickens live in a tractor or a coop? Will you keep a rooster? Do you have an acre or an alleyway?

The average backyard chicken keeper may maintain a flock of as few as two hens, or upwards of 100 birds, depending on their needs. No matter what number you ultimately decide on, bear in mind that chickens are naturally social creatures. A minimum of two will keep their spirits up, as well as provide even more chicken antics for you to relay to family and friends, or to total strangers, as I sometimes do!

SIZE MATTERS

Size, perhaps more than any other characteristic, is what truly differentiates chicken breeds from one another. Size considerations can be paramount. Again, consider the space available for your flock. Is it more suited for bantams, which are small breeds, or for standard breeds?

Bantam Island, located in the Dutch East Indies, is a seaport once heavily trafficked by European sailors. They often selected the small fowl native to the area for long-haul trips, owing to their compact stature, usually somewhere between 2 and 4 pounds (1 to 1.8 kg). The term "bantam" came to be applied to

any small chicken breed, whether from Bantam Island or not. Many bantams have a standard-size counterpart, although several, including Silkies and Bearded d'Uccles, are available only as bantams.

While many bantams are kept purely as show birds, all bantam hens will lay eggs, albeit small ones. (For cooking, in recipes where you might use two large eggs, you'll need three bantam eggs.) Although their output in no way rivals that of standard-size breeds, bantams may be the ideal choice for the would-be chicken keeper with space restrictions. Bantams are typically less than half the size of standard varieties.

These petite birds have correspondingly small appetites, which cuts down on feed costs for their keepers. Bantams love to graze, hunt, peck, dig, and generally happily seek out and annihilate any creepy crawlies, further diminishing their need for feed. Small size and little appetite may be the perfect combination for those keeping an urban flock on a ramen-noodle budget. Do keep in mind, though, that bantams are flighty, with the ability to reach up to 6 feet (1.8 m), and will need to be fenced accordingly.

Brahma
Jersey Giant
Bantam

PURE OR HYBRID?

Deciding on your flock with purebred status in mind may or may not be important. If you someday wish to show your chickens, then they must be purebred. Just as mutt dogs, no matter how flawless and adorable, will never be put on parade at the Westminster Kennel Club, hybrid birds will never make it on the chicken show circuit. It's a harsh, cruel world, I know. Aside from the sheer fun of raising purebred chickens, with all their wild variation and general sauciness, sticking with recognized breeds is a wonderful way to connect with chicken fanciers and breeders.

Even if you have no intention of ever putting Henny Penny on the catwalk, whatever supermodel tendencies she may exhibit, you may wish to keep and preserve a rare or endangered breed. Continuance of numerous so-called heritage breeds such as Araucanas, Dominiques, Dorkings, Spanish, Buckeyes, and Aseels rests in large part on small-scale chicken owners. As interest in backyard chicken raising grows—recent trends point to a nation consumed with chicken fever—perhaps these heritage breeds will cease to be endangered.

Regardless of the many appealing characteristics of purebred poultry, in no way should hybrids be considered inferior. Hybrid chickens are the result of genetically crossing two distinct breeds. While they may lack the silver-spoon pedigree of their purebred cousins, they excel in other ways. They have been bred to possess the best possible traits of the breeds they were crossed from. Hybrids may fall short on some criteria as articulated in the Standard of Perfection, such as length of tail feather or pattern of stripes on their neck, while embodying other desirable attributes, such as generous egg or meat production. Hybrid vigor also makes crosses especially sturdy and resistant to disease. Do bear in mind that hybrid birds will not necessarily bear chicks in their own likeness. In order to obtain a new generation of a particular breed, you will have to go back to original stock.

LAY, LADY, LAY

Many people elect to raise chickens for the singular thrill of gathering up still-warm eggs. Etched forever in my mind will be the first time I tasted, and viewed, eggs from my own chickens. I never knew eggs could be so delicious, so creamy, so, well, orange! When my husband, Glenn, began whisking up the first offerings from our girls, I was convinced he must have added a pinch of turmeric to the bowl to produce that intense hue. He hadn't—the yolks were just that vibrant, enhanced by all the parsley, salad greens, and berries I had been adding to the Ladies' feed. These foods all contain carotenoids, nutrient-rich pigments praised for their immune system-enhancing properties. Supplementing chicken feed with such foods results in almost pumpkin-colored yolks, transferring all that carotenoid goodness to whomever we fire up the skillet and break our eggs for.

If your primary motivation for raising chickens is to be provided with a continuous supply of eggs, consider a breed known for its heavy laying abilities. Of course, all hens will lay eggs; some breeds are merely known for their inclination to lay with a greater degree of regularity. The breed best known for its profusion of eggs is the White Leghorn. Other top laying breeds include Minorcas and Rhode Island Reds.

Egg production will be most abundant during a hen's first two years, after which her laying will become a bit more sporadic. Depending on your needs, this tapering off may work just fine, or you may consider introducing new chicks or pullets to your flock over time to guarantee a continuous supply. Assuming average consumption and production, two hens for each family member should take care of your egg needs. Refer to the chart on page 14 for a listing of breeds suitable for those with a hankering for eggs.

SETTING THE TABLE

Perhaps your interest in raising chickens lies in their ability to keep your table full of safe, clean meat you can feel good about consuming. Factory-raised chickens are exposed not only to antibiotics but often to cruel and inhumane treatment. Birds raised on your own plot, fed by your own hand, offer peace of mind alongside a source of healthy nourishment.

As much as you may care for their well-being, table birds are not pets. Do not allow yourself (or your children, should you have any) to become too attached to chickens intended for the table. Fortunately, table birds are ready for butchering at about six to eight weeks. Such brevity of time on earth makes it difficult to foster too deep a tie with your meat chickens.

The breed most commonly used for table is the Rock-Cornish or Cornish-Rock Cross, a hybrid of the White Rock and Cornish Game. Large commercial meat bird factories favor this breed as it develops quickly and has a good meat-to-bone ratio. With voracious appetites and little interest in getting much exercise, Rock-Cornish Crosses can gain 4 pounds (1.8 kg) in eight weeks. Their rapid growth rate may contribute to health and structural problems, and therefore the need for careful handling. If you do opt for a hybrid table breed, be aware that such birds will not breed true. Should you be interested in breeding more, you will need to return to original stock for desired characteristics.

You can also opt for purebred chickens to use as table birds. Table breeds other than the Rock-Cornish Cross include Jersey Giant, Cochin, and Brahma. Although these birds mature at a slower rate before they are ready for table, their slower growth rate prevents many of the problems affecting the rapidly growing hybrid. As they are generally large and heavy, many table birds will not require much fencing, which may be ideal for those with limited space or funds.

In the interest of full disclosure, I will confess that I don't eat meat. That said, I fully support the decision of anyone—city dweller, suburbanite, or countryside resident—to raise chickens for consumption. I firmly believe it to be inherently empowering and sustainable.

BUTCHERING

Birds intended for table should be butchered around 6 to 8 pounds (2.5–3.5 kg). Do this in the evening, when your flock is calm and relaxed. Butchering chickens, while not difficult, is best performed after witnessing, perhaps repeatedly, someone else do it who has done it before. Perhaps a family member, a neighbor, or a fellow chicken raiser in your community can show you the ropes. If you feel that this is a task you might never be able to perform, there may be a local butcher or mobile poultry processor nearby willing to perform the job at a cost. Ask around at the feed store or solicit a recommendation from your veterinarian.

TWICE AS NICE

Should you be interested in chickens for both eggs and meat, seek out dual-purpose birds. These birds will reliably provide you with an adequate egg supply and are known to be good to eat. Dual-purpose breeds lay fewer eggs than those known for their egg-laying abilities (about 18 to 20 dozen in a laying cycle as opposed

to 20 to 22 dozen) and will put on weight much more slowly than birds raised primarily for table, but are more adept in other ways.

Dual-purpose breeds are generally hardier and more self-reliant than single-purpose breeds. Many are broody, meaning they will sit on a group of eggs (a "clutch" in chicken terminology) to hatch. Broodiness can be beneficial in chickens, whereas broodiness in teenagers can result in such unpleasantness as petulant whining and refusal to make eye contact.

Having been less-intensively selected for specific, narrow characteristics, most dual-purpose birds are also generally calmer than more specialized breeds, making them an ideal choice for the beginner. They are less flighty and will therefore not require high fencing. Dual-purpose birds may begin laying a bit later than other breeds, at around five-and-a-half to six months instead of five months. As for their meat, these breeds purportedly produce more tender meat than exclusively egg-laying breeds.

SHOW ME THE CHICKENS!

Some chickens are kept exclusively for purposes of show. Coddled, preened, and stroked their entire lives, show chickens lead cushy lives anyone might covet. They are hand-groomed, often live in their own separate housing, and enjoy no small amount of attention and, perhaps, fame!

The criteria used in judging at poultry shows in the United States are detailed at length in the Standard of Perfection, published by the American Poultry Association. If you want to know desired breed characteristics for some form of poultry, be it chickens, ducks, geese, turkeys, or bantams, this is your go-to book. Outside the United States, nation-specific rules will apply. An online search should provide the necessary information for judging breeds internationally.

Keeping chickens to show can be great fun, although it requires a bit more elbow grease on your part. Ever given a chicken a bath? Now's your chance! Chicken shows also enable chicken fanciers an opportunity to meet and greet. I love that term, "chicken fancier." I can almost imagine my third-grade teacher Mrs. Pierson asking, "And what do you want to be when you grow up, Ashley?" "A chicken fancier!" I wonder if "chicken fancier" is a vocation listed on the census?

My personal favorite show bird is the Yokohama. The tail length of a mature Yokohama is 2 feet (61 cm)! Fanciers in Japan often keep Yokohamas in conditions preventing molt, thereby allowing their tails to grow to up to 3 feet (91.4 cm). Such proud plumage I imagine must make even a peacock jealous!

If you are considering keeping chickens for show, look for small poultry societies in your area. The American Poultry Association or your local extension office would be good places to seek out these small organizations.

Shows are customarily held in winter, by which time spring-hatched chicks will be fully grown and older birds will have new plumage post-molt. What better way to brighten up the winter doldrums than by gussying up your favorite bird and mingling feathers with fanciers and their fine feathered friends!

Chicken Anatomy 101

points

blade

comb

base of comb

eye

ear

beak

sickles

saddle

ear lobe

wattle

cape

back

hackles

breast

secondaries
(wing-bay)

main tail

saddle feathers

vent

primaries
(flight feathers)

shank

thigh

spur (males only)

toenail

Breeds and Dispositions

Calm, Friendly, and Easygoing

Ameraucana	Cornish	Orpington
Araucana	Dominique	Plymouth Rock
Barnevelder	Dorking	Polish
Belgian Bearded d'Uccle	Faverolle	Silkie
Brahma	Java	Wyandotte
Cochin	Langshan	

Flighty, Nervous, and Aggressive

Ancona	Leghorn
Andalusian	Old English Game
Buttercup	New Hampshire Red
Fayoumi	Rhode Island Red
Hamburg	Sebright
Lakenvelder	Sumatra

Breeds by Purpose at a Glance

PURPOSE	BREED	AVERAGE WEIGHT (POUNDS/Kg)
Table	Brahma	9 lbs/4 kg
	Cochin	9 lbs/4 kg
	Rock-Cornish Cross	8 lbs/3.5 kg
	Jersey Giant	10 lbs/4.5 kg
Dual-Purpose	Plymouth Rock	7 lbs/3 kg
	Australorp	6 to 7 lbs/2.5 to 3 kg
	Orpington	7 lbs/3 kg
	New Hampshire Red	6 lbs/2.7 kg
	Rhode Island Red	6 lbs/2.7 kg
	Wyandotte	6 lbs/2.7 kg
Layers	Ancona	4 lbs/2 kg
	Andalusian	4½ to 5½/2 to 2.5 kg
	Araucana	5½ lbs/2.5 kg
	Black Sex-link	5 lbs/2.3 kg
	Fayoumi	3½ to 4½ lbs/1.5 to 2 kg
	Leghorn	4½ lbs/2 kg
	Minorca	7½ lbs/3.5 kg
	Red Sex-link	5 lbs/2 kg
Show	Crèvecœur	7 to 8 lbs/3 to 3.5 kg
	Faverolle	6½ to 7 lbs/3 to 3.2 kg
	Frizzle	4½ to 6 lbs/2 to 2.7 kg
	Houdan	6½ to 8 lbs/3 to 3.5 kg
	Lakenvelder	4½ to 6 lbs/2 to 2.7 kg
	Polish	4½ to 6 lbs/2 to 2.7 kg
	Sultan	4 to 5 lbs/2 to 2.3 kg

COLOR ME BEAUTIFUL

Chickens lay eggs in a variety of colors. Eggshells get their color from pigments that are deposited as the egg moves through a hen's oviduct. These pigments are genetically determined. Variations in eggshell color are not related to differences in egg flavor, as flavor is determined by diet, not genetics. If you are looking for a particular color, or simply wish to have an array of colors available for use, use this guide in making your selections.

Blue: Araucana

Blue-green: Ameraucana and Easter Egger

Brown (Dark and Light): Australorp, Barnevelder, Black and Red Sex-link, Brahma, Cochin, Cornish, Delaware, Dominique, Faverolle, Hamburg, Jersey Giant, Lakenvelder, Malay, Maran, Naked Neck, New Hampshire Red, Orpington, Plymouth Rock, Rhode Island Red, Welsummer, and Wyandotte

White: Ancona, Andalusian, Campine, Crèvecœur, Dorking, Houdan, Leghorn, Minorca, Polish, Silkie, Sultan, and Yokohama

FROZEN COMBS AND WILTED FEATHERS

Weather plays a significant role in the health of your chickens, as some are genetically better able to withstand summer's swelter while others will gladly frolic in the snow. Bantams generally do well in the heat of summer, except for the feather-footed varieties, whereas the heavier standard breeds will fare better in cold weather, on account of their larger size and denser plumage. The bigger the comb or wattle, the more susceptible a bird will be to frostbite. Knowing which breeds function better in varying climates can prevent discomfort on their part and heartache on yours, should a nor'easter or heat wave cause your fine feathered friend to go claw up.

Cold-Hardy Breeds
(for climates that regularly get below freezing for part or most of the year)

Ameraucana	Hamburg
Araucana	Jersey Giant
Australorp	Langshan
Chantecler	Orpington
Cochin	Plymouth Rock
Cornish	Silkie
Dominique	Sussex
Dorking	Wyandotte
Faverolle	

Heat-Tolerant Breeds

Andalusian	Leghorn
Buttercup	Minorca
Campine	Rhode Island Red
Cubalaya	Sumatra
Fayoumi	

Breeds Hardy in Both Heat and Cold

Aseel

Brahma

New Hampshire Red

RARE BIRD, INDEED!

When selecting your flock, it would be well worth considering rare and endangered breeds. The hybridized uber layers and broilers favored by industrial agriculture have displaced many heritage breeds, and many chicken varieties are now threatened or endangered. The loss of such genetic diversity does us all a huge disservice in the long run, as a reduced gene pool could spell quick and sudden extinction should an especially virulent virus swoop in.

The American Livestock Breeds Conservancy (ALBC) maintains a list of endangered breeds on their website, www.albc-usa.org. Similar organizations exist internationally, each with its own criteria for classifying endangered birds. The ALBC's conservation priority list is based on numerical guidelines as follows:

Critical: Fewer than 500 breeding birds in the United States; globally endangered.

Threatened: Fewer than 1,000 breeding birds in the United States; globally endangered.

Watch: Fewer than 5,000 breeding birds in the United States; globally endangered. Also included are breeds with genetic or numerical concerns or limited geographic distribution.

Recovering: Breeds once listed in another category having now exceeded Watch category numbers but still in need of monitoring.

Study: Breeds of interest but either lack definition or genetic or historical documentation.

Critical	Threatened	Watch	Recovering	Study
Andalusian	Ancona	Brahma	Australorp	Araucana
Aseel	Cubalaya	Cochin	Leghorn (Nonindustrial)	Egyptian Fayoumis
Buckeye	Dorking	Cornish (Nonindustrial)	Orpington	Iowa Blue
Buttercup	Lakenvelder	Dominique	Plymouth Rock (Nonindustrial)	Lamona
Campine Langshan	Langshan	Hamburg	Rhode Island Red	Manx Rumpy
Catalana	Sussex	Jersey Giant	Wyandotte	Modern Game
Chantecler		Minorca		Naked Neck
Crèvecœur		New Hampshire Red		Old English Game
Delaware		Polish		Phoenix
Faverolle		Rhode Island White		Shamo
Holland		Sebright		Sultan
Houdan				Yokohama
Java				
La Fleche				
Malay				
Nankin				
Redcap				
Russian Orloff				
Spanish				
Sumatra				

Chapter 3

Obtaining Chickens

You've chosen your breeds, checked to see if you need a permit to keep chickens in your area, and considered the space available. Now you're ready to start assembling your motley crew! Consider whether you want chicks or more mature chickens, what you should be looking for when selecting birds, where to source your chickens, and what time of year might be best for chicken purchasing.

HERE, CHICK, CHICK!

If your local pet store is anything like most, you won't be finding White Leghorns or Japanese Bantams there any time soon. While most big box pet retailers will sell you salamanders, turtles, finches, and dog sweaters, it's pretty unlikely you'll score any Belgian Bearded d'Uccles there, either. Your local feed store is a much more likely place to begin feathering your nest.

Selection there may be limited, however, especially if you are after a specific exotic or endangered breed. Feed stores can offer a wealth of chicken advice, though. Ask a staff member who supplies them with their poultry and whether their suppliers are nationally recognized as engaging in sound and healthy breeding practices. Participants of such organizations often insure their flocks to be free of once-common diseases such as pullorum and typhoid, nasty bugs your chickens can literally live without.

Mail-order catalogs are a great source for obtaining chicks.

If you don't have a feed store where you live (in, say, midtown Manhattan), or you have your heart set on a Lakenvelder that can't be had at John & Jane Doe's Feed & Seed, then move your search to the Internet. It is possible today to source chickens and chicks online from a number of highly reputable hatcheries. Some offer free catalogs, should you want to take your time ogling and contemplating chicken varieties over your morning cup of joe. These mail-order hatcheries also often sell housing, feed, and reading materials for those desiring a one-stop chicken shop.

Another place to look is the classifieds section of your local newspaper. City newspapers sometimes offer treasure troves of local poultry for sale. Additionally, you may want to seek out poultry clubs in your area, which can be found through a quick Internet search. Club members can recommend trusted chicken suppliers, either in your area or online. A local veterinarian can also be a good source of information and referrals.

Finally, don't underestimate the county fair as a means of procuring a desired breed. Owners of prizewinning birds, or any of the birds on display, might be in the business of selling offspring or could be talked into doing so. Take a gander, see who the chickens belong to, and try to track them down, either by the names listed on the bird's cages or through the fair's livestock coordinators. Score some chickens and ride the Ferris wheel—now that's my idea of a good time!

AGE APPROPRIATE

When you begin assembling your flock, you will have to decide how old your chickens will be when you bring them home. It is possible to purchase freshly hatched chicks, pullets (usually between 16 and 20 weeks old), or mature hens. If you are considering including a rooster in the mix, they may also be purchased as chicks, cockerels (male chickens less than one year old), or mature roosters. Although it's hard to resist the ridiculously cute, fuzzy balls of feathers that are chicks, this decision should not be made lightly, as there are pros and cons to each scenario.

Chicks

If you want the most birds for your money, chicks are the way to go. Depending on the quantity you purchase, chicks usually only cost a few dollars apiece. Some hatcheries require bulk orders of chicks in order to ensure they will remain warm in transit. However, as backyard chicken keeping is on the rise, hatcheries are becoming more responsive to the needs of the small grower. Some will even offer single chicks for purchase.

Chicks bought from a reputable source, either your local feed store or an online commercial hatchery, will generally be in good health when you get them. If you intend to keep your chickens as pets, and not merely as table birds, acquiring them as chicks enables you to develop a relationship with them, building trust as you hold them and feed them by hand. Should you be so lucky, you might one day end up with a chicken that will sit in your lap or perch on your shoulder!

Before you rush to your nearest feed store and gather up the fluffiest chicks you can find, remember that, at least in the beginning, chicks do require more care than older birds. During their first few weeks of life, chicks are at their most vulnerable. Like any young animal, chicks can be rather unruly. Left to their own devices, things could get pretty messy, and potentially hazardous, fairly quickly. They frequently stomp around in their food and water, spreading fecal matter throughout. Savagely enough, they can peck each other to death. Be certain before you purchase your chicks that you will always have someone available for "chick patrol." Furthermore, they are susceptible to a host of illnesses and health conditions.

We will discuss newly hatched chicks and their particular needs in greater detail in chapter 7. Raising chicks requires a significant time commitment. If you don't think you will be able to provide them with what they need, you may want to consider purchasing pullets instead. Conversely, if you do have time to be a chick nanny, little can compare with the

hilarity of watching chick antics and the joy of hearing their little chick peeps.

Another thing to consider is that, unless you purchase sexed chicks, where the sex is determined for you by a poultry sexing expert, the precious chicks you brought home might leave you with several roosters too many, which you don't want. If chicks are your choice, be certain to request sexed chicks and develop an appropriate rooster-to-hen ratio. (Unsexed chicks are also listed as "straight run" and "as-hatched.") If you live in an urban or suburban area, remember that roosters are most likely prohibited, so choose your chicks accordingly.

Started Birds

Although they will cost more than chicks, usually by several dollars apiece, pullets and cockerels require a good bit less care than newly hatched chicks. If your goal is to have a regular supply of fresh eggs to eat, pullets will be that much closer to point of lay—by six months they may already be laying. Accordingly, they will cost you less in feed as they mature. Birds purchased as starts will offer more eggs over their lifetime than those purchased as hens. Also, started birds require less in the way of specific housing and care than do chicks. Pullets can immediately be placed in their run, needing no regulated heat or special chick feed.

On the other hand, started birds are often not as readily available at feed stores as are chicks. If you plan to raise chickens for table, started birds are too old, as table birds are generally slaughtered around eight to 12 weeks. Another down side is that, not having been hand raised from birth, pullets may not be as tame as they might have been had they grown accustomed to you and your environment over time. Furthermore, you may not be fully aware of how an older chicken was handled prior to moving in with you. If you want to ensure yourself stewardship of affable, sociable, guest-and-family-appropriate chickens, then selecting chicks from a breed known for their friendly personalities may be your best bet.

Gender Studies

Professional chicken sexing experts determine chick sex. This occurs by careful observation of the vent for minute gender differences. (The vent is the eliminatory organ through which eggs and feces pass, as well as a chick's genitalia.) These differences are remarkably slight, and chicken sexers develop accuracy through repetition in observation. Even then, sexers are right about 90 percent of the time. This method of gender differentiation is used mostly by large hatcheries. In my case, of the five chickens I received from my nurse friend, all five grew up to become hens. Unfortunately for her, of her five chicks, two turned out to be roosters!

Mature Birds

When electing to purchase a mature bird, as either a hen or a rooster, the clear advantage is that you generally are able to see precisely what you are getting. Older birds are clearly sexually mature and have their plumage in. Like pullets, they require less in terms of housing, critical care, and constant observation than do chicks.

Mature hens, although they will continue to lay, will never produce as many eggs after their first laying season. Older birds are also more susceptible to diseases as they age. Finally, purchasing mature birds will cost considerably more than purchasing chicks, as their entire lifetime up to that point will have been maintained on someone else's dime.

SHINY EYES AND SLICK FEATHERS

When purchasing chickens, be on the lookout for visible cues to the birds' health. If you are purchasing chicks by mail, be certain to open the box in front of a delivery person to make sure your flock all survived the journey. I would not advise bringing children along with you on this errand, as a limp, deceased chick is not an image you'd like to have etched into your child's memories. If purchasing chicks in person, look for alert, energetic birds. Pick them up and examine their rear ends for pasty butt, which is exactly what it sounds like, a backside with excrement dried around it, preventing elimination. Be certain to choose chicks with straight beaks and toes.

Older chickens should have clear, bright eyes, waxy combs and wattles, shiny feathers, and smooth legs. There should be no visible parasites, which an examination under the wings and around the vent should easily disclose. Internal parasites will cause diarrhea, which a quick check at the vent should indicate. Pick up any bird you are thinking of buying. The breastbone should be flexible and covered with flesh. Listen for any coughing or wheezing, as this could be an indication of a sick bird. Examine the entire flock, looking for any listless or isolated birds. One sick bird could affect the entire crew, so pay close attention. Lastly, if you can, try to have a look at the bird's droppings. Healthy birds will have firm, well-rounded feces, brown in color and tipped in white (this is the urine).

WINTER, SPRING, SUMMER, OR FALL?

It is important to consider the time of year when purchasing your chickens. The season in which you assemble your flock will affect their behavior, needs, and laying habits. If purchasing chicks by mail, they will need to be kept warm in transit from the hatchery in cool months. They will then need to remain warm on the way home from the post office or feed store. Feed stores generally have chicks available for purchase in the spring, while most mail-order hatcheries offer chicks every season except winter.

Pullets and mature birds will need to be kept dry in cold, wet weather, and their egg laying will drop off as the daylight

hours shorten. In very cold climates, some chickens' combs will need to have a lubricant rubbed on them to prevent frostbite. Bantams especially will need to be kept out of heavy snow and wind during cold months.

During warmer months, chicks and older birds will need to have access to shade and water. They may also go broody during this time of year, which you may need to discourage if you don't want chicks. Brooding chicks is best done in early spring, as the weather will become increasingly warmer but will remain cool enough in the evenings to ward off diseases. Late summer to early fall is when most chickens molt. Egg laying will lessen or cease altogether during this period.

The Chick's in the Mail

For the best selection, you may opt to purchase chicks by mail. While delivering a box full of live chicks may be an "out of the ordinary occurrence for an urban postal worker, rural post offices are accustomed to express shipments of peeping feather balls. Chicks are shipped by air, with 48 hours elapsing from hatching to delivery at your post office. They are sent in a specially designed chick-shipping box equipped with ventilation holes. It is rare for most hatcheries to ship fewer than 25 chicks per order. The high number is needed for chicks to huddle together and generate body heat, necessary to their survival. If this is the policy of the hatchery you choose, you may want to seek out other members of your community interested in purchasing at the same time. Hatcheries do exist that will send smaller numbers of chicks, but they may either charge an additional insurance fee or throw in extra male chicks for added warmth. You may want to give your local post office a call with a heads-up about your imminent arrival. They will call you once your package arrives either way.

Chapter 4
Housing

Although chickens don't need much square footage (they are rather diminutive birds, after all), they do require appropriate housing. Setting up accommodations will be the largest part of your start-up costs. Once established, the housing should last for a number of years, if cared for properly. The essentials of any henhouse include perches, nesting boxes, security from predators, and access to the outdoors. Beyond the basics, you can customize your flock's housing in an infinite number of ways. Chicken palace or humble abode, the choice is up to you. A number of variables must be considered, though, before hitting the first nail or rolling out the first length of chicken wire. Size of flock, climate, and available space are just a few of the factors that must be taken into account when setting up your coop de Ville.

FOR HERE OR TO GO?

First determine whether you want permanent or mobile housing for your flock. There are advantages and disadvantages to each choice. Permanent housing will be worth considering if you plan on being where you are for some time. If you live in an area subject to extreme heat or cold, permanent housing will provide the greatest amount of protection from the elements. It can be wired for electricity to power heat lamps, water warmers, and ventilation fans, in addition to overhead lighting. With a bit more fortification, permanent housing will also be more predator proof than many mobile setups. Additionally, a greater number of birds may be kept in permanent housing.

Permanent housing can be considerably more expensive to build than mobile housing. If you are planning on building the coop yourself, you may be able to reduce some of the costs. However, providing good insulation, ventilation, fencing, and predator-proof protection will add to the expense, whether you are the builder or not.

Mobile housing may be the ideal choice for those with limited space or budgets. If you intend to keep a small flock, in both number and physical size, and your climate is mild, this may be the way to go. Mobile housing also can help with yard maintenance. Lightweight and bottomless, chicken "tractors" or "arks" are structured to be moved to any location needing weed control and soil enrichment. Your flock gets access to grass, insects, worms, and other slithery soil inhabitants chickens love to dine on, and your yard will be all the greener. If you have flighty birds such as bantams, you won't have to worry about installing pricey tall fencing, as mobile housing is completely enclosed. Furthermore, small mobile coops are often easier to keep clean than larger permanent housing.

If you live in an urban or suburban area and wish to have the ability to move your chickens periodically to avoid having them too near any particular neighbor, mobile housing can be ideal. You may construct your own ark relatively inexpensively, or you may purchase a manufactured version from an online seller. A growing number of mobile pre-fabricated housing units are available in a variety of colors and modern designs. As backyard chicken-raising fever catches on, the design world

A mobile pre-fab chicken enclosure

is rising to the occasion, meeting the discriminating preferences of today's chicken tenders.

BREATHING ROOM

Proper ventilation is essential to chicken health. Chickens have a high rate of respiration and subsequent production of carbon dioxide and moisture, which makes them particularly susceptible to respiratory diseases. Keeping air moving through their coop is therefore fundamental to their vitality. Inevitably, moisture will be introduced into the coop from rain, as well as the chickens' own breath and droppings, and you will need to take steps to remove it.

If you are designing a permanent structure, make sure that at least one-fifth of the wall space has windows that open for air circulation. If you opt for glass windows, simply raise them. Cover

Proper ventilation is essential in the coop.

window openings with ½- to ¾-inch (1.3 to 1.9 cm) galvanized mesh wire on the interior of the coop to prevent interlopers from accessing the coop. Predators can be extraordinarily tenacious in their drive to get into chicken coops; further methods of fortification will be discussed below. Wild birds, which could carry parasites or diseases, must be kept out, as well. Use the right wire in the beginning and save yourself, and your feathered friends, from unnecessary suffering in the long run.

In a small or mobile structure, windows may not be an option. Instead, situate ventilation holes on the north- and south-facing walls near the top of the coop. Cover the holes on the inside with mesh wire. Install a wooden drop-down cover over the screens with hinges at the bottom and a latch or hook at the top. This way you can monitor and adjust the ventilation inside the coop as needed, while keeping wildlife from gaining access. Only close both covers if the weather turns terribly cold. Otherwise, leave the south-facing airholes open at all times, even in chilly weather.

In warmer weather you will need to ensure constant cross-ventilation for your birds, especially for those that spend most of their time in their coop and have minimal outdoor access. This can be achieved either by opening all doors, windows, and covers, or through the use of a fan suspended from the ceiling of the coop or mounted to a wall. Chickens aren't capable of sweating and can go downhill pretty quickly in temperatures over 95°F (35°C). You'll know they are too hot if you see them panting. Keep their coop well ventilated and give them access to the outdoors, shady spots to hide from searing sun, and fresh water at all times, and your flock should cluck along happily all summer long.

SIZING THINGS UP

While bigger isn't always better, having more coop space to start is certainly better than having too little. The less crowded your flock is, the healthier and more content they (and you) will be. You may want to increase the size of your flock over time, and having planned for expansion at the start will save headaches in the future.

That said, there are no hard and fast rules about coop size. In my research, I've found guidelines suggesting everything from 4 to 10 square feet (1 to 3 m²) per bird. Variations account for the size of individual breeds, the number of birds you are keeping, and whether your birds are given access to a large outdoor area or are kept confined in small quarters most of the time. The more space you have available to you, the bigger you can make your coop, if you are so inclined. In my case, I live on 12 acres (48,000 m²) in a relatively rural area. The size limitations of our coop were restricted only by our imaginations! We appropriated an existing 64-square-foot (6 m²) dog shelter built on a platform, put walls on it, installed roosts and nesting boxes, and created essentially a chicken palace for our five Ladies. They also have access to an 800-square-foot (74.3 m²) fenced run, another vestige of the dog shelter. That is an inordinately large amount of coop and run space for a flock so small. It was

what we had available, though, so we simply improvised and piggybacked on an existing structure.

Most folks living in urban, and perhaps even suburban, areas will have limitations on the number of birds they can keep. It would be worth asking town officials about coop size restrictions as well. Before you make your first trip to the hardware store, determine if a building permit will be necessary. More than likely, if you keep your coop small, you won't need one.

For birds with outdoor access, allow 2 square feet (.19 m²) per bird in the coop and 4 square feet (.37 m²) per bird in the run. This will provide ample room for your flock, as they will spend most of the daylight hours outside the coop, hunting, scratching, chatting, fluffing, and doing all the glorious things chickens do. Those numbers can be halved for bantams. For birds kept confined most of the time, or perhaps during lengthy periods of inclement weather, double the interior space, up to 4 square feet (.37 m²) per bird. You will also need to allow for more space if you are keeping heavy breeds, as they simply take up more room.

If at all possible, intensively confined birds should have access to grass. One option is to keep the birds in a tractor and move around each day, returning them to their sleeping quarters at night. The flock's health will fare much better if they are given space to roam and hunt for insects. If this is not an option, however, just be certain to give them a daily ration of leafy greens (lettuce, kale, chard—my Ladies love parsley) in addition to their feed.

In addition to allowing for the birds' needs, be certain to consider your own. Pity the poor chicken tender who has to stoop low to gather eggs and scrape poop! If you are making a larger permanent structure, plan for a person-sized entry door. Otherwise, make sure your small coop or mobile unit has easy access to nest boxes and floors. Plan wisely and you won't need to be a hunched-back chicken keeper.

Some unseemly chicken behavior may result if proper space requirements are not provided. Pecking, biting, egg-eating, and sometimes even cannibalism can be the lot of a flock kept in too close of quarters. Humans get this way, too, usually minus the cannibalism, if packed in together too tightly. Empathize with your crew, and give them the space they need.

KEEP YOUR FRIENDS CLOSE AND YOUR ENEMIES OUT

Predator-proofing your henhouse is of utmost importance. I've heard tales of sly foxes who accessed coops, killing 30 chickens and only taking one. There is little more you can do in terms of flock protection than fortifying their sleeping quarters against four-legged threats. Clever predators can undo latches, find the one crack you failed to notice, and shimmy down roofs. Be mindful of areas of structural vulnerability and you save your flock, not from only stress, but potentially from an untimely demise. Depending on where your flock is housed, danger can come from above, below, or both. Free-ranging flocks are subject to

A well-protected chicken coop

flying predators such as hawks, owls, and eagles, while confined flocks face burrowing predators such as weasels, raccoons, foxes, possums, snakes, and rodents. Most predators stalk for prey at night, or in some cases, dusk or dawn. If you allow your birds to pasture, watch out for hawks, the most brazen daytime predator. Camouflage a pasture flock by purchasing darker colored breeds and ensuring there are bushes or other hiding places for them to run to when trouble soars overhead.

To keep the henhouse safe, think like a predator and take action before they can literally "weasel" their way in. Close up coop doors and windows after the chickens have roosted for the night. Reinforce latches and gates with strong, complex locks. It might be worth placing two types of latches on gates and doors, one at the top and an additional one at the bottom. If a toddler can easily open your closure, so can a predator. Some predators are simply looking for feed, not for chicken meat. If you find your feed has been accessed, either secure it tightly with bungee cords, build a wooden box with a secure lock to keep it in, or store it indoors, scooping out what you need for the flock on your way out each morning.

Deter predators by keeping the grass surrounding your run mowed, and remove nearby piles of debris or objects. Roofs will help keep flocks safe from climbing and flying predators, as well as keep in flighty birds. Permanent housing should have 1/2- to 3/4-inch (1.3 to 1.9 cm) galvanized wire mesh covering all ventilation holes; 1-inch (2.5 cm) chicken wire is too large and will allow a number of predators access. Raccoons can easily pull out regular staple-gun staples, so be sure to use wood staples affixed with a hammer when constructing your housing. Mobile housing should be moved daily and have wire surrounding it that is small enough to prevent weasels and mink from climbing deftly through.

Lastly, if your state permits it, you may want to consider trapping and relocating sneaky pests. You will need to first determine what is getting into your coop and then trap accordingly. If you plan on trapping the predator yourself, please do so in as humane a manner as possible. Remember, what we consider "predators" are simply living creatures looking for food, or in the case of some dogs, playing too aggressively. Check traps several times a day. If you discover an animal, cover the trap with cloth in order to calm it. Either transport the animal to your local animal control facility or relocate it at least 5 miles (8 km) from your home. If you trap more than one of the same species, relocate it to the same area. If you are attempting to relocate and release a wild animal by yourself, read all trapping instructions closely before beginning, and be sure to wear gloves. You may be able to borrow a trap from your animal control and wildlife agency instead of purchasing one yourself, so it might be worth it to call and determine whether this is an option in your area.

FENCE ME IN

Fencing can be an invaluable tool in protecting your flock. If installed properly, it can go a long way toward keeping your crew in and sneaky beasts—intent on ravaging chickens, their offspring, and their eggs—out. Fencing should be no less than 4 to 6 feet (1.2 to 1.8 m) high, depending on the flightiness of your breed.

Honeycomb-pattern chicken wire has its place, but not really as fencing. It is flimsy and acts as little deterrent to a predator determined to get in. It works better as overhead cover from predatory and wild birds in a run. Galvanized chicken wire intended for outdoor use may be suitable for use as fencing. Check how sturdy it is when considering it for purchase.

Ideally, fencing should be made of heavy-duty yard or livestock fencing or netting. Holes in the wire should be no larger than 1 inch (2.5 cm) so that chickens cannot stick

Proper fencing keeps chickens in and predators out.

A typical latch-type gate closure

their heads out and chicks cannot easily slip through them. You may want to consider "double fencing," which consists of an outer layer of heavy-duty fencing and an interior layer, perhaps only a few feet high, of more traditional chicken wire. This helps keep predators out and your feathered crew in. It is advisable when erecting the fencing to bury it 6 to 12 inches (15.2 to 30.5 cm) below ground, bending the end to a 90° angle. By the time a burrowing predator or digging dog reaches the angle, they will most likely determine it's a lost cause and give up. Attach the fencing to posts set about 4 to 6 feet (1.2 to 1.8 m) apart. Posts will need to be buried about 6 to 8 inches (15.2 to 20.3 cm) into the ground, so take that into account when determining the length of posts you need.

Alternatively, consider electric fencing. Affix insulators 6 inches (15.2 cm) from both the top and the bottom of your wire fencing, then thread electric wire through the insulators and around the fencing perimeter. Top wire placement thwarts predators thinking of scaling the fence, while bottom wire deters those thinking of tunneling in or lurking around the exterior. Transportable electric fencing is an option for free-range flocks ("mobile poultry fencing" is the term to search for online or in catalogs). Made of plastic string laced with fine metal wire, netting comes with posts built into it for sturdiness. Mobile fencing may be battery powered or plugged into an electric outlet.

YOU LIGHT UP THEIR LIVES

Chickens need light. The break of dawn is their cue to lay eggs, as morning's light sends a signal to a hen's pituitary gland,

which in turn informs her ovaries to get busy. The darkening at day's end tells the birds to return to the coop for some shut-eye. As their caretaker, you will need light when tending to your chickens. A well-lit coop lets you clean properly, check for eggs, and count your flock for any missing.

During winter, when daylight dips to less than 14 hours per day, chickens may reduce their laying or cease to lay altogether. Having windows in their coop and access to sunlight outdoors may temper this natural response, although it may not prevent it entirely. If sporadic laying simply translates to a few less omelets and custards for you and is no big deal, then it's probably best to let nature take its course. If you are committed to having a specific number of eggs year-round, however, you will need to install artificial lighting.

One 40-watt bulb placed 7 feet (2.1 m) off the ground is plenty of light for a 100-square-foot (9.3 m²) coop; opt for 60 watts if your coop is bigger. In order to mimic longer hours of daylight, you will need to turn the lights

Adequate light is essential.

on either in the morning or the evening to achieve a total of 15 daylight hours. I recommend extending your chickens' day at dawn as opposed to dusk. If you turn out the lights on your flock too quickly, before they're settled onto their roosts, you'll scare the . . . well . . . poop out of them unnecessarily. Either trust yourself to head out to the coop earlier each day or set up a lighting timer to do the work for you.

Pullets need fewer hours than layers, only 8 to 10 as opposed to 15. Giving pullets too much light too soon may cause them to mature too quickly, which can result in prolapse. Prolapse is a condition where tissue just inside the vent is forced out. Eggs may remain attached inside. Remove a prolapsed pullet from the flock as soon as possible, as the visible tissue may encourage other chickens to peck, causing her to hemorrhage. Apply a lubricating hemorrhoid cream, push the tissue back inside the vent, and isolate the pullet until she is healed. Or, save yourself the trouble and use artificial lighting only with layers, never with pullets.

WELL-APPOINTED BEDDING

Bedding, also known as litter, is the absorbent material put down in nesting boxes and poultry housing floors. It is used to provide a cushion for your bird's feet and eggs, offer them insulation, minimize their contact with fecal matter, and absorb their droppings. Any number of materials would be

The most important thing to consider when selecting appropriate litter is that it is completely dry. Any trapped moisture could become a breeding ground for mold and bacteria, which can in turn affect your flock's respiration. Each day, rake over the bedding and, over time, it will break down and begin to compost. You will need to remove the bedding completely several times a year in order to prevent the spread of disease or infection, as well as provide a clean and happy home for your flock. Even chickens appreciate a thorough spring (and fall) cleaning.

Appropriate bedding materials for feathering your girls' nest include wood shavings, sawdust, chopped straw, ripped-up newspaper, dry leaves, even peanut shells. If you opt for wood shavings, be certain to use those designed specifically for this purpose, as some shavings contain fine dust particles that may cause respiratory problems in chickens. Whatever you choose, be sure to put it down at least 2 inches (5 cm) thick in the nesting boxes and 5 to 10 inches (12.7 to 25.4 cm) deep on the floor. For my Ladies, I've put down cedar shavings as bedding. Each nesting box contains shavings about 3 inches (7.6 cm) deep, while the floor has about 6 inches (15.2 cm). Every morning, after I let the Ladies out of the house and feed them, I grab a garden rake kept hanging from the henhouse wall at all times and give the bedding a quick stir. It covers up the droppings

and evens out the smell. In fact, my henhouse almost always smells great!

The method I use, often referred to as the "deep litter" bedding method, allows for the convenience of needing to change out bedding completely only every four to six months. You will need to replenish supplies along the way to maintain a layer between 5 and 10 inches (12.7 and 25.4 cm) at all times. The thickness of the bedding layer, well aerated, will help prevent odor. Some chicken keepers even throw grain on the housing floor to encourage their chickens to scratch. Given incentive, the chickens themselves will stir up the droppings and work them into the bedding. I mean, really, why should you do all the work when you have beaks and claws available to assist?

Alternatively, some chicken keepers use what is referred to as a droppings board or pan. A mesh-wire covered pan or wood board with raised slats is placed underneath the roosts. This allows droppings to fall down through the openings in the board to a place where chickens cannot peck at them. If you use this method, be sure the droppings board is high

enough off the ground to be inaccessible to burrowing animals. Whatever method you elect, remember that chicken poop makes great fertilizer. When you remove droppings and litter, simply toss them into a compost pile. From eggs to meat to garden amendments, chickens are the pets that just keep on giving!

A FOUNDATION TO BUILD UPON

Proper flooring is essential to a safe, healthy, and solid coop. If your housing is mobile, then your "flooring" is simply grass. As long as you rotate the location of your tractor every day, grass flooring will work well. Commonly used types of flooring for permanent housing include concrete, wood, dirt, and the aforementioned droppings boards.

Concrete flooring offers the greatest degree of protection from rodents and burrowing predators, and it's easy to clean. You may elect to mix and pour the concrete yourself or hire a contractor to do the job for you. Either way, concrete is your most expensive flooring option. Concrete isn't a material you can simply move should you become dissatisfied with your chosen location, so make sure your site selection is final before you pour.

Wood floors are great for thrifty builders; you can really use just about any wood to do the job. Recycle wood from an old project, scavenge some from someone's curbside rubbish, or simply buy new from the local hardware store. Your floor will need to be raised off the ground by at least 1 foot (30.5 cm), on either posts or concrete blocks. The downside to wood floors is that they can be difficult to clean and, accordingly, will need to be replaced every few years, based on regular wear and tear.

One solution that I implemented in my henhouse is to line the wood floor with linoleum. Our friend Tom, an amazing handyman if there ever was one, swooped up the linoleum in the corners when he first helped set up the coop, allowing the linoleum to rise up about 5 to 6 inches (12.7 to 15.2 cm) above the floor. This way, come cleaning time, all I have to do is sweep out the deep litter into a wheelbarrow (bound for the compost heap), hose down and mop the floor, and then spread a new layer of deep bedding. No nasty scrubbing of wooden floorboards!

You may also place your coop over a simple bare earthen floor. While this is seemingly the most cost-effective option, it may cause more trouble, and subsequent expense in repair, in the long term. Dirt that is not sandy will simply become too moist and muddy during wet weather. Remember, excessive moisture is public enemy number one with chickens. While a dirt floor will help keep chickens cooler during warmer months, it will pull heat away during cooler times of the year. Dirt floors can also be a challenge to keep free of droppings and can by no means be considered predator or rodent proof. If the dirt where you intend to situate your housing drains well and is sandy, however, such flooring may be a good choice for your needs. You will need to rake the floor daily to remove droppings and cover over holes your chickens may have dug. You may also need to place wood chips or sand atop the dirt to prevent it from getting too mucky.

Chicken housing comes in all shapes, sizes, and materials.

SITE SPECIFIC

Choosing the proper location for your housing is imperative. If you pick a bad spot, you could be faced with multiple inconveniences to both you and your flock. Ideally, permanent housing should be situated on a south-facing slope or slight incline to allow water to drain away during rain and snow, as well as permit ample light for drying out the run and warming up the coop. Windows placed on the south-facing wall let light flood the coop, so your chickens receive sunlight even on short winter days.

Make sure that your coop is located close enough to your home. You will want to be aware of the goings-on in the coop, keeping a watchful eye out for predators and other dangers, including those the chickens might bring on themselves. Also, having your flock nearby allows you to bring them water and food without having to travel great distances, which on cold winter mornings or during wet spring weather will be a godsend. If your coop is not wired, having the housing adjacent to your own will allow you to rig up electric cords, should you have need for them.

Additionally, you will want to make sure that your flock's housing is situated both according to ordinances and setback codes where you live and not too near to your neighbors' homes. Even the tidiest of chicken tenders cannot escape the "aroma" generated by daily chicken droppings. Making certain the coop's site is far enough away from your neighbor's windows will go a long way toward engendering goodwill. I once read of a clever, and prescient, chicken keeper who strategically planted sweet-smelling perennial plants around her coop, allowing the heady perfume of the plants to override the malodorous scent of chicken funk.

If you allow your chickens to free-roam, be mindful of the existing landscaping in your yard. Chickens are not known to traipse gently through the great outdoors, preferring instead to scratch, peck, and otherwise trample whatever they come across. If you have tender shoots or seedlings, prizewinning roses, or carefully manicured borders you would prefer remained as such, plan to either limit the chickens' yard access with a run, or purchase transportable fencing and situate them precisely where you want them to be.

KEEP IT CLEAN

Regular cleaning practices are essential to maintain the structural integrity of your housing and keep parasites at bay. While minor maintenance will need to happen daily or monthly, the "big clean" need only occur once a year. The number of birds kept dictates how often you will need to clean; small flocks are easier to keep tidy than large, hundred-bird

Keep tools at hand for keeping your coop clean.

chicken enterprises. See the appendix (page 78) for a checklist of cleaning and maintenance tasks to be done daily, weekly, monthly, biannually, and annually.

If you have droppings boards, they need to be emptied daily. Failure to do so can result in both a smelly house and hard, caked-on droppings when you finally do get around to emptying them. Those using the deep bedding method will need to rake the droppings over each day, spreading the bedding across the entire floor. Add more bedding over time to maintain a height of around 5 to 10 inches (12.7 to 25.4 cm). Empty out and replenish all the bedding every four to six months. If you use straw in your henhouse, it will need to be removed weekly, especially those areas that become moist and matted. Also, check nesting boxes to see if they have become soiled or need bedding added to them.

Check feeders and waterers daily for droppings or caked up mud. I keep a scouring pad in my coop and give the rim on the Ladies' galvanized waterer a quick scrub-down every few days to remove accumulated dust and debris. A daily scrubbing of roosts and perches is a good idea as well. I use a rake to give a quick run over the perches each morning to prevent the build-up of excrement and to allow droppings to begin to compost in the bedding below. A daily perimeter check will keep you abreast of potential annoyances before they develop into problems. Look for indications of tunneling, tears in the fencing, protruding pieces of wood or nails, and any other needed repairs.

Gear up for the "big clean" once a year. It is a good idea to do this in the spring, before the heat of summer brings out every imaginable parasite. Place your flock safely outdoors, preferably on a sunny day, which will allow for rapid drying in the henhouse. Wear a breathing mask, as a lot of dust can get stirred up during the cleaning process. After you have swept out all bedding and debris, make a solution of one part bleach, one part liquid dish soap, and 10 parts water. I would advise using a non-chlorine bleach along with a natural, nontoxic, biodegradable dish liquid for this job. Toxic chemicals used for cleaning can affect your flock's health, and runoff can pollute local groundwater supplies.

Rent or buy a pressure washer or a backpack sprayer from a hardware retailer, or purchase a small unit for a nominal expense. Fill it up with the solution and saturate every surface of the interior of your coop, taking care to look for nooks and crannies that could easily go unnoticed. Leave all doors and windows opens to dry. Be certain to prevent your flock from entering during the cleaning and drying period.

BUY OR DIY?

These days, it is possible to purchase pretty much everything you need to house your flock. Roosts, nesting boxes, chicken tractors, even complete coops can be purchased through mail-order catalogs and online. If you have the time and tools, you can also craft these necessities yourself.

BUILDING ROOSTS

Chickens prefer sleeping on perches, or roosts, in the evening. After all, they are descended from wild birds, which sleep in trees. While most chickens can't quite make it up into trees (not for lack of trying!), they do feel safer elevated off the ground. Wood is the best material for constructing roosts. Plastic or metal surfaces will not work, as they lack the texture needed in order for chickens to grip the perch with their toes. An old wooden stepladder or tiered towel drying rack will more than suffice. If you opt for new wood, purchase rounded dowels or round off the corners of a square piece with a sander. Roosts should be between 1 and 3 inches (2.5 and 7.6 cm) in diameter, depending on the size of your birds.

If you need more than one perch, position the dowels or pieces of wood in a stair-step fashion with levels at least 12 to 18 inches (30.5 to 45.7 cm) apart. Chickens poop at night and their droppings would otherwise fall right on top of their roommates below. Position roosts 2 to 4 feet (61 to 121.9 cm) off the ground and 18 inches (45.7 cm) from the closest parallel wall. Make sure to secure them firmly to prevent them from turning or falling down.

How Much Space?

Roost Width	Roost Length
1 inch (2.5 cm) for bantams	8 inches (20.3 cm) per bird for
2 inches (5 cm) for standards	lightweight breeds and bantams
	10 inches (25.4 cm) per bird for
	heavy breeds

Homegrown Fertilizer

Chicken manure offers a rich, natural, and free source of soil enrichment. Gardeners pay top dollar for bags of composted manure purchased from the home and garden store. With your own flock of chickens, you now have access to premium fertilizer all year round for no additional cost. Fresh chicken manure is high in nitrogen, and direct application to many plants can "burn" them, although several, such as berry bushes, welcome the heat. For most garden and landscaping plants, a better approach is to toss your chickens' droppings, along with any bedding you are changing out, into your compost bin. Through the alchemy of composting, all that nitrogen gets transformed into a less scorching, abundantly nourishing, organic fertilizer. Composting also helps kill off any harmful bacteria and viruses that may have been lurking in fresh droppings. Alternatively, you can place the fresh droppings and bedding on top of vegetable or flower beds prepped for winter rest. You could even allow your flock to romp around in the area, letting their scratching, digging, and pecking work the manure down into the soil.

left: **Tree branch roost** *middle:* **Painted dowel roost** *right:* **Step ladder roost**

One nesting box for every four hens ensures adequate laying room.

BUILDING NESTING BOXES

Building your own chicken nesting boxes is not much harder than building a simple box. There are infinite variations on how to do it, but this is a simple version that works great. Most poultry experts suggest one box per four laying hens.

The accompanying photo is of the nesting box I have in my coop. We made it larger than necessary so that we can expand our flock in the future. The project below is for a three-hole nesting box, which will easily accommodate 12 chickens.

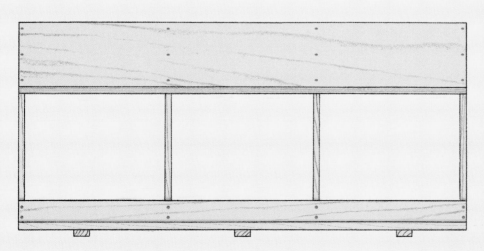

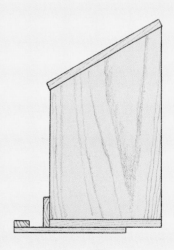

CUT LIST & SUPPLIES

Solid Wood

Number of Parts	Dimensions of each piece	Description	Comments	Ref.
2	1 x 12 board, 4' (1.2 m) long	Top and bottom of nesting box	See the **IMPORTANT NOTE** below on lumber dimensions.	A
4	1 x 12 board, one end cut straight and one cut diagonally to make one side 12" (30.5 cm) long and one 18" (45.7 cm) long	Dividing panels	You'll need about 6' (1.8 m) of 1 x 12 wood in all to make these pieces.	B
1	1 x 3 board, 4' (1.2 m) long	Nesting box lip		C
1	1 x 2 board, 4' (1.2 m) long	Perch railing		D
3	1 x 2 board, 12" (30.5 cm) long	Perch supports		E

¼-inch (6 mm) Plywood

Number of Parts	Dimensions of each piece	Description	Comments	Ref.
1	4' x 18" sheet (1.2 m x 45.7 cm)	Optional backing		F

Other Materials and Supplies

Number of Parts	Dimensions of each piece	Description	Comments	Ref.
4	2" x 2" (5 x 5 cm)	Angle braces		
	1¾" (4.4 cm), 1¼" (3.2 cm), and ¾" (1.9 cm) long	Wood screws		

IMPORTANT NOTE: The dimensions for boards given here are the *nominal* dimensions they are sold by in lumberyards, not the actual dimensions. The actual dimensions are as follows: 1 x 12 = ¾ x 11¼ inches (1.9 x 28.6 cm); 1 x 3 = ¾ x 2½ inches (1.9 x 6.4 cm); 1 x 2 = ¾ x 1½ inches (1.9 x 3.8 cm).

Framing the Boxes

1. Place the square end of the four angle-cut boards (B) on one of the 4-foot (1.2 m) 1 x 12 pieces (A). This will be the bottom of the nesting box. Two of the boards will go on top of the 4-foot (1.2 m) piece, flush with the edge at both ends, and the other two boards will be placed about one foot (30.5 cm) from each end. Draw pencil lines on the 4-foot (1.2 m) 1 x 12 to show where the angle-cut boards will be, then take the four boards off the bottom piece.

2. Attach the angled boards one at a time, each with three 1¾-inch (4.4 cm) wood screws through the bottom of the 4-foot (1.2 m) 1 x 12, two near each end and one in the middle. It is best to drill pilot holes first. Clamp the board to a worktable or have a partner carefully hold the boards in place as you work. For the pilot holes, use a drill bit a little smaller than the diameter of the wood screws. Be sure to carefully center the pilot holes. Drill each pilot hole through the bottom board and about ½ inch (1.3 cm) deep into the angle-cut board. Place a piece of tape 1¼ inches (3.1 cm) from the end of the drill to guide your depth. If you make a mistake and miss the center, don't worry; just drill another hole about a ½ inch (1.3 cm) away.

3. Keep the boards in place after drilling each pilot hole, and drive a 1¾-inch (4.4 cm) wood screw through the pilot hole before making the next one. Screw all four boards in place this way.

4. Line the remaining 4-foot (1.2 m) 1 x 12 piece (A) up with the edges of the 18-inch (45.7 cm) ends of the vertical boards. Drive three 1¾-inch (4.4 cm) wood screws through the top piece into each of the four dividing panels, using pilot holes as in steps 2 and 3. The top may not reach all the way down to the front as in the drawing, but it is not necessary that it does.

Securing the Lip

1. Align the 4-foot (1.2 m) length of 1 x 3 (C) with the bottom of the nesting box on the front (shorter) side.

2. Attach with two 1¾-inch (4.4 cm) screws on each end and one in the middle, using pilot holes as above.

Attaching the Perch

1. One board at a time, place the wider side of each 12-inch (30.5 cm) 1 x 2 piece (E) against the bottom of the nesting box, with two about 6 inches (15.2 cm) in from the sides of the nesting box and one in the middle. Let the perch support stick out 4 inches (10.2 cm) from the bottom of the nesting box.

2. Screw each perch support to the bottom of the nesting box with two 1¼-inch (3.2 cm) screws, using pilot holes as above.

3. Place the 4-foot (1.2 m) 1 x 2 piece (D) on top of the supports, flush with the protruding ends. Connect with one 1¼-inch (3.2 cm) screw for each support, using pilot holes as above.

Fastening to the Coop Wall

1. Attach the nesting box to the side of your coop using four metal angle braces attached with ¾-inch (1.9 cm) screws. Placement will depend on what works best with your particular coop. Sturdy 2-inch (5 cm) metal angle braces with two screws for each side of the angle should xbe fine to safely secure the boxes.

2. You won't need to put a back onto your nesting box if it is up against the wall. If this is not the case, however, simply attach a 4-foot x 18-inch (1.2 m x 45.7 cm) sheet of plywood (F) to the back with screws before you attach the box to the wall.

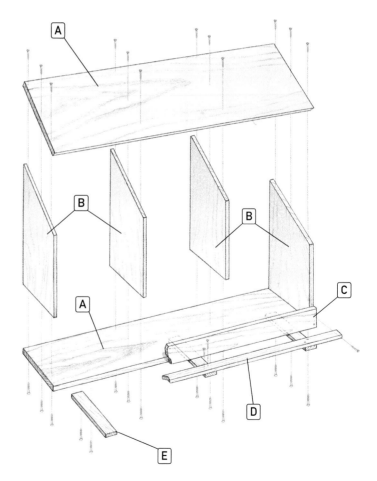

Chapter 5
Feeding

Most people keep chickens in order to get something out of them, literally. In order for chickens to furnish you with well-formed eggs and tasty meat, they need to be properly fed. Age, sex, climate, and intended use all contribute to individualized feeding needs. Just as you wouldn't feed a grown man puréed carrots with peas, or give a baby a filet mignon with a glass of pinot noir, life stages in chickens determine what foods they require. Knowing who needs what and when contributes to the health and longevity of your flock.

EASY TO DIGEST

The digestive system of chickens is an incredible design. As they have no teeth (think of the adage "scarce as hen's teeth"), chickens simply gather up edibles into their beaks. From there, the tongue moves food to the esophagus and then on to the crop. The crop is a pouch in the throat, acting as essentially a holding tank of sorts, where food is packed in and stored for a time. At the end of a day of pecking, you can actually see your chicken's crop bulging. Situated in the middle of their chests, the crop will appear as a small, golf ball–sized protrusion. After it leaves the crop, food travels to the first of a chicken's two stomachs, the proventriculus, also referred to as the "true" stomach. It is here that enzymes and hydrochloric acid are introduced.

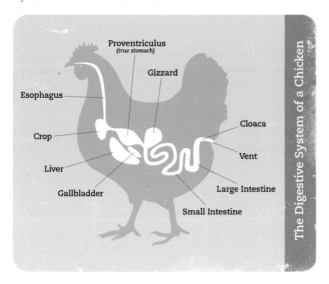

Next, the still-undigested food moves into the second of the two stomachs, the ventriculus, better known as the gizzard. The gizzard serves as a grinding muscle, churning the food with gastric juices from the proventriculus. Any gritty material the chicken has consumed during the day helps the gizzard grind up tougher material. The resulting mass then passes to the small and large intestine, where nutrients are absorbed and water is extracted. Whatever remains moves through the cloaca to be passed as waste out the vent. Amazingly, all of this occurs in a mere three to four hours. Chickens forage and consume food virtually the entirety of their waking hours. The rapid time of digestion, coupled with the prodigious amount of food consumed, accounts for the abundance of poop chickens produce.

THE RIGHT BALANCE

Chickens require a healthy balance of fats, carbohydrates, protein, vitamins, and minerals in order to fulfill their numerous biologic needs. From properly fine-tuning their internal thermostats, to providing energy, to offering the right vitamins for shell integrity, the proper ratio of dietary micro- and macronutrients is essential for optimal chicken output, not to mention a happily clucking bird.

Chickens are innate foragers. Given access to the outdoors, they will search tirelessly for bugs, worms, grass, leaves, grubs, and anything else they can get their beaks on. Their phenomenally acute vision allows them to see microscopic organisms in the soil. While birds in the wild can meet their nutritional needs themselves, domesticated fowl need assistance, even if they are permitted to forage. Commercial feeds remove the guesswork, carefully orchestrating the perfect dietary balance for you. You can further enrich their diet with supplements and treats.

DAILY RATIONS

Commercially prepared poultry feed is customized to meet chickens' daily nutritional requirements. While it is possible to formulate your own feed, it is a daunting task. Feed must include precise amounts of proteins, fats, carbohydrates, vitamins, and minerals. Such a recipe can be concocted at home, but it's a task best left to experienced chicken raisers.

Chicken feed can be purchased at your nearest feed store. Where you live largely dictates the availability of feed choices. Generally, the more rural your location, the greater access you will have to a range of ration options. Those in urban areas may have to look just outside of city limits to find a supplier. It is also possible to order feed online, no matter where you are on the map.

You can also join a buying club in your area. When I was setting up my flock, I was surprised to learn that none of the local suppliers offered organic feed. Through a friend, I became part of a buying club that makes monthly bulk purchases of organic feed from a national distributor. Each month the coordinator sends an e-mail detailing the delivery schedule. Payment is made in advance, and then, on the designated day, we rendezvous in a predetermined location. The whole pickup process feels very covert in a James-Bond-meets-the-farm sort of way. I pull up my car, give my last name, they put the goods in the trunk, and I speed away.

Commercially prepared feeds come in either mash or pellet form. Opinions vary as to which is the preferable choice. Pellets,

which are, in essence, compact cylinders of food, have the advantage of reducing waste. They also help keep show chickens clean. Mash can get messy, as chickens will scatter it on the ground, and more of it will subsequently be wasted than pellets. However, mash is considered ideal for flocks kept in confined quarters. Chickens will quickly consume pellets, while it can take hours for them to eat an equivalent amount of mash. Foraging around for mash keeps them entertained and active, both of which are desirable habits for offsetting winter boredom.

SWEETENING THE POT

In addition to their daily feed, your flock will both enjoy and benefit from supplemental foods. While those with large-scale

left: **Layer crumble** *right:* **Layer mash**

poultry operations may advise sticking to a strictly commercial feed diet to maximize growth and production, backyard flock owners generally don't mind as much if their crew's egg output is occasionally sporadic or they take a bit longer to fatten up for table. Scratch, grit, and table scraps are all options you may want to consider giving to your winged buddies as occasional treats.

Scratch

If you want to see a whole lot of squawking and general merriment occur in your flock, sprinkle some scratch their way. Also known as "cereal feeds," scratch is simply a combination of two or more grains, in whole or coarsely cracked form. Commonly used scratch grains include corn, wheat, milo, oats, millet, rice, barley, rye, and buckwheat. Think of scratch as a treat, though, not a meal replacement. Scratch is high in fat but low in protein. It is imperative that laying hens receive at least 16 percent total protein in their diet daily. Although hens will happily devour fat-rich grains all day, too much fat will throw off their protein consumption, which can be detrimental. Overeating scratch can also result in excess weight for your flock, which can pose its own health risks.

Many chicken tenders provide their flock a meal of mash or pellets in the morning and scatter scratch around for an afternoon delight. Toss the grains directly into their housing and chickens will peck and dig around for the scratch, fluffing up their bedding and "stomp"-composting it in the process. To help them generate and retain heat, feed your flock more scratch in the winter. Oats, which are naturally cooling when

digested, make a nice substitute or addition to scratch during searing summer heat.

Grit

Whether or not you will need to offer grit to your flock depends largely on how they are housed and what they are fed. Grit is any form of small pebble or stone that chickens ingest to assist in digestion. As they have no teeth, grit offers the grinding element needed in the gizzard to break down grain and insoluble fiber. Birds kept in confinement with little to no access to the outdoors will need grit added to their diets. Flocks that are generally range-fed, consuming mostly grass and bugs, will need grit as well, to assist in breaking down plant matter. If your flock eats commercially prepared feed, either in mash or pellet form, you will not need to supplement with grit, as the grains in the feed have already been ground. Also, if your flock has access to a run or yard where stones or small pebbles may be found, adding grit is not necessary. If you are uncertain about the need to add grit or not, you can do as one natural poultry feed distributor advised me. Simply shovel up a scoop of river or streambed dirt and deposit it in your run. Don't substitute yard soil, as it may not offer the needed stones and sand. Replace with a new scoopful every four months or so, depending on your flock size. You may also simply gather up a bag of grit at your local feed store and scatter a handful to your flock or place grit in a container and allow your chickens to take what they need.

left: **Scratch** *right:* **Grit**

Table Scraps

A flock of chickens is a virtual garbage disposal machine. Chickens love to eat what we eat, as well as what's left of what we don't or won't eat. They will gladly gobble up scraps such as apple peelings, carrot tops, heels of bread, leftover cooked meat, and banana peels. Don't give them anything spoiled or moldy, onions or garlic (as they will affect the flavor of eggs), citrus fruit or peels, avocados, raw potato peels, fish, and anything too salty, fatty, or sugary. Pretty much anything else is fair game. At my house, my Ladies get a daily smattering of currants, raisins, blueberries, raspberries, wineberries, or whatever else is seasonally available and on hand. I also give them torn up bits of parsley every few days and salad or leafy greens, depending on the time of year. The chlorophyll in the greens and herbs offer nutrients called carotenoids that aid in coloring their yolks so vibrantly.

If your flock does not have access to grass in their run, consider providing them with fresh greens. Weeds pulled from your yard or vegetable garden will make a fine addition to your flock's diet. I've given mine chickweed, dandelion greens, and plantain, much to their squawking delight! If you really want to treat your flock, plant a garden just for them. Little lettuces and hardy greens are sure to please. Tossing in the occasional slug, cricket, or worm you find lying around never fails to enchant them. After picking hornworms off my tomato plants, any that I gather up go straight to the Ladies. What ensues is the chicken equivalent of a catfight, often with the hornworm as the prize in a game of tug-of-war!

WAY TO GROW!

Nutritional needs for chickens will vary throughout their lifetimes. There are five general feeding classes: chicks, broilers, pullets, layers, and breeders. Commercial feed, also known as "ration," is available for each class. Chicks and their feeding requirements will be discussed in detail on pages 57 to 58.

Broiler feed is high in protein, making up 18 to 22 percent of the feed's volume. This expedites growth, enabling chickens to become table ready quickly. Most birds intended for table are fed a broiler "starter/grower" ration until six weeks of age or so, and then transitioned to a "finisher" ration until slaughter.

Pullet feed contains no calcium and is lower in protein than chick feed. This is to prevent the birds from maturing too quickly, thereby bringing on early laying. Early maturation can result in smaller eggs and potential internal injury to your hens.

Once they are ready, around 18 to 20 weeks of age, pullets graduate to "big girl" food, known as layer rations, which provides sufficient calcium for eggshells to properly harden. Layer feed should be composed of 16 to 18 percent protein, the upper end of the percentage being reserved for birds in particularly warm weather that may be inclined to consume less food.

Kitchen scraps and fresh herbs provide additional nutrients to your flock.

Breeder feed contains extra protein and vitamins for chicken mommas-to-be. It is of the utmost importance that hens destined for breeding be given appropriately formulated feed. Layer feed contains neither adequate protein nor the proper amounts of vitamins and minerals needed for developing fertile eggs. Experts recommend starting breeder rations two to four weeks before you plan on beginning hatching. In the event that you are unable to locate breeder feed, add a handful of dog or cat food two or three times per week to layer rations, starting six weeks before you intend to gather eggs for hatching. You will also need to incorporate a powdered vitamin and mineral supplement into the breeding hen's water.

WATER, WATER, EVERYWHERE!

Chickens need access to clean water at all times. Much like humans, chickens are composed mostly of water. Their bodies as well as their eggs depend on a continual supply of water. Deprived of adequate water for even 24 hours, a chicken will begin to suffer. Any longer and they may never fully recover. While they may not take large gulps at one time, chickens do drink copiously throughout the day, averaging around 1 to 2 cups (240 to 480 mL) per chicken. It is therefore essential to stay on top of both the availability and cleanliness of the water you offer your birds.

In warm climates and during the hottest calendar months, refresh your flock's water supply as necessary. They will consume considerably more fluid when the mercury rises. When the temperature drops, it is essential that you prevent the water supply from freezing. This can be done either by changing out waterers as needed if it's below freezing or by installing a heated waterer. Chickens are notoriously finicky, so be certain their water doesn't become too hot or too cold. Between 50 and 55°F (10 and 13°C) would be their preference. Like Goldilocks, they like things to be just right.

FEEDING FRENZY

There are two methods commonly used for feeding chickens: free choice or by hand, also referred to as restricted feeding. In free-choice feeding, the chickens themselves call the shots on when to eat and how much to consume per feeding session. In

43

PORTION CONTROL

Just how much feed should you dole out per meal? That depends on the age of your chickens, their breed, and the time of year. Smaller chickens and young birds will eat less food than full-grown, heavy breeds. All chickens need increased portions during cold weather. Anywhere between 4 and 6 ounces (112 and 168 g) of feed per day is recommended for adult birds. Again, that amount will vary depending on age, climate, bird size, whether they are laying, whether they have opportunity to forage, and whether they are molting or broody. If you are looking to reduce feed costs and have a suitable location for free-ranging, allow them to forage liberally. No matter what, remember that it is very important your chickens get enough to eat. Underfed chickens won't grow properly, and their ability to lay well will be compromised.

At daily mealtimes, watch to see how quickly the food is disappearing. If they gobble it up like it's their last meal ever, they need more food. Have their droppings examined by a veterinarian to rule out worms or parasites. If the amount of food you offered in the morning looks to be untouched when you return for the evening meal, your birds might not like their feed or you may be providing more than is necessary. Check to be sure it is still fresh and not comprised of mostly vitamin and mineral dust. Sprinkle in some table scraps as temptation to rev up their appetites.

restricted feeding, your flock is fed a limited amount, for only a brief period of time. Each scenario has its own set of pros and cons.

Free-choice feeding makes it more likely that all members of the flock will fill their gizzards. The constant availability of feed allows those lower in the pecking order to feed when higher-status birds may not be around. This feeding style also has the advantage of enabling chicken owners to fill the hopper less often, maybe even have a weekend away if your chickens' housing is predator-proof and self-regulating. On the other hand, chickens waste considerably more rations when they are allowed free-choice feeding. They may also overeat and put on additional unnecessary weight.

Restricted feeding, or feeding by hand, ensures the least amount of feed will be wasted. It is also the preferred method for those keeping show birds, as it keeps them cleaner and increases their enthusiasm for human interaction. Conversely, it is time-consuming and may be prohibitively so for those with busy mornings, like getting to work on time or getting the kids fed and off to school at the break of dawn. Restricted feeding may prevent lower-status birds from getting as much food as they need, as bossy hens tend to hog the feeder. If you opt for a restricted feeding program, you may need to purchase more feeders so that everyone can eat to satiety at the same time.

FEED YOUR CHICKENS WELL

The food and water you provide to your chickens will need to go in containers suitable to their needs and tendencies, which is to say, their inclination to make enormous messes. Specially designed feeders and waterers are commercially available. If you can't swing the cost of feeders or waterers, great ideas for homemade versions can be found online.

Chow Time

One common feeder design consists of either galvanized or plastic tubes, suspended off the ground by chain. Another option is metal or wood troughs that rest on the ground. Whatever you choose, you want to be certain that it discourages waste, prevents your birds from sullying the contents with chicken poop, and is easy for you to both fill and clean. Keep your feeder in a covered area outdoors, just outside the coop. This keeps the feeder out of rain and snow and encourages your crew to venture outside and dig for bugs and other beneficial creepy crawlies.

Galvanized tubes can be handy if you want a weekend away, as they can be filled with several pounds worth of feed at a time. They are also relatively easy to clean, which you should do as often as monthly, or sooner if the feeder is visibly grungy. You will want to suspend tube feeders from the ceiling so that the bottom of the feeder is at the same height as your chickens'

backs. Alternatively, if you are lacking somewhere to hang the tube from, simply place cement blocks under the feeder until it is at the same height as your birds' backs. This aids in keeping the food in the feeder instead of all over the ground and keeps any bedding material out.

Trough feeders should never be filled more than half full, or your flock will waste just as much as they eat. Well-constructed trough feeders, like tube feeders, should keep your chickens from stepping into them or roosting on them. Most are designed to be height-adjustable for lowering and raising based on your flock's age and size. Like tube feeders, they will need to be cleaned regularly to keep the feed hygienic.

Thirst Quenchers

Waterers are available for purchase in quart, and 1-, 5-, and 10-gallon (1 to 38 L) sizes. They are constructed of either metal or plastic. What the metal options add in weight, they more than make up for in durability. Plastic feeders are more likely to crack or break, but they will be lighter to carry if you intend to fill them somewhere other than at the coop. Like feeders, waterers should be suspended just to the level of your chicken's backs.

I have a 5-gallon (19 L) waterer that lives permanently with the chickens. Each morning, as I gather up the Ladies' feed and daily treats, I fill up a plastic plant watering can and schlep

Organic

The term "organic" refers to an agricultural practice that preserves and replenishes soil vitality without the addition of any artificial or conventional pesticides or fertilizers. Furthermore, food that is organically grown must be done so without the use of antibiotics, synthetic hormones, genetic engineering, sewage sludge, or irradiation.

When deliberating feed options for your flock, consider organic feed. Chicken feed that is organically produced is made with grains that have not been treated with chemical herbicides, insecticides, or fertilizers. Chickens fed exclusively organic feed will naturally then provide organic eggs and meat. Evidence suggests that organically grown foods are safer and more nutritionally rich than conventionally grown foods. Organic foods are generally a bit more costly than those produced conventionally. Consider your options, read up on conventional versus organic, and decide what is best for you, your family, and your budget.

everything up to the chickens with my faithful dogs in tow. If the day's heat merits it, or I worry the water will freeze within several hours, I'll bring them more later in the day. This way, I don't have to lug the whole waterer with me up to the house each time.

There are a number of devices available for giving your chickens a continuous supply of water. Automatic waterers can be found at some feed stores and at many online poultry suppliers. Electric warmers are available for those where winter weather is particularly severe. A low-tech trick is to keep two waterers and change them out during the day, allowing the frozen waterer to thaw indoors before exchanging again. Whichever type of waterer you choose, remember to keep it clean, scrubbing it as often as needed.

FRESHNESS IN STORE

It is important to keep your chickens' feed fresh. When purchasing, only buy what you can go through in two to four weeks. This will help prevent spoilage as well as maintain the efficacy of added vitamins, minerals, and supplements. Proper storage is just as important. If storing the feed indoors, place it in an airtight plastic container. Outdoors, use a galvanized steel trash bin, as rodents will often chew right through plastic containers. Secure the lid of the metal pail with a bungee cord to keep feed fresh and pesky varmints out.

Any 10-gallon (38 L) plastic or metal trash can will hold 50 pounds (22.7 kg) of feed, which is terribly convenient, as feed usually comes in 50-pound bags. Be sure the feed remains free of moisture and out of direct sunlight at all times. If kept outdoors, your feed storage bin will need to be protected from rain and snow. Make sure to use up all of the feed in one bag before adding the contents of a new bag to your feed container. If you have just a tiny portion of older feed left, scoop it out of the bin first and place it at the top of the chickens' feed for that day.

> **TIP:**
>
> Refer to the Chicken Care Checklist on page 78 for reminders of daily, weekly, monthly, and annual chicken chores.

Chapter 6 🐔
Hatching Eggs

Whether you are just setting up your flock or simply reach a point where you are ready to expand, a time will come when you may consider hatching chicks yourself. This might be done initially to establish a strong, healthy flock, or perhaps as a science lesson for young children, or even simply by virtue of necessity as aging layers decrease their output. Whatever your particular motivation, consider in advance the essential requirements of successfully hatching eggs to determine if this is the best route for you. Hatching eggs is not an easy feat for the novice. If you have the time and constitution for it, though, the reward of watching an emerging chick peck its way into the world is unparalleled.

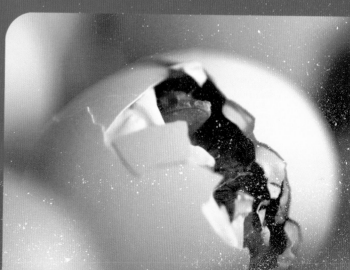

OBTAINING FERTILE EGGS

A rooster is required for fertilizing eggs. Necessarily, without a rooster nearby, any eggs your hens lay will not be fertile. In that case, there are several options available for obtaining fertile eggs. You can either take eggs from a hen in your area that is laying fertile eggs, or you can order freshly laid, fertilized eggs through the mail. To locate a hen in your area with fertile eggs, contact your local feed store, look in the classified section of your local paper, or search online for farmers and chicken enthusiasts in your area.

If you do keep a rooster as a permanent resident of your flock, your eggs are guaranteed to be fertile. If you live in an area where roosters are allowed but do not keep one, consider renting a "stud." In this scenario, a rooster of guaranteed quality breeding stock is housed with your layers for a period of time, usually a month, before he is returned to his owner. This enables you to have the benefits of home-hatched fertile eggs without all the less-desirable "extras" that come with full-time rooster ownership. Make sure that your rooster comes from healthy stock conforming to breed standards, especially if you ever intend to show your birds. Roosters with flawed traits, whether a weak constitution or twisted toes, may pass them on to their offspring. If you plan to borrow a rooster, take a good look to verify that he will be a suitable papa for your Ladies' chicks. He should be neither too old nor too young, but in active breeding age.

EXPIRATION DATE

Fertile eggs remain viable for a finite period of time and only if certain conditions are met. After eggs are collected, incubation is advised within six days, although they may be kept for up to two weeks. The manner in which your eggs will be hatched also factors into their storage time. In general, those that are destined for artificial incubation should be stored no longer than a week, while those a broody hen will sit on can be stored for up to 10 days. The longer fertile eggs are stored, the time it takes for them to hatch increases, while their viability decreases.

Temperature is another important variable when storing eggs destined for hatching. The ideal temperature for stored eggs is 55°F (13°C). The eggs should be kept out of direct sunlight in a cool, relatively dry place. Do not put the eggs in a refrigerator. Too much humidity can create conditions conducive to mold and bacteria growth. Too dry an environment can cause moisture to evaporate through the shell. You can store your pre-incubation eggs in a regular egg carton. Place them pointy-end down and tilted a bit to one side. Each day, you will need to tilt the eggs in the opposite direction. You can easily do this by using a small paperback book to prop up one side of the carton, then simply move it to the other side of the carton around midday.

IT'S THE TIME OF THE SEASON

Time of year is important to take into consideration with hatching eggs. Left to their own devices, hens lay fertile eggs in early spring, when daylight hours are increasing. Hatching in spring is ideal for newborn chicks, as the cooler weather keeps germs and parasites that thrive in warmer weather at bay, allowing their fledgling immune systems to develop. Chicks born in this sort of climate are generally stronger and healthier than those born in the heat of summer.

Decide what time of the year to hatch based on your intentions. If your purpose is to have a supply of eggs, chicks hatched in February and March are the way to go. They will begin laying in late summer, while there are still long daylight hours, and continue laying through the fall and for the following year, although production will wane during days with reduced daylight. Chicks hatched during the winter will lay during the summer months as well but will most likely molt in autumn and may not resume laying until the next spring. If you are interested in hatching chicks to be ready for show, be mindful that it will take standard breeds eight to 10 months to mature, while bantams will be ready to show in six to seven months.

Mother Hens

Some chicken breeds have had broodiness bred out of them. Others are known to be reliable brooders. While the following designations will always have their occasional exceptions, they are fairly trustworthy.

Consistently Broody

Ameraucana, Araucana, Australorp, Belgian d'Uccle, Brahma, Buckeye, Chantecler, Cochin, Cubalaya, Dominique, Java, Langshan, Old English Game, Orpington, Silkie, Sumatra, Sussex, Wyandotte

Occasionally Broody

Aseel, Dorking, New Hampshire Red, Plymouth Rock, Rhode Island Red, Shamo

Rarely Broody

Ancona, Andalusian, Campine, Cornish, Hamburg, Houdan, hybrid layers, Jersey Giant, Leghorn, Malay, Minorca, Polish, Spanish White Face

NEST EGGS

Eggs may be incubated either naturally, under a hen, or artificially, in an incubator. To successfully hatch eggs naturally, you will need to either obtain a broody hen or find the best brooder in your flock. While relying on a hen for incubation puts you in the position of waiting for a hen in your flock to go broody, this method is the most fail-safe

way to supply the best conditions for chick growth. The hen will take care of all the physical requirements eggs need to best hatch, without any effort on your part other than meeting the needs of your brooder, which are few. Top of that list are special breeder rations, begun about two to four weeks before you want to start hatching. Breeder rations contain supplemental protein, vitamins, and minerals, which will improve the hatchability rate of your eggs.

Many of the best breeds of laying chickens had broodiness bred out of them long ago. Once a hen gathers a clutch of eggs and starts sitting, the hormone prolactin is released by her pituitary gland. The release of prolactin provokes the cessation of laying. You can see why commercial egg producers would want to breed out the broodiness trait, as a three-week hiatus from egg laying significantly interferes with the flow of egg income. Consult breed profiles to make sure you have a breed known for broodiness before attempting natural incubation.

Even among breeds with a propensity toward broodiness, some birds are broodier than others. Do any of your hens stay in the nesting box for lengthy stints while the others peck away outside? You may have a broody hen in your flock. Hanging out in the nesting box is not conclusive proof, however. In order to determine for certain who you're dealing with, attempt to remove any eggs under your hen. If she moves off with little fuss, you don't have a brooder. If she tries to peck you, makes growling sounds, puffs out her feathers, or otherwise acts ticked off, you might be dealing with a proud mama. You can either wait for eggs to build up in the nest or place fake eggs made of either wood or plastic in the nesting boxes and see who takes to the throne. Before committing fertile eggs to your suspected brooder, place a few fake eggs under her for the night. If she is still there the next day, looking like she is ready to start hanging curtains and painting the nursery, you've got your broody hen! Go ahead then and replace the fake eggs with fertile ones.

Broody hens will need their nests isolated from the rest of the flock. During her three-week sitting period, other hens may bully her or even attempt to take over her nest when she is out eating or doing her business. After the chicks are born,

they may become a target of their flock mates, getting stomped on or eaten by them. Newly hatched chicks are considered scrumptious, easy morsels by predators from above and below. Keeping your broody hen, her eggs, and the eventual chicks safe should be a top priority.

An ideal nest setting is somewhat dark, well-ventilated, predator-proof, and protected from the elements. It needs to be about 15 inches (38.1 cm) square and 16 inches (40.6 cm) high.

A hen exhibiting broodiness

A cardboard box with 1-inch (2.5 cm) slits cut in the roof for ventilation would be fine. After you are certain your hen will sit, you can remove one side of the box so she can come and go as she desires.

Cedar shavings make an ideal nest material, as they provide both a cushion for the eggs and help keep mites and lice away. It is especially important to keep these parasites away, as they can consume enough blood to easily kill newly hatched chicks. If your hen initially sets up her nest in the henhouse or in some other unsuitable area, you will need to relocate her. Do this at night, when she is calmer, and be sure to wear gloves, as a disturbed brooder can take opportunistic pecks, and hard pecks at that. If you have more than one brooder at the same time, each hen will need her own nesting box in separate and distinct areas.

Once she begins sitting, expect your hen to eat, drink, and move very little, usually no more than 30 minutes per day, sometimes less. She'll be busy feathering her nest, literally. A broody hen will pick off feathers from her breast to keep the eggs, and later, the chicks, closer to her warm body. This also allows moisture from her body to keep the eggs from drying out over the three-week sitting period. You can put small bowls of both food and water in the corners of her nest, or just outside it, to encourage her to eat. If she becomes so fixated on the task of mothering that she neglects to eat, you may need to lift her off the nest. Tempt her with scratch thrown right in front of her nest. Be sure to feel up around and under her wings before attempting to lift her, as she may have an egg tucked in there. Make sure she leaves her nest for no more than 30 minutes daily.

After day 16, don't bother her any further. Make sure her physical needs are met, and then let her go about her business while you go about yours. After the chicks begin hatching, the hen should continue to sit. If she ventures out of the nest before all the chicks have hatched, perhaps heading out to look after some curious and adventuresome firstborns, gather up the hatched chicks and care for them. Return the hen to the nest to continue sitting on the unhatched eggs, then return the hatched chicks to her once the whole clutch hatches.

INCUBATING EGGS

If you have fertile eggs, but no broody hen, you can use an incubator to hatch the chicks. While most current incubators are electric, it is still possible to come across oil- or kerosene-based models. Using an incubator for hatching eggs is a tricky dance and one that requires no small amount of skill and knowledge.

Top Models

There are essentially two major types of incubators: tabletop models, which, as their name implies, sit on tables; and chest models, which rest on the floor. For the small production or backyard chicken enthusiast, the tabletop model will more than adequately meet your needs. For those engaging in large-scale poultry production, the chest model is a more suitable option, holding up to several hundred eggs at a time. Within these two types of incubators, what further distinguishes one from another is the manner in which air is circulated. You can purchase either a forced-air or a still-air incubator. Forced-air models have built-in fans that continually circulate air, while still-air models have vents on their tops, sides, and bottom. The forced-air models are considered to be significantly more reliable. Humidity and temperature—the two absolute must-haves for proper hatching—are easier to maintain in these models. Still-air models do work, however, and are usually less costly than forced-air models; they simply require greater vigilance and oversight, as well as foreknowledge that they have reduced rates of hatchability.

Whatever model you opt for, be certain to situate it out of direct sunlight. Putting it in the sun increases the likelihood of temperature fluctuations, which can be a death knell for incubating eggs. You also want to avoid particularly drafty areas, air-conditioning, or directly in front of heat vents. The three variables that would otherwise be maintained by a broody hen and that are most necessary for successful hatches are temperature, egg turning, and humidity.

Temperature

Your incubator will need a thermometer. Forced-air models usually come equipped with a thermometer, whereas still-air models generally do not. Temperature in most still-air models should be set at 102°F (39°C) and at 99.5°F (37.5°C) in forced-air models. While temperature settings will vary by incubator model, the differences are slight. Fluctuations either way can cause death to your eggs, although raising the temperature more often poses a greater threat than lowering it. Be certain to read the manufacturer's instructions that come with your incubator to learn how to best regulate temperature in your model.

Humidity

Maintaining the proper level of humidity in your incubator is also crucial. During the incubating process, eggs lose a little weight as moisture evaporation through the shell. Keeping a humid environment helps to regulate and prevent some of that loss, allowing the eggs to hatch and the chicks to emerge from the shell free of complication. If the growing embryos receive too much humidity, they will grow too large and struggle to get free of their shells upon hatching. Too little humidity and they end up sticking to the shell inside. I can think of few things sadder than a glued-in chick.

Inside the incubator, humidity will need to be at about 55 to 60 percent from day one until day 18, when it shifts up to 70 percent. Humidity levels can be measured with a hygrometer, also called a wet bulb thermometer. Again, consult the manufacturer's instructions that came with your incubator to ensure you are maintaining humidity levels at the percentage needed during different cycles of embryonic development.

Egg Turning

Eggs must be turned during incubation in order to keep the developing embryo from sticking to the shell membrane surrounding it. In more rudimentary terms, egg turning keeps the yolk in the middle of the white inside the egg. If an egg remains in one position for too long, either the embryo can become stuck and eventually die, a crippled or deformed chick will result, or the hatching chick will not be able to properly emerge from its shell. A hen on her nest performs this task naturally about every 15 minutes, either by using her beak to roll the eggs or moving them as she shifts and resettles her weight on the clutch.

In the absence of a hen, you will need to turn the eggs yourself, at least three times daily, more if possible. If you are turning them yourself, turn them as early as possible in the morning and as late as possible in the evening, so that the time lag between turns is as short as possible.

An egg turning tray

The eggs will be turned from side to side, not top to bottom. Think of the way a hen would move eggs under her on a nest. In order to keep track of which eggs you have turned, mark the tops and bottoms with a pencil with an X on one end and an O on the other.

If you will not be on hand as often as required to turn your eggs, then you will need an automatic turning device. Many incubator models come with automatic egg turners that move the eggs at regular intervals, or you can buy a separate egg turner accessory.

SHINE A LIGHT

If you elect to use an incubator, you should check your eggs weekly to be sure the embryos are developing properly and remove any that have spoiled or are maturing incorrectly. Spoiled eggs give off harmful gases that can be breathed in by the other healthy eggs. Candling will tell you which eggs should stay and which

should go. To candle an egg, a bright light is shined through to get some sense of what might be happening inside. In the past, candling was literal, with eggs being held up to an actual candle to check for fertility. Today, electric candling devices can be purchased from poultry suppliers or homemade.

When candling, you are looking for two things: the existence of a living, viable embryo, and the position of the airspace inside, which is a good indicator of humidity levels. The procedure causes no harm to the embryo as long as you do it quickly and not at all after day 18. First the eggs must be removed from the incubator and allowed to come to room temperature. This is fine at the end of weeks one and two, but not thereafter. In a darkened room, hold the eggs one at a time in front of a bright light shone through an egg-shaped hole in a box. Large commercial production facilities use a horizontal light box that can examine numerous eggs at once. For small-time chicken tenders, a small box with a 40- to 75-watt bulb inside

is sufficient. I've also read about candling by means of a slide projector or flashlight affixed to a toilet paper tube!

Fertility Awareness

Whether you purchase a candling device or improvise your own, your objective is to have light shine through the egg strongly enough that you can gather valuable information. The first bit of information is whether or not you have a fertile egg on your hands. When you shine a light through the egg, you will see one of three basic forms inside. A small black spot with spiderlike radiations out from it indicates a fertile egg. Eggs that look empty with only a light shadow from the yolk visible are eggs that were never fertile. Those eggs containing a darker shadow with a barely discernible blood ring encircling the middle are embryos that have died. Remove infertile or spoiled eggs from the incubator to avoid contamination.

Airspace Indications

The other thing you are looking for when candling is the position of the airspace inside the egg. Examining the airspace is a good way to determine humidity levels inside your eggs. As evaporation causes moisture to flow out of an egg's shell, the contents inside will decrease in size, which in turn causes the airspace to become larger. Use the diagram to see if the airspace in your eggs is similar in size relative to their growing stage. If the airspace inside looks smaller than the diagram, try decreasing humidity in your incubator. If the airspaces look proportionately larger than those in the diagram, you will need to increase humidity levels inside. Getting good at doing this comes with time and practice, so if you have difficulty at first, don't abandon hope for eventual airspace-recognition expertise!

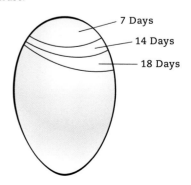

Chapter 7

Raising Chicks

Few things rival the cuteness factor presented by newly hatched chicks. Covered in downy fuzz, peeping nonstop, and weighing about as much as a mushroom, chicks can warm the heart of young and old alike. Like any newborn, they are needy little creatures. In order to ensure your cute fuzzies properly develop into healthy hens and roosters, watchful and informed vigilance will be necessary on your part.

FEATHERY MOMS OR TIN HENS?

The manner in which you will rear your chicks depends largely on whether they were hatched under a broody hen or artificially incubated. Housing for chicks, with or without a hen around, is referred to as a brooder. Chicks with a hen present at hatching will be largely shown what to do by her, although it's a good idea to keep an eye out to confirm that they are drinking and eating.

You will need to provide food and water in chick-sized containers (discussion about these needs forthcoming) that the hen cannot access. She will need her own food and water, suited to her needs, and situated in locations only she can reach; for example, hung from the ceiling or placed on cement blocks or bricks.

Chicks with a hen available will be warmed by her and require no external heat source. Should they be hatched during cooler weather, you will need to protect both hen and chicks from especially chilly temperatures and drafts. Keep the babies separate from the rest of the flock for the first eight weeks of their lives, as the petite size of the chicks makes them particularly vulnerable to being tramped on or pecked at.

If your chicks were hatched in an incubator, you will need to meet all of their needs, including regulating temperature, providing food and water, and keeping their living quarters clean. You can purchase complete brooder housing through poultry catalogs or online, or you can inexpensively fashion a homemade version. In large-scale poultry operations, chicks born in an incubator are often moved to a battery. This style of brooder is made of tiers, sometimes stackable, with each tier containing its own heating coil. Batteries also have feeders and waterers built into their sides.

Those engaged in small production poultry businesses, or simply wishing to add to their backyard flock, can opt for hover, heat lamp, or incandescent bulb brooder setups. These types of brooders provide the heat that is absolutely essential to keeping young chicks alive and thriving. A hover is a large metal umbrella-like heater that hangs from the ceiling literally hovering over the chicks. Hovers can easily provide heat for 100 or more chicks. Many hover models have curtain-like panels hanging over their edges to help in draft protection and heat retention. Many farm-supply stores carry hovers; it is also easy to locate suppliers online.

Heat lamps and incandescent lightbulbs can also be used for heat in brooders. If using heat lamps, you will need to purchase an infrared bulb, either red or clear. Red bulbs are recommended, as they reduce visibility, which in turn helps prevent picking, a potentially serious problem. Select a 75- to 100-watt infrared bulb. If using incandescent bulbs, anywhere between 60 and 100 watts will do, depending on the number of chicks you are brooding. Watch your chicks' behavior to see if the wattage you've chosen is too hot, too cool, or just right. Whether you opt for an infrared or an incandescent bulb,

A homemade brooder fashioned out of a plastic storage bin

suspend it above the brooder housing on a metal chain, not hung by its cord. Either type of bulb also needs to be fitted into a porcelain, not plastic, socket. The lamps will be left on continually in the beginning, and plastic sockets can melt from the heat. Lastly, both styles of bulbs will need to be placed in a reflector with a protective wire cover in the front. Doing so serves as a precautionary measure against fire should the lamp fall over.

CLIMATE CHANGE

Outside of food and water, nothing is of greater importance for your chicks than staying warm. Under the feathered breast of a hen, this need is met. With no hen to warm your little puffs, it will be up to you to keep your chicks toasty. Whether you use a hover, a heat lamp, or an incandescent lightbulb, initially the heat source will need to be placed 18 inches (45.7 cm) from the brooder floor. Every week, move it up about 3 inches (7.6 cm) or so, adjusting the placement depending on your chicks' behavior. If the brooder is too toasty, chicks will spread out to the sides, sometimes piling up on each other, causing suffocation. Too cool and they will pile up in the center, sometimes with the same end result. When temps are just right, the chicks will be spread out evenly across the brooder floor. Be mindful of their actions and adjust the lamp's location accordingly.

In battery or hover brooders, you can regulate the temperature with an adjustable thermostat. Measure the air temperature immediately surrounding the chicks by hanging a thermometer about 2 inches (5 cm) above the brooder floor. When they first hatch and continuing on for one week, chicks will need the brooder temperature to be about 95°F (35°C). Each week thereafter, the temperature can be decreased by 5°F (3°C) until the temperature reaches 70°F (21°C), or room temperature. Thereafter, the chicks should be able to regulate their own temperature, as their feathers will have begun coming in.

DRAFT DODGING

It will also be necessary to keep the chicks away from drafts. Situate your brooder in the least drafty place. Some choose to

One home brooder setup option

place their brooder setup in an outbuilding, such as an unused coop, while others place the chicks in the basement, the garage, in a spare room indoors, or even in the kitchen. No matter where you locate your chicks, be sure there are no obvious drafts coming in on them, either through air-conditioning vents or cracks in the basement wall. Many people opt to place the brooder on a table or some other structure that enables the chicks to be kept off the floor. Cold air falls and can chill little peeps pretty quickly.

A brooder guard or barrier can keep most drafts away. Improvise a barrier by housing the chicks in a cardboard box, a plastic storage bin, an aquarium, or even an animal feeding or watering trough. You can also simply take a large cardboard box and cut out a circle at least 1 foot (30.5 cm) in diameter. Secure the ends with duct tape, and place the cardboard circle about 2 to 3 feet (61 to 91.4 cm) away from the heat source. Replace the circle with a new, larger one as the chicks grow.

Brooder guards help chicks locate their food, water, and heat sources with greater ease when they are just getting familiar with the layout of their new home. Chilled, hungry, or dehydrated chicks can succumb to illness or worse rather quickly. Where chicks are concerned, prevention is considerably easier than cure. Have their setup ready before their arrival to truly ensure you have accounted for any possible oversights. It also goes without saying that whatever housing you use should be predator-proof, whether you are trying to keep out Ricky the raccoon or Fluffy the cat.

HOUSEKEEPING ESSENTIALS

Like any infant, chicks need housing that keeps their diminutive size in mind. A soft bed, adequate space, and somewhere to perch gently are key to helping your little ones grow up strong and healthy.

Bedding

Inside the brooder, the chicks will need some sort of bedding. Chick bedding should be like the perfect pair of winter boots: well insulated, absorbent, and nonslip. Little chickie legs need bedding that doesn't slide around, otherwise they can end up with a condition called spraddle leg, which is exactly what it sounds like. They also need bedding that keeps them warm and wicks away moisture produced by spilt water and droppings.

Ideal bedding materials include pine shavings, peat moss, ground-up corn-cobs or rice hulls, or even old cloth rags. Avoid sawdust, straw, and sand. After a month, you can transition to cedar shavings. Don't do so beforehand, as chicks, in their ever-present pecking, may ingest some, which can be toxic and may cause intestinal blockages. Put down about 4 to 5 inches (10.2 to 12.7 cm) of bedding to begin with, adding more as necessary to keep it fluffy. Stir the bedding daily and remove any moist areas, which can quickly become breeding grounds for bacteria.

Space

The amount of space you will need to provide in your brooder is mostly based on what type you are using. If you are using a battery, your chicks will need 10 square inches (64.5 cm²) each until they are two weeks old, then an additional 10 square inches (64.5 cm²) per chick every two weeks thereafter. If your brooder is a hover or heat lamp, your chicks will need 6 square inches (38.7 cm²) per chick until they are four weeks old and then 1 square foot (77.4 cm²) per chick until they are eight weeks. After they are eight weeks old, they can be moved into the "big house" with the rest of your flock, with each bird needing between 2½ and 3½ square feet (.22 and .32 m²), depending on breed and type (bantam, light, or heavy). Give

them the room they need right from the start. Crowded chicks can turn into pecking and—horror of horrors—cannibalistic chicks. Sad, but true.

Roosts

When your chicks are around three to four weeks old, they will be ready to begin roosting. To get them started, place perches low in their brooder, only a few inches off the floor. As they grow, you can place the roosts higher up. Give each chick about 4 inches (10.2 cm) of roost space. Since their feet are so tiny at this point, use a thin dowel until it becomes obvious the dowel size needs to be increased. Watch your chicks and see who gets the whole roosting idea and who doesn't. For the little peeps that don't seem to get it, gently place them on the roost, removing your hand only after they have gripped the dowel. They may fall off, but that's okay. Eventually, they will literally get the hang of it and never forget how it's done.

FOOD AND WATER

Whether your chicks are hatched under a warm hen, in an incubator, or come to you in a cardboard box via express mail,

they will need to eat and drink fairly soon. The yolk offers nutrients to newly hatched chicks, keeping them hydrated and nourished until everyone in the nest comes pipping out of their shells. This works perfectly for chicks who are shipped just after hatching, arriving one or two days later. When the yolk is gone, your chicks will need to be introduced to food and water, in containers suited to their needs.

Chicks and Food

Baby chickens have unique nutritional needs, which are easily met by specially formulated chick feeds. Both starter broiler and starter layer feeds are available, so make your selection accordingly. Chick feeds are available in mash or pellet form. Medication to prevent coccidiosis, the most common illness chicks face, is

A trough feeder

frequently added to chick feed. The choice to use medicated feed is up to you. In general, if your flock is small, your brooder cleaned daily, and the climate when your chicks arrive isn't sweltering, medicated starter may not be necessary. Conversely, if you are brooding large numbers of chicks, you get started in muggy, warm weather, or you just can't manage to stay on top of daily brooder cleanup, medicated may be the way to go. Chick grit, which is smaller than grit for full-grown chickens, will need to be supplied only if you offer chick scratch.

Place chick feed in troughs, if you are feeding many chicks at once, or in screw-top bases, if your flock is small. Trough feeders either have rods on top that turn in place, discouraging chicks from standing on them, or small openings for chicks to put their tiny heads into. The screw-top bases have several small circular openings and simply screw onto inverted glass jars. Both feeder styles can be picked up

A typical chick waterer

inexpensively either online or at Chicks are notoriously messy, as well as prolifically poopy, so be certain to use feeders specific to chicks. Contamination from droppings in their food or water can make chicks very sick. Chick feeders are specially designed to prevent chicks from stepping into their feeders and have openings small enough to accommodate tiny beaks. Place the feeder no farther than 2 feet (61 cm) from the heat source in the brooder for the first week and never farther than 10 feet (3 m) until they move into the main coop.

Chicks and Water

A dehydrated chick can quickly turn into a sick or dead chick, so providing a constant supply of fresh water is essential. Chick waterers come as either galvanized or plastic screw-top bases, similar to chick feeders, or as plastic tube waterers with small openings. In a pinch, you can devise a homemade version by filling up a glass jar with water, placing a saucer roughly the same size on top, and flipping the whole thing over. You will need to lodge something like a toothpick between the jar and saucer so that the water can trickle out. A quart (liter) jar will meet the water needs of a small flock, while a 1-gallon (3.8 L) waterer can tend 40 to 50 chicks. The lips of some chick waterers are a little deep, posing a threat of drowning, so adding rocks or marbles is advised. Remember to change the water out at least once daily, keep the waterer clean, and never let the water supply run out. Like feeders, keep waterers 2 feet (61 cm) from the heat source for the first week, eventually moving them no farther than 10 feet (3 m) away until chicks are introduced to the rest of the flock.

It may be necessary at first to teach chicks how to drink, especially in the absence of a hen. Simply gather them up one by one and gently dip their beaks into the water. They'll figure it out pretty quickly, and others will catch on by watching the leaders. Some chick aficionados suggest spiking chicks' water with a chick-specific energy booster. Vitamin and electrolyte chick supplements can be purchased through feed stores and hatcheries. As a one-time treat for reviving the energy and diminishing the stress of mail-order chicks, add ¼ cup (56 g) of table sugar to 1 gallon (3.8 L) of water.

IT'S A HARD-KNOCK LIFE, FOR CHICKS

There are a number of ailments posing specific risks to chicks. Keep an eye out for potential problems including coccidiosis, pasting, and picking.

Coccidiosis

Coccidia are protozoa naturally colonizing the intestines of chicks. Exposure to coccidia occurs when chicks come in contact with their droppings. Under normal conditions, coccidia multiply slowly enough that chicks are able to develop immunity to them around 14 weeks of age. The protozoa thrives in damp, warm conditions and can rapidly proliferate in the presence of large amounts of chicken droppings or moist, manure-encrusted feeders and waterers. One of the earliest symptoms of coccidiosis is runny droppings, with bloody droppings showing up later, when the illness is pretty far along. If you have not been feeding your chicks medicated feed and these symptoms present themselves, switch to medicated feed, isolate the sick chicks, and tidy up and sanitize everything. To prevent coccidiosis from ever occurring, either use medicated feed or practice scrupulous brooder hygiene.

Pasting

Pasting (also known as "pasting up," "pasty butt," and "sticky bottom") occurs when a chick becomes stressed from travel, chilled or overheated, dehydrated, or ingests bedding material. Their bottoms subsequently become crusted over with droppings (a mental image best avoided, if there ever was one). This is a very serious condition, requiring immediate action to prevent death, should it occur. You will need to hold the chick's rear end under lukewarm running water and gently dislodge the droppings, or use a warm washcloth. It wouldn't hurt to rub a natural lubricant such as sweet almond, coconut, or vitamin E oil on their bums afterward. They will fuss like their lives depend on it, but don't give up. Attempt to determine what caused the pasting problem to begin with, and make adjustments as necessary.

Picking

Chicks are prone to the unfortunate habit of picking, which is pecking at each other's toes and feathers, sometimes to the point of death. Usually, this is brought on by overcrowding, overheating, lack of food, too much light in the brooder, stagnant air, or insufficient protein in their food. Picking is definitely easier to prevent than to treat, so take steps in advance and curb the habit quickly as soon as you know it is happening. Remove any injured birds, clean their wounds, and apply a healing salve. It might also be worth switching to red bulbs, which impair visibility, and adding grass clippings to the brooder to keep them occupied.

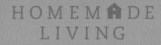

Chapter 8

Health and Wellness

In an ideal world, your flock would remain vibrant, content, and healthy for all the days of their lives. For many small flock owners, this will be the case. Others, however, will encounter the occasional chicken health crisis. While this chapter is by no means comprehensive, it does address the most common major and minor illnesses that may befall your feathered friends. Many of the conditions listed here are rare in small flocks, but are good to be informed of nevertheless.

A CLEAN BILL OF HEALTH

Perhaps the single most important thing you can do toward ensuring the health and safety of your flock is to stay on top of coop hygiene. Dirty chickens and dirty coops can quickly spell sick chickens, or worse. A little daily elbow grease on

your part acts as preventative care. Should something manage to make them ill anyway, having a clean coop will work in their favor toward fighting the illness off.

Remove droppings daily, or, when using the deep litter method, stir droppings and add litter if needed.

Make sure food and water bowls are clean and free of droppings or other debris. Always have clean food and water available. Be sure the coop is well ventilated but free from any cold drafts. Perform a thorough coop cleaning once or twice a year, complete with changing all bedding, scrubbing roosts and nesting boxes if needed, and disinfecting the entire area. In short, do whatever you can to maintain the cleanliness and integrity of your coop.

Limit your flock's exposure to other poultry and wild birds. Only introduce new chickens you know to be disease-free and healthy. Do as much as you can to minimize stress on your flock, whether that stress comes in the form of a terrorizing family pet, exposure to loud and startling noises on a daily basis, or a child who hugs their tender bodies too tightly.

STOP, LOOK, AND LISTEN

In addition to staying on top of your daily cleaning routine, take time to listen to and look at your flock each day. Chickens are fairly consistent in their behavior. They also generally stay together in their activities; you know, "birds of a feather flock together." If a member of your crew looks listless or lethargic

and isn't keeping up with everyone else's goings-on, it might spell trouble. Or it might not, but it's worth it to take the extra minute or two and examine the bird in question.

I make a point of checking feet, eyes, and sounds everyday. As they gather around the feeder for their breakfast, I squat down and make sure all feet and toes are straight and flat on the ground. Next I look them square in the eye, slowly moving my gaze across the entirety of their bodies, noting anything that might give me pause. Then, I listen. Any rasping? Any sniffling? Anything other than the standard soft clucking and "that piece of dried corn is mine, fool!" reproach overheard? Finally, I look at their droppings, checking for anything short of compact, firm plops with white peaks. So, take a daily long, hard stare and give a good listen. Some things are easy to catch early if you stay in touch with your flock.

HEALTHY CHICKEN CHECKLIST

In order to determine when something is amiss, you need to know what a healthy chicken should look and sound like. Make a mental checklist, or even write it down when you are first starting out, and give it a daily rundown as you feed your flock and gather up eggs. Catch symptoms when they first surface, before they have time to advance to a genuine health crisis. From comb to toes, here's what to look for:

Anatomy	Ideal Appearance
Comb and wattles	Glossy and plump
Eyes	Shiny, bright, absent of fluid
Nostrils	No obstructions or sounds
Breast	Full and rounded
Feathers	Smooth and slick, well groomed
Vent	Clean, a bit of moisture is fine
Droppings	Firm, white-capped
Body weight	Appropriate for age, neither over- or underweight

Additionally, healthy chickens hold their heads and tails up high, often craning and turning their heads to follow sounds and movements.

PROPER HANDLING

You will occasionally need to pick up your chickens, whether to examine them for mites, administer medications, or simply to give (and get) a hug. Handling them in advance of this need makes them more acquainted with the whole experience and can abate the stress such handling may incur. Think of it as the poultry equivalent of taking the dog along on errands in the car so that when the time comes for the annual visit with the veterinarian, Fido doesn't suddenly decide to freak out on you.

To pick up a chicken, you can do one of several things. I'll start with what works for me. Since I visit my flock often, they are accustomed to the sight of me and gather around my feet. Actually, they sometimes cluster in so tightly that I am immobilized for a few seconds until they decide to free me from their chicken circle. In any event, because of their closeness, it's usually pretty easy for me to simply squat down behind one of them, place my right hand across her back, stretching the thumb and pinkie over each wing, and then, cradling the underside of her body with my left arm, lift her up to my chest (reverse hands if you're a lefty). You must keep your right hand over their wings to keep them from flying away. I'll usually stroke their necks and backs while I have them this way, to relax them, and tuck them a bit into the crook of my arm.

Alternatively, you can corner a chicken or drop some tasty food treats near you, and once one approaches, pick her up with both hands, tucking her under your arm with her beak toward your back. This is a helpful position if you need to examine feet or vents. Other tactics for catching less tame chickens include simply picking them up off their perches while they are resting at night (when they are very docile), gathering them up in a fishing or butterfly net, and utilizing a device called a catching hook, which is basically a long pole with a V-shaped hook at the end that grabs hold of a chicken's leg, like the hook you might use to pull limelight-hogging clowns offstage, only scaled down to chicken size.

Eventually, you will likely have to make physical contact with chickens whose time on earth has come to a close. Mortality rates in healthy flocks are about 5 percent annually. Should you suffer several deaths in close sequence, though, you might have a problem on your hands. Properly disposing of deceased chickens

is extremely important. If the cause of death was attack by a predator or some other cause not related to disease, it may be unnecessary to contact the authorities. Depending on where you live, you may be able to burn the chicken in an enclosed container, such as a barrel. If your chicken met its demise from a known or suspected disease, however, you may be legally required to notify your local extension or agricultural office. In some instances, they will give you the go ahead to burn your afflicted bird. On occasion they will want to examine the bird to determine what the disease is. Several poultry diseases pose a severe enough threat as to potentially endanger the rest of your flock or the greater community as a whole. When in doubt, call up your local extension agent and find out the proper protocol for your area. Never bury a dead chicken that was sick, as an animal could dig it up, thereby exposing itself and wild and domesticated animal populations as a whole to whatever did your bird in, or disease organisms could leach into groundwater supplies.

TIME OUT

Sick or injured birds need to be separated from the rest of the flock until they heal. Other flock members sometimes even pose the greatest threat to a chicken's recovery. Injured birds can fall victim to picking and general bossing around by their flock mates. One of the best means of sequestering I have discovered is a dog crate.

On one terribly unfortunate afternoon, I'd gone out for a few hours, and upon returning found the gate to my chicken's coop open and the chickens spread out in the forest surrounding their quarters. My German Shepherd saw this situation at precisely the same moment I did and tore off after the flock, as I ran screaming behind her. She caught my Buff Orpington,

A dog crate makes a great portable shelter for a bird in need of time alone.

appropriately named Buffy, and removed a fairly sizable portion of her back feathers, skin, the whole shebang. While my husband rounded up the dogs, I gathered up Buffy and cradled her close, talking softly to her. Chickens can weather pretty horrific injuries, but succumb much more easily to stress, so I wanted to calm her as much as possible. After pouring hydrogen peroxide over her wound, I kept her in a large dog crate for about a week, administering poultry antibiotic by beak twice daily. If you think children can be stubborn about taking their medicine, try a chicken, but that's a whole other story. For the first few days, I kept her in the henhouse all day. We threaded a dowel through the crate to provide her with a perch and gave her fresh food and water in small metal bowls. Two days later, I felt comfortable moving the crate outside during the day, removing its plastic floor so that she could peck at bugs and grass. After one week, the wound had begun to heal over, so I allowed her to rejoin her flock mates. Of course, within the first few minutes of her release, two of them pecked at her still-open wound. She replied in a high-pitched squawk that I can only imagine meant "Don't even *think* about doing that again, or I will have to take you down!"

Consider keeping a dog crate on hand, or some similar housing, for placing sick or injured birds into. A chicken tractor works well for this purpose also. Such a setup could also be suitable housing for a broody hen. Keeping housing for isolating a chicken readily available saves you the added stress of a last-minute scramble and gives your feathered friend somewhere safe to go, fast!

IN SICKNESS AND IN HEALTH

Most of the maladies that may affect your flock will come from diseases, parasites, or other flock members. While the cause of diseases and parasites is usually from an external source (often-times wild birds), they can also be introduced to a healthy flock when new chickens are acquired. Only buy birds as chicks from a reliable hatchery, or as older birds from a seller of outstanding repute. Sometimes, even in the best of circumstances, birds that are healthy in one flock will cause illness in another. Keep a close watch on your flock when introducing new members, and deal with any problems as soon as they present themselves.

Disease

Though many flocks will likely not encounter any of these illnesses, the following diseases are witnessed more often than others.

Aspergillosis

Also known as "brooder pneumonia," aspergillosis is caused by the fungus-like organism *Aspergillus fumigatus*. This organism grows easily on a number of substances and surfaces, including bedding material, feed, and rotting wood. While most healthy chickens can withstand repeated low-dose exposure, inhalation of a large volume of the spores can cause infection, as can exposure in those chickens with compromised immunity. In

young birds with acute infection, symptoms include gasping, fatigue, reduced appetite, and, occasionally, convulsions or even death. High mortality is associated more with acute cases in younger birds. Older birds seem to fare better, with the same symptoms but greatly reduced mortality. There is no treatment,

so prevention is key. Remove any moldy bedding, feed, or other decaying matter. Clean feeders and waterers routinely.

Avian Influenza

The Influenza A virus subtype H5N1, also known as "bird flu," is a type of highly contagious virus occurring mostly in birds. Wild birds carry the virus naturally in their intestines and are generally unaffected by them. However, in domesticated birds, the viruses can prove especially virulent and even fatal. The virus is shed through the bodily fluids of birds, including saliva, nasal secretions, and feces. Birds then spread the virus between themselves when exposed to their secretions or excretions.

H5N1 infection manifests in two ways. The "low pathogenic" form usually produces mild symptoms, including ruffled feathers and possibly a drop in egg production, and is likely to go undetected. Conversely, the "highly pathogenic" form causes much more damage, rapidly sweeping through flocks, producing symptoms that ravage multiple organs, and incurring about 100 percent mortality within 48 hours. The virus does not usually affect humans, although a few cases have been reported. Most instances of interspecies spread of the virus occurred in individuals having close contact with birds infected with H5N1 or surfaces contaminated by the virus. As of this writing, most instances of the virus affecting both birds and humans have occurred in Southeast Asia. A vaccine has recently been approved for the prevention of human infection by one strain of the H5N1 virus. Should you have any suspicions about avian flu presenting itself in your flock, you must contact your nearest animal control agency immediately. They will assist you in determining what steps to take next.

Bumblefoot

Appearing as a large, bulbous growth on the underside of a chicken's foot, bumblefoot is caused by a cut or abrasion on the footpad becoming infected. Consider this malady to be the poultry version of getting a splinter frustratingly lodged in your foot. Once injured, whether a large cut or a tiny abrasion, the footpad begins to swell within a matter of days. It may also become reddened and hot to the touch.

Calling the Shots

Deciding to vaccinate or administer antibiotic feed or medications should not be done without careful consideration. Overuse of any antibiotic can cause drug-resistant strains of bacteria. Vaccinating for diseases that pose no perceivable risk to your flock may prevent them from developing natural immunity to threats within their environment. While many large-scale poultry operations employ the use of both antibiotic feed and a litany of vaccinations, they often do so because they are unable to keep housing conditions as sanitary as the small flock owner will be able to. Talk to your veterinarian for information about what poultry diseases pose risk in your area, and vaccinate accordingly. Stay on top of coop cleanliness, and antibiotics may be unnecessary.

The opportunistic bacteria that set in could be any one of the following: *Staphylococcus aureus, E. coli, Corynebacterium* spp., and *Pseudomonas* spp. These bacteria are also aggressive in humans, so take caution when treating a chicken with bumblefoot. Wear disposable latex gloves, and wash clothing after contact.

It is possible to prevent your chickens from ever getting bumblefoot by keeping their feet safe from abrasion. Be certain all roosts and perches are smoothed and free of splinters. Additionally, check your coop frequently and remove any broken glass, nails, rough metal edges, or anything that could injure a chicken's feet. Heavier breeds are especially susceptible, as their weight puts extra strain on footpads. Couple that with a rough roost, and bumblefoot may not be far off.

Key to treating the illness is catching it early. If the foot is visibly swollen but is soft, wash the foot and leg, drain the abscess, rinse with hydrogen peroxide, apply an antibiotic ointment, and wrap in a bandage, changing the dressing daily. If the injury goes unnoticed and the footpad becomes hard, surgery is the only option.

Campylobacteriosis

This infection is caused by the campylobacter bacterium. One of the most common bacterial infections affecting humans, often as a foodborne illness, campylobacteriosis can be treated with antibiotics once contracted. In chickens, symptoms include shriveled or shrunken combs, bloody or mucousy diarrhea, and even sudden death. It is possible, though, for no symptoms to be present other than a drop in egg production.

Broiler chickens contract the bacteria in the external environment, bringing it into their housing via insects, untreated drinking water, livestock and farm equipment, or on workers' clothes or boots. Once introduced to the remainder of the flock, campylobacter spreads quickly. If it causes no symptoms, it is possible to go undetected, remaining in the birds' flesh after processing. The poultry industry is trying its best to control exposure on their end but encourages consumers to protect themselves from the bacteria by thoroughly cooking all poultry and practicing scrupulous household hygiene when handling raw poultry.

Chronic Respiratory Disease

Also known as mycoplasmosis, chronic respiratory disease (CRD) is caused by bacterial organisms in the genus *Mycoplasma*. While not usually fatal, chickens that recover will remain infected for life, and future stresses may produce a recurrence of the disease. Symptoms include coughing, nasal discharge, reduced egg production, diminished appetite, sneezing, slow growth, and potentially reduced rates of hatchability and chick longevity. Outbreaks of the bacteria typically occur at times of stress when the flock's ability to resist infection may be compromised, such as when they are moved, vaccinated, too cold, or exposed to poor ventilation, ammonia buildup, or moist litter. Treatment is administered through antibiotics.

Fowl Pox

This slow-spreading viral disease can affect members of your flock at any age and at any time. Fowl pox is evidenced by wartlike nodules on the skin and in the mouth—the poultry version of chicken pox, if you will. The virus does not usually cause death, unless it impairs respiration by growing in the respiratory system itself. Since it is slow growing in nature, the virus may be present for months before symptoms appear. Once present, it affects birds for about three to five weeks. Often transmitted initially by mosquitoes, the virus spreads within the flock by both direct and indirect contact with infected birds. Chickens that recover do not remain carriers of the virus. As routine sanitation and hygiene practices will not prevent it, vaccination is often performed as a proactive measure. There is no treatment for fowl pox.

Fowl Typhoid

This is a highly infectious, contagious bacterial disease caused by the bacteria *Salmonella gallinarum*. Mortality is often 100 percent. Although occurring most often in young birds, the disease can affect chickens of all ages. Signs of infection include lethargy, reduced appetite, increased thirst, pale combs and wattles, green or yellow diarrhea, or sudden death. Fowl typhoid is spread by droppings from infected birds, as well as by contaminated food, water, clothing, and equipment. Antibiotic treatment exists, although it will not remove the infection. A vaccine may be preventatively administered.

Infectious Bronchitis

Caused by a virus affecting only chickens, infectious bronchitis is a highly contagious respiratory disease. When it appears, any and all susceptible birds around will become infected. The disease spreads through airborne transmission and can also be carried on clothing, equipment, and metal surfaces. Symptoms include coughing, gasping, rattling, sneezing, nasal discharge, and severely reduced egg production. If it affects young birds, it may damage reproductive organs, rendering them unable to produce normal eggs. An outbreak affecting a laying flock halts egg production to almost zero. Those eggs that are laid may be small, soft-shelled, and oddly shaped. As there is no treatment, prevention through vaccination is the only means of keeping the illness at bay.

Infectious Coryza

A respiratory disease caused by the bacteria *Hemophilus gallinarum*, infectious coryza typically occurs in semi-mature or adult birds. It may present as slow growing in nature,

affecting only a few birds at a time, or spread quickly, infecting a greater number of chickens at once. Telltale characteristics of the disease include swelling of the face and wattles, smelly nasal discharge, watery discharge from the eyes (which may cause the eyelids to stick together), a drop in egg production, impaired vision, and reduced food and water consumption. The disease is usually introduced via carrier birds added to healthy flocks. Once a chicken is infected, it remains a carrier and shedder of the bacteria for life. Infectious coryza may be treated with antibiotics. For disease prevention, an all-in, all-out policy is advised, which basically means culling existing birds before adding to your flock. Otherwise, either breed your own chicks or purchase new birds and chicks only from highly reputable hatcheries and sellers.

Infectious Laryngotracheitis

Infectious laryngotracheitis (ILT) kills cells lining the airways of a chicken's windpipe, resulting in varying degrees of impaired respiration. ILT is caused by a herpes virus, and birds that recover may become lifelong carriers, often transmitting the disease in flocks. While ILT does not affect humans, they can spread the disease to chickens via clothing, dirty footwear, or poultry equipment. Symptoms include coughing, gasping, discharge from eyes and nostrils, or even death. The disease is highly contagious, and mortality can be up to 70 percent. There is no treatment, so prevention is essential. Only buy birds from a reputable hatchery whose birds are known to be ILT-free. If adding birds to your flock, quarantine them first for up to a week to see if any disease symptoms manifest.

Marek's Disease

Caused by a virus in the herpes family, Marek's disease usually affects young birds. It is believed to live in the feather follicles and shed in dander or sloughed-off skin and feather cells. Spread of the infection is usually respiratory, and the rate of contagion is high. Marek's disease may manifest in a number of ways. Neurologically, it results in various forms of paralysis. Viscerally, tumors infiltrate numerous organs, including the heart, reproductive organs, muscles, and lungs. If the disease presents itself on the skin, tumors of the feather follicles may result. In acute cases, the disease may advance very quickly, killing birds previously exhibiting vibrant health. Most hatcheries vaccinate one-day old chicks against Marek's disease.

Newcastle Disease

Newcastle disease is a widespread, highly contagious viral respiratory disease affecting all species of poultry. One strain of the virus, referred to as "exotic Newcastle disease," is considered such a threat that strict border control measures exist to prevent its entry into various countries around the world. Once exposed, almost all birds in a flock will become infected in a number of days. Symptoms are similar to other respiratory diseases in poultry and include coughing, sneezing, gasping, difficulty breathing, and, if allowed to advance, paralysis. Mortality rates vary widely, from zero to 100 percent. No treatment exists for Newcastle disease. Vaccination is widely practiced by large-scale poultry producers. The disease can survive for long periods in normal temperatures, so be sure to thoroughly clean coops with disinfectant and hot water if you have an infected chicken.

Parasites

Various parasites, both internal and external, are known to infect chickens.

INTERNAL

Coccidiosis

Coccidia are protozoan parasites that live in the cells lining the intestines of all poultry. In most instances, it lives in a symbiotic relationship with chickens. However, under unsanitary conditions, it can proliferate extremely quickly, resulting in potentially grave danger to birds. As it most commonly affects chicks, refer to chapter 7, Raising Chicks, for more information.

Worms

Transmitted by wild birds, rodents, and insects, worms are fairly common in chickens and don't always pose a problem. However, if one or more of your birds exhibit diarrhea, listlessness, weight loss, and a drop in egg production, you might have a worm situation that has gotten out of hand. Roundworms, tapeworms, and cecal worms are the most common types of worms associated with chickens. If you suspect worms, don't worm indiscriminately. Doing so can result in the development of drug-resistant colonies of parasites, as well as keeping your chickens from forming their own resistance to parasites. Bring a sample of droppings in to your veterinarian for testing first.

EXTERNAL

Lice

In chickens, lice can be found either on the head or on the body. They are visible to the naked eye and resemble small, tiny to almost transparent organisms. When the chicken's feathers are parted, you will see lice scurrying about if your bird is infested. Symptoms indicating you may have a lice problem include witnessing one or more of your chickens trying to pull out their feathers (to stop the itching and irritation), a reduction in egg production, weight loss, and a dirty backside. If one bird exhibits symptoms, then treat your entire flock, as they will likely all

It is important to check for external parasites on a regular basis.

have lice. These nasty critters are more often an issue for birds permitted to free-range or having access to the outdoors than for birds kept intensively. Encourage your birds to dust bathe, as dust clogs louse pores. Treatments include dousing your flock with louse powder or a chemical spray. Check with your local agricultural extension office or veterinarian for an approved poultry insecticide. Other natural options I have encountered include liberally dusting with sulfur, diatomaceous earth, and wood ashes.

Mites (Red, Northern Fowl, and Scaly Leg)

Mites are parasites that live either in the blood of chickens, or burrow deep into their skin or in their feathers. Once they infest a chicken, they cause delayed growth, a drop in egg production, irritation, blood loss, diminished fertility, and on occasion, death.

Red mites, found mostly in warmer weather, come out at night. They live in henhouse crevices and can be seen crawling over walls, roosts, and chicken's bodies with the help of a flashlight. Red mites are so named on account of the way in which their normally grayish-white bodies turn red when engorged with blood. Treat them by cleaning your coop thoroughly and liberally dusting with an approved mite insecticide.

Northern fowl mites appear during cold weather and crawl on birds during the day. Discourage these mites by placing cedar chips, a natural mite deterrent, in nesting boxes as bedding.

Scaly leg mites invade the legs and feet of chickens, burrowing in and causing scales to protrude and fall out. An affected chicken, if left untreated, may eventually have difficulty walking. One treatment involves rubbing the legs with an equal mixture of kerosene and linseed oil. If the thought of rubbing kerosene on a bird and the subsequent fire hazard that doing so presents scares you off this treatment, alternatives include rubbing petroleum jelly or some other lubricant over the infected bird's shanks weekly for up to two weeks, or dipping their shanks weekly in some form of vegetable oil. Telltale signs of the presence of mites other than actually viewing them include "egg spotting," which are specks of blood on egg shells where mites were squashed by sitting hens, and "salt and pepper" deposits underneath perches.

Dusting Themselves Off

Dust baths are essential for maintaining health and wellness in your flock. A dust bath is an area of dry, sandy soil. Your chickens will either create this area themselves, in the warmest, sunniest portion of their coop, or you can provide it for them. If space is limited in your yard, you'll want to keep their dust baths confined to a certain area (and out of your veggie beds!); or if your birds are intensively kept, simply fill up a deep tray, wooden box, or even a shallow terracotta planter with loose dirt and dry sand. Dust bathing clogs the breathing pores of parasites that prey on chickens, serving as the most perfectly natural and organic insecticide imaginable. Accordingly, this habit should be encouraged. Don't worry, dust baths don't result in dirt-crusted chickens. To the contrary, after digging themselves as far down into the dirt as possible, chickens puff out their feathers, shake themselves off, then begin preening.

Cannibalism

As alarming as it sounds, several forms of cannibalism are common among chickens. Naturally, you will want to stop these behaviors in their tracks for a healthy, unmolested flock.

Egg Eating

Egg eating is a form of cannibalism that starts when a hen accidentally breaks open an egg, samples the goods, and realizes she likes the taste. After that, others may get in on the action and begin breaking open eggs deliberately. Egg eating may result from too crowded living quarters or from eggs left in nesting boxes for too long. Discourage this nasty habit from ever beginning by emptying nesting boxes early and relocating the instigator (the one with the yellow goop festooning her beak and the "who, me?" look across her guilty face) to a new home. You can discourage future egg eating by placing bogus "eggs" that have been blown empty and filled with mustard inside the nesting boxes.

Feather and Toe Picking

Chickens pick and peck, 'tis their nature. This is normally all good and well, but when the picking and pecking occurs on each other and not on grains of corn or bits of a wriggling grub, an otherwise natural habit can quickly become lethal. If you notice one of your birds missing feathers, attempt to determine if she is doing it to herself. If she is, try to find out what is giving her the itchies. If you have a rooster, the loss in feathers could be the result of a particularly passionate leading man. Also, consider that your bird may be molting. Ruling out roosters, critters, and molt, the cause of feather loss might be a hen's flock mates.

A chick's toes can look a good bit like little yellow worms. A curious chick might pick at his or her own toes or those of their flock mates and, at the sight of blood, go on a pecking free-for-all. Older chickens are more inclined to pick the heads and tail areas of other birds. Either way, once there is blood, curious picking can spiral into cannibalism. Picking can be caused by cramped living conditions, a nutritional deficiency, lack of sufficient feeders and waterers, harsh lighting, too much

heat in a brooder, external parasites, inadequate ventilation, or some other stressing variable such as inclement weather, improper handling, or moving to new living quarters. A cannibalistic bird might also simply be a bored bird. While this is not usually the case in birds permitted access to the outdoors, those kept indoors or in cages for extended periods of time denied the opportunity to express their natural inclination to scratch, dig, hunt, forage, and otherwise pick will manifest this urge in less desirable ways.

If you discover cannibalism within your flock, curb it immediately. Attempt to discover the root of the problem. Consider giving your birds distractions by tying pieces of fruit or vegetables to strings and suspending them from the coop ceiling or offering scratch grains for them to turn their picking attention toward. Always sequester injured birds as discussed early in this chapter. Try rubbing vinegar or a poultry-specific ointment on the feathers and wound of the chicken on the receiving end of the bullying; flock mates will get a mouth full of nastiness when they take an opportunistic peck. If all else fails, you may have to resort to either removing the instigator from your premises or permanently rehousing the injured bird in separate quarters.

Other Ailments and Conditions

Although this list is not comprehensive, there are several other things to watch out for in terms of your flock's health and wellness.

Acute Death Syndrome (Flip-over Disease)

Have you ever heard about someone who "up and died"? Chickens who meet their end this way are said to have flip-over disease. Occurring most often in intensively confined male birds bound for table, the illness causes sudden death, prefaced by a brief wing-flapping convulsion. Although the cause is unknown, it is believed to be metabolic in origin, most likely the result of overfeeding. Many broilers overeat, growing rapidly all the while, causing sudden heart failure from ventricular fibrillation. No warning signs foretell an impending demise. Otherwise healthy chickens, sometimes in midstep, literally flip over and die on their backs. Incidents of occurrence may be reduced by changing the diet of broilers to mash (thereby lowering carbohydrate consumption), restricting feed availability, introducing artificial light that mimics daylight and evening hours, and reducing stress.

Crop-binding

It is possible for a chicken's crop to become obstructed, or blocked, preventing food from moving out of the crop and into the proventriculus. When this occurs, it is usually the result of consuming long blades of grass, bedding material, or feathers. The blockage will be visible as a large bulge in the center of a chicken's breast, but only in the evening, after the chicken has had a full day to eat and fill up their crop with other material. Left unattended to, the affected bird's breathing may become difficult, potentially resulting in death.

If you notice a large bulge in the evening that is still there the following morning and is accompanied by a lack

of appetite, try giving your chicken either a little warm water or vegetable oil and then gently massaging the surface of the bulge. Use caution when attempting to put any liquid down a chicken's throat, as they can asphyxiate if given too much liquid too quickly. It the lump does not loosen and break up, a visit with the veterinarian may be necessary.

Egg Binding

If a chicken attempts to pass an egg that is especially large, it can become lodged inside her vent. Also, chickens receiving inadequate exercise can be susceptible to becoming egg bound, as lack of activity may cause the buildup of a fatty layer around her reproductive organs. This in turn impedes the ability of the oviduct to push eggs down toward the vent. Should you witness one of your birds squatting with nothing coming out, hanging out in the nest all day, or looking as though she may be, well, constipated, it's possible she may be egg bound. Cover your finger with mineral oil, warm olive oil, or some other lubricating substance safe for human skin, and insert it into the vent. If you can feel an egg inside, rub the lubricating substance all around the vent, which should assist her in passing the egg.

Attempt to get the egg out of your chicken, carefully massaging her abdomen in the direction of the vent. You didn't know you signed up for this when you took on chicken raising, did you? As a measure of last resort, you may need to puncture the egg while it is still inside the chicken, carefully removing it in small pieces. This carries the risk of injuring her vent, though, and should only be done if nothing else seems to get the egg to move. Clean the vent afterward with hydrogen peroxide in a spray bottle to prevent possible infection.

Molting

You know how snakes shed their skins every year and some dogs shed their winter undercoats come spring? Well, chickens also have an annual shedding period, called molting. During this process chickens gradually lose their feathers. Prompted by waning daylight hours, molting takes place in most chickens around late summer to early fall, although some molt in early winter. As their feathers fall out, new feathers called "pinfeathers" come in, resembling short, hollow drinking straws at first. Molting follows a sequence, beginning at the head, then moving down the neck, to the body, on to the wings, and finishing at the tail. In most chickens, the process takes about six weeks; however, it is not unheard of for some to take up to 12 weeks to molt. While some chickens molt so slowly you may not even be aware the process is occurring, others, perhaps the more scandalous of your flock, toss off all their feathers at once, running around partially nude with abandon. Egg production customarily drops off during this time and can even halt completely in some chickens. Molting is stressful, so don't be surprised if an otherwise happy-go-lucky hen suddenly turns a bit skittish and cross; the attitude generally dissipates with the arrival of the new plumage.

Chapter 9
Eggs

Whether served up tableside, hidden outdoors for Easter, or artfully crafted into decoration, eggs are an integral part of cultures the world over. From folklore to holiday games, people have woven eggs into the fabric of their lives. Nutritious, versatile, and awe-inspiring, it's easy to see why we hold eggs in such high esteem.

WHICH CAME FIRST?

Female chickens are born with two ovaries. When she is still young, the right ovary stops maturing, leaving the left to carry on the work involved in egg formation. This left ovary contains 4,000 or so ova, which are undeveloped yolks. As a pullet reaches the point where she is ready to begin laying eggs, these ova begin to mature, one after the other. Ova are mature once they have acquired sufficient layers of yolk. They then slip into the oviduct, a long tube terminating in the vent, which is the same exit point for droppings. This process is called ovulation.

As it travels along the oviduct, a number of things happen to the yolk. If a hen has recently found herself the recipient of a rooster's passionate embrace, sperm may be present and the yolk will become fertilized. Otherwise, the yolk becomes shrouded in egg white, technically referred to as albumen, gets wrapped up in fibers called chalazae that anchor the yolk within the white, and lastly is enclosed in a pigmented shell.

The turnaround time of egg production varies slightly from hen to hen, averaging 25 hours, with some hens laying closer to every 24 hours and others preferring 26 hours. My Ladies all lay at different times of the day. Since each one proudly announces her success with barely contained enthusiasm, I am inundated with joyful proclamations all day long. Hens prefer not to lay in the evening, causing them to occasionally miss a day and lay the following morning. How many eggs a chicken will lay depend on a number of factors, including breed, age, climate, and stress level. Chickens intended to be heavy layers are bred to have the shortest turnaround time between eggs. Such chickens can produce 300 eggs a year when they are at peak production age. Purebred chickens will more often lay approximately 250 eggs annually. Production will wane as daylight decreases in the winter months.

SIZE, SHAPE, AND COLOR

Size and shape of eggs is informed by a chicken's age. A pullet's first eggs may be tiny, somewhere between the size of a marble and a grape. As she ages, the size of her eggs will increase, eventually weighing 2 ounces (56 g) on average.

As for shape, irregularities during formation can result in some odd-looking eggs, including those with wrinkles, exaggeratedly pointed ends, or thin shells. Eggs may also gain odd appearances as a chicken ages or if she becomes scared. Don't be distressed if you find the occasional goofball eggshell, especially if you are dealing with pullets or seasonal weather variations. These are fine to eat, but don't hatch them, as you don't want to pass on that trait.

The color of a chicken's eggs corresponds to the color of her ear lobes, which are found just behind the eyes on each side of the head. As a rule of thumb, hens with white ear lobes will lay white eggs, while those with red ear lobes will lay brown eggs, although some variations to this exist. Generally speaking, Mediterranean-originating breeds will lay white eggs, while Asiatic and most American breeds will lay brown eggs. In the middle, you find a spectrum ranging from almost pink to blue-green.

UNUSUAL EGGS

Occasionally, you will come across an abnormality in an egg. Most of the time, it will be a one-time occurrence, requiring no further action on your part other than monitoring your eggs to see if the anomaly returns. Sometimes, though, weird eggs can be a sign of distress in your birds. When a pullet first begins laying eggs, she may produce an egg missing a yolk. These are called no-yolkers, dwarf eggs, or wind eggs. This rarely happens in mature hens, but it certainly isn't outside the realm of possibility. Pullets can also produce eggs with two yolks, aptly known as double-yolkers, at the beginning of her laying cycle. Don't be concerned about no-yolkers or double-yolkers. Your pullets are merely setting up their production cycles. If this continues, though, you may consider a visit with your veterinarian to rule out potential problems.

Several other unusual features can show up inside the eggs from time to time. Blood spots or meat spots, while they may look unappetizing, do not compromise the integrity of an egg. Both are remnants of reproductive tissue that broke free from a blood vessel during egg formation. They may be indications that your hen is receiving inadequate vitamin A in her diet. A

Salmonella

Salmonella enteriditis is a type of bacteria present in the feces of many animals, including chickens, that is known to cause severe food poisoning in humans. The bacteria can be transmitted to eggs either through the porous shell or inside of the egg itself, perhaps when eggs are being formed inside a chicken's ovaries. Salmonella poses a risk if ingested raw, so cooking eggs to 160°F (71°C) is considered essential, especially if your eggs are purchased from a large-scale egg producer. For the most part, though, the likelihood of contracting salmonella through a small, home-based operation is rare. Staying on top of coop cleanliness drastically minimizes the risk of exposure. Prompt removal of eggs from their nest boxes, followed by refrigeration, also lessens the chances of salmonella contamination, as the bacteria multiplies at room temperature. Be sure to wash any utensils that have come into contact with raw eggs thoroughly after use, and always wash your hands with hot, soapy water when handling eggs.

tendency to produce eggs with blood spots can be hereditary, so depending on whether your eggs are for your own personal use or for sale to the public, you may opt to cull the responsible party. Nature isn't always fair, I know.

If you come across funky-tasting eggs, consider what table scraps you have given your flock recently. Flavors from garlic, onions, and fish can be imparted to eggs, resulting in an off flavor. As eggs are porous, they can also pick up strong odors from any chemicals near the chicken coop, such as kerosene, gasoline, mold, or dank scents. Lastly, if you come across (so sorry for having to write this) worms in an egg, take immediate action. You're dealing with parasites here and need to get the

afflicted bird on the mend pronto and do all you can to curtail the same fate befalling the remainder of your flock. Call your vet, and disinfect your coop.

QUALITY CONTROL

If you have free-ranging hens, you may find eggs in assorted and sundry locations whose freshness is questionable. There are a few tools available for determining whether the egg is fit to consume. Using a candling light, you can do one of two things. First, you can check yolk visibility by spinning the egg in front of the light. A fuzzy-looking yolk means the egg is fresh, whereas a clearly defined yolk indicates aging. Also, you can look for airspace size. A fresh egg has no airspace, while the size of an airspace increases as the egg contents cool and shrink. Refer to page 53 for more information about candling.

Other means for determining freshness include floating, smelling, and simply examining the contents by cracking the egg open. Floating is exactly what it sounds like. A fresh egg will sink to the bottom of a bowl of water and lie there horizontally. An egg that is around one week old, thereby containing a growing airspace, will rise up on a slight diagonal. Eggs two to three weeks old will lift vertically, with the tip resting against the bottom of the bowl. Older eggs will float right up to the top on account of their large airspace. You can also simply sniff for any rotten-egg odors, which indicates the presence of hydrogen sulfide and an egg that is long past its prime. Finally, cracking open an egg will give you ample information about its age. In general, fresh eggs have firm yolks and cloudy whites while older eggs have yolks that are more likely to break and watery, runny whites.

WELL-ROUNDED MEALS

Eggs are absolute nutrient powerhouses. They are often referred to as the perfect food, and for good reason. Although a large egg contains only about 75 calories, it is laden with all eight essential amino acids; vitamins A, B_{12}, D, and E; folic acid; phosphorus; and zinc. One egg contains roughly 15 percent of the U.S. recommended daily allowance of protein. This protein is widely considered to be of superior quality among food proteins, second only to that found in human breast milk. Egg

Fresh eggs are full of nutrients.

yolks are composed of fats, cholesterol, and pigment, along with several other nutrients. One of the fats, lecithin, purportedly plays a crucial role in brain function. Eggs also contain the nutrient choline, which is said to play a pivotal role in fetal brain development and the prevention of birth defects. The carotenoids lutein and zeaxanthin are present in eggs, which research suggests assist in eye function and integrity.

There are some people who refrain from eating eggs, believing them to cause elevated blood cholesterol levels and subsequently increasing the risk of heart disease. Cholesterol is a fat required by humans for a number of functions, including regulating hormones, assisting in brain function, and converting sunlight into vitamin D. Most cholesterol present in humans is produced internally, with only about 20 percent coming from dietary sources. A healthy body regulates dietary cholesterol, eliminating or adding it as needed. Numerous studies have shown that eating eggs has no effect on blood cholesterol. A growing number of scientists believe trans fats and saturated fats are the more likely culprits in raising blood cholesterol levels than are dietary sources of cholesterol. Furthermore, the choline present in eggs works to break down the amino acid homocysteine, which research has indicated may contribute to an increased risk of heart disease.

Sharing and Selling

Depending on the size of your flock, it's possible you may have more eggs than you can reasonably scramble, poach, or curd. Selling your eggs to coworkers or neighbors is a time-honored way to unload your Ladies' bounty. Better yet, consider trading or bartering with those neighbors or coworkers. Everyone has a skill or service they can offer, even if it's something as simple as exchanging your eggs for a loaf of someone's homemade bread. Ask around and see what folks might be willing to trade.

Perhaps you have enough surplus eggs that you are thinking of selling them at a local farmers' market or corner grocer. If you intend to market them in any particular way, such as "free-range" or "certified organic," be aware that laws exist related to such labeling claims. Contact your county extension office to learn what the regulations are in your area before you start proffering your eggs on a large scale.

STORAGE

Gather up your flock's eggs at least once a day, if not twice (or more!). Doing so not only prevents egg eating, but also keeps the eggs from getting sullied and ensures quality. Eggs that are soiled can be wiped off with a dry cloth, rough paper towel, or a bit of superfine sandpaper. It's best not to get eggshells wet, as water will rinse off the protective covering, or "bloom." Truly soiled eggs are better disposed of than rinsed. If you keep your nesting boxes clean, this really shouldn't be an issue anyway. As a stay-at-home writer, I have the luxury of checking on my Ladies three times a day. I realize that most people aren't home all day, though, so gathering eggs first thing in the morning is your best bet.

Stored in a cool, dark place at about 70 to 75 percent humidity, eggs will keep for up to five to six weeks. If you store your eggs in the refrigerator, place them on the lowest shelf, as this is generally the coolest place. Most refrigerators have low humidity, causing foods to dry out, so eggs kept in a fridge will last for about four weeks. Always store eggs in a closed container with the pointed end facing down to keep the yolk centered. If you have a surplus of eggs that you know you won't use in time, crack the eggs into a freezer-appropriate container and store frozen for up to one year. Alternatively, you can separate yolks and whites and freeze in ice cube trays, allowing you to thaw out only what you need. Either way, sprinkle a pinch of sugar or salt to keep the eggs from getting gummy when they thaw. Never freeze eggs in their shells, or they are likely to explode. I don't know about you, but I can think of, oh, a thousand things I'd rather be doing than removing frozen eggshell bits from the interior of my freezer.

A Good Way to Dye

Naturally dyed eggs make a colorful addition to any festive occasion, whether you celebrate Easter, Beltane, or Passover. Eggs can be dyed using many household fruits, vegetables, herbs, and spices, creating subtle shades that are nonetheless striking in their simplicity. To create a dye bath, add the dyeing agent of your choice to a large stainless-steel pot filled with 1 quart (.95 L) cold water and 2 tablespoons (30 mL) white vinegar. Bring to a boil, then reduce heat and simmer for 25 minutes. Next, add however many raw eggs you would like to dye to the bath, and boil at least 30 minutes. Remove eggs from bath and dry gently with a paper towel or old cloth. Need ideas? Here's a color chart to get you started:

Color	Agent
Pale yellow	Orange marigold leaves
Golden yellow	Turmeric
Pale purple	Cranberries
Blue-purple	Blueberries
Lavender	Raspberries
Pale pink	Beets
Dark pink	Red cabbage
Dark brown	Coffee grounds
Copper	Onion skins

Appendix

CHICKEN CARE CHECKLIST

While most care for your flock will occur on a day-to-day basis, some tasks are reserved for weekly, monthly, biannual, and annual attention. Daily and weekly tasks will quickly become habits, while those performed less often might need to be jotted down on your calendar. Although routine care doesn't necessarily guarantee your crew will never succumb to any unpleasantries, it sure goes a long way toward achieving that goal.

Daily

- Let chickens out of henhouse in the morning
- Fill waterers
- Remove frozen water during cold weather
- Fill feeders
- Remove any branches, leaves, or other matter from waterers and feeders as needed
- Remove eggs
- Store eggs, pointed end down
- Fluff up litter if using deep litter method
- Give a quick glance at your flock for any signs of distress or injury
- If there are any damp spots in the henhouse, remove them
- Lock chickens up at night

Weekly

- Scrub rim of waterer
- Clean feeder as needed
- Examine fence perimeter for any signs of burrowing
- If providing grit, refill supply as needed
- Add litter to nesting boxes or henhouse floor as needed
- Replace any soiled bedding, and empty droppings tray
- Scrape any droppings off of roosts

Monthly

- Check that roosts are sturdy and have no rough edges
- Examine entire coop for any signs of wear or rot, and repair as needed
- In the winter, check for drafts and remove source if found
- Check that all latches and locks are secure
- Place orders for feed and scratch or purchase from local feed store
- Purchase bedding material as needed
- Empty and refresh nesting box litter
- If needed, mow grass in run

Biannually

- If using deep litter method, empty out and compost all bedding; replace with fresh bedding
- Check for leaks in roof and repair as needed

Annually

- Remove all bedding, feeders, waterers, and nesting materials
- Disinfect living quarters with a 1:10 bleach and water solution administered in a spray bottle
- Scrub floor with disinfectant solution
- Allow everything to dry completely before putting materials back in
- Add fresh bedding material to floor and nesting boxes
- Put a fresh coat of paint on coop, if needed
- Repair any openings or worn parts of fencing

Book 2
Canning & Preserving

Some folks measure wealth by the type of car they drive or the size of their home. For me, I feel wealthy when my pantry is well stocked with a plethora of jams, jellies, pickles, and more. In this section, we'll cover the basics of what it takes to get started with water baths and pressure canners. From equipment selection and tools of the trade to the science involved, as well as ingredient selection and primers on the particulars of preserving jams, pickles, and whole fruits and vegetables, we'll discuss and explore in photographic detail the most vital aspects of home canning. My hope is that if you're just getting started with home canning, you'll come away comfortable with "putting a lid on it" solo, and that if you're already an experienced home canner, you'll find troubleshooting tips and inspiration to further you in your canning adventures.

Chapter 1 🍶
Why We Can

Capturing the heady sweetness of ripe peaches, bottling up the juiciness of sun-ripened tomatoes, transforming crisp apples into spicy, buttery spreads—all acts of food alchemy made possible to you through canning and preserving. By putting up the best of the season's flavors when they are at their peak, you can revel in a parade of culinary delights all year round. Imagine the pleasure of savoring fragrant cherry marmalade on crispy toast when snow is falling outside, or devouring pickled asparagus alongside a smoky Gouda during an autumn picnic. While sublime flavor is the ultimate goal in any form of cooking, in the case of canning, safety must also be considered paramount. Here we'll take a quick peek at the origins of home canning and how that history has led us to where home canning is today.

TIME IN A BOTTLE

Consuming preserved foods and beverages has never been as easy as it is today. Pad into the kitchen in your slippers, open the fridge, drink orange juice straight from the carton, and your thirst is quenched, the beverage remains at a hospitable temperature to prevent spoilage, life is good. Before bottling and canning methods were invented, let alone refrigeration, food preservation was achieved through drying, salting, smoking, and pickling in vinegar. Those methods preserved well but could only be applied to certain types of foods.

Who'd have guessed Napoleon Bonaparte would have so much to do with culinary history? The prolonged and far-reaching Napoleonic Wars prompted the need for a new means of extending the shelf life of foods. The Little Corporal once famously stated, "An army marches on its stomach." In order for those stomachs to be satiated and battle-ready, they needed nonperishable, easily transported foods. At the end of the 18th century, Bonaparte's government placed an ad in the French newspaper *Le Monde* offering 12,000 francs to anyone able to invent a new means of preserving food for his army and navy. The stipulation was that the end product must be inexpensive to manufacture in large quantities, easy to transport, and offer soldiers a more nutritious meal than their current ration of salted meat and hardtack. The MREs (Meal Ready to Eat) of modern armies wouldn't make their appearance on the military meal scene for some time to come.

Enter French confectioner and chef Nicolas Appert. After initially beginning his career experimenting with preserving fruits, he later concentrated his work on bettering preserving methods for all types of foods. Borrowing from and building on the experimentation of chefs and chemists preceding him, Appert devised the wide-mouthed glass-bottle water bath method of preserving that underlies home canning as it exists today. Reports on the success of the French navy's experiment with his canned goods gained the attention of the French government, ultimately securing him the cash prize on the condition that he put down in words a detailed description of his methods. After the publication of Appert's book in 1810, a timely and, some argue, cunning London entrepreneur named Peter Durand purchased a patent in England for preserving foods, the means of which were strikingly similar to Appert's. He did make a number of alterations and substitutions to Appert's method, however, like also allowing the use of pottery and tinned iron canisters, later shortened colloquially to "cans."

Several decades later, after tin cans were in widespread use in America, an inventor and metalsmith from New York named John L. Mason upped the home-preservation ante by developing the appropriately titled glass "mason" jar. What distinguished Mason's jar from those previously used in home canning was a threaded top, to which a zinc lid with a rubber ring was screwed on. It was the rubber surrounding the lid that created a vacuum seal, protecting food from spoilage. Until Mason's invention, home canners used a flat tin lid topped with sealing wax. Thanks to the ease of use and low cost of Mason's jars, the practice of home canning opened to a wide audience, from city slickers to country folk. By the end of the 19th century, as the cost of cane sugar fell and the development of wood stoves made the process of cooking less physically cumbersome, mason jars were put to increasingly greater use. Summer gardens were planted to produce abundant yields, the surplus of which was "put up" for winter consumption. The Ball family began purchasing small glass-bottle makers, eventually becoming the largest manufacturer of mason jars in

Vintage jars, while not suitable for use now, make an attractive collection.

the United States. The new technology, coupled with widespread manufacture, brought home canning into every kitchen.

WAR AND PEAS

Then along came grocery stores. The year 1916 brought the first "cash and carry" food store. For the first time ever, shoppers were permitted to peruse store shelves at their leisure, selecting from a wide variety of items. When large-scale grocery stores opened their doors, the way people interact with their food was forever changed. "You mean there's more than one brand of canned corn out there?" The advent of the grocery store marked a reduction in the number of home canners. Housewives of the time questioned the merits of home canning, and understandably so, when so many convenience foods were now available for purchase.

Home canning resurfaced during both world wars only to then retreat from public view for several decades. It appeared again among back-to-basics advocates in the 1960s and 1970s. Truthfully, though, it never really disappeared. Homemakers have been making relishes and putting up preserves for as long as home processing has been possible. There is an inherent logic found in preserving your own foods, I'd argue. I'm not alone in this attitude either. For a growing number, the questionable nutritional quality and safety of many packaged foods, coupled with an increasing awareness about the distances foods are shipped to reach consumers, have kindled a desire to take up home canning and preserving. Some gather up their ingredients fresh from their own backyard gardens, while others visit nearby orchards, farmers' markets, and grocers for seasonally available, local foods.

Chapter 2

Tools of the Trade

Much of the equipment needed in order to properly can at home is most likely already in your kitchen. Investing in a few specialized items will make the process both easier and safer. The good news is that home canning needn't break the bank. Many people opt to start canning in the first place because of the long-term savings incurred by doing so. Take a look around your kitchen and determine what you already have and what might be missing. If you lack an item, consider asking around before you buy new. Chances are, you'll find a neighbor, relative, or fellow canner in your community who would gladly loan, barter, or sell the necessary item to you. Used-goods and thrift stores can also be a reservoir of gently worn kitchen items yearning for a second chance. Yard and estate sales are also worth checking out for canning treasure.

CANNING JARS

Come summertime, you can find canning jars in just about every grocery store. Many hardware stores will also have packages of them on hand. The only type of jar that I recommend for canning is the mason-style jar with a threaded top. Mason jars are made of tempered glass and are able to withstand the high temperatures that are reached in both boiling water baths and pressure canning. Best of all, they can be used again and again. Each time you get ready to put up a batch of something, inspect your jars to ensure that they have no cracks, breaks, or chips and are safe to use. Otherwise, you might find yourself dealing with a canner full of leaked pickles or jam or a lid that fails to seal.

Mason jars are available in a variety of sizes, from 4 ounces to quarts (120 mL to 1 L). Gallons (3.8 L) are also available, but they are bulky and cumbersome and, because of their size, need a long processing time to ensure that all microorganisms packed in the center have been destroyed. As such, they are suggested only for processing highly acidic juices, such as grape juice. If you're into appearances, like me, and want a range of looks, rest assured that there is a canning jar out there to suit any style, from traditional to modern. Square jars with platinum-colored lids, my personal favorite, are now available in several sizes. Although I love the look of European jars with rubber gaskets and clamps, I cannot in good conscience recommend them here, as they are not considered safe by all federal food agencies.

So, how do you know which size to use? While most recipes will tell you how many pints or half-pints a recipe will make, consider the quantity of the preserved food that your family is likely to quickly consume, and select your jar size accordingly.

If you are a household of one, stick with half-pints. Larger families may wish to use larger jars. Mason jars are available with either wide or tapered mouths. Wide-mouthed jars are suggested if you will be packing large items such as whole tomatoes, dill pickles, or peach halves, as they are easier to both fill and to empty.

Although you might be tempted to repurpose mayonnaise, applesauce, or pickle jars from commercially produced foods, I would suggest you resist the urge. Such jars are made for a single use and may crack or break when up against the temperatures used in home canning. It would be a real shame

Canning jars come in a variety of sizes and shapes.

to spend hours preparing apples and cooking them down to a lovely applesauce, only to be left with a sloppy mess inside your canner from a cracked jar. Instead, repurpose such jars in your pantry, where you can use them to safely store grains, legumes, and baking items. Similarly, antique canning jars, while fabulous for holding cotton balls and swabs in the bathroom, ought not be used for modern home canning. These jars may not be tempered properly or have minute flaws in them, making them susceptible to breakage during processing.

Assorted lids and screw bands

A stainless-steel stockpot

CANNING LIDS AND SCREW BANDS

Modern home canning closures are comprised of a two-piece lid and screw band. The flat lids are fashioned from tin-plated steel that has been covered in a food-grade coating. Running the circumference of the underside of the lid is a rubber compound, specially formulated for vacuum-sealing foods canned at home. After processing, the vacuum seal produces a permanent impression in the lid, thereby rendering it unsafe for reuse. Once you've used a lid, it cannot be used in canning again. It doesn't have to go into the trash can, however. Use the jar for storing dry goods in your pantry, or save up lids and give them to a local elementary school for arts and crafts projects. (I remember making canning-lid Christmas ornaments!)

The lid doesn't go it alone, but completes its task with the aid of its trusty partner, the screw band. This threaded metal band fits atop the lid, securing it in place over the neck of the glass jar. During processing, the screw band holds down the lid, allowing the sealing compound to work its magic and secure the lid to the jar. Once the jar has been processed and allowed to cool, the screw band may be removed. In fact, it should be, at least temporarily. Moisture may be present under the screw band and, if not removed and dried, rust may occur, prohibiting reuse of the band for future processing. If cared for properly, screw bands may be used multiple times. Once they show signs of wear, such as warping or rusting, it's time to safely discard or recycle them. Canning lids are made from tin-plated steel covered with brass plating or a platinum finish. Call your local recycling company to see if tossing them in with cat food cans is safe or if they should be taken to a metal scrapyard.

BOILING WATER CANNER

Jars intended for boiling water bath canning can be processed in either a large enamel pot specifically designed for home canning or a large stockpot. Ideally, whatever vessel you choose should be deep enough to provide 1 to 3 inches (2.5 to 7.6 cm) of space above the jar lids, to accommodate both the boiling water itself and the attendant splashing. The enamel canning pots found in grocery and hardware stores often come with their own racks, which are metallic disks with handles. The purpose of a canning rack is to keep the jars out of direct contact with the bottom of the pot, which would prevent water from circulating underneath

An enamel stockpot

A pressure canner

the jars. The rack handles also allow you to raise and lower jars into the boiling cauldron with ease. If you are using a stockpot from your home collection and lack a rack, you can purchase one separately, or try fashioning one from either a round cake cooling rack or by attaching extra canning screw bands together with metal ties to form a circle. In lieu of handles to lift the entire rack out, use a jar lifter or tongs to individually remove jars from the canner.

PRESSURE CANNER

A pressure canner is a tall metal pot equipped with a locking lid containing a pressure-regulating gauge. This type of canner creates steam inside the pot, allowing temperatures of 240 to 250°F (115 to 121°C) to be reached. If you intend to can any low-acid foods, a pressure canner is absolutely essential. Don't even let yourself think that it might be possible to do otherwise. The risks posed by processing low-acid foods, unless pickled, in a boiling water bath are not worth it. Read more about low- and high-acid foods on page 93.

Pressure canners come in either weighted-gauge or dial-gauge models. Some models, like mine, actually have both dials and weighted gauges on their lids. Weighted-gauge pressure canners are fitted with a 5-, 10-, or 15-pound (2.25, 4.5, or 6.8 kg) pressure adjustment. These models allow small quantities of steam to escape from the lid every time the gauge whistles or rocks back and forth during processing. Altitude adjustments must be made on weighted-gauge pressure canners, as their accuracy is affected by changes in elevation. They are considered more durable, seldom requiring replacement or servicing. Dial-gauge pressure canners give exact numeric readings of the pressure inside the canner. If the pressure is too low or too high, raising or lowering the heat level of the burner adjusts it. Dial-gauge pressure canners must be checked annually for accuracy. This is often done at a local extension office, where you can check their instruments against your own. If a dial-gauge canner is giving incorrect pressure readings, it must be replaced.

LITTLE THINGS MEAN A LOT

While jars, lids, and canners are the most essential items needed to can food at home, a number of other kitchen items can speed up and simplify the process. Many of the items listed below can be found in most well-stocked kitchens. The first items on the list are the most specific to canning and, while not required, definitely help make the entire endeavor operate more smoothly.

KITCHEN SCALE Helpful for when recipes call for ingredients by the pound.

LID MAGNET Essentially a plastic stick with a round magnet attached to one end, lid magnets, or magnetic wands, as they are also known, make the task of fishing lids out of hot water considerably easier.

POT HOLDERS Be sure to have these nearby when lifting any heavy, hot, water-filled pots.

JAR LIFTER These resemble regular tongs, but the grabbing ends are covered in soft plastic. Not only do they make inserting and retrieving jars from boiling canners safer, but jar lifters also reduce the chance of scratching either the glass or the lid surface.

CLOTHS You will need clean cloths for wiping down the rims of filled jars, as well as for wiping up spills.

CANNING FUNNEL Designed specifically to fit inside either narrow- or wide-mouthed canning jars, these funnels help to keep messes and overfilling to a minimum.

KITCHEN TIMER Setting a timer will take the guesswork out of how long your pot has been boiling.

KNIVES A basic tool in any kitchen, knives in a variety of sizes are essential for processing foods for home canning.

NONMETALLIC SPATULA While bubble-removing tools can be found wherever canning supplies are sold, any long, thin, rubber spatula or wooden chopstick can be used for removing trapped air bubbles from filled jars.

MIXING BOWLS You'll need an assortment of bowls for holding prepared ingredients.

DRY AND LIQUID MEASURING CUPS A glass liquid measuring cup with a pouring spout can be an indispensable aid when transferring your cooked preserves from stovetop to jar.

MEASURING SPOONS For measuring out salt, spices, and so on.

CUTTING BOARD In addition to its more obvious role in chopping up fruits and vegetables, a cutting board is great for placing underneath jars while filling. It keeps the jars stationary and keeps spills off the counter.

FOOD MILL This less-common tool can be handy for puréeing apples for applesauce.

FOOD PROCESSOR This kitchen workhorse is truly wonderful when you have a good amount of slicing or chopping to do.

COLANDER For rinsing produce, draining off cooking liquid, and so on.

MEDIUM AND LARGE, HEAVY STAINLESS-STEEL POTS Many canning ingredients are first cooked before being packed in jars, so having good-quality pots on hand is essential.

APPLE PEELER/CORER A countertop-mounted peeler saves vast amounts of time when you're peeling by the bushel.

LABELS You may think you have the memory of an elephant, but after canning all summer, remembering the contents of each jar can be daunting. Label and date what's what and when it was made.

MUSLIN TEA BAGS Used for creating herb bundles/sachets to prevent dried or loose herbs from direct contact with liquids. They're quite inexpensive and can often be found in stores where bulk herbs or teas are sold.

CHEESECLOTH A finely woven fabric used in home canning to either fashion into herb and spice sachets or separate solids from liquids in jelly-making.

JELLY BAG A cloth bag made of tightly woven cheesecloth, cotton flannel, or unbleached muslin used to strain solids from liquids. The bag is set into a 12-inch-high (30.5 cm) three-legged stainless-steel stand. The stand fits over the rim of a pot, thereby allowing juices to drip out and collect.

Chapter 3
Canning
Concepts

When it comes to starting out with home canning, it's really best to take things slowly. Aim for more of a water-creeping-up-your-swimsuit-slowly than a dive-right-in approach. While there are certainly amazing rewards to putting up foods yourself, those rewards can only be reaped when the correct steps and cautionary measures have been taken. So, brush up a bit on the fundamentals of canning before getting started. Once you know what to look for, you'll be that much more confident every time you break out the mason jars and fire up the stovetop!

CANNING CHEMISTRY 101

The world we humans inhabit keeps close quarters with a vast array of other living organisms. From the furry friends who share our homes to the microscopic life forms that live in our digestive tracts, many of these relationships and interactions are symbiotic. Microorganisms live in soil, in water, and in the air. While they are necessary and vital in their given functions, they do contribute to decay, especially when it comes to the deterioration of foods. Anyone who has had the immense displeasure of finding forgotten potatoes morphed into a gelatinous stew in the pantry has, regrettably, witnessed this natural deterioration firsthand.

Molds, yeast, and bacteria are, in most cases, the enemies of food preservation. Under controlled conditions, specific microorganisms can be welcome guests in the manufacture of wine, cheese, and pickles. Left to their own devices in canned goods, however, molds, yeast, and bacteria will render your food unsafe and inedible. Done properly, home canning stops these microorganisms in their tracks. By exposing them to heat and hermetically sealing glass jars, the little beasties are killed and the environment inside the jar becomes inhospitable to pathogen growth. Exposure to high temperatures also prevents naturally occurring enzymes present in food from speeding deterioration and decomposition. By killing off microorganisms and giving the kibosh to enzymes, home canning holds foods in a sort of suspended animation.

How does it work, exactly? Well, to begin, food is placed into a sterilized glass jar (more on sterilization ahead), capped with a two-part flat lid and metal ring, and allowed to boil for a period of time, as directed by your recipe, in either a boiling water bath or a pressure canner. The heat makes the food and gases inside the jar expand, causing a buildup of internal pressure. Air begins to escape from the food and from the headspace (see page 99), which is the area between the top of the food and the underside of the lid left unfilled, relieving this buildup of pressure. The buildup and release of gases recurs continually during the canning procedure,

resulting in the formation of a vacuum inside the jar. As the jar cools, external pressure will be greater than the pressure inside the jar. The greater external pressure helps to keep the lid pushed down, while the compound surrounding the lid acts as glue, completely sealing in the contents of the jar and keeping hungry microorganisms out. Memorizing this process to expound upon at length at social gatherings is completely optional. What matters is that, if done properly, it keeps your lovingly preserved food from spoiling and keeps you from getting sick.

Fully processing foods according to directions is absolutely imperative. If any step is skipped, or done only partially, microorganisms may still be present inside the jar. Flavor can be compromised, your foods may spoil, and, of greatest concern, serious risks to health may be presented, including death! I say this not so that you bury your canning jars deep in the recesses of your basement in defeat, but instead to encourage you. Years of rigorous scientific research have resulted in tried-and-true, and inherently safe, home-canning methods, which you will learn about here. Done properly, you can feel confident that the fruits of your labor are safe for consumption.

A STERILE ENVIRONMENT

Perhaps you are a member of the club whose motto is "God made dirt and dirt don't hurt." Be that as it may, dirt, or more specifically, microorganisms in the environment, can be undesirable in home canning situations. If you are making any product that is to be processed in a boiling water bath for less than 10 minutes, you will need to sterilize your canning jars in addition to simply cleaning them.

To sterilize jars, place them upright on a canning rack inside a boiling water canner. Fill the canner with hot water, allowing water to flow into the empty jars, bring it to a boil, and process for 10 minutes. If you live at an elevation above 1,000 feet (300 m), add 1 minute for each extra 1,000 feet (300 m) above sea level (we'll discuss elevation in greater detail on page 94).

Once the required boiling time has been met, keep the jars in the canner with the lid on until you are just about ready to fill them. Using tongs, carefully remove the jars and drain the water back into the canner one at a time. This way the water in your canner will already be hot and ready to begin boiling again as soon as your jars are filled, fitted with lids, and returned to the canner for processing. Sterilization of canning jars is generally only required for items such as jams, jellies, and pickles. Any item requiring more than 10 minutes in a boiling water bath or that will be processed in a pressure canner does not need pre-sterilized jars.

ACID TEST

Knowing whether a food is low or high in acid is crucial to canning safety. This is because relative acidity determines the temperature at which microorganisms present on a food will be killed. The pH scale is used for measuring acidity. Those foods with a pH of 4.6 or lower are considered high acid, whereas those whose pH is above 4.6 are considered low acid. High-acid and low-acid foods will be processed differently.

Microorganisms on high-acid foods will be killed at 212°F (100°C), the temperature achieved by a boiling water bath. Microorganisms on lower-acid foods can survive at temperatures up to 240°F (116°C), so a boiling water bath cannot guarantee that pathogens on such foods will be destroyed. Pressure canning is an absolute must to ensure safety when canning low-acid foods.

Jams, jellies, chutneys, marmalades, butters, and most fruit spreads are generally higher in acid, and therefore may be processed in a boiling water bath. Some fruits, however, straddle the high/low acidity fence. For example, tomatoes can have variable acidity, and on occasion may have a pH higher than 4.6. Unless you plan on putting all your tomatoes to a litmus test, adding an acidifying agent like vinegar, lemon juice, or citric acid will provide enough acidity to allow tomatoes to be safely boiling water bath processed.

Otherwise, if you are intending to preserve any vegetable, meat, seafood, or poultry products through canning, they must be pressure canned. These foods are all low in acidity and therefore require a temperature of 240°F (116°C) in order to kill off spoilage-inducing microorganisms. The organism that poses the gravest concern to home canners is the bacterium *Clostridium botulinum*, also known as botulism toxin. This nasty beast, the cause of botulism food poisoning, can lurk in canned or bottled foods. Colorless, odorless, and tasteless, the spores of this microorganism are potentially lethal if consumed.

MIXING IT UP

So what if you want to make a product that combines both low- and high-acid foods? Will you need to process through a boiling water bath or a pressure canner? The answer is pretty straightforward. If you are pickling or adding an acidifying agent to your recipe, then you're safe to use a boiling water bath. Otherwise, you'll need to fire up your pressure canner.

ACIDITY (pH) OF SELECT FRUITS AND VEGETABLES

Strong Acidity

0

2 Plums (Damson and Blue)

3 Apples, Apricots, Blackberries, Blueberries, Cherries, Gooseberries, Lemons, Peaches, Pears, Plums (Greengage, Red, and Yellow), Sauerkraut

4 Tomatoes

4.6 Safety threshold

5 Asparagus, Beets, Cabbage, Carrots, Cauliflower, Celery, Eggplant, Green beans, Lima beans, Okra, Pumpkin, Spinach, Turnips

6 Corn, Peas

14

Strong Alkalinity

(Data from the U.S. Food and Drug Administration, 2007)

ALTITUDE ADJUSTMENT

As we move from sea level up to higher elevations, the temperature at which water boils changes. This occurs because of changes in surrounding atmospheric pressure. Essentially, the higher up you go, the less dense the air will be, and air with reduced density exerts less pressure. You know how your ears pop when flying in an airplane? That's because you have gone up in elevation and your body is recalibrating with the change in air pressure inside the cabin. So, at sea level, water will boil at 212°F (100°C), whereas on top of Mount Everest, it will boil at 156.2°F (69°C).

If you live at an elevation of over 1,000 feet (300 m), you can't simply trust your eyes and assume that since the water is boiling, it must be above the temperature necessary to kill off molds and yeasts and to inactivate enzymes inside your jars. The truth is that it is boiling at a lower temperature, since it is responding to reduced air pressure. Whether you are using a boiling water bath or pressure canning, you will need to make adjustments if you live over 1,000 feet (300 m) above sea level. Use the chart on page 338 to determine how much extra time you will need to tack on to the time suggested in the recipes in this book.

SIZING UP THE COMPETITION

I love to eat. You love to eat. Everything that lives loves to eat, including those organisms that want to eat whatever it is you're eating. Although you often can't see those other living entities (or, for our purposes, "beasts"), they are certainly there. From soil, air, water, and on every surface in between, microorganisms are moving along through their lives just as surely as you are through yours. Three classes of microorganisms pose health and quality concerns to canned foods: mold, yeast, and bacteria. Let us examine each and consider the ways in which they are affected by acidity and temperature.

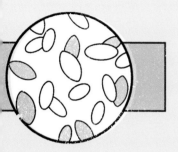

Mold

Mold is fairly easy to spot. No doubt you've found a patch greedily hugging the inside of a long-past-its-expiration-date container of cream cheese, or on a forgotten bit of zucchini buried in the bottom of the crisper drawer. Fuzzy and customarily green, gray, or white, mold is a type of fungus that grows in a multicellular filament. Molds prefer and thrive on high-acid foods such as fruits and pickles. Fortunately, they are destroyed at temperatures between 180 and 212°F (82 and 100°C), which is readily achieved in a boiling water bath.

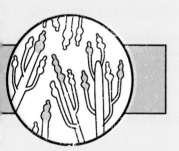

Yeast

Yeast is also a type of fungus. However, unlike molds that grow together in clusters, yeasts grow as single units. Many types of yeasts are highly valued in foods, as it is their presence that helps transform barley into a malty ale and grapes into a full-bodied Cabernet. This metamorphosis occurs as a result of yeast-induced fermentation. While fermentation is desirable in, say, converting cabbage into sauerkraut, it is not something you want occurring inside your canned goods. Yeasts are fond of high-acid foods, as well as those with ample sugar. Like molds, they will be destroyed in a boiling water bath.

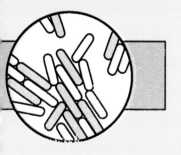

Bacteria

Bacteria are the most pernicious microorganisms of the lot. Temperatures that would easily cause molds and yeasts to bite the dust can actually be hospitable to bacteria. Some bacteria can even survive being boiled for a while in water. Worse yet, most bacteria are invisible to the naked eye. So while mold announces its presence as a fuzzy clump and yeast says "howdy do" with a pungent scent and tingly taste, bacteria can lurk, unnoticed, in your food. Salmonella and *Staphylococcus aureus* can cause food poisoning and general physical discomfort, but it's botulism that is the most menacing of bacterial threats to the home canner.

Clostridium botulinum doesn't particularly care for high-acid foods and instead thrives in low-acid environments such as those found on vegetables, meats, seafood, and poultry. The one and only way to kill off *C. botulinum* spores naturally found on these low-acid foods is to process them in a pressure canner. This bears repeating, so I'll say it again. If you're canning any low-acid foods without pickling them, then you must use a pressure canner. I don't know about you, but when I go, I don't want it to be on account of a nasty critter lurking inside an unscrupulously packaged jar of green beans.

The Methods

Now that you know the equipment you'll need to get started with home canning, we'll examine some of the methods used for getting the job done. The ingredients and end product will always dictate which technique is utilized. While many recipes will indicate what method is needed, it's good to be well acquainted with all the modes available for home processing. Make yourself something tasty to drink, find a quiet spot, and read over this chapter before you start mixing up a batch of marmalade or pickled okra. Here we'll explore boiled water bath and pressure canning.

Boiling Water Bath

The boiling water bath processing method is applied to high-acid foods including jams, jellies, marmalades, preserves, pickles, relishes, chutneys, salsas, ketchup, and some sauces. These items require a temperature of 212°F (100°C) in order to kill off harmful microorganisms, and the boiling water bath provides just such an environment. Follow these simple steps, and you'll be stocking your larder with delectable delights in no time!

1   **Assemble all your equipment.**

Gather up jars, lids and screw bands, canner and rack, jar lifter, funnel, spatula, recipe ingredients—everything you'll need to concoct your recipe, bottle it up, and process it. Doing so in advance saves you from last-minute scrambles. While you're at it, go ahead and read through your recipe. Know what you're getting into, how many jars it yields, and how much time you should be prepared to spend on the entire process.

2 Clean all jars, lids, and screw bands.

Give your gathered jars and their closures a good wash in hot, soapy water. Rinse them thoroughly, and set aside. Whether you are using brand-spanking-new jars or canning veterans, inspect the rims for cracks, nicks, or uneven edges. The easiest way to do this is by running your index finger around the circumference of the jar. Although it is unlikely that new jars will have faults, it is not entirely outside the realm of possibility. Weeding out the duds at this point will save you from leaks or jars that fail to seal properly. Check your screw bands, too. If you're reusing any, discard those that have rusted or show signs of wear such as scratches or scuff marks.

3 Heat the jars.

Fill your canner with enough water to cover the jars by 3 inches (7.6 cm). Depending on what sort of rack you are using, you can either put it into the canner at this point or fill it with jars and use the handles to lower it into the canner. Place your cleaned jars in the canner atop the rack, allowing the jars to become filled with water. It can be handy to have a teakettle with hot water ready in the event that you find yourself needing extra water to cover the jars once they have been submerged into the boiling water bath. Cover the pot and heat until almost boiling, around 180°F (82°C). Whatever you do, don't put cool jars into a boiling pot of water. By warming up the canning water and jars at the same time, you eliminate the risk of the jars cracking in response to a rapid change in temperature. Keep the jars hot and the canner covered until you are ready to begin filling. Alternatively, you can sterilize your jars in the dishwasher, but only if your model has a sterilization setting.
NOTE: If you will be processing your jars for less than 10 minutes, then you will need to boil the jars for 10 minutes to sterilize them. Otherwise, just keep them warm, with the lid on.

TIP:

I can't tell you how many times I've been up to my elbows in jam and discovered I have fewer jars prepped than I have jam to fill them. You really can't have enough "just in case" jars ready. If you end up not needing them after all, no harm done. Simply dry them off and store them back in your pantry. As far as extra lids go, though, I'd keep a "wait and see" approach. Once lids have been exposed to high heat, the sealing compound is activated and they shouldn't be used later. Monitor whether it looks like you might need an extra lid or two as you begin filling. If you do, simply submerge the new lids in the pot on the stove holding the other lids, and allow them to sit for several minutes before pulling them out and applying them to jars.

4 Prep the lids.

Fill a small pot with about 4 inches (10.2 cm) of water. Place the lids into the pot, cover, and heat until just simmering, around 180°F (82°C). Turn off the heat at this point and keep the pot containing the lids covered until you begin filling the jars. The screw bands don't need to be warmed up, just cleaned as described above and set aside until it's time to start filling the jars.

5 Prepare your recipe.

Work your magic on the stovetop, chopping, mixing, and cooking as your recipe indicates. If you're making a recipe with an especially lengthy cooking and preparation time, wait until you are finished, or at least on the home stretch, before you start warming up your jars and lids. Otherwise, you'll be using unnecessary energy keeping everything simmering the entire time.

6 Fill the jars.

Using a jar lifter or tongs, carefully remove one jar at a time from the canner, taking care to tip out the water away from you to avoid splashing.

Place the empty jar on a kitchen towel or wood cutting board on the counter. Any heat-protected surface will work. What you're looking to avoid is direct contact between a hot jar and a cold surface, such as a stone countertop, which could cause the jar to crack.

If your recipe has a pourable consistency, you may wish to transfer the hot mixture into a pitcher or large glass measuring cup with a pouring spout. This way, you can more easily and safely fill your jars with a minimum of mess.

Place a canning funnel over a jar, and fill the jar with your concoction until there is either ¼ inch (6 mm) or ½ inch (1.3 cm) of headspace, depending on what your recipe indicates. Headspace is the space between the top of the food in the jar and underside of the lid. Generally, whole fruits and any pickled or acidified foods such as chutneys, relishes, pickles, condiments, and tomatoes require ½-inch (1.3 cm) headspace, while fruit spreads and juices need ¼-inch (6 mm) headspace. Altitude has no effect on headspace requirements.

Using a nonmetallic spatula, a bubble releasing tool, or a chopstick, release any trapped air bubbles inside the jar by running your tool of choice inside between the food and the jar. Trapped air bubbles can prevent proper sealing, creating leaks and encouraging the growth of pathogens. After you have released any trapped air bubbles, check the headspace again and add or remove contents to adjust as needed.

> **TIP:**
>
> If you do end up scalding yourself, slather on some aloe vera pronto. It will help soothe the burn and expedite healing. Or try this tip from my old days as a baker at a natural foods store and rub a few drops of lavender essential oil onto the burn.

Check Your Head(space)

Headspace accuracy is vital to creating a proper seal and for keeping your jar's contents inside where they belong. Too little room and the contents could spill out

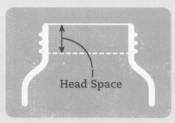

Head Space

when processing; too much air can prevent a complete seal from forming. Using a canning funnel definitely

helps, in my experience, as it serves as a visual gauge when the jar is getting full. If you are just getting started with home canning, know that the value of this simple step cannot be stressed enough.

7   Clean the jar rims.

Using a clean, dampened cloth or a paper towel, wipe the rim and threads of each jar, removing any food debris that may have dripped when filling. This step is very important, since food left on the jar rim can interfere with proper sealing.

8   Place the lids and screw bands on the jars.

Remove lids one at a time from their pot using either a magnetic jar lifter or tongs. Center a lid atop each jar, and secure with a screw band. Turn each screw band until you feel a little bit of resistance, and then continue twisting on until it is fingertip-tight. Don't overtighten the screw bands, since doing so can prevent the jars from venting properly during processing, which in turn can prevent a proper seal from forming.

10 Cool the jars.

After the processing time is complete, turn off the heat and take the lid off of the canner. Allow the jars to rest for 5 minutes, and then remove them one at a time using a jar lifter. Try to avoid tilting the jars as you remove them from the canner. Place the jars on a towel, and allow them to cool, untouched, for 24 hours. You might want to drape a kitchen cloth over your jars to keep them from catching drafts, which could cause the jars to cool too quickly, making them susceptible to cracking.

9 Process the jars.

Using a jar lifter, place your filled jars one at a time into the canner. Be certain they are sitting on top of the rack and aren't touching each other, since you want the boiling water to circulate underneath, over, and in between each jar. Once all of your jars are in, adjust the water level in the canner as needed to ensure that all jars are well covered. Place the lid on the pot, and bring the water to a rolling boil. Once a sustained boil is reached, you can begin timing. Processing times vary widely and are based on what type of food item you are preserving. Process for the amount of time specified in your recipe, adjusted for altitude if necessary (see Altitude Adjustment on page 338). The water must continue boiling rapidly for the entire duration of the processing. Check the water level periodically during processing, and add more boiling water as needed.

11 Check the seals.

Once your jars have had their cooling-off period, you'll want to ensure that they have sealed properly. If you heard lots of popping and pinging coming from your jars as they cooled, you're looking good, although you'll still need to determine whether each jar is sealed. Remove the screw bands from the jars, dry them thoroughly, and return them to the pantry.

(Screw bands serve no immediate function after processing, and should be removed and stored to help prevent rusting caused by water drops between the screw band and the jar threads.) Dry off your jars completely, including the lid, threads, and body. Next, view your jars from the side, looking for a slight indention in the center of the lid. Press down on the lid with your fingertips and feel around for a downward curving dent. A properly sealed lid will remain in place once

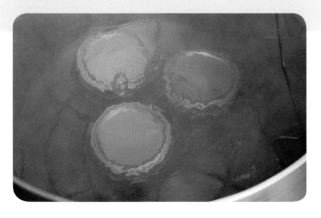

you remove your finger, refusing to yield. Still not fully convinced? Grasp your jar by the lid only, checking to see if it remains firmly attached. If your lid springs back when pushed on, slips off either partially or completely, shows no indentation, or displays a stream of tiny bubbles inside (an indication that air is getting into the jar), you have a faulty seal.

12 Reprocess or refrigerate if needed.

Should one of your jars fail to seal properly, you can either reprocess the jar and its contents, or set it aside for immediate use. Reprocessing will compromise the quality of your finished product, as the contents will have been subjected to high temperatures twice. Alternatively, you can simply put the jar, unsealed contents and all, in the refrigerator and eat it up within the week. If you opt to reprocess, you will need to begin at the beginning, warming up the contents of your jar, cleaning and heating another jar, and using a new lid. Before you start, though, check the rim of the jar that failed to seal for nicks or cracks. If it's fine, go ahead and use the same jar again. Otherwise, begin with a new jar. Next, fill the jar, check the headspace, remove air bubbles, and process again in the canner for the amount of time specified in the recipe. If you have several bad seals and don't have the time, energy, or temperament to reprocess, simply empty the contents into freezer-proof containers and freeze until needed. I wouldn't suggest freezing pickles, though, as the amount of liquid they contain makes them less crunchy when returned to room temperature.

13 Label and store.

Finally, label and date your jars while their contents are fresh in your mind. Dating the jars is equally as important. When you begin amassing an impressive arsenal of home-canned goods, it will be necessary to know which need eating soon and which can be left to stew in their own juices for a bit longer. For the best flavor and texture, eat your wares within one year.

While those items older than one year might not have gone bad, their quality will begin to suffer. Many home canners use a permanent marker, writing directly on the lid for easy identification. You can also use labels and stickers if you'd like to adorn your goods for quick gift giving (see Finishing Touches, page 104).

Store your jars in a cool, dry, dark location, such as a pantry or cabinet. If you're lucky enough to have a basement, you've hit the storage jackpot. Home-canned goods need to be kept between 40 and 70°F (4 and 21°C) in an area free from high humidity. If you are storing your jars in a garage and think the temperature out there might approach freezing, wrap the jars in newspaper or cloth, put them in a cardboard box, and cover the box with a blanket, providing an added layer of insulation against the cold. If your storage area reaches over 70°F (21°C) or is very humid, consider relocating your canned goods. Too much heat or humidity can cause seals to fail, resulting in spoilage.

Some items, such as tomato juice, might separate during storage. This is normal and no need for concern.

🥘 Pressure Canner

All low-acid foods must be canned in a pressure canner, unless they have been acidified. The steps are similar to water bath canning but with a few unique twists. As discussed in Tools of the Trade, page 88, pressure canners come in either weighted- or dial-gauge versions. While the following directions apply to both models, always consult the manufacturer's directions provided with your model to ensure proper and safe use. If you picked up your pressure canner at a yard sale or via a no-longer-canning aunt, write or e-mail the manufacturer and request a manual, or simply check their website for an online version. Read it thoroughly before firing up your pressure canner for the first time.

2 Prep your pressure canner.

Put about 2 to 3 inches (5 to 7.6 cm) of water in the bottom of your pressure canner. Place the rack in the bottom of the canner. Begin warming the water over medium heat with the lid off.

3 Clean and heat your jars and lids, prepare your recipe, fill the jars, clean the rims, and put on the lids and screw bands.

Refer to steps 2 through 8 of Boiling Water Bath for detailed instructions.

1 Assemble all your equipment.

Gather up jars, lids and screw bands, canner and rack, jar lifter, funnel, spatula, recipe ingredients—everything you'll need to concoct your recipe, bottle it up, and process it. Read through your recipe. Know what you're getting into, how many jars it yields, and how much time you should be prepared to spend on the entire process.

4 Exhaust the vent.

Take your filled jars and, using a jar lifter or tongs, place them one at a time into the pressure canner. Be certain they are sitting on top of the rack and aren't touching each other. Once all of your jars are in, place the lid on the canner and lock it into place according to the manufacturer's directions for your model. If using a dial-gauge canner, be sure the petcock, the small tube sticking out of the lid, is open. If using a weighted-gauge canner, leave the weight off of the vent pipe. Bring water to a boil over medium-high heat. Once you see steam coming out of the vent pipe, set a timer for 10

minutes. This process is known as *exhausting*. Its purpose is to force all the air inside of the canner out. You will want to time this to be certain that you have allotted 10 minutes and no less, as failure to do so could alter temperatures inside the canner and result in improperly sealed jars. Exhausting is necessary every time you use a pressure canner.

5 Process the jars.

After you have exhausted the vent for 10 minutes, close the petcock on dial-gauge canners by putting the counterweight on it. For weighted-gauge canners, close the vent by placing the weight over the vent pipe. If you are at sea level up to 1,000 feet (300 m) elevation, position the weight at the number (5, 10, or 15) indicated by your recipe. If you are more than 1,000 feet (300 m) above sea level, refer to Altitude Adjustment (page 338) and amend canner settings accordingly. Depending on the model you are using, you will either watch the dial until it reaches the desired pressure (dial-gauge) or listen and watch for the weight to begin to jiggle and sputter and rock (weighted-gauge), indicating pressure has been reached. Once that level is achieved, set a timer for the number of minutes listed in your recipe.

It is essential that the pressure in your canner remain constant during processing. Significant fluctuations can cause food inside the jars to leak out, ruining the seals in the process. You will therefore need to keep an eye on your canner for the entire duration of the processing time. Dial-gauge models should read at the same number the entire time, and weighted-gauge models should continue to emit a hissing sound and jiggle one to four times per minute. If something takes you away from the stovetop and you return to find a reduction in pressure, you will have to start timing from the beginning. The only way to ensure food safety, and prevent the dreaded botulism, is to guarantee that you have processed your items at the correct pressure for the full duration of the suggested time.

6 Cool down the canner.

Once you are absolutely certain that your canner has continually remained at the correct pressure and your processing time is complete, turn off the heat and allow the canner to cool. When the pressure gauge returns to zero (consult the instructions included with your model to determine when this occurs), it is then safe to remove the weight from the vent. Do not remove the weight, however, before the pressure returns to zero. Depending on your model, it could take between 15 minutes and one hour for the canner to cool completely and pressure

to reach zero. After you take off the vent, wait another few minutes (again, refer to your model's instructions) before removing the lid. As you take the lid off, be certain to tip the steamy side up away from you, as the steam that will rise out of the canner, along with any water droplets accumulated on the underside of the lid, will be very hot.

7 Remove the jars.

Using a jar lifter or tongs, remove the jars one at a time. Try to avoid tilting the jars as you remove them from the canner. Place the jars on a towel, and allow them to cool, untouched, for 24 hours. You might want to drape a cloth over your jars to keep them from catching drafts.

8 Check the seals, reprocess if necessary, label, and store.

Refer to steps 11 to 13 of Boiling Water Bath for detailed instructions.

THE HOME CANNING CANON

- Use the boiling water bath processing method for high-acid foods only.

- Process low-acid foods in a pressure canner, unless you acidify them.

- Always check jars for nicks or scratches before use.

- Be certain your equipment and preparation areas are thoroughly cleaned between each use.

- Leave the amount of headspace per jar as indicated in the recipe.

- Use new lids each time. A used lid cannot be trusted to seal properly.

- Only begin timing processing once the water surrounding your submerged, filled jars is at a rapid boil or your pressure canner has emitted steam for 10 minutes.

- Don't use jars larger than 1 quart (.95 L). It is more difficult to guarantee the contents of larger jars have been uniformly heated during processing.

- Adjust for altitude when necessary.

- Always follow recipes to the letter. Adding even just one ingredient can alter the pH.

- Examine used screw bands for signs of wear before use.

- If a lid fails to seal, remember the two Rs: Reprocess or Refrigerate. Freezing is another option if your entire batch failed to seal and you're not quite feeling up to the task of processing the whole thing over again.

- Never use a dishwasher to sterilize jars unless your model has a sterilization setting.

- Avoid temperature fluctuations between your jars, their contents, and hard surfaces, as this may cause the jars to crack.

FINISHING TOUCHES

If you intend to give away any of your canned goods, there are numerous options for dressing up the jars in gift-worthy garb. Wax seals, labels, ribbon, raffia, and decorative cloth are but a few of the ways in which your jars can go from functional to fabulous.

Cloth, Paper, and Scissors

Quickly transform your jars with handmade paper, printed paper, or fabric. Using straight-edged craft scissors or decorative-edged scissors, cut a circle of paper or cloth ½ to 1 inch (1.3 to 2.5 cm) larger than the circumference of the jar you wish to decorate. Secure the cloth or paper to the lid with ribbon, raffia, twine, or whatever your imagination suggests.

You can also use inexpensive waxed or parchment paper for jar toppers with great results.

A Fashionable Label

Labels (page 90) are another way to gussy up your jars in minutes. You can pick up blank labels at an office supply store, and design labels to your liking on your home computer. Alternatively, you could search for preprinted labels with space to handwrite information about the jar's contents. Canning-appropriate labels can be found online on sites such as Etsy.com or MyOwnLabels.com, where you can custom-design labels. Round, metal-rimmed tags are a simple yet unexpected way to festoon your wares. There are no limitations when it comes to labeling your jars. Just remember to include the date in addition to a description of the contents.

The Science of Sugar

More than simply making your preserves taste sweet, sugar plays a critical role in making your jam, well, jam. That is to say, without the right amount of sugar in a recipe, you'll have a runny goo on your hands, not a firm, stable spread. This is because of the chemical interaction that occurs when sugar and fruit pectin get together. Pectin is a type of polysaccharide, which is a complex carbohydrate. When the pectins in whatever fruit you are using interact with sugar, chemical bonds are formed that bolster the stability and smoothness of the mixture.

Sugar also serves as a natural preservative. This happens because sugar is hygroscopic, meaning it pulls moisture out of the air. In home canning, this is desirable, since any moisture that is drawn into the sugar molecules means less moisture available in the jar for microorganisms to invade and contaminate. Whether you are using granulated sugar or sugar syrup made from fruit juice, be sure to use the proper amount indicated in a recipe to prevent the mold brigade from feasting on your carefully crafted preserves before you do!

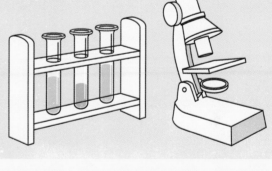

The Science of Salt

While salt is used primarily for flavor when canning vegetables, it is essential to quality, texture, and safety when home-canning seafood, quick pickles, and fermented foods.

Salt is made up of the chemicals chloride and sodium. Like sugar, salt is hygroscopic, pulling water out of the air and into itself. This happens through the process of osmosis, a type of diffusion causing solutes to move from an area of high water concentration (such as a diluted solution) to one of low water concentration (such as a concentrated solution). A salty brine has a lower concentration of water than the water present inside the cells of a vegetable such as a cucumber, causing the water inside the cuke to flow out. When this principle is applied to pickling, salt helps pickles be crunchier, as the water and moisture that would otherwise flow into them is being drawn instead into the salt molecules.

Salt also acts as a preservative. In addition to pulling moisture out of foods, salt pulls moisture away from bacteria, making it difficult for them to survive.

Undesirable beasties are killed off, keeping your pickles safe until you're ready to eat them. When making fermented foods, salt is absolutely vital. While salt discourages some bacteria, it encourages the growth of others that are desirable, such as lactic acid bacteria. This type of bacteria is a group of related bacteria that produce lactic acid as the result of carbohydrate fermentation. It is lactic acid that gives pickles their characteristic puckery twang. When salt is at a certain concentration in a solution, lactic acid grows more abundantly and more quickly than any other bacteria present. If there is too little salt in a solution, other bacteria may thrive and outcompete lactic acid for survival, spoiling your pickles in the process. Too much salt and the lactic acid isn't able to really do its thing, leaving your vegetables unpickled.

Chapter 4

Ingredients

Experienced cooks know that a dish is really only as good as its ingredients. You can't expect stellar results from subpar supplies. For a recipe to end up spectacular, it must begin with the best-quality ingredients you can find. It might take a little more time, as you learn to carefully select the most ideal specimens, but I'd argue that the extra five minutes required to find the ripest, smoothest peaches for a batch of buttery, fragrant jam is well worth it.

NATURAL SELECTION

In an ideal world, every fruit, vegetable, herb, and spice would be available only in its purest, cleanest, most natural form. The world in which we live, however, is far from ideal. Unless you grow your food yourself and are aware of its treatment during its entire life cycle—from seed, to germination, growth, and harvest—you will have to rely on labeling to make informed food purchases.

Organic foods are grown without the use of toxic pesticides and fertilizers. Such foods must be free of antibiotics, artificial growth hormones, genetically modified organisms (GMOs), irradiation, and sewage waste. Furthermore, the production of organic foods cannot involve the use of cloned animals, artificial ingredients, or synthetic preservatives.

In the United States, federally mandated standards require that third-party state or private agencies oversee organic certification for producers. The U.S. Department of Agriculture (USDA) in turn accredits these agencies. In order for a farm to become certified organic, the land must not have had any prohibited materials applied to it for three years. Scrupulous records must be on hand to prove this, in addition to a detailed plan for preventing contamination by prohibited substances. Outside the United States, a number of agencies perform similar organic certification testing around the world. Requirements, regulations, and oversight vary from country to country but are, for the most part, quite similar.

Why search out organic ingredients for home-canned goods? Put simply, they're healthier—for you, your family, and your planet. Research indicates organically grown foods are higher in a number of nutrients, containing more vitamin C, iron, magnesium, phosphorus, and antioxidants than their conventionally grown counterparts. Furthermore, foods grown organically yield greater amounts of omega-3 fatty acids and conjugated linoleic acid (CLA). These essential fatty acids are necessary in order for the immune, cardiovascular, reproductive, and nervous systems to function optimally. Since your body can't manufacture essential fatty acids on its own, they must be obtained through the diet.

Finally, organically grown foods simply taste better. Take celery, for example. The conventionally grown version most people are familiar with has an acrid and somewhat bitter aftertaste.

Organic celery is sweet, crunchy, and delicious. It's just one example of how the absence of artificial pesticides and fertilizers is truly manifest in the flavor of many organically grown foods.

Not too long ago, organic foods weren't terribly easy to come by. Today, however, as consumers gain more information about the detrimental effects of toxic agents on their health, the demand for organics has increased. From local grocery stores, food co-ops, farmers' markets, and even big-box retailers, organic foods are not hard to find. For many, though, the cost of organic foods may be out of reach. While organic foods do not have to be more costly than those that are conventionally produced, many organic options currently are. As demand continues to grow, the price will fall. In the meantime, acquaint yourself with those foods whose conventionally grown versions tend to contain the highest levels of pesticide residue and should always be purchased organic. Other foods tend to be generally low in pesticide application even when conventionally grown, and these may be a lower priority to buy organic.

According to the Environmental Working Group (EWG), a nonprofit organization dedicated to using public information to promote public health and environmental protection, the following items, dubbed the "Dirty Dozen," show the greatest traces of pesticides:

"Dirty Dozen"		
	apples	nectarines
	celery	peaches
	cherries	spinach
	cherry tomatoes	strawberries
	cucumbers	sweet bell peppers
	grapes	tomatoes

The following produce items were shown to contain the smallest amounts of pesticides, designated by the EWG as the "Clean 15":

"Clean 15"		
	asparagus	kiwi
	avocados	mangoes
	cabbage	onions
	cantaloupe	papayas
	cauliflower	pineapples
	eggplant	sweet corn
	grapefruit	sweet peas (frozen)
	honeydew melon	

These results were based on 43,000 tests for pesticide levels conducted by the U.S. Department of Agriculture (USDA) and the U.S. Food and Drug Administration (FDA). You can download a wallet-sized version of this list from EWG's website, www.ewg.org. As a nutrition consultant, I like to keep copies of this list available for clients who want to go organic but just can't afford to make the switch completely. I find myself returning to my own copy, safely tucked into my wallet, again and again.

PROPERLY SEASONED

I was at my local grocer the other day and found fresh strawberries and blueberries, carefully cradled in plastic clamshells, in the produce department. While that discovery seems rather innocuous, what makes it noteworthy is that it was January.

January! While the first month of the year is associated with many things, among them winter squash, iced-over windshields, resolutions, and hot chocolate, it is generally not associated with fresh berries—at least not in the Northern Hemisphere. Innovations in transportation and refrigeration technologies have made some foods available without regard to their traditional growing seasons. While that might be an ideal advancement for things like Earl Grey tea, dark chocolate, and vanilla beans, for others, especially perishable items, it can mean compromised flavor, as well as a reduction in nutrients.

Foods grown in far-flung locales must be picked before they are fully ripe in order to allow for transit time. As soon as any produce item is harvested, it begins to lose nutrients. Pick any fruit or vegetable and consider the days that have elapsed from harvest, to packaging, transit, and finally shelf time once it reaches the grocery store. When those New Zealand apples reach Iowa in March or a cluster of Chilean grapes shows up at your market in Maine during a New England nor'easter, many of the nutrients originally present are either greatly reduced or nearly gone. Why spend your hard-earned money on foods that in theory seem nutritious, only to have them depleted of so many of the health benefits you're eating them for?

Every season naturally offers a bounty of delicious foods. Nothing compares to cooling strawberries, freshly picked, in the heat of summer, or a hearty bowl of root vegetable soup bringing comfort on a cold winter night. Eating in season offers unrivaled flavor in addition to complete nutrients. Don't think of it as depriving yourself. Instead, consider eating seasonally to be the most culinarily rewarding act possible. When you eat seasonally, you eat the best available. In my book, that trumps lackluster midwinter strawberries every time!

CLOSE TO HOME

Inextricably linked with eating seasonally is eating locally. Yes, it is possible to find apples at your local grocer that were grown 3,000 miles (4,800 km) away even when they are in season in your area. You can also find corn shipped in from several states over at the same time you see it crowding the fields of nearby farms. Trucked-in produce is lacking more than just flavor. Those foods, while technically in season where they originated, were harvested before peak ripeness in order to be shipped. Precious nonrenewable resources were used to transport produce that could be easily found at your local farmers' market, U-pick farm, or, even better, in your own backyard. (Talk about local!) What's more, eating locally allows you to meet the people who grow your food. You can ask them direct questions about how they grew the goods they're offering. Carrots in a plastic sack at the store don't answer back.

Eating locally also creates a viable market for small farmers, who, tragically, are a dying breed. In fact, the number of individuals currently employed in farming in the United States is so low that it is no longer listed as a vocation with the Census Bureau. That's set to change, though, as increasing numbers of young people, concerned about environmental stewardship and healthy foods, are literally entering the field. When you purchase your foods from a local supplier, you provide a reliable customer base for them while ensuring nutritious, delicious foods for yourself and your family.

Eating and buying locally produced foods is an amazing way to meet and connect with your wider community. Some farmers put aside items they know particular customers would appreciate, while others even keep treats on hand for canine companions. I can't think of a more ideal means of obtaining the best possible ingredients for home canning use and making some new friends in the process.

INCREDIBLE EDIBLES

If you want your home-canned goods to be sublime, you truly must begin with the best available ingredients. When searching for ideal produce, be on the lookout for items that are ripe and free from blemishes and bruises. Bear those criteria in mind at all times. You want your fruits and vegetables to be at their peak of ripeness and in the best condition possible. If you find that the ingredients you were hoping to use are past their prime or show signs of wear, it's best to simply count your losses and either eat them fresh or cook and eat them straightaway. Many organically grown fruits and vegetables can be less "perfectly" shaped than their conventionally grown counterparts, which is fine. What you want to avoid, though, is signs of wear or aging. For example, when purchasing some locally grown apples intended for apple butter, I left behind those with visible bruises, worm holes, and cuts. Those apples would be fine for an apple crisp or slathered with peanut butter; they're just not the right choice for home canning.

Take care that your fruit isn't overripe, either, as that can affect pectin levels. Overripe fruit can also make a mushy mess, especially if you're attempting to can fruits in whole form. If you are harvesting the produce yourself, try not to stack the fruits on top of each other, as this can cause bruising. Instead, lay them out flat in a basket or even a cardboard lid. Be especially careful if you are harvesting soft fruit such as berries, cherries, and stone fruits such as peaches. If they are at peak ripeness, they can crush quite easily. If you're going to go to all the trouble of getting tangled up with thorns (berries) and ladders (cherries and stone fruits), you really don't want to be crushing the goods on their way back to your kitchen. You'll also want to give your produce a gentle scrub and washing before use. Wait until you're ready to begin your recipe before

you do this, though, to ensure no lasting damage results should you have a less than gentle hand.

Never use waxed produce items such as shiny, glossy apples or cucumbers for home canning. The wax affects flavor and is hard to remove, which makes it difficult for liquid to penetrate while pickling. If an acid, such as lemon juice or vinegar, is not able to fully penetrate a low-acid item, dangerous bacteria can develop if processed only in a boiling water bath.

Not every produce variety is optimally suited for home canning. Some varieties simply hold up to the rigors of processing better than others. At the grocery store, rarely will varietal names be listed except for sturdy fruits like apples and pears. Some farmers' market sellers do list the specific names of what they've grown. If you don't see what you're looking for, don't be afraid to ask. Many farmers can easily tell you the name of the cucumbers or peppers they are selling.

If you plan to grow your own produce, seek out canning-worthy varieties. Ask your local county extension agent for recommendations on good varieties of produce to can. In the United States, all counties have agents available for answering a wide range of agricultural questions. You can find yours online or in the phone book under state listings. Abroad, local farmers, universities, and agricultural organizations would be good resources for produce-related questions.

Use the following list as a guide for selecting produce varietals known to hold up well when canned. These varieties work equally well whether you are putting up fruits and vegetables whole or incorporating them into condiments. Consider this guide as suggestive, not definitive or comprehensive. The varieties of produce available to the home gardener are truly endless. Consult your seed catalog and feel free to experiment.

Fruit

Apples: Golden Delicious, Granny Smith, Gravenstein, McIntosh, Newton, Pippin, Winesap
Apricots: Blenheim, Early Gold, Moongold, Royal
Cherries: Bing, English Morello, Golden Sweet, Meteor, Montmorency, Royal Ann, Windsor
Citrus: Most citrus withstands canning without problem
Figs: Black Mission, Brown Turkey, Celeste, Everbearing, Kadota, King, Magnolia
Grapes: Concord (seedless), Flame, Reliance, Thompson
Peaches: Belle of Georgia, Champion, Elberta, Golden Jubilee, Madison, Red Haven, White Heath
Pears: Bartlett, Duchess, Kieffer, Moonglow
Plums: Burbank, Greengage, Laroda, Mariposa, Mount Royal, Santa Rosa, Satsuma, Seneca, Stanley

Vegetables

Beets: Big Red, Detroit Supreme, Little Ball, Red Ace, Ruby Queen
Black-eyed Peas: Queen Anne
Butter Beans: Dixie
Carrots: Falcon II, Minicor, Little Finger
Corn: Flavor Queen, Golden Jubilee, Merlin
Cucumbers: Amour, Diamant, Northern Pickling
Lima Beans: Fordhook 242
Okra: Annie Oakley II, Cajun Delight, Red Velvet
Peas: Alaska Early, Alderman
Peppers: Anaheim, Cherry Sweet, Jalapeño M, Super Red Pimento

Tomatoes

Crushed: Amish Paste, Bellstar
Soup: Bellstar, Roma, Ropreco, San Marzano, Super Fantastic
Whole: Glamour, Halley, Heinz 1350 VF, Marglobe, Ole, Red Plum

YOU SAY TOMAYTO, I SAY TOMAHTO

Tomatoes hold a special place in the world of home canning. Not only are they canned more than any other item, they are exceptionally versatile and take well to processing. In fact, the only tomato varieties that aren't so keen on being canned are grape and cherry tomatoes. When you consider there are over 7,500 members of the *Solanum lycopersicum* species out there, that restriction shouldn't crimp your style.

Tomatoes were once considered a reliably high-acid food, and processing in a boiling water bath was the preferred route of putting them up. That's no longer the case. The growing environment of tomatoes, influenced by fluctuations in weather and soil composition, their maturity level at time of sale, and normal differences between tomato varieties is so variable that many end up straddling the low-/high-acid fence. As a result, it is suggested that an acidifying agent be added to tomatoes to alter their pH. Lemon juice or citric acid are the customary additives, as vinegar can alter the flavor. If you want to put up a batch of balsamic-infused tomatoes, however, then vinegar will certainly do the job. No additional acid is needed when canning tomatillos and green tomatoes, as they are naturally high acid.

The USDA notes that use of a pressure canner will result in higher quality and more nutritious canned tomato products.

When deciding which type of tomatoes to use, consider your recipe. Are you canning tomatoes that will eventually be made into sauce? If so, go for plum tomatoes, as they're generally less juicy, making them ideal for thick, hearty marinaras. If you'll be using your canned tomatoes in salsa, round fruit will work just as well as plum.

Acidifying Tomatoes

Lemon juice: 1 tablespoon per pint

Citric acid: ¼ teaspoon per pint

For quarts, simply double the amount of acidifying agent.

Bottled lemon juice is preferable as it has a more consistent pH than fresh squeezed, which can vary from one fruit to the next.

SUGAR AND SPICE AND EVERYTHING NICE

While it is possible to put up fruit and vegetables with nothing more than added liquid, many home canners elect to jazz up their provisions, creating culinary concoctions rivaling the finest store-bought goods. Below we'll explore some of the common, and not so common, additives every home canner should know about.

Sweeteners

Sugar

Sugar is essential for jelling jams, jellies, marmalades, and chutneys. It interacts with pectin and acid to give preserves body and prevent runniness. Additionally, sugar acts as a preservative, preventing spoilage. Without adequate sugar in a recipe, the shelf life of a home-canned item is seriously compromised.

Most recipes calling for sugar require regular granulated white sugar, as it is neutral in both taste and color. In my

home canning, I use organic cane sugar. The texture is the same as granulated white sugar, but organic cane sugar is less refined, retaining more vitamins and minerals. Brown or muscovado sugars are best for use in chutneys and darker marmalades, as their brown hue and molasses flavor can mask colors and flavors in more subtle recipes. Superfine sugar, also known as castor sugar, is sometimes called for in curd recipes. Curds require low heat, and superfine sugar is perfect for dissolving quickly at low temperatures, due to the small size of the sugar granules. If you cannot locate superfine sugar, whip up some of your own by pulsing granulated sugar in a food processor or blender for several seconds.

Honey

Honey can be used as a sweetener in homemade preserves where its distinct flavor is welcome. Honey contains moisture not found in granulated sugar, and for this reason preserves made with honey will generally have a softer texture, not firming up quite as well as those made with granulated sugar. That said, if honey is your favorite sweetener and you don't care if it masks the gentle flavors of the fruit it is mixed with, then by all means use it. Honey is more dense than granulated sugars, so it cannot be substituted cup-for-cup. Instead, replace every 1 cup of sugar with ⅞ cup of honey, and don't alter any other liquid amounts in the recipe.

Fruit Juice

It's possible to reduce the amount of granulated sugar in recipes considerably by using fruit juice concentrates. Most often, 100 percent apple, pineapple, or white grape juice is used to replace most or all of the sugar called for in traditional sugar-based recipes. However, as sugar acts as a thickening agent, recipes made exclusively with fruit juice as a sweetener will need added pectin. The one exception is when the recipe is composed almost entirely of high-pectin fruits, for example, an all-fruit recipe for apple butter. Do not attempt to alter existing recipes calling for granulated sugar. Instead, seek out those written expressly for fruit juice–based sweetening. Several companies now offer a "no-added-sugar pectin," allowing low-sugar recipes to successfully gel. Many include recipes on the box itself.

If you wish to can whole fruit, fruit juice is a wonderful natural sweetener that can be used in place of a sugar syrup. Be sure to pick mild-flavored juices for this purpose, as anything with too pronounced a taste might end up masking the fruit itself. White grape juice or apple juice work well.

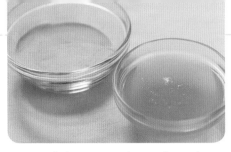

Pectin

Pectin is a naturally occurring, water-soluble type of carbohydrate that is found in the tissue, skin, and seeds of fruit. It reacts with sugar and acid to create a gel, or bond. Without it, your exquisite strawberry jam would be little more than a runny red puddle. Fruits contain varying degrees of inherent pectin, ranging from low to high (see Pectin Portion). While underripe fruits contain more pectin, they are inferior in flavor and are not recommended.

If you are cooking with a high-pectin fruit, such as apples, adding additional pectin might be unnecessary. When cooking a low-pectin fruit, it is normally possible to achieve a gel without added pectin, simply by cooking for a longer duration. This doesn't always work, however, and extra pectin may be required, either by the addition of a high-pectin fruit or incorporating commercial pectin. Care must be taken, however, as pectin is a fickle muse, deteriorating quickly if a fruit is too ripe or if it is allowed to cook for too long. In addition to breaking down pectin content, prolonged cooking can result in a darkened color and diminished flavor.

Commercial Pectin

Made from tart apples or the pith found under the peel of citrus fruit, commercial pectin is 100 percent natural. It is available in both powdered and liquid forms. Powdered pectin is incorporated into a recipe before cooking, whereas liquid pectin is generally incorporated into the fruit and sugar mixture after it has been heated. Prepared pectin is also available in low- and no-sugar forms, enabling you to control the amount of sugar added to a recipe and still achieve a firm gel. Commercial pectin supplies will need to be replenished annually, as they don't hold up well over time.

Homemade Pectin

Making your own pectin from fruit is a great step toward food self-sufficiency. That said, it is also a time-consuming process producing a perishable item. Sour apples are the source of choice for making homemade pectin. You will need to verify that the apples used in your recipe are fresh, as pectin content decreases with age. Don't just assume apples in the produce section of your local market were recently harvested, especially if they aren't from a local source. Ask the produce manager, or only make homemade pectin in autumn, when apples are in season. If you have your own apple trees or a nearby U-pick farm, pectin production might be an ideal way to make use of a bushel or a peck.

Making Your Own Pectin

You can make as much or as little pectin as you would like. One pound of apples will yield around 1 pint of pectin. When choosing apples, the more tart varieties are preferable.

Wash the apples and then cut them into quarters. Be sure to hang onto the core and peel, as these parts contain high amounts of pectin. Place the apples into a stainless-steel pot. Add 2 cups of water and 1 tablespoon bottled lemon juice for each pound of apples.

Bring to a boil, then reduce the heat, cover, and simmer for 35 to 40 minutes, stirring occasionally to prevent the apples from sticking to the bottom of the pan.

Remove from heat. Drain the mixture through a large sieve, removing solid pieces; discard the solids. Next, strain the apple liquid through either a jelly bag or several damp layers of cheesecloth. Return the strained liquid to a stainless-steel pot, heat to boiling, ladle into sterilized jars, and then process for 10 minutes in a boiling water bath. Refer to Boiling Water Bath on page 96 for detailed processing instructions.

Pectin Portion

High-pectin Fruits: Apples (sour); cherries (sour); crabapples; cranberries; black, white, and red currants; gooseberries; grapefruit; Eastern Concord, Muscadine, and Scuppernog grapes; kiwifruit; lemons; limes; sour oranges; Damson and other tart plums; quince

Medium-pectin Fruits: Apples (sweet); apricots; blackberries; blueberries; boysenberries; loganberries; raspberries; tayberries

Low-pectin Fruits: Bananas; cherries (sweet); elderberries; figs; grapes (except varieties listed above); melons; nectarines; peaches; pears; pineapple; pomegranates; rhubarb; strawberries; sweet and Italian plums

Acids

Acid is the final part of the trinity that, along with sugar and pectin, improves flavor and combats growth of microorganisms in home-canned goods. Achieving the proper amount of acid is imperative in order to safely process items in a boiling water bath. Furthermore, acid helps jams, jellies, and preserves to gel properly while keeping pickles crispy. It also adds characteristic zip to relishes and salsas. The type of item you are preparing determines which variety of acid you will use.

Vinegar

Often used in pickling, a dash or two of vinegar can also be added to jams and jellies for unexpected flavor. Use only commercially prepared vinegars that can guarantee a

A medley of vinegars

consistent level of acidity. When vinegar is used as an acidifying agent, it must contain at least 5 percent acetic acid, also known as "50-grain." Homemade vinegars have unknown acidity levels, presenting possible health risks if used in the home canning of low-acid foods processed in a boiling water bath. Stay on the safe side and look for vinegars at your local grocer with labels reading "5% acidity" or higher. Apple cider vinegar and white vinegar are recommended, as their acidity levels are usually right on target, but they are by no means the only options available. Balsamic, red and white wine, sherry, and many flavored vinegars may also be suitable; simply check the label to determine if the acidity label makes it safe for use.

If you have difficulty finding flavored vinegars with acidity levels at 5 percent or higher, start with a mild-flavored vinegar, such as distilled white or white wine, and infuse it for two to three weeks with whole spices. Strain out the spice at the end of the infusing period. Cloves, black pepper, cumin, fennel, juniper, cardamom . . . the options for homemade flavored vinegars are limited only by your imagination. Try adding your infused vinegar to pickles, relishes, and chutneys for extra pep.

Lemon Juice

Lemon juice is often the acid of choice when making jams, jellies, marmalades, and conserves. Only bottled lemon juice

Lemon juice and citric acid

should be used, as its acidity level is more consistent than that of fresh juice. Just like other fruits, the acidity level of lemon juice can vary from one lemon to the next. Stick with the yellow bottle and definitely never use fresh lemon juice for low-acid items such as tomatoes or figs if you intend to process them in a boiling water bath.

Citric Acid

Citric acid is a powdered substance made from citrus fruit. It has a strong sour taste, so it's better used as an acidifying agent for tomatoes than for fruit spreads. To use citric acid in place of lemon juice, use ¼ teaspoon per pint and ½ teaspoon per quart of tomatoes. Citric acid is commonly available at drugstores and natural foods stores.

Salt

It is entirely optional to use salt in many home-canned items. It serves no function in preservation for jams, jellies, chutneys, marmalades, conserves, butters, or curds. It is, however, essential in relishes, pickles, salsas, fermented foods like sauerkraut, and

Using the right kind of salt is essential.

smoked foods, where it contributes to both flavor and texture, since salt draws out moisture. When a canning recipe calls for salt, be sure to use only salts labeled "canning," "pickling," or "kosher." Never use table salt, as it is likely to contain anticaking agents that will turn the brining water cloudy. Table salt usually contains iodine, as well, which can darken your canned goods. Salts specifically indicated for home-canning use are free of iodine and anticaking additives and are very fine-grained, making them dissolve easily.

Herbs and Spices

When using herbs and spices in your home-canned goods, fresh is always best. The flavor and aroma produced by fresh basil or just-ground cardamom simply dwarfs that produced by their dried and preground cousins. Buy spices in small quantities as often as needed to ensure freshness. Many natural food stores sell herbs and spices in the bulk section, which is a fantastic way to save money, as purchasing entire jars can quickly add up. Simply scoop out the amount you need, label your bag, and use your supply without delay. If you are pickling, stick to whole spices, as adding them ground will cloud the brining solution. Spices added to jams, jellies, chutneys, marmalades, conserves,

or butters are better in their whole form, as well. Make a spice bundle out of cheesecloth or a muslin drawstring tea bag, and let it infuse the mixture as you cook. Remove the bundle from your finished batch before filling jars.

When using herbs, the volatile oils present in the plant's tissues are released as soon as they are broken, making both the taste and fragrance of dried herbs nowhere near as robust as that of those just harvested. Packaged fresh herbs can get costly rather quickly. If you anticipate you'll be using a lot of herbs, consider growing your own. You don't even need a yard to enjoy fresh tarragon, thyme, or rosemary. Got a sunny windowsill? That's really pretty much all you'll need in order to successfully grow fresh herbs all through the winter, spring, summer, or fall. If you are an experienced gardener, start your herbs from seed. Otherwise, keep an eye out at garden stores, nurseries, farmers' markets, or grocery stores for potted herbs.

Any herb or spice works well in home canning. Don't limit yourself to old standbys like mustard seed and chili flakes. In my kitchen, I love big, bold, unexpected culinary elements. For herbs consider lemon verbena, rosemary, dill, tarragon, thyme (of which there are many varieties worth sampling), geranium, lavender, mint, lemongrass, marjoram, and basil. Spices I adore include star anise, fennel seed, coriander, cumin, celery seed, nutmeg, ginger, cinnamon, juniper berries, all-spice, whole cloves, and peppercorns.

Prep School

Some ingredients will need to be prepped in advance of cooking. Reading through a recipe in advance will give you a heads-up on preliminary steps to be dealt with before starting a recipe. While most food prep in home canning is fairly straightforward, there are two techniques meriting a bit of elaboration: washing and blanching.

Washing

When cleaning produce to be used in home canning, removing every last bit of dirt should be your top priority. Botulism spores live in dirt and soil, so it is imperative that you get out all traces of dirt before preparing your recipe. Even if you don't see any soil on the surface of the produce items you will be using, it is still a good idea to give everything a good rinse and a thorough scrubbing with a vegetable brush just prior to use. For delicate items such as berries, simply rinsing well with cool water will loosen up any remaining debris.

Blanching

The skins of some produce items will need to be removed before they are ready for use in a recipe. Otherwise, the skin's texture can become chewy and rubbery after cooking, not at all what you want people to notice when enjoying your peach chutney at brunch or digging into the jar of tomato jam you gave them as thanks for pet sitting. Blanching is also used with some vegetables in order to keep their color vibrant once canned. Fortunately this cooking technique couldn't be easier. Follow these simple steps to remove skins or boost color.

Blanching Peaches, Plums, Onions, and Tomatoes

Wash your produce under cool water. Prepare an ice bath by filling a large bowl with cold water and ice and setting it in the sink. Fill a medium stainless-steel pot two-thirds full with water. Bring to boil over high heat. Using a slotted spoon, gently place one item at a time into the boiling water. Boil for 30 seconds, remove the item with a slotted spoon, and immediately plunge it into the ice bath. Continue until each item has been blanched. The skins should slip off easily.

Prepare your ice bath in advance.

Blanching Vegetables for Color

The items most suited to blanching for color retention are listed at right, accompanied by blanching times. Follow the instructions above for removing skins, substituting blanching times as appropriate.

Asparagus: 2 minutes

Beans (green and wax): 2 to 3 minutes

Beets: 20 minutes

Broccoli: 2 minutes

Brussels sprouts: 3 minutes

Carrots: 2 minutes

Cauliflower: 3 minutes

Corn (cut): 4 minutes

Okra: 3 minutes

Onions: 1½ minutes

Peas: 1½ minutes

Chapter 5

A Jams, Jellies, and Preserves Primer

I can think of few culinary experiences more transcendent, more deeply palate pleasing, than jam on toast. Crispy, crackly, almost caramelized toast, smothered in fragrant, tart-sweet strawberry jam or spicy apple butter paired with a warm mug of tea or fresh glass of juice—is there anything better? Jams, jellies, and preserves have a way of bringing us back to childhood, when peanut butter and jelly sandwiches ruled the lunch box and jam left its sticky traces on faces and hands.

Jams, jellies, and preserves can be as sophisticated or as simple as you like. Beginning with fruit, sugar, and, on occasion, added pectin, these condiments are sublime when pared down to showcase the fruit, or glorious when made complex and heady with spices, herbs, and flavorings. Their versatility has established them as staples in all kitchens. Any way you stir the pot, these condiments never fail to tickle the taste buds.

WHAT'S IN A NAME?

Jams, jellies, preserves, conserves, marmalades, fruit butters, and fruit curds are close kin. All contain a mixture of fruit and sugar that is cooked until thickened. What distinguishes these fruit concoctions from one another is the type of fruit used, the size of the fruit pieces, the addition or omission of flavoring ingredients, and the manner in which the fruit and sugar mixture is processed. Let's examine each.

Jam A cooked mixture of fruit and sugar, in jam the fruit is finely chopped, mashed, or crushed. Jams should hold up firmly but still be spreadable. When fruit is cooked only with fruit juices and no added sugar, the resulting mixture is sometimes called a "fruit spread" instead of a jam.

Jelly Jelly is a cooked mixture of fruit and sugar that is strained, resulting in a clear spread. Jellies should be completely solid and easy to cut and spread with a knife. To make jelly, strain cooked fruit through a mesh fabric bag (known as a jelly bag) or cheesecloth-lined sieve that is suspended over a bowl. Once the liquids have drained out, they are returned to the stovetop and cooked with sugar until a gel is formed.

Preserves A cooked mixture of fruit and sugar, preserves are made from fruit left in large pieces or chunks. Aside from the size of the fruit bits, preserves are otherwise very much akin to jams. To be considered a preserve, the fruits mustn't be crushed, minced, chopped, mashed, or cut into small bits. Small whole fruits, especially berries, or larger fruits cut into big chunks, are used in preserve making.

Conserves This spread is a cooked mixture of fruit, sugar, nuts, raisins, and often, dried fruits and spices. Conserves are similar in texture to jam, where the fruit is cut finely, mashed, or crushed, and then cooked. Most conserves contain more than one fruit and contain some sort of citrus.

Marmalade Marmalade is a cooked mixture of fruit (most commonly citrus) and sugar that is somewhere between jam and jelly in consistency. Pieces of lemon, orange, tangerine, lime, or grapefruit peel are suspended in a jellylike base. Most recipes will direct you that the pith be completely removed from citrus peels prior to cooking, otherwise a bitter taste will be imparted. If you enjoy a bitter flavor, as I do, you need not be as fastidious about removing the pith when making marmalade to your own taste.

Fruit Butters Fruit butters are a fruit and sugar mixture where cooked fruit such as apple or pear is puréed and then combined with sugar and heated until smooth and velvety. The resulting spread should be thick and contain no runny juices. Cooking times for butters are highly variable, depending in large part on the juiciness of your fruit.

Curds Fruit curds are a mixture of citrus fruit, sugar, butter, and eggs, cooked to a smooth, thick, pudding-like texture. As curds contain eggs, they require either refrigeration (where they will keep for about four weeks) or pressure canning. If you opt to pressure can, try to eat, or gift, your curds within three to four months, as the flavor diminishes over time. In my experience, consuming curds in a timely manner has never been an issue.

Troubleshooting Tips

If you follow the directions in this book and practice safe and hygienic home canning practices, the likelihood of mishaps will be considerably reduced. Nevertheless, snafus may occur. Learning what caused your seal to fail or your jelly to refuse to set will hopefully help prevent repeat performances the next time you decide to whip up some sweet spreads.

If your spread won't set:

◪ You may have used either too much or too little sugar. Follow recipes exactly as written, as adjusting the sugar content can negatively affect the spread's ability to gel.

◪ You may have had insufficient pectin, or the commercial pectin you used may have expired. Use the amount indicated in a recipe. If your pectin was coming from the fruit itself, you may need to add some supplemental pectin to create a gel.

◪ You may have used fruit that was overripe. Always choose fruits that are just at the peak of ripeness, but not past. Plan your canning for days when you will either be purchasing ripe fruit or harvesting fruit that is at peak ripeness.

◪ You may have not provided enough acid for a gel to occur. Add supplemental acid in the form of lemon juice.

◪ You may have cooked your mixture for too long after commercial pectin was added, or for too long after the intrinsic pectin in the fruit was released. Boil your mixture for only as long as indicated in the recipe.

◪ You may be dealing with a jelly that takes time to set up; be aware that some jellies set over time, needing as much as two weeks to firm.

If your spread is too tough:

◪ You may have overcooked your mixture, causing too much liquid to evaporate. Cook your mixture for only the amount of time indicated in the recipe.

◪ You may have used underripe fruit. Always choose fruits that are just at the peak of ripeness.

◪ You may have provided either too little sugar or too much acid. Follow the measurements in the recipe exactly.

If your jelly becomes cloudy:

◪ You may have used underripe fruit and the starch present in it caused the juice to cloud. Always use fruits that are just at the peak of ripeness.

◪ You may have squeezed the jelly bag or cheesecloth while it was dripping. Tempting as it may be, don't squeeze your extractor, as doing so can cloud the juice.

◪ You may have allowed your jelly to cool a bit in the pan before pouring it into the jars. Have all jars and lids ready and your boiling water bath prepared so that you can pour the mixture into jars as soon as it is done cooking.

If your spread darkens:

◪ You may have overcooked your mixture. Always follow cooking times as written in the recipe.

◪ You may have stored your preserves in too bright a location. Keep your canned goods in a dark spot after processing, such as a pantry, cupboard, or basement.

◪ You may have stored your preserves in too warm a location. Keep your canned goods in a cool location, ideally between 40 and 70°F (4 and 21°C).

If your spread has mold or mildew:

◪ You may have failed to process your jars properly in a boiling water bath after cooking. Always process for the amount of time indicated (remember to adjust for altitude), and only begin timing after water is at a full, rolling, and sustained boil.

◪ You may have failed to provide adequate sugar or acid. Always measure ingredients as indicated in the recipe.

◪ You may have stored your preserves in too warm a location. Keep your canned goods in a cool spot, ideally between 40 and 70°F (4 and 21°C).

If your spread has crystals:

◪ You may have failed to dissolve the sugar completely before bringing the mixture to a boil. Always allow the sugar to completely dissolve in the fruit juice or water over low heat before bringing to a full boil.

◪ You may have added too much sugar. Measure out and use only the amount of sugar indicated in the recipe.

◪ You may have insufficient acid in your mixture. Add supplementary lemon juice until the crystals dissolve.

Strawberry Jam

Strawberry jam is pretty much the rock star of the jam world. Everyone seems to like it, it's easy to make, and you get an incredible return for rather little effort. The only advance preparation required in this recipe (short of prepping the fruit) involves allowing the strawberries, sugar, and lemon juice to sit together for 2 hours before cooking. This causes the natural juices of the strawberries to be released, which in turn helps the pectin in the berries to be more available when you begin cooking.

Yield: 3 half-pints

YOU WILL NEED:

- 4 pints strawberries, hulled and sliced
- 2 cups granulated sugar
- 2 tablespoons bottled lemon juice

top: Skimming foam from the surface   bottom: Test for gelling

TO PREPARE:

1. Place two small plates in the freezer. These will be used later to test for gelling.

2. In a large nonmetallic bowl, add the strawberries, sugar, and lemon juice; stir, cover loosely with a kitchen cloth, and set aside to macerate at room temperature for 2 hours.

3. Sterilize three half-pint mason jars, lids, and screw rings (refer to page 97 for detailed instructions). Fill a canner or large stockpot with water, and set over medium-high heat. Bring just to the boiling point. Place the lids in a small saucepan, fill with water, bring to a boil, turn off the heat, and set the pan aside.

4. Transfer the strawberry mixture to a medium stainless-steel pot. Bring to a boil over medium-high heat and boil for 20 to 25 minutes, until the mixture begins to thicken. Stir frequently and watch the pot carefully to prevent the contents from boiling over. Skim off any foam that rises to the top.

5. Test for gelling. Remove a plate from the freezer and spoon about 1 teaspoon of the strawberry mixture onto it. Place the plate back in the freezer and wait 2 minutes. Remove from the freezer and push the edge of the jam with your fingertip. If the jam has gelled properly, the surface will wrinkle a bit. If it fails to wrinkle, or is obviously still runny, boil the jam for 5 minutes longer, and then repeat the test.

6. Place the hot, sterilized jars on top of a kitchen cloth on the counter. With the help of a canning funnel, ladle jam into the jars, reserving ¼-inch (6 mm) headspace. Use a nonmetallic spatula to remove any trapped air bubbles, and wipe the rims clean with a damp cloth. Place on the lids and screw bands, tightening only until fingertip-tight.

7. Using a jar lifter, place the jars into the canner. Process for 10 minutes in a boiling water bath (refer to page 100 for detailed instructions). Remember to adjust for altitude.
Variation: If you'd like to give your strawberry jam an herbal undertone reminiscent of summer, add 1 tablespoon fresh mint or lemon verbena. If fresh herbs aren't available, use 2 teaspoons dried.

Apple Butter

Apple butter invokes the most ideal elements of a crisp autumn day. You can almost smell piles of leaves being burned, feel the heat from steaming mugs of cider, and see resplendent foliage in fiery shades of orange, yellow, and red. This recipe makes an incredibly fragrant mixture with a rich, velvety texture. Your kitchen will smell amazing, and, if you're anything like me, you'll feel as though you are truly embracing the full splendor of the autumn season. Cooking apples work best; good choices include Golden Delicious, Granny Smith, Gravenstein, McIntosh, Newton, Pippin, or Winesap.

Yield: 4 half-pints

YOU WILL NEED:

5	pounds cooking apples
2	cups granulated sugar
2	teaspoons ground cinnamon
½	teaspoon ground cloves
½	teaspoon ground nutmeg
½	teaspoon ground ginger

An apple peeler is quite the time-saver.

TO PREPARE:

1. Peel, core, and roughly chop the apples. Place in a large stainless-steel pot along with 2 cups water. Simmer over low heat for 45 minutes. Stir occasionally to prevent sticking, and add water in ¼-cup increments if sticking occurs. Remove from heat.

2. Press the cooked apple mixture through a food mill or fine-meshed sieve, purée in a food processor once slightly cooled, or use an immersion blender and purée the mixture in the pot.

3. Return the apple purée to the pot, add the sugar and spices, and bring to a gentle boil over medium heat. Reduce the heat to low, and simmer for 25 to 30 minutes. Stir often to prevent sticking. Remove from heat.

4. While the apple butter cooks, sterilize four half-pint mason jars, lids, and screw rings (refer to page 97 for detailed instructions). Fill a canner or large stockpot with water, and set over medium-high heat. Bring just to the boiling point. Place the lids in a small saucepan, fill with water, bring to a boil, turn off the heat, and set the pan aside.

5. Place the hot jars on top of a kitchen cloth on the counter. With the help of a canning funnel, ladle apple butter into the jars, reserving ¼-inch (6 mm) headspace. Use a nonmetallic spatula to remove any trapped air bubbles, and wipe the rims clean with a damp cloth. Place on the lids and screw bands, tightening only until fingertip-tight.

6. Using a jar lifter, place the jars into the canner. Process for 10 minutes in a boiling water bath (refer to page 100 for detailed instructions). Remember to adjust for altitude.
Variation: Use only cinnamon, or omit the spices altogether, for a basic apple butter where the flavor of the apples shines through.

Grape Jelly

A perennial favorite of children and adults alike (not to mention budget-wise college students), grape jelly is the perfect solution for tempering the innate tartness of grapes. Spread heavily over peanut butter, grape jelly aids in producing what is arguably the ultimate quick and tasty sandwich. It also pairs flawlessly when matched with a spicy chili sauce and poured over meatballs, producing a robust appetizer. Of course, it's also quite good straight out of the jar, thank you very much!

Yield: 4 half-pints

3½ pounds Concord or red grapes

4 teaspoons dry pectin

3 cups granulated sugar

A jelly bag or cheesecloth

TO PREPARE:

1. Rinse grapes under cool water. Remove from stems and place in a medium stainless-steel pot. Don't bother removing the seeds, if present, as they will be strained out later in the jelly bag or cheesecloth. Add ¾ cup water, crush grapes lightly with a wooden spoon or mallet, and place over high heat. Bring to a boil, reduce heat, cover, and simmer 12 minutes, stirring frequently to prevent scorching. Remove from heat.

2. Pour the grape mixture into either a moistened jelly bag or a strainer lined with several layers of cheesecloth. Place over a large bowl, and allow juice to drip out overnight or for a minimum of 2 hours.

3. Place two small plates in the freezer (these will be used later to test for gelling).

4. Sterilize four half-pint mason jars, lids, and screw rings (refer to page 97 for detailed instructions). Fill a canner or large stockpot with water, and set over medium-high heat. Bring just to boiling point. Place lids in a small saucepan, fill with water, bring to a boil, turn off heat, remove from the stovetop, and set aside.

5. Mix ¼ cup sugar with pectin in a small bowl. Transfer the collected grape juice to a medium stainless-steel pot, add sugar-pectin mixture, and bring to a boil over medium-high heat. Once juice has reached a full boil, add additional sugar, and boil rapidly for 2 minutes. Skim off any foam that rises to the top of the boiling mixture.

6. Test for gelling. Remove a plate from the freezer and spoon about 1 teaspoon of the grape mixture onto it. Place back in the freezer and wait 2 minutes. Remove the plate from the freezer and push the edge of the jelly with your fingertip. If it has gelled properly, the surface will wrinkle a bit. If it fails to wrinkle, or is obviously still runny, continue cooking the jelly for 2 minutes longer, and then repeat the test.

7. Place the hot jars on top of a kitchen cloth on the counter. With the help of a canning funnel, ladle jelly into the jars, reserving ¼-inch (6 mm) headspace. Use a nonmetallic spatula to remove any trapped air bubbles, and wipe rims clean with a damp cloth. Place on lids and screw bands, tightening only until fingertip-tight.

8. Using a jar lifter, place the jars into the canner. Process for 10 minutes in a boiling water bath (refer to page 103 for detailed instructions). Remember to adjust for altitude.

Variation: To impart a bit of unexpected herbal vigor to your jelly, consider adding herbes de Provence. Named after the sunny region in southern France, the herbal blend consists of varying amounts of bay leaf, thyme, fennel, rosemary, chervil, oregano, summer savory, tarragon, mint, marjoram, and lavender. Place 1 tablespoon dried herbes de Provence in a muslin pouch, secure at the top, and add to the grape mixture after the sugar has dissolved. Remove once the mixture begins to gel, and process as above.

Chapter 6

A Pickle, Relish, and Chutney Primer

Pickles, along with relishes and chutneys, help appetizers, salads, and entrees become more fully energized, enlivened, and complete. These condiments add twang and puckery perfection to the fruits and vegetables they are preserved alongside. The common element connecting pickles, relishes, and chutneys is that they are all preserved in an acid solution, most commonly based on vinegar.

PICKLES

Pickles are commonly processed in one of two ways: fermented or fresh pack. While the cucumber is pickling's star, everything from okra to watermelon rind to pears can be pickled. Fresh-pack and fermented pickles are markedly distinct entities. If you are unsure whether you've actually had a "pickled" pickle, you most likely haven't. Once you have, you'll know. The flavor and aroma of fermented pickles is distinctly sour and pungent. While it can overwhelm delicate nasal passages, I find it intoxicating.

To create fermented pickles, also called crock or barrel pickles, vegetables or fruits are covered in a brine. Pickling brine is simply a solution of water, salt, vinegar, and varying herbs and spices. The brine-covered mixture is then left to cure at around 70°F (21°C) for two to six weeks. During this time, the atmospheric conditions inside the container will allow bacteria to produce lactic acid. It is this lactic acid that serves to preserve the vegetables or fruits, keeping them from rotting and imbuing them with their characteristic "pickley" essence. Many enthusiasts rave about the benefits of lactic acid, including improved digestion. I won't be offering any fermented pickle recipes in this book, as a proper discussion of fermentation truly merits an entire book of its own. I do suggest further exploration for those who are curious. The website of the National Center for Home Food Preservation is a wonderful resource on fermentation: http://uga.edu/nchfp.

If you don't have the patience to wait for fermented pickles, fresh pack may be the best pickling method for you. Fresh pack also involves creating a brine. This brine is then poured over fresh vegetables or fruits packed in canning jars, after which the jars are processed in a boiling water bath. You'll find a recipe for fresh-packed dill pickles on page 133.

Fermented pickles (right) show a cloudy brine.

RELISHES

Relishes are similar to pickles in their use of acid to preserve foods. What distinguishes both relishes and chutneys from pickles is that ingredients are chopped and cooked before they are jarred. Relishes can be sweet, spicy, savory, or all three. While the first relish you might think of is the sweet, bright green pickle relish of hot dog fame, many other relishes exist. Relishes aren't limited to vegetables, either. Fabulous condiments can be made from many fruits, including pineapples, apricots, and cranberries.

CHUTNEYS

Chutneys tend to be primarily fruit-based, although vegetable-based recipes are not unheard of. This condiment is characterized by its spiciness, ranging from the mild heat produced by ginger to the fiery blaze of cayenne and chili peppers. Chutneys tend to be saucier than relishes; some are smooth while others are chunky. Although most commonly associated with Indian foods, chutney can highlight the flavors of any cuisine. Spread on a sandwich, served alongside cheese and pickles, or paired with a pork loin, chutney instantly adds zip and interest.

Troubleshooting Tips

Sometimes, things just don't turn out right when making pickles, relishes, and chutneys, even for experienced home canners. The pickles get mushy, the color is off, the brine turns cloudy—the pickles are just not cooperating. Knowing in advance what to be aware of during prep and processing can help limit mishaps. The following pickle problems are those most frequently encountered in home pickle making. With relishes and chutneys, I've found that if you stick to the recipe, few things go wrong. Do make sure to always follow suggestions for headspace. If you fill your jar too full, it's likely to overflow during processing.

If your pickles are soft:

◧ You might have added too little salt or vinegar with low acidity. Be sure to use commercial vinegars with 5 to 7 percent acid; it will be marked on the bottle as such.

◧ You might have left the blossom end on the cucumbers. These must be removed before processing, as an enzyme in them can make pickles soft once jarred.

◧ You may have left the pickles in too warm an environment. The ideal temperature for storing fermented pickles is between 70 and 75°F (21 and 24°C).

If your pickles are hollow:

◧ You might have used cucumbers too long off the vine before pickling. Ideally, pickling cucumbers should be harvested no more than 48 hours before processing, with 24 hours being ideal. To test whether your cucumbers are hollow, put them in a bowl and cover with cold water. If they float, use them for relish, instead. Sinkers should be fine for pickling whole.

◧ You might have made your brine either too strong or too weak for fermentation to occur. Follow your recipe expressly as indicated, and be sure to use vinegar with 5 to 7 percent acidity.

If your pickles are tough:

◧ You might have used too much salt. Carefully measure all salt to be used in recipes; "winging it" can sometimes result in too little or too much.

◧ You might have processed your pickles too long. Set a timer so that you only process as long as necessary.

◧ You might have used cucumbers harvested some time before pickling. Ideally, pickling cucumbers should be harvested no more than 48 hours before processing, with 24 hours being ideal.

If your pickles are dark:

◧ You might have used ground spices in the brine. When pickling, it's best to use whole spices.

◧ You might have used table salt. Only use pickling or kosher salt in pickling, as anticaking agents in table salt can cause an off color.

◧ You may have hard water containing iron or other metals. Use either soft or distilled water.

If your pickles are moldy:

◧ Your fruits or vegetables might not have been washed thoroughly before processing. Give every item you intend to pickle a thorough wash and scrub before use.

◧ You might have used cucumbers harvested some time before pickling. Ideally, pickling cucumbers should be harvested no more than 48 hours before processing, with 24 hours being ideal.

If your brine is cloudy:

◧ You might be witnessing the presence of lactic acid. If you are making fermented pickles, cloudiness indicates that the lactic acid is doing its thing.

◧ You might have spoiled pickles. If you are making fresh-pack pickles, cloudiness could indicate the presence of bacteria. Check for stinky smells or mushy texture. If neither is present, your pickles are safe to eat. Otherwise, toss them into the compost.

◧ You might have used table salt. Use only pickling or kosher salt in pickling, as anticaking agents in table salt can cause an off color.

◧ You may have hard water containing iron or other metals. Use either soft or distilled water.

Basic, All-Purpose Brine for Pickling

This delicious and easy three-step pickle recipe can be used for a wide range of summer's bounty. The formula is three parts vinegar to one part water; the amount of sugar and salt can vary according to taste. Anything that's crisp and fresh can be put up in this well-balanced solution. Favorites are okra; green or yellow wax beans; carrots; cherry peppers; small onions; cauliflower; baby summer squash such as zucchini, yellow, or pattypan; and, of course, cucumbers. Adjust or change seasonings according to your taste or desired spiciness. This recipe makes enough pickling liquid to fill approximately 4 pints of packed jars.

YOU WILL NEED:

3 cups white vinegar

½ cup sugar (may use less, but don't omit entirely)

3 tablespoons pickling salt

Prepared horseradish

Peppercorns (may use a blend of black, white, and green)

Celery seed

Fresh dill or tarragon

Garlic cloves, peeled

Hot cayenne pepper (optional)

2. Sterilize four pint or two quart mason jars, lids, and screw rings (refer to page 97 for detailed instructions). Fill a canner or large stockpot with water, and set it over medium-high heat. Bring just to the boiling point. Place the lids in a small saucepan, fill with water, bring to a boil, turn off the heat, and set the pan aside.

3. Combine vinegar, 1 cup water, sugar, and salt in a small saucepan. Bring the brine to a boil. Reduce heat and hold at a simmer, covered, while packing your jars.

4. Place your hot jars on top of a kitchen towel on the counter. Into the bottom of each sterilized jar, add the following: ½ teaspoon horseradish, 6 peppercorns, ⅛ teaspoon celery seed, a sprig of dill or tarragon (or ¼ teaspoon dill seed or ⅛ teaspoon dried tarragon), 1 garlic clove, and 1 cayenne pepper (whole, halved, or quartered lengthwise).

5. Pack the vegetables tightly into the jars, and add hot pickling liquid. Slip a nonmetallic spatula down the side of each, and carefully tip the jar slightly to allow brine to fill any voids. Leave ½-inch (1.3 cm) headspace. Wipe the rims clean with a damp cloth. Place on lids and screw bands, tightening only until fingertip-tight.

6. Using a jar lifter, place the jars in the canner. Process pints 10 minutes and quarts 15 minutes in a boiling water bath (refer to page 100 for detailed instructions). Remember to adjust for altitude.

TO PREPARE:

1. Wash, scrub, and chop whatever vegetables you will be using. Hard vegetables such as cauliflower, squash, carrots, and cherry peppers can be packed more tightly into jars if slightly softened beforehand. Simply pour boiling water over the vegetables and allow them to soften for 5 to 10 minutes, just until they are resilient, then rinse in very cold water.

Dill Pickles

For many, a sandwich just isn't a sandwich unless it's accompanied by a dill pickle. In my opinion, their pungent saltiness is the perfect lunchtime companion. Aside from an overnight soak, this canning classic is ready in no time. **Yield: 8 pints**

YOU WILL NEED:

6	pounds pickling cucumbers
¾	cup pickling salt (divided)
4	cups white vinegar
	Garlic cloves, peeled
	Dill seed
	Fresh dill heads (if unavailable, use dried dill)
	Black peppercorns

TO PREPARE:

1. Rinse the cucumbers in cold water. Scrub gently with a vegetable brush to loosen any hidden soil. Remove a thin slice from the blossom end of each cucumber (if you can't tell which end is the blossom end, just take a thin slice off of each end). Place the cucumbers in a nonreactive glass or ceramic bowl, add ½ cup pickling salt, cover with water, place a plate or towel over the top, and set in a cool place or the refrigerator overnight or for 8 hours.

2. Drain off the brine. Rinse the cucumbers thoroughly to remove salt residue. Set aside.

3. Sterilize eight pint mason jars, lids, and screw rings (refer to page 97 for detailed instructions).

4. In a medium stainless-steel pan, combine vinegar, 3½ cups water, and ¼ cup pickling salt. Bring the brine to a boil, reduce heat, and simmer for 5 minutes. Remove from heat, and set aside.

5. Into each sterilized jar, place 1 garlic clove, ½ teaspoon dill seed, 1 dill head or ½ teaspoon dried dill, and 8 black peppercorns.

6. Pack cucumbers into each jar, and cover with the vinegar solution. Leave ½-inch (1.3 cm) headspace. Use a nonmetallic spatula to remove any trapped air bubbles, and wipe the rims clean with a damp cloth. Place on lids and screw bands, tightening only until fingertip-tight.

7. Process for 10 minutes in a boiling water bath (refer to page 32 for detailed instructions). Remember to adjust for altitude.

Removing the blossom end of the cucumber

Sweet Pickle Relish

Classic southern deviled eggs and hot dogs pretty much owe their very existence to sweet pickle relish. Add a tablespoon or two to potato salad, and it's instantly elevated to new culinary heights. Sweet pickle relish harmoniously marries sweet and sour tastes, each flavor balancing and tempering the other. There's a reason this union has endured the test of time—its puckery sweetness punctuates and embellishes every dish it is paired with. *Yield: 6 half-pints*

YOU WILL NEED:

- 4 medium cucumbers, peeled, seeded, and diced
- 2 1/2 cups sweet onion, diced
- 1 cup green pepper, diced
- 1 cup sweet red pepper, diced
- 1/4 cup pickling or kosher salt
- 3 cups granulated sugar
- 2 1/2 cups apple cider vinegar
- 1 1/2 tablespoons yellow mustard seed
- 1 1/2 tablespoons celery seed
- 1 teaspoon turmeric

TO PREPARE:

1. Combine the cucumbers, sweet onion, green and red peppers, and salt in a large bowl. Toss to combine, cover with a kitchen towel, and let stand in a cool area overnight or for at least 4 hours.

2. Drain and rinse the vegetables in a colander. Rinse several times, pressing the vegetables with the back of a wooden spoon to remove all liquid and salty residue. Set aside.

3. Sterilize six half-pint jars, lids, and screw rings (refer to page 97 for detailed instructions).

4. In a medium stainless-steel saucepan, combine the sugar, vinegar, mustard seed, celery seed, and turmeric. Add the vegetables, and bring the mixture to a boil. Reduce heat to low, and simmer for 15 minutes.

5. Pack relish into the jars, leaving 1/2-inch (1.3 cm) headspace. Use a nonmetallic spatula to remove any trapped air bubbles, and wipe the rims clean with a damp cloth. Place on lids and screw bands, tightening only until fingertip-tight.

6. Process for 10 minutes in a boiling water bath (refer to page 100 for detailed instructions). Remember to adjust for altitude.

Quick Persian Pickles

Enjoy the heady fragrance and spicy zip of cumin, fennel, black pepper, and other Persian spices in this easy pickle recipe. Served alongside a hummus sandwich, homemade falafel, or even your basic burger, these crunchy goodies might become your new favorite thing. **Yield: 2 quarts**

3	pounds pickling cucumbers
2 1/2	cups white vinegar
1/4	cup granulated sugar
2	tablespoons pickling or kosher salt
6	whole garlic cloves, peeled
1	tablespoon fennel seed
1	tablespoon cumin seed
1	tablespoon coriander seed
1	tablespoon mustard seed
2	teaspoons whole cloves
1	tablespoon black peppercorns

TO PREPARE:

1. Thoroughly clean whatever containers you will be using to store your quick pickles once refrigerated. You can use any ceramic or glass container with a lid. Avoid metal and plastic vessels, as they can impart an off flavor.

2. Wash and gently scrub your cucumbers to remove any dirt or debris. Cut about ¼ inch (6 mm) from each end. Cut each cucumber in half, and place in a large bowl.

3. Next, combine 2½ cups water with the vinegar, sugar, salt, garlic, and spices in a medium saucepan over medium-high heat. Bring the brine to a boil, then reduce heat to low and simmer for 5 minutes. Remove from heat and cool for 15 minutes.

4. Pour the brine over the cucumbers. Cover the bowl lightly with a cloth and allow to cool for one hour. Transfer the pickles to refrigerator-bound containers, cover with a lid, and refrigerate.

5. Your pickles will need at least 24 hours to absorb the flavors of the spices. For the zestiest, best-tasting results, wait for one week, at which point the flavor will be much more pronounced. Quick Persian Pickles will keep for four weeks in the refrigerator.

Quick Pickles

Perhaps what you have is a hankering, not a mission. Possibly you have merely a cuke or two, not a bushel, and you've got a pickle itch that must be promptly scratched. Well, look no further; your healing balm has been found. If you crave the puckery twang of a pickle but don't want the time commitment involved in boiling water bath processing, then a quick, or refrigerator, pickle is just the thing you're after. The process goes something like this: you stir up a brine, chop up your veggies, add them to the brine, and park the whole thing in the fridge. Pickled ecstasy is yours within a week. Your quick pickles will stay fresh for about 3 weeks thereafter. It really is that easy.

Chapter 7

A Whole Fruits and Vegetables Primer

For many, the motivation for home canning comes from a very real need to preserve a bounty of produce. Whether your bumper crop comes from your own vegetable patch, an irresistible bounty at a nearby farmers' market, or a too-good-to-pass-up sale at the grocery store, it's easy to suddenly find yourself swimming in green beans, tomatoes, peaches, or any number of fresh fruits and vegetables. A wonderful way to make the deliciousness of these items available year-round is to preserve them in simple syrup or water for vegetables.

Fruit, owing to its high acidity, can be safely canned in a boiling water bath. The pH of whole tomatoes tends to straddle the low-/high-acid fence; they can also be processed in a boiling water bath so long as the proper amount of lemon juice or citric acid is added (see Acidifying Tomatoes, page 111). All other vege-tables must be processed in a pressure canner unless supplemental acid is provided. If you'd love to put up some corn, green beans, or asparagus, you'll need to get yourself a pressure canner. Detailed instructions for using a pressure canner can be found on page 102. Be sure to familiarize yourself with the specific instructions accompanying your particular model, as well.

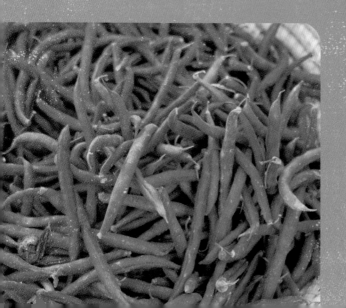

FRUIT

From peaches to plums and beyond, putting up fruits in their whole form affords great versatility for fruit-inspired concoctions during the off-seasons. In addition to providing you and your family with a pantry full of provisions, preserved fruits are lovely items for gift-giving, whether the occasion is a housewarming get-together, a birthday, or simply a thank-you.

Preparation

Naturally high in acid, fruit does not require pressure canning and can be safely processed in a boiling water bath. Figs are perhaps the one exception to this, with a pH around 4.6. As such, they'll need a bit of supplemental acid for water bath canning. If processing figs whole, add 1 teaspoon lemon juice per jar for safety.

To prep items for processing, gently scrub them with a vegetable brush in a sink of cold water, taking care not to bruise the flesh or puncture the skin. You may need to change the rinsing water several times if a good amount of dirt and debris is coming off of the fruit. Only wash as much fruit as can be canned in a single batch, as exposing fruit to water causes deterioration. Prep and can the first batch, and then move on to the next batch.

Some fruit will also need to have its skin removed. For apples or pears, use a vegetable peeler or paring knife to gently remove the skin. For peaches and apricots, blanch the fruit for easy removal of the skin (see page 116 for detailed instructions on blanching). Plums, grapes, and cherries need not be peeled but do best if their skins are gently pricked with a needle or fork tine; this helps prevent the skins from bursting when subjected to the high temperatures of the boiling water bath.

Preventing Browning

Some light-colored fruit, such as apples, pears, peaches, and apricots, will brown once its flesh is cut and exposed to oxygen. While not affecting the taste or quality, this discoloration makes the fruit less appealing once canned. To prevent discoloration, soak your fruit in an antibrowning solution. Commercial

---

TIP:

While simply placing your fruits and vegetables in a jar, ladling preserving liquid over them, and firing up the boiling water bath or pressure canner are all that's truly required to put up produce, adding a few special touches makes your labor of love that much more appealing. Whether you will be the sole recipient of your wares or you intend to gift friends and family with jars of home-canned peaches or green beans, the addition of herbs or spices goes a long way toward imparting flavor and making the contents especially lovely. Whole star anise, cloves, and cinnamon sticks are aromatic and striking in their unique forms, perfectly complementing most fruit. Fresh basil, dill, tarragon, thyme, or marjoram will enliven vegetables and provide a punch of color.

solutions can be found wherever home canning equipment is sold. Alternatively, you can make your own version one of two ways: dissolve 1 teaspoon powdered citric acid in 1 gallon (3.8 L) of water, or crush up six 500 mg water-soluble vitamin C tablets and add to 1 gallon (3.8 L) of water. Make the solution before you begin peeling, cutting, or blanching the fruit. Add the fruit pieces to the solution as you are prepping your batch for canning. Never leave fruit in the solution for longer than 20 minutes, as doing so can compromise flavor. Before processing, drain the liquid off in a colander and give the fruit a quick rinse. As long as you remember to drain and rinse the antibrowning solution, it won't impart any flavor to your fruit.

Canning Syrups

While it is certainly possible to can fruit using only water as your preserving liquid, your fruit will become soft and darken within a matter of months. If you plan to polish off your jars quickly, a shortened shelf life might not be a problem. If you hope to keep your canned fruit for some time, however, then sugar syrup or fruit juice should be your canning liquid of choice. The inclusion of sugar helps fruit retain texture, shape, and color. Homemade sugar syrups can range in sweetness from extra light to extra heavy according to personal preference. If you wish to keep fruit inside the jar from floating to the top, use either light or medium sugar syrup.

Sugar Syrups

Type	Sugar	Water
Extra Light	1 cup	1 quart
Light	2 cups	1 quart
Medium	3 cups	1 quart
Heavy	4 cups	1 quart
Extra Heavy	5 cups	1 quart

To make simple syrup, combine sugar and water in a medium saucepan over medium heat until sugar crystals are dissolved. Raise the temperature to high and boil for 5 minutes. Keep warm until needed.

Hot Pack and Raw Pack Methods

The terms "hot pack" and "raw pack" refer to the manner in which the contents are placed in the jar, either raw with hot liquid poured over it (raw pack) or cooked with liquid before packing in the jar (hot pack).

Delicate fruit, such as berries, will lose their shape if first cooked prior to canning. In their case, it is best to use the raw pack method, pouring hot liquid over the berries after they are gently placed into jars. Other fruits should be simmered lightly for several minutes in the liquid of your choice prior to processing. This helps force some of the air trapped inside the fruit's tissues out, replacing it instead with liquid, thereby weighing the fruit down and removing the tendency for it to float to the top of the jar. If you would prefer to use a heavy sugar syrup, water, or fruit juice, be advised that the fruit is more likely to float to the top of the jar unless the hot pack method is used.

The amount of liquid each jar will require depends on the size of the fruit pieces, but generally runs between ¾ cup and 1¼ cups per pint. Canned fruit requires ½-inch (1.3 cm) headspace.

> ### TIP:
>
> It is absolutely essential that you always avoid using waxed produce in home canning. The wax coating makes it difficult for fluids to sufficiently penetrate the tissues of fruit and vegetables, posing the risk that deadly botulism spores may remain in produce even after pressure canning.

VEGETABLES

Imagine pints of corn, peas, and green beans lining pantry shelves, always at the ready for cooking up impromptu casseroles, stews, and soups. With a modest amount of effort, this vegetable fantasy can be your kitchen reality. Once canned and properly stored, vegetables no longer require refrigeration or freezing, providing nonperishables for up to a year.

Preparation

Ideally, vegetables intended for canning should be preserved as close to harvest as possible. If you are canning vegetables you grew yourself, then you are, of course, in the best possible position to guarantee a speedy transit from harvest to jar. Otherwise, if you are purchasing produce from a farmers' market or roadside stand, inquire as to how long ago the vegetables were harvested. Deterioration begins just after harvesting, so acquiring the freshest produce possible is imperative.

If you develop a close relationship with the produce manager at your local grocer, it may be possible to learn when the vegetables available for purchase there were harvested. Wherever you source your produce from, give it a gentle scrub with a vegetable brush in a sink of cool water to remove any hidden dirt or debris. Change the soaking water several times if necessary. Any vegetables that float to the top (especially cucumbers) may be hollow and would be better used in recipes where they are chopped instead of being canned whole.

Canning Liquid

The liquid most often used for canning vegetables is simply water and salt. Adding salt helps the vegetables keep their consistency and flavor over time. If dietary sodium is a concern for you or your family, feel free to leave it out. Be advised, however, that vegetables canned without salt may lose a bit of color and become softer than those preserved with salt.

As with fruit, hot pack and raw pack methods may be used, although the hot pack method tends to produce better results with vegetables. Boil the vegetables in a bit of salted water for several minutes and then pack them into heated jars. Place the vegetables into the jars first and then ladle the hot liquid over them. Remember to leave headspace, which, in the case of vegetables, should be 1 inch (2.5 cm). Avoid overcrowding, as this can make it difficult for the water inside the jars to reach the temperature required to kill off nasty botulism spores.

When canning vegetables without added acid, you must process in a pressure canner. This is the only way to assure that botulism spores have been destroyed. Play it safe with vegetables and either pick up a pressure canner or acidify your veggies into relishes, pickles, chutneys, and salsas.

Choose the freshest produce available.

Troubleshooting Tips

Mistakes can be fabulous teachers. Sometimes you just don't know that you're doing something wrong until obvious clues present themselves. Once the error has been made, you know what not to do in the future, which only helps in making you a better home canner over time. The following is a guide for some of the most commonly occurring problems when canning whole fruit and vegetables.

If your jars fail to seal:

◻ You may have had some traces of the jar's contents on the rim. Always wipe the jar rim clean with a wet cloth before placing the lid and screw band on.

◻ You may not have had adequate water covering the tops of the jars in the boiling water bath. Be sure to have between 1 and 3 inches (2.5 and 7.6 cm) of water covering your jars at all times.

◻ You may have been using a jar with a cracked or chipped rim. Each time you can, check the rim of every jar by running your index finger around it before use.

◻ You may have left too much headspace in your jars. Leaving too much headspace can prevent a proper vacuum from forming, so always leave only the amount indicated in the recipe.

◻ You may have forgotten to adjust the processing time for altitude. If you live at an elevation above 1,000 feet (300 m), remember to add on to processing times as necessary (refer to page 338 for altitude adjustment amounts).

If your jars leak during processing:

◻ You may have filled your jars too full. Remember to always leave enough headspace to account for expansion that occurs during processing.

◻ You may have crammed in too many fruits or vegetables. You want to pack the jar closely, but not too closely; there needs to be space for the preserving liquid to move in between the jar's contents.

If your jar's contents float to the top:

◻ You may have used the raw pack method for items needing to be hot packed. For the most part, when canning fruit (except berries) and vegetables, use the hot pack method.

◻ You may have used produce that wasn't properly ripened. When selecting fruit and vegetables for canning, look for ripened, yet firm, pieces.

If your jar's contents become cloudy:

◻ You may have used overripe produce. When selecting fruit and vegetables for canning, look for ripened, yet firm, pieces.

◻ You may have cooked your fruit or vegetables for too long in the preserving liquid before canning. Only cook your items for as long as specified in the recipe before packing to jars. Use a timer if you think you might get distracted.

◻ You may have used table salt in your preserving liquid. Table salt contains fillers and anticaking agents that can cause liquids to become cloudy. Use only pickling or kosher salt in the preserving liquid.

◻ You may have failed to process your jars long enough to prevent the growth of bacteria. Follow recipes stringently and according to the processing manner they require. If the cloudiness is accompanied by an off odor, dispose of the jar's contents without tasting.

If your food darkens at the top of the jar:

◻ You may have failed to put in an adequate amount of preserving liquid. After placing the fruit or vegetables in the jar, ladle the preserving liquid over the contents until the proper amount of headspace is reached: ½ inch (1.3 cm) for fruit or 1 inch (2.5 cm) for vegetables.

◻ You may have failed to remove any trapped air bubbles in the jars. Always remember to use a nonmetallic tool for removing air bubbles around the interior circumference of the jars, before wiping down the rims and applying the lids and screw bands.

◻ You may have left too much headspace in your jars. Leaving too much headspace can prevent a proper vacuum from forming, so always leave only the amount indicated in the recipe.

◻ You may have failed to process your jars long enough to kill off enzymes. Follow processing times exactly as written in the recipe, adjusting as necessary for altitude.

Whole, Crushed, or Quartered Tomatoes

If you're looking for an ideal way to pack away the exquisite taste of one of summer's most beloved fruits, look no further. In a few short steps you'll be on your way to enjoying tomato deliciousness year-round.

Yield: 12 to 14 pints

YOU WILL NEED:

18 to 20 pounds meaty tomatoes, such as Roma

Pickling salt

Bottled lemon juice or citric acid powder

 Pressure canner

TO PREPARE:

1. Wash 14 pint-sized mason jars, lids, and screw rings (refer to page 97 for detailed instructions). Remember to inspect the jars for cracks, chips, or scratches, and ensure that the screw bands are rust-free. Although you don't need to sterilize jars that will be pressure canned, you will need your jars to be hot when filled in order to prevent them from cracking. You can either run the jars through the dishwasher, keeping them warm until ready for use, or place jars in a stockpot or boiling water bath canner, cover with water, and keep simmering until ready for use.

2. Wash tomatoes. Make a small crosshatch score across the bottom of each fruit. Fill a large metal bowl with ice water, and place in the sink.

3. Put the rack in the bottom of the pressure canner, fill with 2 to 3 inches (5 to 7.6 cm) of water, and set over low heat (adjust as needed, according to the manufacturer's instructions for your model). With the lid off, bring just to the boiling point. Place the jar lids in a small saucepan, fill with water, bring to a boil, turn off the heat, and leave on the stovetop until needed.

4. Bring a large pot of water to a boil over high heat. Drop the tomatoes into boiling water for 30 to 60 seconds, or until the skins split. Using a slotted spoon, ladle the tomatoes into the ice water bath. When they are cool enough to handle, slip off the skins and cut out the cores. Depending on your preference, quarter, halve, or leave tomatoes whole.

5. Place the hot mason jars on top of a kitchen cloth on the counter. Into each jar, place ½ teaspoon salt and either 1 tablespoon bottled lemon juice or ¼ teaspoon citric acid powder.

6. With the help of a canning funnel, pack tomatoes tightly and evenly into the jars, reserving ½-inch (1.3 cm) headspace. Use a nonmetallic spatula to remove any trapped air bubbles, ensuring that all voids in the jar are filled with juice. Wipe the rims clean with a damp cloth. Place on the lids and screw bands, tightening only until fingertip-tight.

7. Using a jar lifter, place the jars in the canner. Remember to exhaust the vent first. Process at 15 pounds (6.8 kg) pressure for 15 minutes if using a weighted-gauge canner, or at 11 pounds (5 kg) pressure for 25 minutes if using a dial-gauge canner (refer to page 103 for detailed instructions). Remember to adjust for altitude.

A jar funnel can be a great time-saver.

Whole Peaches

Nothing says summertime quite like peaches. With home canning, you can enjoy the taste of peaches when autumn leaves cover the ground, snow blankets the streets, and buds burst into bloom. Make sure your peaches are at the peak of ripeness and bruise-free in order to capture these heady fruits at their finest.

Yield: 6 pints or 3 quarts

TO PREPARE:

1. Sterilize six pint- or three quart-sized mason jars, lids, and screw rings (refer to page 97 for detailed instructions).

2. Fill a canner or large stockpot with water and set over medium-high heat. Bring just to the boiling point. Place the jar lids in a small saucepan, fill with water, bring to a boil, turn off the heat, and set the pan aside.

3. Combine the sugar and 4 cups water in medium saucepan over medium heat until all sugar crystals are dissolved. Raise the heat to high, and boil for 5 minutes. Keep the syrup warm until needed for packing.

4. Blanch the peaches (refer to Prep School on page 116 for detailed blanching instructions). When they are cool enough to handle, cut the peaches in half and remove the pits. Add the peaches to an antibrowning solution as you prep them. Once all the peaches are prepped, drain and rinse the fruit completely to remove any traces of antibrowning solution.

5. Add the peaches to the sugar syrup, and warm over medium-high heat for 2 minutes. Remove the peaches with a slotted spoon, and pack into hot jars; ladle sugar syrup over the peaches until covered, reserving ½-inch (1.3 cm) headspace.

6. Process pint jars for 20 minutes and quart jars for 25 minutes in a boiling water bath (refer to page 100 for detailed instructions). Remember to adjust for altitude.

Variations: Instead of sugar syrup, you can use 100% white grape or apple juice as the preserving liquid. To imbue your peaches with a subtle spiciness, add one cinnamon stick, two whole cloves, and two whole allspice to each jar. These peaches, evocative of a Middle Eastern spice bazaar, would be heavenly paired with fresh whipped cream, rice pudding, or vanilla ice cream, or alongside a warm slice of coffee cake.

Whole Kernel Corn

Smothered in butter, nestled into cornbread, or tucked into succotash, everything really does seem to go better with crunchy, sweet kernels of corn. When the season is high and corn can be found fresh at farmers' markets, local grocers, and backyards, grab a bushel or two and put up several pints. The reward is being able to brew up a steaming pot of corn chowder anytime! As the sugars in corn quickly turn to starch, plan on processing your ears as close to harvest time as possible, otherwise the corn begins losing some of its sweetness. *Yield: 6 pints or 3 quarts*

YOU WILL NEED:

- 16 ears sweet corn
- 4 cups boiling water
- Pressure canner

TO PREPARE:

1. Husk the corn, remove the silk, and wash the ears under cool water. Using a sharp knife (a serrated knife works quite well), cut the kernels off the cob, taking care not to cut into the cob itself. Place into a bowl, and set aside.

2. Wash six pint or three quart-sized mason jars, lids, and screw rings (refer to page 97 for detailed instructions). Remember to inspect jars for cracks, chips, or scratches, and ensure that screw bands are rust-free. Although you don't need to sterilize jars that will be pressure canned, you will need your jars to be hot when filled in order to prevent them from cracking. You can either run the jars through the dishwasher, keeping them warm until ready for use, or place the jars in a stockpot or boiling water bath canner, cover with water, and keep simmering until ready for use.

3. Put a rack in the bottom of your pressure canner, fill with 2 to 3 inches (5 to 7.6 cm) of water, and set over low heat (adjust as needed, according to the manufacturer's instructions for your model). With the lid off, bring water just to the boiling point. Place lids in a small saucepan, fill with water, bring to a boil, turn off the heat, and leave on the stovetop until needed.

4. Combine the corn and 4 cups boiling water in a large saucepan. Bring to a boil, reduce heat to medium-high, and simmer for 4 minutes. Remove the saucepan from the heat and drain corn, reserving liquid.

5. Place the hot jars on top of a kitchen cloth on the counter. With the help of a canning funnel and slotted spoon, pack corn evenly into the jars, leaving 1-inch (2.5 cm) headspace. Take care not to press the corn down or pack too tightly.

6. Ladle reserved cooking liquid over the corn, again leaving 1-inch (2.5 cm) headspace. Use a nonmetallic spatula to remove any trapped air bubbles, and wipe the rims clean with a damp cloth. Adjust headspace, if necessary, by adding more hot water. Place on the lids and screw bands, tightening only until fingertip-tight.

7. Using a jar lifter, place jars in the pressure canner. Remember to exhaust the vent. Process pints for 55 minutes and quarts for 85 minutes, selecting 11 pounds (5 kg) of pressure for dial-gauge models or 10 pounds (4.5 kg) of pressure for weighted-gauge models (refer to page 103 for detailed instructions). Remember to adjust for altitude.

Notes

MARKET FRESH

Freshness counts. I can't emphasize it enough. Just-picked fruits and vegetables are at their peak in terms of flavor, texture, and nutrition. For some items, such as cucumbers and corn, home canning is successful only if the items are put up right after harvest, as intrinsic enzymes can compromise their ability to maintain quality once jarred. That is why shopping, growing, and canning of fruits and vegetables are best done when they are in season. The following lists offer a season-by-season guide to what is available to the home canner. Keep these seasonal offerings in mind when you head out to the market or start eyeballing seed catalogues. Be advised that these listings may differ for those not living in North America.

Winter

- Brussels sprouts
- Celeriac
- Citrus fruits
- Fennel
- Kale
- Leeks
- Parsnips
- Rutabagas
- Turnips

Spring

- Apricots
- Artichokes
- Asparagus
- Broccoli
- Celery
- Peas
- New potatoes
- Radishes
- Ramps
- Rhubarb
- Scallions
- Spinach
- Strawberries

Summer

- Blackberries
- Blueberries
- Cherries
- Corn
- Cucumbers
- Currants
- Eggplant
- Garlic
- Green beans
- Melons
- Nectarines
- Okra
- Onions
- Peaches
- Peppers
- Plums
- Raspberries
- Tomatoes
- Yellow squash
- Zucchini

Autumn

- Apples
- Beets
- Cabbage
- Cauliflower
- Collard greens
- Cranberries
- Figs
- Grapes
- Mushrooms
- Pears
- Pomegranates
- Potatoes
- Pumpkin
- Sweet potatoes
- Swiss chard
- Winter squash

AS THE CANNER BOILS

Sometimes it's nice to look back over the years at all you've managed to put up. While your pantry shelves will reveal more recent contributions, keeping notes affords you the opportunity to reflect back on the last time you canned peaches, say, or made fig jam. Use this journal to chronicle your efforts and to provide some backup in the event that you should overlook dating your jars.

Year: _____

Canned: _____

_____

_____

_____

_____

_____

_____

_____

_____

Year: _____

Canned: _____

_____

_____

_____

_____

_____

_____

_____

_____

Year: _____

Canned: _____

_____

_____

_____

_____

_____

_____

_____

Year: _____

Canned: _____

_____

_____

_____

_____

_____

_____

_____

Book 3

Home Dairy

In all of my homesteading adventures, I've found that few things invoke as much awe and wonder in both others and myself as making dairy products. Something about the transformation from liquid to solid, fluidity to permanence is simply captivating and enthralling. Watching the metamorphosis of cream into butter, or the coagulation of milk into yogurt, or the shift as curds stretch into mozzarella is literally watching a change in physical state—an alchemical reaction occurring. I find it fascinating to witness so much wonder, all in the comfort of my kitchen. Plus, it's just plain fun! In this section, we'll examine the history behind homemade dairy goods, discuss what equipment and ingredients are necessary in the home dairy, and explore a bevy of recipes, all intended to get you comfortable with dairy dabbling.

Chapter 1

Creamery Origins

From the fields of Provence to the cliffs of Greece, from Turkish herders to Swiss milkmaids, dairy products are prized, lovingly crafted, and consumed with gusto the world over. In this chapter we'll explore the origins of our love affair with dairy and examine how dairy-making moved from the kitchen to the factory and back again.

IN THE BEGINNING

Humans have been dabbling with dairy products longer than we've been practicing agriculture. Our hunter-gatherer ancestors began animal domestication sometime around 11,000 B.C., starting with sheep and moving on to goats about 10,000 B.C. These animals, being small, nimble, and amenable to eating whatever scrubby, scraggly vegetation they encountered, could easily navigate cliffs, mountains, and other rugged terrain. Furthermore, they adapt readily to challenging weather, faring just as well in cold climates as more balmy ones.

While still nomadic, our tribal forebears would store surplus milk gathered from these sheep and goats in animal stomach pouches and head out on their daily hunts. Legend has it, one particularly auspicious day an Arabic nomad (or herder, or wandering merchant, depending on who's telling the tale) set out in the blazing heat of the desert sun, equipped with the day's milk ration. So the story goes, the heat of the sun interacted with the nomad's movements and the enzyme rennin (found inside the animal pouch), turning the milk to solid curds. Whether motivated by sheer curiosity or compelled by an empty stomach, the herder purportedly downed the foreign substance, immediately becoming the world's first *turophile*, or lover of cheese. I can't say I wouldn't have done the same.

The dawn of agriculture, when people literally started putting down roots (plant roots, that is), occurred around 9,000 B.C. in the Fertile Crescent, an area encompassing present-day Iraq, Syria, Lebanon, Israel, Kuwait, Jordan, southeastern Turkey, and parts of Iran. The permanence of these newly forming societies allowed for domestication of the larger, albeit fussier, cow. Though generous in terms of milk production, cows' needs are greater than those of the blithe sheep or the sprightly, make-do goat. Cows need shelter in poor weather and large tracts of verdant pasture for grazing. Its output being far superior to any of the other mammals humans attempted to milk, however, the sensitive cow became the go-to milker of choice.

SPREADING THE GOSPEL

Information on the nutritious, not to mention delicious, nature of milk began to spread. Manipulation of the milk provided by cows, sheep, goats, and other ruminants such as buffalo and yaks (that's right, yaks) began in earnest. While fresh milk is highly perishable, aging it not only preserves milk for later use, it arguably improves its flavor. What our ancestors couldn't use the same day, they could transform into a stable product to be stored for consumption or trade at another time. Use of dairy went global—a significant enough factor in ancient diets that it was etched onto walls, caves, and works of art. A Sumerian frieze from about 5,000 B.C. depicts cows being milked, the milk in turn being strained, and then the resulting substance being churned into butter. Later clay tablets show milk being rendered into cheese. Ancient Egypt was in on the dairy action, as well. Unearthed artifacts depict cheese and dairy products as staples of daily life.

Greek mythology also includes reference to cheese, most notably in Homer's *Odyssey*. When investigating Cyclops's cave, Odysseus and his men discover pens holding an abundance of goats and sheep, wicker baskets for molding cheese, and racks of curing cheese. The typical cheeses being produced in that hot, humid region at that time were highly salted in order to preserve them. These early cheeses would have been similar to feta and cottage, or other soft, salty cheeses, served fresh and intended to be eaten soon after they were made.

Dairying made its way to Rome, where inventive Romans expanded and improved on cheese-making techniques. They designed a type of cheese press, developed the process of ripening, and experimented with flavor enhancements such as smoking. Home cheese-making was widely practiced by Roman citizens, so much so that a number of larger homes contained kitchens expressly reserved for the production of cheese and other areas devoted to cheese ripening. Additionally, the Romans developed the practice of adding rennet to milk to hasten coagulation. This discovery, along with the cheese press, allowed curds to be pressed into hard cheeses. At the height of the Roman Empire, Italy was unquestionably the epicenter of cheese-making, for both home and market. Perhaps the secret to the Romans' seemingly infinite inventiveness was abundant cheese and dairy consumption!

BLESSED ARE THE CHEESE-MAKERS

Roman colonization took cheese out of Italy and across all of Europe. As the legions conquered outlying territories, they adapted, invented, and spread agricultural and culinary practices. When the Roman Empire began to decline, much of the trade of commodities over long distances fell apart as well. Cheese-making was a casualty of Rome's demise, with few advances in technique or production occurring during the Middle Ages. Fortunately, however, Catholic monasteries served as repositories of information for all things food related, from growing to harvesting to preserving. Monks revived cheese- and dairy-making practices, and crafted beers and wines with ingredients indigenous to their locale (and you thought monasteries were all vespers and lauds). They also experimented with new methods of curing, leading to advancements in ripening techniques and mold-rind cheeses such as Brie and Camembert.

GOD SAVE THE CHEESE

Monasteries and abbeys left a profound and enduring legacy of cheese-making in the British Isles. England, Scotland, Wales, Ireland, and the outlying smaller islands possess ideal conditions for dairying. The temperature, terrain, elevation, and highly fertile grasslands are eminently conducive to the needs of grazing animals (not to mention languid picnicking and Jane Austen novels). Some of the most famous English cheeses include Wensleydale (Yorkshire), Cheshire (Cheshire County), Stilton (Leicestershire), and cheddar (Somerset).

COTTAGE (CHEESE) INDUSTRY

By the later Middle Ages, the production and manufacture of cheese and other dairy products began making their way out of monasteries and home kitchens exclusively and into modest cottage industries. It was during this time, and in the ensuing years, that cheddar, Parmesan, Gouda, and Camembert showed up on the global cheese board. In mountain communities of the Jura and Alps, dairy associations and cooperatives were formed to exchange information about the best ways to craft a quality cheese.

Later, whole villages and even regions caught cheese-making fever, realizing the potential benefit of having a regionally recognized commodity of fine repute. Cooperatives formed during the 13th through 16th centuries introduced cheeses such as Gruyère and Emmentaler, both from Switzerland. The reputation and legacy of these items provided Swiss cheese-makers with the confidence to begin making their dairy products en masse in the early 19th century, opening the world's first cheese factory in Bern in 1815.

BRAVE NEW WORLD

In the early 17th century, several waves of English immigrants arrived in North America, bringing their dairying and cheese-making practices with them. They also brought cows, first to Jamestown Colony in 1611 and then to Plymouth Colony in 1624. British influence on the practice of American cheese-making has been particularly strong. Many cheeses made in New England are reflective of British styles, most notably cheddar.

In other areas of North America where Swiss, German, and Scandinavian immigrants settled, such as the Midwest states, dairy products produced there similarly reflect a European heritage. Emmentalers and other Swiss styles were among the first cheeses to be regularly manufactured and consumed in that region. Italian, German, French, English, and Dutch immigrants brought their offerings to the upper Midwest states, as well, including mozzarella, Muenster, Brie, cheddar, and Gouda. Enterprising Wisconsin-based cheese-makers also experimented with new cheese-making styles, creating brick and Colby cheeses. In Quebec, where a number of French immigrants settled, Francophile cheeses are the order of the day. Other areas of Canada reflect a British influence, crafting a number of cheddars.

A DAIRY-MAKING REVOLUTION

During the late 18th and 19th centuries, advances in industrial technology introduced a huge shift that occurred in the way goods were created and labor was performed. Coal-fired steam power was followed by the invention of the internal combustion engine and, later, electric power. Work previously performed manually was given to machines. Waterways were more easily dug and roads chiseled through heretofore impenetrable mountains, allowing agriculture to flourish and perishable commodities to be shipped from one location to another.

The new technologies moved dairy-making out of small farms, creameries, and home kitchens and into factories, where vast machines could crank out thousands of pounds of butter and cheese daily. Refrigeration allowed milk to be preserved until ready for use, allowing processing to occur far from remote dairy farms. Cold shipping and rapid transit allowed dairy products to be sold and consumed far from both pasture and factory.

COMMON GROUND

There was a time when keeping a family cow was an everyday practice, witnessed as commonly as the sight of chickens scratching in the yard and laundry drying in the breeze. In Britain, and to a lesser extent in early colonial America in areas such as Boston, those who couldn't afford to own property were allowed to make use of common land, sometimes referred to as the "commons." Many peasants used the commons to graze livestock, ensuring access to a reliable source of milk and meat for their families.

Over time, however, many commons were appropriated from public use and developed into areas of private ownership. As public access to grazing lands decreased, those who couldn't purchase property lost the ability to keep milking animals. Purchasing milk could be prohibitively expensive, and the ability to craft homemade dairy products was out of the reach of many. In the United States, the family cow in the backyard was supplanted by the subdivision and suburban landscape. Land just off the fringes of urban areas was parceled up and converted to housing. Backyards were modest and could hardly accommodate the needs of a cow.

In more recent years, a renewed interest in locally sourced, artisan, and homemade foods has sparked a return to home-based dairy production. Regardless of the presence of a milking animal in the backyard, home cooks are once again practicing the craft of DIY dairy, culturing yogurt and ripening feta cheese in their kitchens. Furthermore, small creameries continue to crop up in every region, with a host of enthusiastic fans ready to gobble up their products and learn about the practice of small-scale dairy-making.

Chapter 2

Ingredients:
Milking the Subject

When selecting ingredients for home dairy-making, seek out the best quality items you can find. Your finished product can only be as good as its component parts, so be certain to start with premium offerings. Milk is a highly perishable food (before it's preserved, that is). Select the freshest, cleanest milk you can find from a supplier you trust, and get ready to be amazed by the flavor, texture, and diversity of dairy deliciousness coming out of your kitchen. Patting yourself on the back upon completion of said dairy products is entirely optional.

MILK

The basis of all dairy products, milk is the most essential ingredient in the home dairy kitchen. Just as grain is necessary to produce bread and fruit to create wine, milk is indispensable for making cheese, yogurt, kefir, ice cream, and more. All this delicious diversity arises from one basic ingredient: animal milk. (While nondairy options made of everything from soy to nuts to hemp may be found at your local market, they are made through different processes that are beyond the scope of this book.)

Dairy products the world over are made from a variety of milks. If an animal produces milk, humans have tried their hand at extracting it: cows, goats, sheep, water buffalo, caribou, camels, donkeys, moose, reindeer, horses, buffalo, and even llamas. The composition of milk, while varying from animal to animal, is largely made up of the same basic elements in differing quantities: water (comprising the bulk of milk's composition), proteins, fat (butterfat), lactose (milk sugar), vitamins, and minerals. The recipes herein were developed and tested using cow and goat milk.

For many of you, the milk you'll be using to make home dairy items will be picked up at your nearest grocer. In that case, it's likely to have been both pasteurized and homogenized. **Pasteurization**, named after French chemist and biologist Louis Pasteur, is a process that greatly slows the growth of microbes in food. Introduced in the 19th century, pasteurization doesn't completely kill microorganisms in the same way that sterilization does. Instead, it curtails the number of pathogens (microorganisms likely to cause disease), so long as a food, once pasteurized,

is refrigerated and consumed in an expedient manner. Beyond killing the bacteria that can make you sick, pasteurization also kills beneficial bacteria in milk that are necessary to certain chemical reactions in the process of making cheese or cultured dairy products. Therefore, if you intend to make these products using pasteurized milk, it will be necessary to add starter culture to replace the missing bacteria.

Homogenization is the process used to combine two insoluble substances into an emulsion. You know how oil and vinegar have a natural tendency to separate from each other in your bottle of homemade vinaigrette? That's on account of their lack of homogenization. Had they been homogenized, the oil would have been broken up into particles small enough to penetrate the vinegar. The same thing happens with milk. Homogenization punctures the butterfat particles in milk, which are then made small enough to no longer separate from the water, creating a uniform distribution of butterfat within the liquid.

It is homogenization that creates the percentage designations indicated on grocery store milk. **Skim milk** (also referred to as "fat-free" in some countries, as the remaining percentage of fat is considered negligible) literally has the cream skimmed off the top and, once homogenized, contains a butterfat content of no more than 0.5 percent. Skim milk is used in making starter culture, as well as in hard cheeses like Romano and Parmesan. **Low-fat milk**, after homogenization, has between 1 and 2 percent butterfat remaining, while **whole milk** retains all of its original butterfat, with a percentage between 3.5 and 4 percent.

If you have access to fresh, raw, unadulterated, unprocessed milk, consider yourself blessed by the dairy gods. Raw milk possesses a number of attributes that are otherwise destroyed or reduced during pasteurization, including beneficial bacteria (such as lactic acids), heat-sensitive enzymes (including lactase, lipase, and phosphatase), and vitamins A, B_6, and C (all heat-sensitive nutrients). That said, if you have any reservations whatsoever about the purity of your milk or sanitary practices at its dairy of origin, you will want to pasteurize it. Potentially harmful bacteria can be found in raw milk, including mycobacterium (responsible for tuberculosis—characterized by difficulty breathing, wheezing, and chest pain), brucella (responsible for brucellosis—characterized by fever and joint pain), and salmonella (responsible for salmonellosis—characterized by abdominal pain, vomiting, and diarrhea). Some of these bacteria have also shown up in pasteurized milk.

Essentially, the hygiene standards practiced on the farm will determine what sort of opportunistic bacteria can contaminate the milk. These bacteria pose the greatest health threat to children, seniors, and those with vulnerable immune systems. That said, if you are utterly certain about the cleanliness of your milk—either because you are well-acquainted with your dairy supplier or you keep dairy animals yourself and are a hygiene ninja—you may choose to forgo pasteurization. Many raw milk advocates say pasteurization compromises flavor and texture, as the process destroys enzymes and makes proteins, vitamins, and minerals less available chemically.

Rules and regulations concerning the sale and consumption of raw milk and raw milk products vary widely. To learn about raw milk in your area, visit www.realmilk.com (U.S. and international information is provided). Consider the pros and cons of raw versus pasteurized milk to make the most informed decision for yourself and your family.

Home Pasteurization

Pasteurizing raw milk at home is easy, as long as you make certain to practice scrupulous hygiene. Prepare all of your equipment in advance by washing it in hot, soapy water and then allowing it to air-dry, make sure your kitchen is as clean as it can possibly be (no need to bust out the bleach, simply make sure countertops are clean; I use a homemade vinegar and water solution), and keep your raw milk refrigerated until you're ready to begin.

TO PREPARE:

1. Sterilize a stainless-steel stockpot by rinsing your pot with the hottest tap water. Add several inches of water to another, larger, stockpot. Add the milk you'll be using to the smaller pot. Place the smaller pot inside the larger one, making sure the water doesn't touch the bottom of the interior pot.

2. Gradually heat the milk to 145°F (63°C), checking the temperature with a dairy thermometer. Once the milk has come to temperature, set a timer for 30 minutes. Keep the milk at a consistent temperature the entire time, stirring the pot every so often to ensure even distribution of heat. If an interruption takes you out of the kitchen and you return to find the temperature has fallen, you'll have to start the timing from the beginning.

3. While your milk heats, clean your sink to a sparkle and fill it with ice and cold water, about as deep as your milk pot, to make a water bath. When the timer goes off, submerge the pot containing the milk into the bath.

4. Stir the milk continually until the temperature drops to 40 to 45°F (4 to 7°C). You want this to happen fairly rapidly, so be sure the water bath is really cold and full of ice when you submerge the milk-filled pot.

5. Once the milk has cooled, transfer it to a clean, covered container. Store in the refrigerator for up to two weeks.

STARTER CULTURES

The name gives away the role of this essential dairy-making ingredient. Used to make everything from cheese to yogurt, kefir, and sour cream, starter cultures are what get things started, as it were, in your pot of milk. Bacteria in the culture gobbles up lactose (milk sugars) and gives off lactic acid, jump-starting the acidification process. Lactic acid is essential for curdling milk, the first step in many home dairy recipes. Starter cultures also greatly influence the taste, smell, and physical structure of finished dairy products.

While there is a great deal of variety in the actual cultures used in home dairy-making, there are two basic types: mesophilic and thermophilic. Within those two categories, starter cultures may be referred to as traditional (mother culture) or direct-set (DVI). Let's examine the two main categories and both forms they come in.

Mesophilic Cultures

Mesophilic starter cultures don't do well if heated beyond 103°F (39°C). Just remember, mesophilic "loves cool." Mesophilic cultures are therefore used to make buttermilk and cheeses preferring low milk and curd temperatures, such as Gouda, cheddar, and feta. When this form of starter culture is required, the recipe you are using will indicate it.

It's acceptable to use any mesophilic culture; however, there are some specified varieties available within the broader category. So, for example, you might use one culture to make Brie, Camembert, Havarti, Gouda, Edam, feta, blue cheese, or chèvre, whereas a completely different culture might be more suitable for making cheddar, Colby, or Monterey Jack. It's not as confusing as it seems. Most suppliers specializing in cheese-making equipment will provide information for choosing the best mesophilic culture to create whatever product you have in mind (see page 341 for a list of suppliers).

Thermophilic Cultures

These starter cultures can take the heat. Thermophilic cultures are fine at temperatures up to 132°F (56°C). Just remember, thermophilic "loves warmth." Thermophilic cultures are key to the production of yogurt and hard Italian cheeses such as Parmesan and Romano, as well as Swiss-type cheeses. Whatever recipe you are following will indicate if you should be using a thermophilic culture. Also, thermophilic cultures have variations especially suited for achieving the best possible form of whatever dairy product you might be creating. Chat with your local cheese-making vendor or read over the options listed on dairy-making websites to find the option that best suits your needs.

Traditional (Mother) Cultures

Throughout history, part of the cheese-maker's art has been in the care and feeding of a "mother" bacterial culture. Once the "mother" is ready, she can produce "offspring" for as long as she is "fertile," to really stretch the metaphor. Traditional cultures can be a bit more demanding than direct-set cultures, as they require a lengthy culturing time before they can be used, usually somewhere between 15 and 24 hours for mesophilic cultures and 6 to 8 hours for thermophilic cultures. Once made, frozen mother culture will keep its vitality for up to one month. After that, you'll have to make up a fresh batch.

Starter cultures

DIY Mother Culture

If you'd like to make your own batch of traditional culture, follow these simple instructions. Either thermophilic or mesophilic mother cultures can be made using this method, although each type requires a different incubation temperature.

TO PREPARE:

1. First, sterilize your vessel: Fill a large stockpot with enough water to cover a 1 quart (.95 L) mason jar. Submerge a clean jar in the pot, allowing water to fill it, and cover the jar with a lid and screw band. Bring the water to a boil over high heat, and boil rapidly for 5 minutes. Remove the jar from the pot, uncap, and empty the water inside back into the pot.

2. Allow the jar to cool slightly. Fill the jar with skim milk, leaving ½-inch (1.3 cm) headspace between the top of the milk and the underside of the secured lid. NOTE: Be sure to give the jar a little bit of cooling-off time before filling with milk, otherwise the temperature variation between the hot jar and the cold milk may cause the jar to crack.

3. Place the milk-filled jar back into the stockpot. Bring the water to a boil over high heat, reduce heat to medium-high, and boil for 30 minutes. This will sterilize the milk, killing off unwanted bacteria while allowing the mother culture to thrive.

4. Remove the jar from the stockpot and place on a kitchen cloth in a protected area away from drafts. Let the milk cool to 108 to 110°F (42 to 43°C) for thermophilic culture or 70 to 72°F (21 to 22°C) for mesophilic culture.

5. Add the contents of one freeze-dried packet of mesophilic or thermophilic culture (depending on what type of mother culture you intend to produce) to the jar of cooled milk. Place the lid and screw band back on, and shake the jar lightly for a couple of minutes, just enough to distribute the culture throughout the milk.

6. Keep the jar in an area where its internal temperature can remain somewhat constant, such as a kitchen pantry or cabinet. If it seems too cool, consider wrapping the jar with a towel. Allow the milk to inoculate at 108 to 110°F (42 to 43°C) for 6 hours if making thermophilic culture or 70 to 72°F (21 to 22°C) for 18 hours if making mesophilic culture. See Incubating Ideas on page 194 for ideas on regulating temperatures. Check the culture after those respective inoculation periods. If it doesn't seem to be coagulating, leave it for another 6 hours or so, making sure to regulate the temperature. This part of the process is known as "ripening."

7. Once the mother starts to look like yogurt, sort of gelatinous and firm, and pulls away easily from the jar's edge, put it straight into the refrigerator. If you don't get to making cheese right away, that's fine; you can keep your mother in the fridge for up to 3 days. After that, it needs to be frozen.

8. To freeze your mother culture, run five or six empty ice cube trays under extremely hot tap water (wear rubber gloves!) for about 1 minute. Spoon the refrigerated mother into the trays, and cover the trays with plastic wrap. Place the trays in the freezer and allow to freeze solid, which should take 3 to 4 hours. Don't forget about them, because once they're firm, you'll need to transfer them to a resealable freezer bag.

9. Mark the bag with the date. Frozen mother culture will be good for about a month.

Direct-set Cultures (DVIs)

Developed in the 1980s, this time-saving technology is to home dairy makers what commercially produced pectin is to home canners. Direct-set cultures, also known as direct-vat inoculants (DVIs), are made in a laboratory and contain all of the important characteristics found in traditionally made cultures without the need to first be cultured. Available in powdered form and stored in the freezer until you need them, direct-set cultures are simply added to warmed milk. Many come in single-use packages, intended to work in 2 gallons (7.6 L) of milk. It is also possible to purchase direct-set cultures in bulk, measuring out the amount of powder required for larger or smaller batches. If measuring from bulk powder, use this guide to determine how much you'll need:

Bulk Direct-set Culture

⅛ teaspoon per 1 gallon (3.8 L) milk
¼ teaspoon per 2 to 5 gallons (7.6 to 19 L) milk
½ teaspoon per 5 to 10 gallons (19 to 38 L) milk

RENNET

A collection of naturally occurring enzymes, rennet is found in the stomach of any mammal, helping it to digest mother's milk. One protein-digesting enzyme in particular, chymosin (or rennin), coagulates milk, separating curds, or solids, from whey, the liquid portion of milk. Essential for mammalian digestion, the role of rennet is equally important in cheese-making. While milk would naturally separate into curds and whey if left alone for several days, it would also become a bit tangy and acidic, not the ideal flavor to begin with when making cheese (although such a flavor is desirable later, during ripening and maturing). Adding rennet to milk while it is still sweet and fresh expedites coagulation while keeping the fresh flavor intact.

As discussed in the opening chapter, the action of rennet is rumored to have been discovered by a wandering nomad, who found solids in his milk pouch when he'd started his

Organic

Organic foods are produced without the use of chemicals. Crops must be grown without the use of pesticides, herbicides, and nonorganic fertilizers. All organic products, including those derived from animals, must be free of antibiotics, artificial growth hormones, genetically modified organisms (GMOs), irradiation, and sewage waste. Furthermore, the production of organic foods cannot involve the use of cloned animals, artificial ingredients, or synthetic preservatives.

Organic milk is certified to be free of rBGH (or rBST), a bovine growth hormone used to boost milk production in cows; addi-tionally, milk may only be organically certified if the cows were given no antibiotics, their feed was free of pesticides, and they were permitted access to pasture. Cows that have been treated with rBGH produce such an exaggerated amount of milk that they must be milked three times a day. As a result, many cows experience mastitis, an infection of the udder, and a reduced lifespan. Furthermore, the milk from rBGH-treated cows has been shown to contain IGF-1, a growth hormone shared by humans. Human ingestion of dietary IGF-1 via hormone-addled milk may cause a proliferation of cancer-causing cells, especially affecting reproductive organs sensitive to hormonal fluctuations.

In the United States, federally mandated standards require that third-party state or private agencies oversee organic certification for producers. The U.S. Department of Agriculture (USDA) in turn accredits these agencies. In order for a farm or dairy to become certified organic, the land and animals must not have encountered any prohibited materials for three years. Scrupulous recordkeeping must be on hand to prove this, in addition to a detailed plan for preventing contamination by nonorganic materials. A number of agencies around the world perform similar organic certification testing. Requirements, regulations, and oversight vary from country to country but are, for the most part, quite similar.

day with liquid. This discovery led to widespread use of animal stomachs for cheese coagulation. Along the way, it was discovered that the fourth chamber (abomasum) of a young kid or calf was particularly adept at producing rennet. After animals were slaughtered, the abomasa were cut up into strips, salted, dried, and added in small portions to milk to speed up the separation of curds and whey. This bit of dried stomach was later dubbed *rennen* by the Germans, defined as "running together," eventually becoming known in modern parlance as rennet. Rennet is now sold in powdered, tablet, and liquid form. Rennet is standardized, so all forms work equally well. Personally, I prefer liquid, as it's quite easy to measure. Rennet is perishable; store tablets and powder in the freezer and liquid forms in the refrigerator.

Animal Rennet

Though largely abandoned in favor of standardized, synthesized rennet, some cheese-makers in parts of Europe still use rennet in the traditional manner. The stomachs of young calves are cut and then added to either saltwater or whey, along with vinegar or wine. The addition of acid allows rennet production to flourish. The solution is left for several days and then filtered. The pieces of stomach are dried and then broken into small pieces to be reconstituted as needed for cheese-making.

Vegetable Rennet

Throughout history, when animal sources of rennet have been scarce, plant-based sources of coagulating enzymes have been sought out as alternatives. The ancients used everything from fig juice to nettles, thistles, and mallow. Today, commercially available vegetable rennet is made with an enzyme produced by the mold *Mucor miehei*. This mold contains chymosin (the active constituent responsible for causing the separation of curds from whey) and is identical to animal rennet in chemical structure.

Genetically Manufactured Rennet

Right up until the early 1990s, rennet was made in the tried and true fashion, with either abomasa or vegetables known for their coagulating properties. Nowadays, however, most rennet is genetically manufactured via bacteria into which the enzyme for rennet has been introduced. Grown in huge vats, these bacteria produce rennet as a by-product, which is then extracted, purified, and sold for cheese-making.

LIPASE

Lipase is an enzyme made by certain animals (including humans) to break down dietary fats during digestion. In the home dairy, the role of lipase is to impart certain types of cheeses with their characteristic strong flavors. Raw milk naturally contains lipase enzymes, which act on triglycerides found in milk fat, freeing up fatty acids. Add in ripening time and you've got nuanced flavors that distinguish certain cheeses.

Pasteurization deactivates lipase, however. If you're using pasteurized milk in home cheese-making, then the addition of commercially prepared lipase is essential. Without it, the flavors associated with many types of cheeses will be almost completely absent. Vegetarians should know that most commercially produced lipases used in cheese-making are animal derived, although microbially sourced varieties do exist.

Two of the most commonly available varieties of lipase are Italase (mild), which is customarily added to blue, mozzarella, Parmesan, and certain other cheeses, and Capilase (sharp), which is used for Romano, provolone, and other strongly flavored cheeses.

BACTERIA & MOLDS

Some cheeses require the artificial introduction of specialized molds to give them their characteristic flavor and appearance. These molds are really fungi or bacteria that are crucial in making, say, the Roquefort cheese taste and look as we've come to expect. Added molds will appear either internally, such as the mold that makes "eyes" develop in Swiss cheeses, or externally, evidenced by the bloomy rind on Brie. Molds used in cheese-making can be purchased through a cheese-making supplier.

Thin white rind of *Penicillium camemberti*

Penicillium candidum

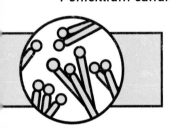

When you think of the rind on a wheel of Brie, you're thinking of this mold. *Penicillium candidum* is used to ripen Brie, Coulommiers, Sainte-Maure, and some French-style goat cheeses. After the mold is sprayed onto the surface of the curd, it spreads and grows incredibly quickly, keeping other molds from developing in the process. It is then allowed to age, during which time its characteristic white bloomy rind forms. The rind actually begins as tiny, fine, white hairs that grow and overlap and come to resemble what the French call *poil de chat,* or cat fur. Tasty, no? This fur is then rubbed away, leaving only a thin white rind behind that acts as a protective enclosure for the cheese's soft interior. *Penicillium candidum* also contributes to the development of flavor during the ripening stage. This surface mold, given the proper salt and moisture, will develop a rind that breaks down amino acid chains from the outside in, creating an increasingly soft, buttery texture with time.

Penicillium camemberti

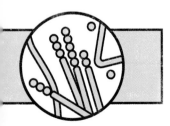

This mold is quite similar to *Penicillium candidum*, producing many parallels in characteristic flavor and appearance. *Penicillium camemberti*, however, is used more often in producing goat's milk (as opposed to cow's milk) soft cheeses.

Penicillium roqueforti

When the first blue cheeses were made, *Penicillium roqueforti* was literally in the air. Early European cheese-makers found the mold on and in their cheeses when they were left in caves, such as those in Roquefort, France, to

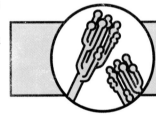

age. Now available in both fast and very-fast growing forms, *Penicillium roqueforti* is used in the manufacture of Stilton, Roquefort, Gorgonzola, Danablu, and other blue cheeses. The mold imparts the characteristic blue-green ripple typical of such cheeses, along with a smooth, creamy, spreadable texture. Enzymes created by *Penicillium roqueforti*

The telltale blue veins of *Penicillium roqueforti*

are responsible for the pleasingly pungent flavor and aroma associated with blue cheeses. These enzymes break down complex molecules into simple ones, changing the fibrous chemical structure into a smoother one and imbuing it with piquant flavor and smell.

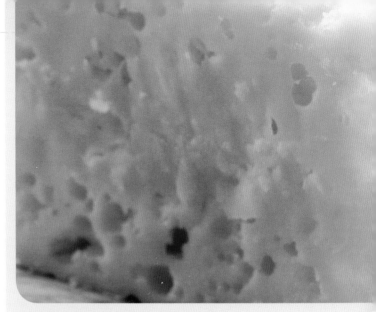

The "eyes" formed by *Propionic shermanii*

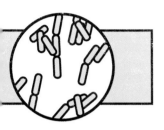

Brevibacterium linens

Brevibacterium linens is a red mold, used to create orange and yellow coloration on cheese surfaces. Often referred to as "red cultures," it develops quickly and assists with ripening. The mold is added to the brining mix and sprayed onto washed-rind cheeses during aging. The sulfurous aromas produced by the mold are characteristic of brick, Limburger, and Muenster cheeses. Which is to say, when you smell "stinky cheese," *Brevibacterium linens* are shouting "Hello! We're here!"

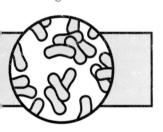

Propionic shermanii

Propionic shermanii is responsible for putting the holes (or "eyes"), smell, and taste into Swiss, Emmentaler, and Gruyère cheeses. Without it, many "hole-y" cheeses would be downright secular!

Geotrichum candidum

This mold plays a key role in cheese ripening. Used in conjunction with other molds, *Geotrichum candidum* contributes to both flavor and physical integrity during the ripening process of cheeses such as Brie and Camembert. It is also used in ripening for some goat cheeses. The mold helps to create a neutral environment in which *Penicillium candidum* and *Brevibacterium linens* can flourish and do their thing.

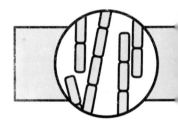

FLAKE SALT

Salt is an essential ingredient in the home dairy, especially when making cheese. Through its hygroscopic properties, salt is able to pull liquid out of cheese curds and into the whey, which is then drained off. Flake salt is usually added right before pressing to help pull out any remaining moisture left inside the curds. Salt also reduces the size of curds, making them easier to press and retain their form.

When it pulls moisture out of foods, salt also pulls moisture away from bacteria, making it difficult for them to survive. Added near the end of the cheese-making process, flake salt prevents any opportunistic bacteria that may

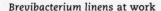

Brevibacterium linens at work

Flake salt

Bottled lemon juice and citric acid

have sneakily made their way into the milk from thriving. It also slows down the growth rate of lactic bacteria. And, of course, salt adds flavor. Some cheeses, such as feta, simply wouldn't be themselves without the addition of salt.

In home dairy-making, you'll need to use flake salt, the granules of which are slightly larger than table salt or sea salt. Flake salt (also known as cheese-making salt) is a coarse, non-iodized salt that dissolves completely in water, leaving behind no grit, grains, or residue of any kind. Selecting salt without added iodine is particularly important, as its presence can kill off some cultures and slows down the cheese aging process. Flake salt can be obtained from cheese-making suppliers; you can also use ground kosher or canning salt with equal success. Whichever salt you use, be sure that it contains no anti-caking ingredients.

ACIDS

A number of supplemental acids may be called for in home dairy-making, including vinegar, citric acid, tartaric acid, and lemon juice. Citric and tartaric acids can be found at dairy-making suppliers, as well as at some natural foods stores. When using lemon juice, I suggest bottled organic juice, as its acidity level will be more consistent than fresh-squeezed juice.

HERBS, SPICES & FLAVORINGS

A number of homemade dairy products benefit from the addition of herbs and spices. I'm thinking of a particular Gouda I'm crazy about that is studded throughout with cumin seeds. Then there's that cheddar with the sage . . . I could go on and on. The point here is that, since you're in charge of your home dairy, you can be as extravagant or as judicious as you'd like with flavor flourishes. For added heat, toss in dried chili flakes. Try cumin, caraway, mustard seeds, or juniper berries in hard cheeses, or basil, marjoram, oregano, chives, thyme, dill, garlic, sage, tarragon, or chervil in soft cheeses. Explore and discover which flavors speak to you. Herbs are best used fresh, but if fresh herbs are hard to come by, dried can work reasonably

well. For each tablespoon of fresh herb called for, use one teaspoon dried.

Consider add-ins to yogurt or ice cream. Fresh fruit or a spoonful of jam is absolutely scrumptious stirred into plain, whole-milk yogurt. Ice cream truly shines when kissed with nuts, herbs, fresh and dried fruits, extracts, and liquors. Let your imagination hold court when deciding how to jazz up homemade dairy items.

CALCIUM CHLORIDE

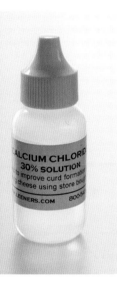

Unless you own your own milking animal or otherwise have access to raw milk, the milk used in your home dairy-making will be purchased from your local grocer, which means that it will be homogenized and pasteurized. These processes can interfere with the calcium present in milk, which, in turn, can hinder the ability of rennet to coagulate properly. You might end up with an oozy, gooey, milky mess that fails to firm up and cooperate like a good cheese should. The shortcut around this difficulty is to add calcium back in the form of calcium chloride. For each gallon of milk called for in your recipe, add ¼ teaspoon of calcium chloride, diluted in ¼ cup of cool water. Stir the mixture into warmed milk before you add in your starter culture. Calcium chloride is available in both powdered and liquid forms from cheese-making suppliers.

ASH

Historically, the ash used in cheese-making came from an actual fire. These days, the ash more likely is sourced from salt and vegetables that are dried and powdered. The ash serves a number of different functions. It creates a hospitable environment for surface mold growth, desirable in certain cheeses.

Adding ash, an alkaline substance, works to neutralize the acidity found in cheese, which might otherwise slow down ripening and, consequently, flavor development. Ash also provides a bit of visual interest, providing a darkened contrast to the paleness of the cheese. Also known as activated charcoal, ash can be purchased from cheese-making suppliers as well as drugstores.

KEFIR GRAINS

Kefir (a fermented beverage we'll discuss at greater length in chapter 5, Cultured Dairy) can be made from either a starter culture or from "live grains." The grains, looking a bit like cauliflower florets,

are a jellylike community of bacteria and yeasts mixed with proteins, lipids, and sugars (yum, right?). The grains can't be made, but must be obtained from actively fermenting kefir. You can purchase kefir grains, or look for someone making kefir nearby who might be able to part with some.

Chapter 3

Equipment: Creamery Necessities

As with any new venture, a few tools specific to the task will be in order. Fortunately, for home dairy-making, many of those essential items are most likely already hanging out in your kitchen. Many of you will find it surprisingly easy to get started culturing yogurt and churning out butter. Once you've assembled the necessary equipment, crafting cream cheese for your morning bagel, mozzarella for a pizza dinner, or vanilla ice cream for that birthday party will be a breeze. In fact, you might just wonder why you didn't join in on the DIY dairy adventure sooner!

There's a great deal of overlap in the tools and materials used in home dairy-making. Equipment used in making cheese will also be used in making yogurt, and so on. I'll detail all of the basic gear you'll need on hand first, then walk you through those items specific to creating certain products. Depending on your budget, time constraints, and personal preferences, you might choose to substitute cleverly appropriated everyday items for costly specialized equipment and tools (check out pages 194, 224, and 327 for DIY options). Everyone's needs are different, so when the time comes to start your own homemade dairy adventure, read through a recipe first, consider all of your equipment options, and then choose what feels best for you.

ESSENTIAL SUPPLIES

The following items are the go-to tools you'll visit, revisit, and then visit once more whenever you make homemade dairy products. Most likely, you've already got these objects on hand. For those you lack, a quick trip to the nearest kitchen supply store or online dairy-making supplier will get you suited up in no time.

Cheesecloth and Butter Muslin

You'll find these cloths to be indispensable in your home-dairy tool kit. Cheesecloth, as its name implies, was originally used to wrap cheeses for preserving. While still used for this purpose, it is more routinely used to drain whey from curds and for lining cheese molds intended for hard cheeses. The loose-woven fabric doesn't shed any fibers or lint into curds and won't retain flavors. Butter muslin is similar in use to cheesecloth, yet quite different in structure, possessing a finer, tighter weave.

In order for it to hold up to the rigors of regular home dairy-making, be sure to start with good-quality cheesecloth right out of the gate. While you might be tempted to opt for the packaged variety available in grocery stores, I urge you, buyer beware! Such offerings are flimsy and shabbily made, not to mention possessed of holes large enough for smaller curds to slide right through. Source quality cheesecloth and butter muslin from a dairy-product supplier. Fortunately, it can withstand repeated use with proper cleaning.

To sanitize cheesecloth or butter muslin, boil a pot of water, add the soiled cheesecloth or butter muslin, and boil for 2 minutes. Remove the pot from the heat, drain off the water, and rinse the cheesecloth in cold water until all food debris is removed. Wring it out thoroughly and allow to air-dry.

Colander

You'll return to your colander again and again, so be sure to use one that can withstand the test of time. Plastic or metal isn't as important a consideration as is sturdiness. You will want your colander to be able to accommodate a large volume of curds at one time, so make it a big one. Don't worry too much about the size of the drainage holes, as you'll be lining the colander with butter muslin or cheesecloth.

Dairy Thermometer

Because reaching or holding specific temperatures is crucial to many home dairy processes—a few degrees variation can render curds into completely different products— a reliable thermometer will be necessary. Dairy thermometers range from 0 to 220°F (-18 to 104°C) and show 2-degree increments. Whichever style you choose, it must have a stem at least 2 inches (5 cm) long in order to reach into the milk and produce an accurate reading. In my experience, and in researching feedback from others, I've found a digital thermometer with a stainless-steel clip-on and a built-in timer to be the best option. Setting the timer to sound when the desired temperature has been achieved frees you up to do other things while your milk warms. Besides, we all know a watched pot never boils.

Double Boiler

Basically just another way of saying "a pot inside a pot," a double boiler is useful when you need to warm milk gradually and evenly. It needn't be anything fancy. If you'd rather not purchase a dedicated double boiler set, a double boiler can be fashioned by putting a smaller stockpot into a larger one to which 1 to 1½ inches (2.5 to 3.8 cm) of water has been added. Make certain the bottom of the mixing bowl doesn't come in contact with the water, otherwise the bowl's contents will overheat, defeating all of your efforts.

Glass Jar and Lid

When making yogurt and butter, you will need a glass mason or canning jar, along with a lid. For yogurt, the glass jar is simply the vessel that will hold the mixture as it warms and cultures. In the case of butter-making, the "shaken jar" method is a low-tech, calorie-burning means of rendering cream into butter. While a variety of jar sizes are available, those most often used in butter- and yogurt-making are half-pint, pint, and quart.

Saucepan

You will need a medium, heavy-bottomed stainless-steel pot for warming up milk for making yogurt, ice cream, and some soft cheeses. Ideally, it should hold up to 1 gallon (3.8 L) of milk. Be sure to use only stainless-steel or chip-free enameled pots, as the acids present in milk can interact with aluminum, drawing the metal out of the pot and into the milk.

Measuring Cups

A glass measuring cup with a pouring spout is best. I like to have two sizes available: 8 ounces and 64 ounces is ideal. It is recommended that your equipment be completely sterile each time you fire up the home dairy. This is easier to achieve, in my experience, with glass equipment, as plastic can become scratched and retain residues, rendering it susceptible to contamination.

Sieve

A sturdy sieve will be needed in certain dairy-making processes, such as straining buttermilk off of butter and straining custard when making ice cream. Choose a medium version, as anything too small will just be a nuisance and an especially large sieve can be cumbersome.

Skimmer or Perforated Ladle

Your skimmer will be one of the tools you reach for most when making homemade dairy goods, especially in cheese-making. Utterly indispensable for transferring curds from the pot into the colander for draining, its large, flat diameter allows for easy lifting without breaking up curds. Stick with stainless steel, as it offers greater durability and assurance of sanitization than that offered by plastic utensils.

Measuring Spoons

Keep a sturdy set of metal measuring spoons on hand. I've found them to be less susceptible to breakage than the plastic variety, unlikely to melt if they get too close to the stove, and less likely to become scratched, thereby making them easier to properly clean and sterilize.

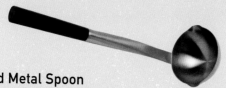

Long-handled Metal Spoon

A long spoon is helpful for stirring and combining liquids. Again, metal is advisable, as plastic and wood can absorb flavors and residues, posing risks for contamination. If you're going to spend time, attention, and money on making homemade dairy products, you don't want opportunistic bacteria to spread all over your lovingly prepared goods on account of a cheap utensil.

String or Twine

Some dairy products will need to be swaddled in cheesecloth or butter muslin and suspended to allow the whey to drip off. That's where string comes into play. Any kitchen string or butcher's twine will work here. You can also get creative and use craft twine or even strong raffia in a pinch. Whatever you choose, just make sure it's sturdy. Should a phone call, unexpected house guest, or other need draw you out of the kitchen, few things might make you cry into your curds and whey more than a poorly secured bundle of dairy deliciousness, plunged to an untimely demise all over your kitchen floor.

CHEESE TOOLS

The type of cheese you are making factors heavily into the type of equipment you will need to make it. For example, a cheese press will only come into play when making hard cheeses. If you opt to jump completely into the dairy vat, as it were, read up on all types of equipment and then make your purchases (or make the equipment yourself) accordingly.

Cheese Trier

This device is what allows cheese-makers to sample a bit of cheese from the center of a wheel to test for ripeness. Made of stainless steel and used only when making hard cheeses, the trier lets a cheese-maker check on where their cheese is in its aging process without having to cut a wedge out of the wheel itself. The trier removes a core of cheese (similar to the core removed by an apple corer); a bit of the core is sampled and then the remaining portion is repositioned in the hole, allowing the aging process to continue.

Cheeseboard

Not to be confused with marble or granite boards used for serving finished cheeses, this type of cheeseboard is an integral component to the aging process. It is basically a cutting board, used here as a drying platform. Cheeseboards are also used in aging and, when needed, as drainage stands for certain cheeses. Either plastic or wood cheeseboards are both acceptable for use, so long as fastidious cleaning hygiene is practiced. If you decide to use a wooden board, seek out one made of birch, maple, or bamboo, as the tannins in cherry and oak can be harmful to your cheese, potentially imbuing it with a bitter, astringent taste.

Cheese Press

A cheese press is needed when making hard cheeses. Presses work by applying continued pressure onto curds that have been placed into a mold. The pressure squeezes whey from the curds, forming them into a solid mass. You can purchase a cheese press or make your own (see page 237 for DIY plans). Either way, your press should be easy to put together and take apart, making the process easy from start to cleanup.

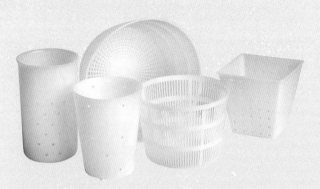

Cheese Molds

Molds are used for forming curds into specific shapes. They are used in the final stages of cheese-making and determine the ultimate shape of your cheese. From rounds to pyramids, columns to hearts, cheese molds come in a variety of shapes and sizes. Commercially purchased cheese molds are made from wood, stainless steel, ceramic, and food-grade plastic. It is also possible to make your own molds from appropriated containers. See Bend Me, Shape Me, Anyway You Want Me on page 224 for DIY cheese mold options.

Cheese Wax

This type of wax is made especially for use in cheese-making and is deliberately soft and pliant. Used to keep hard cheeses from drying out during aging, wax also keeps harmful bacteria out of cheese while it is ripening. You may want to devote a used or worn-out pot expressly to cheese waxing, as attempting to remove the hardened wax can be a colossal challenge.

Curd Knife

You'll need a long knife, at least 10 inches (25.4 cm) in length, for cutting curds in some cheese-making recipes. The knife should be able to reach the bottom of the pot containing the curds without its handle touching the curds. It should also be relatively thin and capable of cutting straight lines. If you lack a curd or "cheese-cutting" knife such as those sold by cheese-making suppliers, a long, flat kitchen knife or cake spatula may be used.

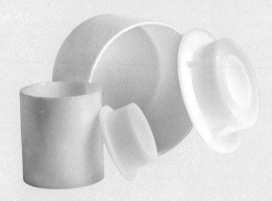

Cheese Followers

Used primarily when making hard cheeses, followers are flat disks of wood or plastic that sit snugly atop cheese molds. Without them, cheese curds would spill and seep out when subjected to the rigors of pressing. As pressure is applied, followers sink into the cheese mold, compressing the cheese in the process.

Drip Tray

A drip tray is simply the container into which whey will drain during cheese pressing, keeping whey from running all over your countertops. Most commercially made cheese presses will come with their own tray. Should yours break, it can be replaced with an aluminum pie plate.

Drying Mats

Similar in use to cheeseboards, drying mats are made of bamboo or food-grade plastic. Mats can be purchased from cheese-making suppliers, Asian supermarkets (sushi mats), or craft supply stores (food-grade plastic in varying sizes). Drying mats are necessary for draining cheeses such as Brie, Camembert, and Coulommiers, and also aid in the aging and air-drying process following pressing.

Spray Bottle

This is used in making mold-ripened cheeses. A light mist of mold solution is sprayed over the surface of the cheese, providing just the right amount of inoculant to get things ripening properly. Care must be taken not to over-mist, as doing so can turn a little bit of mold into a nasty beast. To prevent cross-contamination, each type of mold or bacteria will need its own spray bottle. To keep things sanitary, use only newly purchased bottles as opposed to repurposing a spray bottle you currently own.

Ripening Refrigerator

A number of hard cheeses need to age, some for a handful of days, weeks, or months, and some even for years. While aging, the temperature and relative humidity in the aging environment must be carefully maintained in order for proper acidity to develop, as well as to control mold growth. If you have a basement whose temperature never goes over 68°F (20°C), then you've got the equivalent of a cheese cave. If your basement is too warm or nonexistent, a dedicated, dormitory-sized refrigerator can do the job. Put a bowl of water in the bottom, set the temperature to 55°F (13°C), add your cheese, and, presto, consider yourself the proud owner of a modern-day cheese cave!

Stockpot

A large stainless-steel stockpot will be one of your most frequently used items in home dairy-making. Anything holding between 1 and 4 gallons (3.8 and 15.2 L) of milk will work, depending on the size of your family and the frequency with which you consume dairy products (my house of two can put back a lot of dairy). An unchipped enamel pot works equally well.

BUTTER TOOLS

Making homemade butter is really quite simple. It can be as high- or low-tech as you'd like it to be. If you'd like to streamline the necessary equipment, simply use your muscles to shake the cream into whipped submission. Otherwise, a food processor takes care of the work in short order.

Butter Churn or Food Processor

There are a number of different means of creating homemade butter. An electric churn makes butter from cream in about 30 minutes and involves no greater effort than pouring the cream into a large glass jar. A motor rests atop the jar and, once switched on, a plunger (also known as a "paddle" or "dasher") agitates the cream, separating water molecules from oil molecules. The resultant liquid is buttermilk, and the solid substance is butter. An electric model can be a great investment if you plan to make large quantities of butter on a regular basis. These can be expensive, though, so I'd suggest purchasing one only if you intend to sell your butter or otherwise market it.

A hand-cranked churn produces the same result as the motorized version, only with a little more elbow grease. Cream is poured into a glass jar and then whipped via a crank secured onto the lid of the jar. Less costly than electric models, its only drawback (if perceived as such) is its need for physical labor. Otherwise, it's an electricity-free way to make butter and, perhaps, give a task to squirmy children.

Asked to conjure up images of butter churns, likely an old-fashioned dasher-style churn will comes to mind. A small, tapered barrel holds a dasher that is moved up and down repeatedly to make butter. Not ideal for regular use, they can be difficult to clean and are susceptible to leaking. Antique dashers are more often kept as collector's items than for actual butter-making these days.

Finally, butter-making can also be accomplished with the help of a food processor. Although many home cooks may already possess a food processor, it is absolutely optional when making butter, although it can certainly expedite the process.

Butter Molds

A variety of molds exist for fashioning butter into all sorts of whimsical shapes, from stars, to hearts, to pineapples. I'm a fan of the asterisk/swirl myself. Made from plastic, food-grade silicone, or wood, butter molds are perfect tools for those times when gussying up your butter is in order.

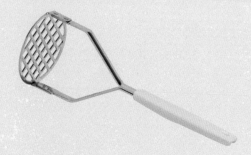

Potato Masher

A potato masher (or even simply two forks) is helpful when making butter by hand (i.e., without a machine). It needn't be fancy, requiring only a handle that will permit comfortable repeated kneading.

ICE CREAM & YOGURT TOOLS

While making yogurt or ice cream at home might never have occurred to you before, it should. It's easily done with the right equipment. As with other dairy-making endeavors, making yogurt or ice cream can involve repurposing basic equipment you already have, or acquiring specialty equipment suited expressly to the task at hand.

Electric Ice Cream Maker

These can be immensely handy for those pressed for time or short on hand-cranking labor. I love mine and use it all summer long. An electric ice cream maker operates with little assistance outside of plugging it in, filling the bowl, and turning the switch on. A little bit of advance planning is required, however. A double-walled bowl containing a solution capable of freezing below the freezing point of water must be frozen in a regular kitchen freezer for 24 hours before you begin. After the pre-freeze period, the bowl is placed inside the machine cavity, the cream mixture is poured in, the machine is turned on, and an interior paddle begins to churn the concoction. The cream begins to freeze as it makes contact with the frozen bowl, and, about 20 or so minutes later, the ice cream is frozen. I plan ahead for ice-cream urges by leaving the double-walled bowl in the freezer at all times, ready to receive a creamy mixture should the mood strike.

Hand-crank Ice Cream Churn

These are the ice cream machines our forefathers (and foremothers) used, cranking and churning out frozen delicacies with the aid of ice, rock salt, and good old-fashioned elbow grease. In this configuration, the cream mixture goes into an inner bowl, which is placed inside the larger churn. A layered mixture of ice and rock salt is then sandwiched between the cream-containing bowl and the interior wall of the churn. Salt causes the ice to melt more quickly and water to freeze faster. A paddle inside the inner bowl is activated when the hand crank atop the churn is turned. As the salt begins to melt the ice, heat generated by the paddling action is pulled out of the cream mixture and into the salt and ice mixture, freezing the cream. Depending on the model and manufacturer, and the size of the churn, a hand-crank model can be less expensive than an electric ice cream maker. However, it can also become rather messy, as the melting ice creates a pool of salty water that must be disposed of and replaced before a fresh batch can be made.

Electric Yogurt Maker

These machines regulate the temperature during your yogurt's incubation. This can be especially handy if your house temperature is too variable, you don't have the right setup for keeping the temperature consistent, or you don't want to be bothered with babysitting your yogurt (although it's a pretty docile ward, as far as caretaking responsibilities go). Otherwise, a number of means exist for incubating yogurt without use of a yogurt maker. See the sidebar on page 194 for suggestions on rigging up your own incubating device.

Chapter 4

Butter & Ghee:
Butter Me Up!

Butter, in my opinion, is downright swoon-worthy. It possesses a flavor so divine, a mouthfeel so rich and creamy, an aroma so promising of scrumptiousness that I've yet to meet a pat of butter I didn't like. Whether it's found in flaky piecrusts or melted into rich hollandaise and béarnaise sauces, slathered on hot biscuits or drizzled on straight-out-of-the-tandoori-oven naan, butter has captivated and transfixed taste buds the world over.

Now it's time to whip up this homemade dairy delight yourself, delivering butter's timeless tastiness to those gathered 'round your table. For those of you into homemade gifting, never underestimate the power of festooning friends and loved ones with butter (so long as your recipient lives nearby). I can all but guarantee that a multitude of doors will be opened up when fresh, creamy, whipped-with-love butter is offered.

FARM WIVES & FACTORIES

Butter has been consumed with delicious enthusiasm by humans for millennia. Derived from the Greek word *bou-tyron* (loosely translated as "cow cheese," from *bous* "ox or cow" and *tyros* "cheese"), butter use has been documented as far back as 2,000 B.C. From India to Norway, Japan to Britain, and many points in between, butter now makes its appearance on the global dining table.

Historically the work of farmers' wives and milkmaids, butter was once formed by hand-agitating cream via a plunger or dasher-style churn. If it was to be consumed shortly, the butter would be pressed into molds resembling sheaves of wheat or other decorative motifs. Otherwise, it was stored in wooden or ceramic tubs that could be taken to the local mercantile store for sale or bartering. Surplus butter was also stored in wooden casks called "firkins." Just prior to being shipped, small holes were made into the top of the firkins and salty brine was added to fill any airspace remaining between the butter and the cask. The brine acted as a preservative; butter stored this way could be stored in perfect condition for several months.

The production of butter began making the move from farm to factory during the late 19th century. In the traditional butter-making process, cream is allowed to naturally separate from milk, floating to the top in a thick layer, and fermenting, or "ripening," slightly. The ripening imbues the finished butter with a more complex flavor profile. This method of cream extraction, like many time-honored traditions, can take a while. For those looking to produce butter on a large scale, it was a costly, lengthy, yet necessary step.

Enter Swedish engineer Carl Gustaf Patrik de Laval, inventor of the centrifugal cream separator. This device enabled cream to be extracted from milk much more expediently. The first cream centrifuges were expensive, cumbersome contraptions, so farms shipped their milk whole to factories, which separated the cream there. Over time, advances were made in the size and cost of the separators, permitting farmers to swiftly extract cream in the comfort of their own farm-based creameries. This cream is then shipped out to factories, which transform it into butter in giant mechanical churns.

NUTRITIOUS & DELICIOUS

By definition, butter is an emulsion of butterfat, water, air, and possibly salt. A foodstuff composed almost entirely of cream—no wonder so many people love it, right? When cream is churned or otherwise seriously agitated, granules of butterfat glob together and separate from the whey, now known as buttermilk. The butterfat is then washed with water and kneaded until all excess liquid is removed. In commercial creameries, cream is churned with huge revolving blades at a very high speed, quickly forming butterfat that, in turn, is then mechanically kneaded. In home butter making, however, the churning and kneading are achieved through old-fashioned elbow grease.

Butter, as you may well have guessed, is rather high in fat. In fact, it's made almost entirely of milk fat: 80 to 86 percent, depending on the diet of the animal from which it was sourced. As far as nutrients go, butter contains protein, calcium, phosphorus, potassium, and vitamins A, D, and E. On a chemical level, butter consists of a mixture of triglycerides, or fatty acids, that form a bond. Melting at just below body temperature, somewhere between 90 and 95°F (32 and 35°C), butter can be spread easily at room temperature.

Old-fashioned butter churns

HOT 'N' BUTTERED

A somewhat fickle fat, once the short-chain fatty acids in butter are heated, its structure completely changes. So, let's say you're making a cookie dough and want to warm up some butter in the microwave to make it easier to cream with the sugar. Oops, you overheat it, resulting in a runny soup. Even if you put the melted butter back in the refrigerator and re-solidify it, its structure will never return to its original form, as its emulsion has been broken. This structural change will, in turn, affect just how well your cookie dough performs (word for the wise— not well at all!).

Cooking with butter also requires care. The milk solids in butter will burn at a pretty low temperature, around 250°F (121°C), making it fairly easy to scorch your butter over high heat. If you want to heat butter over high temperatures without scorching, you need to clarify it first. Clarifying butter involves melting it over a low temperature until the butterfat and milk solids form separate camps in your pan. Pour off the milk solids, and the remaining butterfat can be placed over high heat and won't burn. Clarifying butter does affect butter's taste, as many of its characteristic flavor elements reside in the milk solids.

COLOR THEORY

You may have wondered about the color of butter. Cow's milk is white, right? So, what's up with the yellow in butter? The greatest reason for the presence of a yellow hue in butter is carotene. Carotene is the vegetable form of vitamin A, which shows up not just in carrots, sweet potatoes, and cantaloupe, but also in grass. Butter made from the milk of cows that are allowed to pasture will have a greater degree of yellowish hue than from those fed on grain. The color will vary during times of the year when weather prevents cows from grazing or when grass is not growing in abundance. You can even see such seasonal variation in the milk of grass-fed cows, with more yellow milk in spring and summer and lighter toned milk during other times of the year.

Carotene contributes to the yellow hue in butter.

That's not to say that grain-fed cows don't also possess carotene in their butterfat; they do, only not as much. Because many people have become accustomed to yellow-hued butter (without really knowing why), a bit of annatto is often added to commercially produced butter. A natural coloring, annatto is produced from the reddish-tinted pulp that surrounds seeds of achiote tree fruit. Used to color everything from cheese to margarine and even lipstick, the inclusion of annatto mimics the yellow that would be found in summer milk from grass-fed cows.

STORING BUTTER

There are a number of different ways to keep your butter fresh and tasty—whether store-bought or homemade. If you make a large batch, you might even want to divide it into portions and employ several storage options at once. The addition of salt to homemade butter is entirely optional and mostly a matter of taste, although salted butter remains fresh a bit longer than unsalted butter.

Fresh

The best means I've found for storing butter at room temperature (ideal for spreadability!) is to employ the use of a butter crock. Developed long before the existence of refrigerators, butter crocks (also known as "French" or "Acadian" butter dishes) are simply two-piece earthenware containers. The lid of the crock has an interior bowl into which butter is packed. This lid is then inverted and placed inside the bottom bowl, into which cold water has been added. The water forms an airtight seal, preserving the butter by keeping it safe from bacteria in the air, while simultaneously holding the butter at room temperature. I've found that being fastidious about keeping crumbs out of the crock and changing out the water every two days keeps the butter fresh for about a week without spoilage. Sweet cream and cultured butter work equally well in a butter crock, so long as you are certain to keep it filled with cold water and consume the butter relatively quickly (never an issue in my house!).

A butter crock

Chilled

If you intend to refrigerate your homemade butter until ready for use, it's best to wrap it up or store it in an airtight container. Butter begins to deteriorate when exposed to air, so securing it tightly is paramount. Waxed or parchment paper are perfect for wrapping, while lidded glass containers keep butter fresh without imparting any residual food flavors or aromas that can sometimes show up in plastic containers. Butter stored in the refrigerator will last for four months, if held at temperatures between 32 and 38°F (0 and 3°C). Personally, I've found butter to taste considerably fresher if consumed within two months and butter made from raw milk to taste best if refrigerated for no longer than one month.

Storage vessels for fresh butter

Wrap butter in parchment or waxed paper for long-term storage.

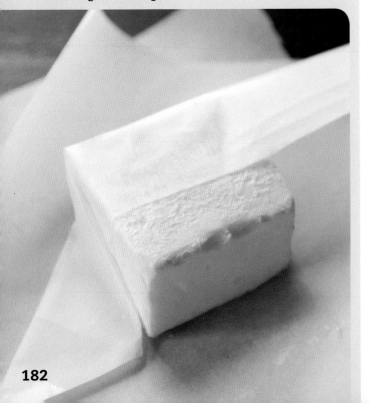

Frozen

If you have butter you'd like to freeze, you'll need to wrap it up or store it in an airtight container, much like refrigerator-bound butter. If you opt to wrap, I'd suggest you then slide it into an airtight freezer bag, to offer further protection against the formation of ice crystals. Frozen butter, if held at temperatures between -10 and -20°F (-23 and -28°C), will keep for up to one year. Its flavor will be best if used within six to eight months.

Butter Recipes

A number of different means of making butter at home exist. Depending on the type of equipment you own, and the flavor profile you prefer, it's possible to create butter manually, mechanically, or in a European "cultured" style, all from your kitchen. How cool is that? I have to warn you: the flavor of homemade butter is incomparable. When I first began making butter, I found myself daydreaming about it when doing something totally unrelated, such as folding laundry or planting my fall garden. Simply put, it's delicious. You'll wonder why you hadn't treated yourself to homemade butter much, much sooner!

Whipped Butter

For modern households, the mixer and food processor take on the responsibilities previously held by dashers, plungers, and barrel churns. Delicious butter can be yours in a fraction of the time provided by other means (although you won't get the same champion butter-making biceps you might have otherwise acquired).

Yield: *Approximately 1 cup*

YOU WILL NEED:

1 pint heavy cream

¼ teaspoon salt, optional

    Food processor or stand mixer

TO PREPARE:

1. Allow the cream to come to room temperature, right around 72 to 74°F (22 to 23°C). To do this, simply take the cream out of the refrigerator, set it on the counter, put a dairy thermometer into it, and check on it every 30 minutes or so until the temperature rises. This allows the cream to ripen and raises its acidity slightly, making it easier to whip and full of flavor.

2. Place the cream inside either a food processor or mixer bowl, and begin operating at medium speed. Turn the machine to high and process the cream through the butter-forming stages: first sloshy, then stiff, then finally dividing ranks and forming separately into butter and buttermilk. Depending on your machine, this could take between 6 and 9 minutes (I average around 8 minutes using a food processor).

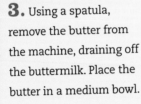

3. Using a spatula, remove the butter from the machine, draining off the buttermilk. Place the butter in a medium bowl.

4. Run cold water over the butter. Empty the water out, and repeat several times until the water is clear in the bowl. Strain off any remaining water. If using salt, stir it in with a metal spoon.

5. Place the butter on a cutting board. Using either clean hands, a wooden spoon, plastic pastry scraper, or a potato masher, begin pressing

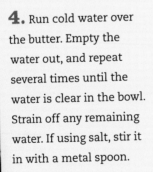

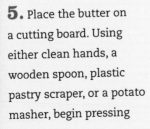

the butter repeatedly, allowing any liquid inside of it to drain off. Continue pressing until you no longer see liquid coming from your butter.

6. Depending on whether you intend to use your butter now or in the future, you can store it at room temperature in a butter crock, or chilled or frozen in waxed or parchment paper, or a covered container in the refrigerator or the freezer.

Shake, Rattle & Roll

It is entirely possible to make butter simply by shaking a jar of cream. Take turns passing the jar to helping hands around the house (including children), shake it while listening to your favorite radio program, agitate it as you play fetch with your dog—whatever it takes to make the time pass and the cream transform. When making butter, I like to hold on to all of the heavenly buttermilk that oozes out of the creamy mass during straining and pressing. Perfect for biscuits and cornbread, it also works well in waffles and pancakes.

Yield: *Approximately 1 cup*

TO PREPARE:

1. Allow the cream to come to room temperature, right around 72 to 74°F (22 to 23°C). To do this, simply take the cream out of the refrigerator, set it on the counter, put a dairy thermometer into it, and check on it every 30 minutes or so until the temperature rises. This allows the cream to ripen and raises its acidity slightly, making it easier to whip and full of flavor.

2. Place the cream and the marble inside your jar, secure the lid tightly, and begin shaking vigorously. Continue shaking, about once per second, until the cream begins to thicken. You'll hear it, as it changes from a constant sloshing sound to a heavier thud. This process will take anywhere between 5 and 30 minutes, depending on the intensity and frequency of the shaking.

3. Using a spatula, remove the butter from the jar, draining off the buttermilk. Take the marble out, and place the butter in a medium bowl. Finish the butter following steps 4 through 6 on page 184, and store as desired.

YOU WILL NEED:
1 pint heavy cream
1 glass marble
1 quart-sized jar with lid
1/4 teaspoon salt, optional

Cultured Butter

Cultured butter has a rich, mildly tangy flavor, and is far more common in Europe than in the United States, where sweet cream butter is preferred. This type of butter is made from fermented cream or cream that has had bacterial cultures added to it. During fermentation, bacteria present in the milk and air transform lactose (milk sugar) into lactic acid. This produces a product higher in butterfat than sweet cream butter (around 85 percent to sweet cream butter's 80 percent), providing a richer and, arguably, fuller butter flavor. Cultured butter purchased in stores is most often made with added *Lactococcus* and *Leuconostoc* bacteria. Homemade cultured butter is allowed to ferment naturally. **Yield: *Approximately 1 cup***

YOU WILL NEED:

1 pint heavy cream

3 tablespoons plain whole milk yogurt, sour cream, or crème fraîche

1/4 teaspoon salt, optional

Food processor or stand mixer

TO PREPARE:

1. Combine the cream and yogurt in a glass or ceramic bowl. Using a metal spoon, slowly and gradually incorporate the two until well mixed. Sealing the top with either plastic wrap or a plate large enough to cover the top of the bowl, let the mixture sit at a warm room temperature (75°F [24°C] is ideal) for 12 hours.

2. Place the fermented cream in a food processor or mixer bowl, and begin operating at medium speed. Turn the machine to high and process the cream through the butter-forming stages: first sloshy, then stiff, then finally dividing ranks and forming separately into butter and buttermilk. Depending on your machine, this could take between 6 and 9 minutes.

3. Using a spatula, remove the butter from the machine, draining off the buttermilk. Place the butter in a medium bowl. Finish the butter following steps 4 through 6 on page 184, and store as desired.

Oh Ghee, Oh My

A type of clarified butter, ghee is widely used in Indian cooking. It is formed by simmering unsalted butter until its water cooks away and three layers form: whey protein, liquid fat, and casein. Simply strain the clarified fat out from the whey protein casein particles, and you have ghee. Because the substances that would otherwise promote rancidity have been removed (the casein particles and water, and their attendant microbes and enzymes), ghee can remain without refrigeration for several months, so long as it is stored in an airtight container. It's important for ghee to remain free of moisture, so don't use a wet or moist spoon when extracting some from its container. Ghee is ideal for use in high-heat or deep-frying, as it will not scorch.

Yield: Slightly less than 2 cups

Homemade Ghee Recipe

YOU WILL NEED:

2 cups (4 sticks) unsalted butter

TO PREPARE:

1. Place the butter in a medium stainless-steel saucepan. Melt the butter, and bring to a boil over medium-high heat.

2. Once the butter begins boiling, reduce the heat to medium. Watch for a foam to appear on the surface of the melted butter. After the foam disappears, watch for a second foam to form and for the butter to turn a darker, golden color. At this point, you should be able to see brown particles (milk solids) on the bottom of the pan and detect a popcornish scent.

3. Using either several layers of coffee filters, a very fine-meshed sieve, or butter muslin, drain the mixture into a heatproof container. The strained liquid is clarified butter, or ghee.

4. Cover your container with a tight-fitting lid, and store out of direct sunlight at room temperature. Ghee solidifies when cool, but melts quickly when exposed to heat.

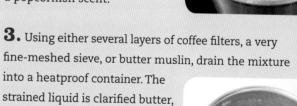

Compound Butters

Butter on its own is all well and good, but butter with flavorings added to it is transcendent! Butter can have any given number of helpful taste agents mixed in, creating what is called a "compound" or "composite" butter. Spices, herbs, liquors, dried fruits, powders—let your imagination go to town! Compound butters are delicious spread on bread and absolutely stellar atop hot vegetables or meats, and sweeter versions will make any dessert shine. The four variations below reflect a year's worth of seasonal offerings. Compound butter will keep in the freezer for up to two months.

Yield: Slightly more than ½ cup

YOU WILL NEED:

½ cup (1 stick) butter

Flavoring of your choice

TO PREPARE:

1. If you are beginning with chilled butter, it will first need to come to room temperature. Place it in a medium bowl for around 30 minutes to soften up.

2. If necessary, chop your flavorings finely and evenly. Combine with the butter and mash with a fork until well mixed.

3. Using a spatula, transfer your compound butter to a sheet of waxed paper. Wrapping the waxed paper around the butter, shape it into a cylinder approximately 6 to 8 inches (15.2 to 20.3 cm) long. Twist up each end of the waxed paper, as though it were a piece of candy, to secure the contents inside. Alternatively, place compound butter into individual butter molds.

4. Place the roll inside a plastic bag in the freezer and allow to firm up. Use as needed.

SEASONAL VARIATIONS

 SPRING

Lemon and Dill

This would be delicious spread onto steamed or pan-sautéed asparagus, spooned atop piping hot new potatoes, or dolloped onto grilled salmon. Add 1 tablespoon finely chopped fresh dill and the grated zest of 1 lemon.

☀ SUMMER

Herbal Bouquet

Try this compound butter spread liberally atop hot baguettes, tucked into mashed potatoes, or dolloped onto roasted root vegetables; you could also slice a coin onto a freshly seared steak. Finely chop 2 teaspoons each fresh marjoram, rosemary, thyme, tarragon, basil, and fresh or dried lavender buds. Mix the herbs with softened butter as described at left.

🍁 AUTUMN

Spice of Life

Tuck this butter into hot apple-walnut muffins, spread it on pumpkin pancakes, or add to straight-from-the-oven sweet potatoes. Yum! Mix together ½ teaspoon ground cinnamon, ¼ teaspoon ground nutmeg, ¼ teaspoon ground cloves, and ¼ teaspoon allspice. Combine the spices with the softened butter.

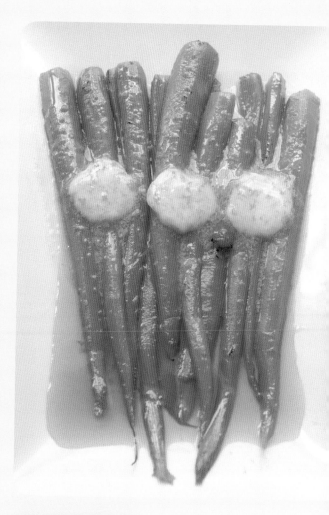

❄ WINTER

Triple Orange Compound Butter

This would be divine spread over hot waffles, nestled inside a poppy seed scone, or melted over glazed carrots. Combine 1 tablespoon orange juice, 2 teaspoons freshly grated orange zest, and 1½ tablespoons triple sec with the softened butter.

Butter & Ghee   **189**

Browned Butter

Literally translated as "hazelnut butter," *beurre noisette* (browned butter) adds a nutty, complex dash of deliciousness to both sweet and savory dishes and is an essential component in classical French cooking. Creating browned butter is somewhat similar to making ghee, or clarified butter, except that the milk solids aren't strained out. As delicious in pastries and desserts as it is spooned over fish, chicken, eggs, or vegetables (think broccoli and brussels sprouts), browned butter will "butter you up" and leave you begging for seconds.

Yield: Slightly less than ¼ cup

YOU WILL NEED:

4 tablespoons (½ stick) unsalted butter

TO PREPARE:

1. Create an ice-water bath by filling either the kitchen sink or a large metal bowl with cold water and a few ice cubes.

2. Place the butter in a medium stainless-steel saucepan. Melt, then bring to a boil over medium heat.

3. Once the butter begins boiling, monitor it closely. Stir continually, watching for the butter to turn a darker, golden, hazelnut-like color and a nutty, but not burned, smell.

4. Remove the saucepan from the heat, and dip the bottom into the waiting ice-water bath. This stops the browning process and prevents any continued in-pan cooking.

5. Serve immediately or store in a covered jar in the refrigerator and use within one week.

Variations: Browned butter possesses a seemingly infinite capacity for variation. Squeeze in the juice of half a lemon and 3 tablespoons chopped fresh parsley to create *beurre meunière*, perfect over fish, eggs, or steamed veggies. For a kiss of sweetness, add 1 tablespoon maple syrup and ¼ teaspoon ground nutmeg; serve over pancakes, waffles, or crepes.

Chapter 5

Cultured Dairy:
Cultivated Tastes

From Greece to Germany, Australia to the Americas, cultured dairy products are integral parts of numerous food cultures. The puckery twang characteristic of these foods is only part of their appeal. Containing a veritable bounty of beneficial bacteria, cultured foods are both good to eat and good for you. The best part is how easy they are to make at home. Get ready to learn just how delicious it is to sample the world's cultures.

FERMENTING CHANGE

Cultured dairy products are, by definition, those that have undergone fermentation. Fermentation in foods is a result of the action of yeast and bacteria. Chemically, carbohydrates are transformed into alcohol and carbon dioxide (as well as other organic acids) in an anaerobic environment (one that is lacking oxygen).

As discussed in the recipe for cultured butter (page 186) in chapter 4, during fermentation, bacteria found in milk and air interact, turning milk sugar (lactose) into lactic acid. The bacteria responsible for this conversion can include *Streptococcus*, *Lactobacillus*, *Lactococcus*, and *Leuconostoc*. When exposed to temperatures around 90°F (32°C), these bacteria begin to proliferate very, very rapidly—as in, doubled-in-size-in-20-minutes rapidly.

The presence of these bacteria result in a number of features specific to fermented foods. The development of a characteristic "cultured" flavor is one such feature. Fermented dairy products also offer increased digestibility, as the proteins and sugars in the milk have already begun to break down, rendering them "predigested." For this reason many people who avoid drinking milk due to lactose-intolerance find that they have no problem digesting dairy products that have been cultured. There is also evidence that consumption of fermented dairy products may lower cholesterol, protect against bone loss, and bolster the immune system against illness.

CULTURAL STUDIES

Culturing dairy is nothing new. People have been fermenting dairy products for just about as long as they've been domesticating animals. You've got to do something with all that milk, right? Before the age of refrigeration, warm milk from animals was gathered and allowed to ferment, using the remains of previously cultured batches as the "starter." Common strains of *Streptococcus* and *Lactobacillus* did all the work, beating out the microbial competition in a bacterial smackdown.

Kefir, buttermilk, and yogurt are all examples of cultured dairy products.

As a result, the milk was prevented from spoiling and could be stored for several days—or possibly even weeks—without refrigeration.

Various strains of culturing bacteria can now be prepared in the laboratory and are available commercially to the home dairy-maker, permitting a wide range of cultured dairy alchemy. In many of the recipes in this chapter, it is possible to use an existing batch of cultured dairy (either purchased or made at home) as your starter, such as yogurt you made or gathered up at the grocery store. Alternatively, you can use a purchased starter, available from dairy-making supply companies, to inoculate fresh milk and get the party started.

Yogurt

Spooned into granola, mixed with cucumber and spices for a cooling raita, or blended into a refreshing fruit shake, yogurt has a long and storied reputation as a cross-cultural palate-pleaser. Yogurt's pudding-like texture, coupled with an intense tanginess, makes it perfect for any meal, from breakfast to dinner (think chilled yogurt soup) to dessert. This cultured treat is a treasure trove of vitamins and minerals, containing generous amounts of iodine, calcium, phosphorus, potassium, zinc, pantothenic acid, and vitamins B_2 and B_{12}. It is also a great source of protein, with 8 ounces supplying around 8 grams.

Prior to the 20th century, yogurt was consumed primarily in the Middle East, Asia, Russia, and several eastern European countries. During the 1900s, research conducted by Dr. Ilya Mechnikov brought yogurt to the attention of the Western world. The Ukrainian-born doctor was given a Nobel prize for

his work on the role of beneficial bacteria—now commonly known as probiotics—in digestion. Based on the dietary habits of some of the world's longest-lived individuals, such as inhabitants of eastern Europe, known for their regular consumption of cultured dairy foods, he theorized that lactic acid could prolong life, and consumed soured milk and yogurt daily. His research inspired a new generation of yogurt makers and eaters, introducing the puckery treat to the entire world.

Yogurt Recipe

When you're just starting out, you have the option of using a packet of commercially prepared yogurt starter or a dollop of prepared yogurt, purchased from the market. If you decide to use prepared yogurt, make certain it indicates somewhere on the label that it possesses "live, active cultures." The existence of these cultures is absolutely crucial to the success of your batch. While you can use milk of any type, the higher the butterfat in your ingredients, the thicker and creamier the end product will be.

Yield: *Slightly more than 4 cups; 5 half-pints, if jarred*

TO PREPARE:

1. If you are using a thickening agent, whisk the dried milk or gelatin into the milk until combined. Warm the milk gently in a medium saucepan over medium-high heat until it almost reaches the boiling point, right around 180°F (82°C).

2. Remove the milk from the heat and allow it to cool to 110 to 115°F (43 to 46°C). Using a metal spoon, stir in the yogurt or dried yogurt culture. Mix until well incorporated.

3. Transfer the mixture to whatever container you will be culturing it in, such as yogurt machine glass jars, mason jars, lidded glass bowl, or a thermos.

4. Hold the yogurt at 110 to 115°F (43 to 46°C) for the next 6 hours. Consider any of the "Incubating Ideas" options as a way to maintain the necessary temperature for proper yogurt formation.

5. Store the yogurt in an airtight container in the refrigerator, and use within one to two weeks.

"Incubating Ideas": DIY Yogurt Makers

Try any one of these ideas for successfully regulating yogurt without the aid of an electric yogurt maker.

OVEN

Preheat an oven to 120°F (49°C). Place the yogurt mixture in a glass or ceramic bowl, and cover with a lid or plate. Turn the oven off, and place the yogurt inside for 6 hours.

COOLER

Place the yogurt mixture into one (or several, depending on volume) glass jars. Place the jars in a small to medium insulated cooler overnight, along with several jars of hot water.

SLOW COOKER

Preheat a slow cooker on low. Add glass jars of yogurt to the pot. Turn off the heat, cover with a lid, and allow to incubate 6 hours or overnight.

SUN

Let the sun do all the cooking for you. Place your yogurt mixture in a ceramic or glass bowl, cover with a lid, and put in a spot that will be consistently sunny for 4 to 6 hours. During the dog days of summer, when the sun is seriously scorching, it might be wise to either start this means of incubating quite early in the morning (7-ish), or wait for a more hospitable, balmier day to make yogurt. This technique can be used year-round, as you'll be culturing your yogurt indoors, so long as the ambient room temperature remains between 68 and 74°F (20 and 23°C).

THERMOS

Simply fill an insulated thermos with your yogurt mixture, put the lid on, wrap a couple of kitchen towels around it, and put in an area away from drafts, such as a pantry or cabinet, for 6 hours or overnight. The ambient temperature should be somewhere between 68 and 74°F (20 and 23°C) for your yogurt to culture properly.

Buttermilk

My grandmother was absolutely wild about buttermilk. It was always in her refrigerator and, if pressed to choose, was probably her favorite beverage, bar none. Nanny's buttermilk was the store-bought kind, but making it at home couldn't be easier. In fact, when you make butter, you produce one type of buttermilk as a by-product, hence the original meaning of the term. This is considered "traditional" buttermilk. Store-bought buttermilk, or cultured buttermilk, is a fermented beverage, unrelated to butter-making. Similar in flavor to yogurt, buttermilk's texture is thicker, coating the entire tongue. If cultured, or allowed to ferment like yogurt, buttermilk becomes imbued with lactic acid, giving it the telltale sour flavor. (Buttermilk that is simply the liquid left behind in making butter at home isn't cultured.) Commercially prepared buttermilk is made by adding bacterial culture to warmed milk and then holding the mixture at a low temperature for 12 to 15 hours. Homemade buttermilk will be made in the same manner, either by using remnants of the last batch of cultured buttermilk you created, or by inoculating milk with a buttermilk starter culture.

Buttermilk Recipe

Once you get on board with using buttermilk, you'll find all sorts of opportunities to sneak it in. This recipe would be delicious served ice cold (my grandmother's preference), incorporated into biscuits (my preference), or rendered into an ice cream with some serious kick (everyone in the world's preference). Check the label and make sure that your starter buttermilk contains live, active cultures.

Yield: _Slightly more than 4 cups_

YOU WILL NEED:

4 cups whole or skim milk

¼ cup cultured buttermilk or 1 packet dried buttermilk culture

TO PREPARE:

1. Warm the milk gently in a medium saucepan over medium-high heat until it reaches 85°F (29°C).

2. Transfer the milk to a glass or ceramic container. Using a metal spoon or a wire whisk, stir in the buttermilk or dried buttermilk culture. Mix until well incorporated.

3. Cover the container with a plate or lid, and leave it at room temperature for 12 hours.

4. Store the buttermilk in an airtight container in the refrigerator and use within one to two weeks.

Kefir

Whether you pronounce it *ka-fear*, *kef-ur*, or *key-fur* makes no difference. Similar in a number of ways to yogurt, kefir's difference lies in the bacteria it possesses. Kefir contains *Lactobacillus Caucasus*, *Acetobacter* species, and *Saccharomyces* (yeast), all known for their ability to penetrate the mucosal lining of the digestive tract. These microbes colonize the intestinal lining, giving the boot to harmful intruders potentially residing there. As a result, it becomes easier for your body to ward off pathogens like intestinal parasites and *E. coli*.

You can make kefir from any type of milk, including animal (cow, sheep, goat, what have you), coconut, rice, and soy. While the milk used can be variable, the invariable part of the recipe is kefir grains—a fascinating blend of bacteria and yeasts in a protein/lipid/sugar base. These grains look like cauliflower or white coral and can be as tiny as a grain of rice or as large as a human hand. The grains activate the fermentation process and are strained out before consumption. Kefir made at home is allowed to culture at ambient room temperature for up to a day. As it ferments, the kefir sours and becomes mildly carbonated, becoming very

mildly alcoholic in the process (although you won't be getting drunk off of kefir, at levels of 1 to 2 percent!).

Kefir Recipe #1 (Using Live Grains)

Many find kefir perfect completely unadorned, without any flavor additions. It is also delicious blended with fruit, nuts, spices, and fresh herbs. (Strawberries and vanilla bean flecks mixed into fresh kefir is a personal favorite). Kefir is also an ideal candidate for inclusion in cornbread, its puckery punch a perfect foil to corn's sweetness!

Yield: *Slightly more than 3 cups*

YOU WILL NEED:
3 cups whole, skim, or low-fat milk
4 tablespoons live kefir grains

TO PREPARE:

1. Place the milk in a glass or ceramic container, and add the kefir grains.

2. Stir the grains gently, cover the jar loosely with a kitchen cloth, and leave it at room temperature for 18 to 24 hours.

3. At the end of the culturing time, once the mixture begins to thicken up a bit, give the jar a gentle stir. Strain off the liquid through a sieve or small-holed colander, taking care not to press on the grains while straining.

4. Transfer the strained liquid to a clean glass jar with a lid, and store in the refrigerator for up to three weeks.

5. To store the grains for future use, do not rinse them after straining. Instead, gently place the still-moist grains in a clean, lidded jar, and store them in the refrigerator. When you are ready, follow recipe steps 1 through 4 to make a new batch. With each subsequent batch, the number of kefir grains will continue to multiply. You can either choose to share some kefir booty with friends and family, or store the grains in your refrigerator for future use.

Kefir Recipe #2 (Using Dried Starter Culture)

Kefir made from powdered starter culture will be slightly less fermented than that made from live grains. It will possess all of the same health benefits, however. Kefir made from starter culture can be used to make successive batches up to six or seven times. After that, you'll need to make a fresh batch using a new packet ofpowdered culture. Kefir made from live grains can be used to start new batches pretty much indefinitely.

Yield: Slightly more than 1 gallon

YOU WILL NEED:

1 gallon milk

1 packet dried kefir culture

TO PREPARE:

1. Warm the milk gently in a medium saucepan over medium-high heat until it reaches 85°F (29°C).

2. Transfer the milk to a glass or ceramic container. Using a metal spoon or wire whisk, stir in the dried culture. Mix until well incorporated.

3. Cover the container with a plate or lid, and leave it at room temperature for 12 hours.

4. Store the kefir in an airtight container in the refrigerator, and use within three weeks. Once you've made your first batch of kefir, you can use that kefir to make successive batches before a new packet of culture will be required. To make successive batches, simply follow the recipe as above, replacing the starter culture packet with 1 cup kefir.

Sour Cream

Thick, tangy, and creamy, sour cream is a cultured dairy hall of famer. You begin with cream, which is, really, where all good things begin. To cream you add a starter culture, you provide a bit of heat, and end up with a product of a tartly sublime nature. Appearing in various incarnations worldwide, sour cream makes cameos in dishes as varied as Russian blini and ranch dressing.

Sour cream is quite high in butterfat, averaging between 12 and 18 percent. It is particularly well suited to thickening soups and sauces or as an ingredient in a thick dip. Sour cream can be made at home either by the addition of a prepared cultured product (in this case buttermilk) or a purchased dried starter culture. I'd make a strong case for whipping up your own sour cream, as many store-bought varieties include additional thickening agents and acids to artificially mimic the characteristic lactic-acid-derived sourness.

Sour Cream Recipe

From Hungarian goulash to seven-layer bean dip, sour cream crosses all cultural divides. Try it as a baked potato topper, to impart a tart touch to coffee cake, or as a means of tempering the fiery heat of enchiladas.

Yield: *Slightly more than 1 cup*

YOU WILL NEED:

1 cup heavy cream

¼ cup buttermilk*

*You can also make sour cream using a packet of dried starter culture. Simply increase the cream to 4 cups and follow the recipe as written, substituting your packaged culture for the buttermilk.

TO PREPARE:

1. Warm the cream gently in a small saucepan over medium-high heat until it reaches 85°F (29°C).

2. Transfer the cream to a glass or ceramic container. Using a metal spoon, stir in the buttermilk or dried culture. Mix until well incorporated.

3. Cover the container with a plate or lid, and leave it at room temperature for 12 hours.

4. After the culturing time has passed, your cream should have noticeably thickened. Store the sour cream in an airtight container in the refrigerator, and use within one to two weeks.

Crème Fraîche

Similar in flavor to sour cream, crème fraîche (pronounced "krem fresh") is cultured heavy cream, French-style. Developed before the time of refrigeration, crème fraîche cultured itself, as it were. As raw, unpasteurized cream sat at ambient temperature in buckets awaiting transport to market, lactic acid cultures formed and mild fermentation began to occur. The resultant tangy, soured taste became an intrinsic component of the French culinary landscape—and the world is all the better for it, in my opinion. Pasteurized cream won't develop lactic acid in the same manner if left to sit at room temperature, as the viable cultures were killed off during the pasteurization process. It will need to have cultures introduced to it in order for fermentation to occur.

Exceptionally velvety, the high fat content of crème fraîche prevents it from curdling when added to hot sauces and soups, making it a favorite of professional and home chefs alike. The bacterial cultures found in this cultured dairy product, introduced via either buttermilk, sour cream, or dried starter cultures, impart both flavor and thickness. Crème fraîche will be almost runny once first made but gains body and solidifies over time. Flowing and oozy or firm and substantive, crème fraîche holds its own in the pantheon of cultured dairy delights.

Crème Fraîche Recipe

Its applications seemingly infinite, crème fraîche is exquisite incorporated into sauces for pork or chicken, whipped with a smidge of confectioners' sugar and dolloped over hot fruit crisps, or stirred into hot pasta with fresh herbs.

Yield: Slightly more than 1 cup

YOU WILL NEED:

1 cup heavy cream

2 tablespoons buttermilk or sour cream*

  *You can also make crème fraîche using a packet of dried starter culture. Simply increase from 1 cup heavy cream to 4 cups cream and follow the recipe as written, substituting your packaged culture for the buttermilk or yogurt.

TO PREPARE:

1. Warm the cream gently in a small saucepan over medium-high heat until it reaches 85°F (29°C).

2. Transfer the cream to a glass or ceramic container. Using a metal spoon, stir in buttermilk, sour cream, or dried culture. Mix until well incorporated.

3. Cover the container with a plate or lid, and leave it at room temperature for 12 hours.

4. After the culturing time, your cream should have noticeably thickened. Store the crème fraîche in an airtight container in the refrigerator, and use within one to two weeks.

Quark

A relative newcomer to the U.S. culinary landscape, quark has a long history of hearty consumption in Europe. It is typically described as an unaged curd cheese, although the fact that it is made with lactic acid renders it a cultured product. German quark is typically served creamy, containing a good deal of the quark's whey, while other countries prepare theirs with less whey, forming a drier, firmer product. Quark can be made with either cultured buttermilk or yogurt. It is really quite easy to prepare and acts as an incredibly versatile ingredient in a wide variety of dishes.

Quark Recipe

Try mixing quark into dips or sauces, especially creamy salad dressings. It also makes a tasty dessert if drizzled with a bit of honey and served alongside fresh fruit; throw in some buttery shortbread cookies if you're feeling especially decadent!

Yield: *Slightly more than 4 cups*

YOU WILL NEED:

- 4 cups whole, skim, or low-fat milk
- 4 tablespoons cultured buttermilk or yogurt

TO PREPARE:

1. Warm the milk gently in a medium saucepan over medium-high heat until it reaches 105°F (41°C).

2. Transfer the milk to a glass or ceramic container. Using a metal spoon, stir in the buttermilk or yogurt. Mix until well incorporated.

3. Hold the mixture at 105°F (41°C) for the next 4 hours. Consider any of the "Incubating Ideas" discussed on page 194 for a way to maintain the temperature.

4. After 4 hours, place the container in the refrigerator. The mixture will thicken slightly during this time. Allow the mixture to cool completely, 2 to 3 hours.

5. Once it is chilled, transfer the mixture to a colander lined with butter muslin. Set the colander inside a larger bowl, which will serve as a drip pan. Ladle the curds into the colander, tie the ends of the butter muslin into a knot, and return to the refrigerator. Allow the bag to drain for at least 8 hours or overnight.

6. Once drained, transfer the quark from butter muslin to an airtight container, and keep covered in the refrigerator. Use within one to two weeks.

Chapter 6

Cheese

Cheese is quite possibly *the* universal dairy product. Cultures the world over have nuanced it, celebrated it, and given it their own signature twists. Now you can put your spin on this beloved global food, feeling confident in the knowledge that your end product will be free of the additives and preservatives often added to commercially prepared cheeses.

Home cheese-making is an exceptionally good way to get a bit closer to the cheeses you have known and loved for so long. It's also much easier than many people think. Grab a gallon or two of milk, follow my home-kitchen-tested recipes, and you'll be savoring homemade mascarpone, Swiss, and mozzarella in no time. Invite friends or family over for a cheese-centered dinner, and watch their jaws drop in wonder when you tell them you crafted it yourself!

BASIC TECHNIQUES

Cheese-making involves many of the same steps, no matter if you're making paneer or provolone. The constants include milk, heat of some degree, bacteria, and often rennet. The variation comes in temperature, how the curd is handled, types of cultures and milk used, and whether you will be pressing or drying your cheese.

The basic techniques involved in making cheese at home are detailed below. Those steps that are used only in certain types of cheese, such as hard cheeses, will be noted accordingly. When you start making your cheese, refer back to these instructions as needed. They'll provide more detailed explanations of each step than those offered in individual recipes.

 ## Heating the Milk

The first step in cheese-making, whether you're making a soft or hard cheese, is heating the milk. The increase in temperature helps to expedite the conversion of lactose to lactic acid. This enables the bacterial cultures added to the milk to grow, helping coagulation (the formation of curds) and helping curds to later separate from whey.

It's very important to closely monitor the temperature of the milk as it heats. If allowed to overheat, the milk's ability to interact properly with the starter culture will be compromised. So, while it's said that a watched pot never boils, a watched pot of milk never overheats! Keep your dairy thermometer handy and check often, stirring frequently to ensure the even distribution of heat.

Milk can be heated in one of two ways: directly or indirectly. (In the recipes in this book, I will indicate whether direct or indirect heating is to be used.) In direct heating, milk is warmed in a pot set directly over a heat source. Indirect heating warms milk to the desired temperature by means of a double boiler or a sink filled with hot water. If you opt to use a double boiler, remember that the water in the bottom pot shouldn't make contact with the underside of the pot on top. Also, keep water to a gentle simmer, instead of a full, rolling boil. To use the water bath method, put a pot or metal bowl containing the milk in the sink and fill the sink with water warmed to approximately 10 degrees hotter than the target temperature.

2 Adding Starter

Next up in the cheese-making process is the addition of a starter to the warmed milk. Starters include mesophilic and thermophilic cultures in their various forms (see Starter Cultures on page 162 for more information). Other recipes call for vinegar or cultured dairy products, such as yogurt, sour cream, or buttermilk. Starters aid in coagulation and begin the acidification process, imparting the flavors characteristic to certain cheeses.

3 Including Additives

For some types of cheeses, additives such as calcium chloride, annatto, lipase, molds, or flavorings may be used. These additives all must be diluted in sterilized water before use. (Using nonsterilized water runs the risk of introducing nasty contaminants such as chlorine that have no place in cheese.) Simply boil the amount of water you'll need, allow it to come to room temperature, and then store it in a clean, sterilized bottle in your refrigerator until needed. When a recipe in this book calls for an additive requiring dilution, it will be noted in the ingredient listing.

4 Adding Rennet

Rennet is used in cheese-making to separate the curds from the whey. It's a fickle muse, however, so take care when adding it to your heated milk. Follow the recipe and measure carefully, or you could end up with a cheese that refuses to set or an acrid, noncompliant curd.

As with additives, rennet will need to be diluted prior to use, regardless of whether your rennet is a liquid, a powder, or a tablet (see page 164 for more information on available forms of rennet). When called for in a recipe, instructions to dilute rennet will be noted

in the ingredient listing. Once diluted, rennet must be evenly dispersed within the milk. This is achieved by stirring the milk constantly for 30 seconds, being certain that your stirring spoon reaches all the way to the bottom of the pot. You'll then cover the pot with a lid, leaving the curd to set.

5 Setting Curds

This is a rest step. Letting your pot sit allows the milk to properly sour. Temperature variations and too much jostling and movement can upset the acidification process, so no dance parties in the kitchen once your curd begins its slumber! Take note of the curdling time indicated in the recipe, and let the pot sit undisturbed the entire time.

6 Cutting Curds

Once your curds have set, it's time to cut them. Cutting the curds releases the whey from the curd, allowing the curd to form a mass that will dry out and solidify into one block during aging. You'll know you've reached the right stage for cutting when you achieve what's known as a "clean

break." This is what is seen when you insert your finger, a knife, or a thermometer into the curd and it breaks away cleanly and clearly. If you test and a clean break doesn't form, wait 5 or so minutes and then check again.

Once you're sure your curd has set, it's time to start cutting. The manner in which your cheese will be cut is determined by what type of cheese it will ultimately become—soft or hard. Adhere to the following cutting instructions depending on what you are making.

6A Soft Cheese Curd Cutting

With soft cheeses and bacteria- and mold-ripened cheeses, it's best to not disturb the curd too much. The less interference at this stage, the more velvety your cheese will ultimately be. Using a large perforated ladle, gently scoop out spoonfuls of curd. Transfer the curds to either a cheese mold or a butter-muslin-lined colander, as indicated in your recipe.

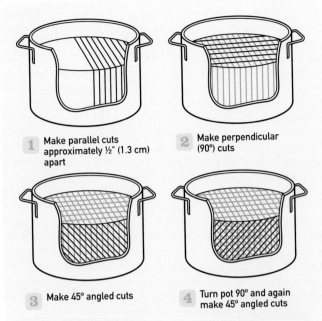

1 Make parallel cuts approximately ½" (1.3 cm) apart

2 Make perpendicular (90°) cuts

3 Make 45° angled cuts

4 Turn pot 90° and again make 45° angled cuts

6B Hard Cheese Curd Cutting

To cut the curds effectively, you'll need to be able to cut all the way to the bottom of your pot. This is best achieved by using a knife with a long blade, such as a bread knife or a curd knife, whose sole purpose in life is this very task. To the best of your ability, form straight cuts ½ inch (1.3 cm) apart, slicing at a 90° angle from one side of the pot clear across. Once you've cut across horizontally, turn your pot 90°and begin cutting vertically, in the same consistent-width manner, until you've cut a checkerboard pattern. After you've cut in both directions, turn the pot back to the original direction and begin cutting again, on a 45° angle this time. Turn the pot one last time and cut again along those lines, again on a 45° angle. You have now successfully cut your cheese!

7 Stirring Curds (Hard Cheeses Only)

When making hard cheeses, the curds will need to be stirred just a bit after they are cut, but before they are heated. This allows any residual whey to drain out of the curds. After cutting the curds, allow them to rest for 5 minutes. Then, using a perforated metal spoon, give the curds a gentle stir. Turn them over each other, being certain to reach all the way to the bottom of the pot. If you see any oversized curds, cut them into ½-inch (1.3 cm) cubes.

8 Heating Curds (Hard Cheeses Only)

After the curd has been cut and stirred, it will be lightly heated. This forces any remaining whey from the curd, resulting in a firmer curd when it is eventually molded and

pressed. Firmer curds are what you want, as they provide the body needed for the cheese to meld together into one mass during pressing. Heat is introduced to the curds very slowly using a double boiler or a hot water bath, incrementally raising the heat by 2 degrees every 5 to 10 minutes. As they warm, the curds will begin to shrink and force out the whey. The curds are held at the temperature indicated in your recipe for the specified period of time and then removed from the heat for draining.

9 Draining

Draining is the next-to-last attempt at removing any sneaky, hold-out whey remaining in the curd. The manner in which your curds will be drained is determined by what type of cheese you are making: hard, soft, or mold- or bacteria-ripened.

9 A Hard Cheese Draining

Transfer the curds to a cheesecloth-lined colander, strainer, or large sieve. Place the colander inside a large bowl to collect the dripping whey. Make sure the colander sits high enough above the bottom of the collecting bowl

not to touch the gathering whey as it rises. Allow the curd to drain for the duration indicated in your recipe.

9 B Soft Cheese Draining

For soft cheeses, the curds are drained just after you cut them, skipping the steps for stirring and heating. Carefully transfer the curds to a butter-muslin-lined colander, strainer, or large sieve. Next, tie the four corners of the butter muslin into a strong, secure knot. Suspend the knotted bag either

over the sink, using the faucet to secure it, or thread a wooden spoon through the center of the knot and hang the bag over a pot large enough to collect the dripping whey. I like to wrap a bungee cord around my bag and hang the cord from the sink faucet. Allow the bag to drain for the duration indicated in your recipe.

9 C Mold- and Bacteria-ripened Cheese Draining

Transfer the curds directly to cheese molds. Place the filled molds over open racks that are in turn placed over a rectangular collecting container, such as a baking pan or a plastic bin. You can use old refrigerator racks, broiler pan racks, cookie cooling racks, or any other similar rack. Allow the cheese to drain for the duration indicated in your recipe.

10 Milling Curds (Hard Cheeses Only)

After the curds have drained, gently transfer them to a large glass, metal, or ceramic bowl. Using your fingertips, very delicately break up the curds into smaller pieces. The required size will be indicated by your recipe. Be very gentle here, as rough-handling the curd at this point could cause a potentially disastrous loss of butterfat, a definite no-no. Whatever you do, don't squeeze the curd. You need all the moisture to stay inside where it belongs.

11 Salting

As discussed in the Ingredients chapter, salt serves a number of vital functions in home cheese-making. It helps draw out moisture, puts the kibosh on opportunistic bacteria, and, of course, contributes to flavor. Additionally, it slows down growth of lactic acid, beneficial when you are getting ready to age your cheese. Two methods of salting are used: direct salting and brining. Consult your recipe to determine which method you will be using.

11 A Direct Salting

This manner of salting involves adding salt granules directly to the curds. Salt soft cheeses directly by transferring the drained curd to a bowl, adding the amount of salt indicated in the recipe, and stirring with a metal spoon. For hard cheeses, transfer the curds to a bowl, sprinkle the amount of salt indicated over the curds, and then, with clean hands, gently incorporate salt throughout. Mold- and bacteria-ripened cheeses are salted after the curd comes out of its mold. Salt is rubbed over the surface of the cheese just prior to the drying stage.

11 B Brining

Only certain types of cheese are salted by brining, usually those with relatively short aging times. A brine is simply a salt and water solution. The curd is submerged in the solution for a specified length of time. Feta is one of the most widely known brined cheeses, its salty taste giving away its vacation spent at the saltwater spa.

12 Molding and Pressing

Molding and pressing are the final attempts at ridding a cheese of any residual whey. Nearly all cheeses are molded, whether into a hand-shaped log, as with chèvre, or packed into a round mold with a follower on top, as with cheddar, for instance. The mold used is determined both by personal preference and requirements of individual cheeses. According to your recipe, allow your curds to reach 65 to 70°F (18 to 21°C). Next, line your mold with cheesecloth if necessary (some cheeses don't require the use of cheesecloth during molding; individual recipes will indicate when the use of cheesecloth is recommended). Spoon the curds into the mold. If your cheese will not be pressed for long, or not at all, pack the curds in loosely. If your cheese will undergo a long pressing time, pack the curds in tightly and snugly.

For hard cheeses, the mold, filled with curd, is now placed into a cheese press. A follower (a top that fits into the mold and is slightly smaller than its circumference) is placed atop

the mold. Pressure is incrementally applied to the mold for a specified period of time. Be careful when applying pressure. Too much could cause the outer rind of your cheese to split, letting bacteria in. Too little could prevent whey from being squeezed out, resulting in cheese that is too dense. Specific pressures and pressing times will be indicated in individual recipes. Generally speaking, the harder the finished cheese, the longer the pressing time.

13 Misting and Aeration
(Mold- and Bacteria-ripened Cheeses Only)

If you are making a mold- or bacteria-ripened cheese, you will need to inoculate your curd. Depending on the variety of cheese you are making, inoculation will occur either before or after molding and pressing. For blue cheeses, holes are made in the inoculated pressed curd with a sterilized tool (the pointy end of a dairy thermometer works dandy). The mold grows rapidly, spreading into the cheese's interior. For rind mold-ripened cheeses, such as Camembert and Brie, mold is misted onto the outside of the pressed curd. In either case the curd is then placed in a ripening refrigerator and kept at a certain temperature for a specific duration to allow the mold to develop.

14 Drying (Hard Cheeses Only)

After pressing, most hard cheeses require a bit of room-temperature drying. If it's the dog days of summer and your kitchen lacks air conditioning, room temperature might be too warm. Schedule your cheese-making activities so that the drying can be achieved overnight, when it's cooler, or in the coolest part of your house (anything cooler than about 72°F [22°C] is fine). Gently remove the pressed curd from the mold, and place it on a cheese board or drying mat (refer to the

Equipment chapter for cheese board and drying mat recommendations). Allow the cheese to rest for several days until it feels dry to the touch. In the event that any mold should form on the surface (as in, mold that you didn't intend to be there!), dip a bit of cheesecloth into some vinegar or saltwater, wring it out, and lightly rub the cheese until the mold is gone.

15 Waxing (Hard Cheeses Only)

Once fully dried, some cheeses are waxed to keep them from drying out or molding during aging. Place the cheese in a refrigerator until completely cool. When it is ready, remove it from the refrigerator and rub the entire surface with white vinegar to deter the growth of mold. Next, turn the fan of a stove hood to high. Melt the wax in a double boiler over medium heat (as mentioned in the Equipment chapter, it is best to dedicate a used or worn-out pot exclusively to this purpose, as removing wax from a pan can be difficult, if not impossible). Cheese wax vapors are rather flammable, so take caution. You know the wax is ready when it's fully melted, but never let it boil.

You can apply wax with a brush or by dipping the cheese fully into the wax. Dip a cheese brush or other natural-bristle brush into the wax and brush it over the cheese, completely covering one side. Let it cool, then turn and repeat on the other side. Once the second side has cooled, repeat the process. To dip, quickly dunk the entire cheese mass directly into the wax, coating one side. Take care, as the wax can get quite slippery. Allow the wax to cool and then repeat on the other side. After the second side has cooled, repeat the process. If any mold appears on the wax during aging, just cut it off. Your cheese is fine, nestled snugly inside.

16 Aging

The final step in the home cheese-making process, aging finishes off your cheese, imparting characteristic flavor, texture, and aroma. Just as with wine, a little maturing time allows the cheese to become nuanced and distinctive. Aging times are highly variable, depending on the cheese you are making. Amounts range from a few days to years.

Controlling temperature and humidity during the aging process is essential. Accordingly, you'll need to ensure an environment conducive to the needs of your cheese. Refer to the discussion of a ripening refrigerator, or "modern-day cheese cave," on page 175 for ideas on achieving the proper climatic conditions needed for cheese-making. If you use

a basement, you'll need to monitor the temperature and humidity levels routinely. This can be done with the aid of a thermometer and a hygrometer (a device that measures humidity). You can find a combined meter at a hardware or home building supply store. Hygrometers are also available at pet stores, where they are sold for monitoring the humidity level of reptile tanks.

If you use a refrigerator, set the temperature to 55°F (13°C) and place a bowl of water in the fridge's bottom. Make sure it is always filled with water; otherwise, your humidity level could become imbalanced.

You will need to turn your cheese periodically as it ages to ensure that the moisture, fat, and proteins in the cheese are distributed evenly and don't end up all smushed together on one side. Turning also prevents the buildup of moisture on the cheese bottom, which could in turn lead to rot. You don't want to have come this far along in the game only to be outdone by a bit of moisture, do you? Turn your cheese as indicated in your recipe, and stop moisture in its tracks.

S oft, unripened, unaged cheeses are the very best place to begin your cheese-making adventures. They're easy to make, most are ready to eat within several hours, and all are generally quite forgiving. Fresh milk is simply curdled, drained, and in some cases molded, with little additional processing. These cheeses are generally spreadable, creamy, and milder in both flavor and aroma than aged cheeses, which develop sharper, more piquant, pungent tastes and scents over time.

Queso Blanco

Prep Time: 45 to 60 minutes
Draining Time: 3 to 5 hours
Heating Method: Direct

If you're a fan of Central and South American cuisines, chances are you've rubbed shoulders with queso blanco. Mildly sweet, this soft cheese is a perfect partner to spicy foods, providing a creamy, cool counterpoint to the heat of chilies. It is also rather firm, making it perfect for frying or broiling, as it retains its body and shape. Queso blanco is ideal if you want to make your own cheese but find yourself short on time, as it can be made and used the same day.

Yield: Approximately 1 pound

YOU WILL NEED:

1 gallon whole goat's or cow's milk

¼ teaspoon calcium chloride mixed with ¼ cup cold, sterilized water*

5 tablespoons apple cider vinegar

*Omit if using raw milk.

TO PREPARE:

1. In a medium saucepan, gradually warm the milk to 175 to 180°F (79 to 82°C) directly over medium-low heat. Monitor the temperature closely with a dairy thermometer to avoid overheating. Expect this to take 30 to 35 minutes.

2. Once you reach 175°F (79°C), hold the milk at that temperature for 10 to 12 minutes. Stir the pot frequently to keep the milk from scalding. Add the calcium chloride, if using, and stir for 1 minute.

3. Add the vinegar a little bit at a time, stirring continuously. Within 5 to 10 minutes you will see curds begin to form. Continue stirring until all the vinegar has been added and curds are visibly forming.

4. Ladle the curds into a colander, drainer, or large sieve lined with butter muslin or a double layer of cheesecloth. Allow the curds to drain for 3 to 5 hours, until you no longer see any whey dripping from the bag.

5. Consume the queso blanco immediately or place it in a lidded container and store in the refrigerator. Use within one week.

Cream Cheese

Prep/Cook Time: 20 to 30 minutes
Ripening/Draining/Aging Time: 36 hours
Heating Method: Indirect

Creamy, light, and couldn't be any easier to make, homemade cream cheese proves that there really is no substitute for handcrafted dairy goods. Cream cheese is infinitely adaptable—try it whipped into pumpkin cheesecake, slathered atop poppy seed bagels, or blended with herbs and veggies and stuffed into mushroom caps. This recipe requires a 24-hour ripening time and a 10-hour draining period, so if you plan to incorporate it into a dish, you'll need to get cracking a couple of days before.

Yield: Approximately 1½ cups

YOU WILL NEED:

3 cups whole milk

3 cups heavy cream

½ teaspoon (1 packet) direct-set mesophilic starter culture or 2 ounces fresh mesophilic starter culture

¼ teaspoon calcium chloride mixed with ¼ cup cold, sterilized water*

2 drops liquid rennet

*Omit if using raw milk.

TO PREPARE:

1. Combine the milk and cream in the top half of a double boiler or a metal bowl and indirectly warm it to 72°F (22°C), using either a double boiler or a warm water bath.

2. Add the starter culture to the milk, and stir the mixture with a metal spoon to fully incorporate. Add the calcium chloride, if using, and stir for 1 minute. Add the rennet and stir again to combine. Remove the pot from the heat source, cover with a lid, and place in a draft-free spot at room temperature. Allow it to sit for 24 hours.

3. The next day, the curds should look like very firm pieces of yogurt. Transfer the curds and whey into a colander, drainer, or large sieve lined with butter muslin or a double layer of cheesecloth. Tie the four corners of the butter muslin or cheesecloth into a knot. Either hang the bag over a sink to drain, or place a wooden spoon or chopstick through the knot and suspend the bag over a catch bowl. Allow the curds to drain for 10 hours at room temperature.

4. Once you no longer see any whey dripping from the bag, remove the curds from the cheesecloth and transfer them to a small, lidded bowl. Give the curds a good stir until they look spreadable and creamy.

5. Cover your cream cheese and place it in the refrigerator for at least 1 hour. You can use it immediately or store it in the refrigerator and use within one to two weeks.

Mascarpone

Cook Time: 20 to 25 minutes
Aging Time: 12 hours
Heating Method: Direct

This soft cheese lends itself to a wide variety of uses beyond tiramisu, the Italian dessert combining mascarpone with espresso and ladyfingers. The flavor and texture of mascarpone can be found at the intersection of a mildly tangy sour cream, whipped cream, and cream cheese. Spread it on quick breads (pumpkin in winter, zucchini in summer) or try it in a tart (caramelized apple in autumn, rhubarb and strawberries in spring)—there's no end to the opportunities presented by this subtly sweet-and-sour cheese. It needs half of a day to set up, though, so if you intend to serve it with dinner, you'll need to get started early.
Yield: Approximately 1 pound

YOU WILL NEED:

4 cups half-and-half or light cream*

¹/₄ teaspoon (1 packet) direct-set crème fraîche starter culture

*You can also make your own half-and-half by combining 1 cup heavy whipping cream with 3 cups whole milk. Whisk the milk and cream together to fully incorporate before use.

TO PREPARE:

1. In a medium saucepan, gradually warm the half-and-half to 86°F (30°C) directly over low heat. Monitor the temperature closely with a dairy thermometer to avoid overheating.

2. Stir in the starter culture with a metal spoon, and then remove the pan from the heat. Cover, and allow the mixture to rest at room temperature for 12 hours. When your curds have set, they will look like a very thick yogurt or cream.

3. At this point, depending on your desired thickness and consistency, the mascarpone is done. If you'd like it to be a bit firmer (as is necessary for dishes such as tiramisu), ladle the curds into a colander, drainer, or large sieve lined with butter muslin or a double layer of cheesecloth. Put a catch bowl underneath the colander, place in the refrigerator, and allow the cheese to drain for 2 to 3 hours.

4. Use the mascarpone immediately, or place it in a lidded container and store in the refrigerator. Use within two to three weeks.

Feta

Prep Time: 3 hours
Draining Time: 4 to 5 hours
Heating Method: Indirect

Feta is one of my personal must-haves when it comes to cheese. It is almost always found in the cheese drawer of my refrigerator, ready to adorn the humblest of salads, be tucked into fish tacos, or be crumbled atop a homemade pizza. Traditionally made from both sheep's and goat's milk, this salty cheese has been a Mediterranean culinary staple for centuries. In this recipe I use goat's milk alone; unless you keep sheep or have a neighbor who does, collecting the required quantity of sheep's milk can prove challenging.

Yield: Approximately 1½ pounds

TO PREPARE:

1. Warm the milk to 88°F (31°C) indirectly, using either a double boiler or a water bath in the sink (see page 202 for water bath instructions).

2. Add the starter culture, and stir with a metal spoon to fully incorporate. Remove the mixture from the heat source, cover, wrap with a kitchen towel, and allow to sit for 1 hour.

3. Add the calcium chloride, if using, and stir for 1 minute to combine. In a small bowl, mix the rennet into the water. Stir to thoroughly combine, then whisk the rennet into the milk, making certain that it is distributed evenly. Cover the pot again, and allow it to sit for an additional hour. The curd is ready when a clean break forms (see page 204).

4. Cut the curds into 1-inch (2.5 cm) cubes. Allow the curds to rest for 15 minutes, then gently stir the curds for 20 minutes using a metal spoon. This allows the curds and whey to separate more fully from one another, resulting in a firmer feta.

5. Transfer the curds and whey into a colander, drainer, or large sieve lined with butter muslin or a double layer of cheesecloth. Tie the four corners of the butter muslin or cheesecloth into a knot. Either hang the bag over a sink to drain, or place a wooden spoon or chopsticks through the knot and suspend the bag over a catch bowl. Allow the curds to drain for 4 to 5 hours.

6. Unwrap the bag, place the ball of curd on a cutting board, and cut the curd into 1½-inch (3.8 cm) slices. Cut the slices into approximately 1-inch (2.5 cm) cubes.

7. Place the cubes into a lidded container, sprinkle with salt to taste, cover, and place in refrigerator. I like a salty feta, so I tend to opt for the upper amount of suggested salt. If you prefer an even stronger, extra-salty feta, prepare a brine by mixing 8 cups warm water with 1 cup cheese salt. Stir until the salt is completely dissolved in the water. Add unsalted 1-inch (2.5 cm) feta cubes to the brine, cover with a lid, and store in the refrigerator.

8. Allow the feta to cure for four days and then use within three weeks. If brined, use within one month.

Paneer

Prep Time: 25 minutes
Draining Time: 3 hours
Heating Method: Direct

Saag paneer is one of my all-time favorite Indian dishes, made from a savory blend of cream, spinach, spices, and cubes of this soft cheese. We often make it at home, especially during the spring when my garden is exploding with fresh spinach. Served alongside a bit of tandoori spice–rubbed salmon or catfish and a piece of ghee- and chutney-laden naan, it's quite possibly the perfect meal. Paneer is also delicious in any type of curry, or simply cubed up and pan-fried in a bit of ghee or butter.

Yield: Approximately 1 pound

TO PREPARE:

1. In a medium saucepan, heat the milk to a gentle boil. Stir the pot every few minutes to keep the milk from scorching. Add the calcium chloride, if using, and stir for 1 minute to combine.

2. Reduce the heat to low and stir in the lemon juice. The milk should begin to coagulate. If that fails to occur, add an additional 1 tablespoon lemon juice and watch for the whey to become clear, as opposed to milky. Once curds begin to form, remove the pot from the heat, cover, and allow to rest for 5 minutes.

3. Ladle the curds into a colander, drainer, or large sieve lined with butter muslin or a double layer of cheesecloth. Place a catch bowl underneath to collect the whey as it drains off.

4. Tie the four corners of the butter muslin or cheesecloth into a knot. Give the knot a light squeeze to remove the whey. Place the knotted bag onto a rimmed cookie sheet. On top of the bag, put a heavy board, such as a wooden or thick plastic cutting board. Place a weight on top of the board. You could use a stack of heavy books, a gallon-sized jar filled with water, or a brick or two. You're simply trying to weigh down the curd to force any whey out. Leave the curds to drain and firm for 3 hours.

5. Remove the paneer from the cheesecloth, and transfer it to a lidded container. Use it immediately or store in the refrigerator and use within one week.

Ricotta

Prep/Cook Time: 1 hour
Draining Time: 20 to 50 minutes
Heating Method: Direct

Soft, creamy, easy ricotta—is there anything better? Minimum processing produces maximum satisfaction with this delicious cheese. Traditionally, ricotta is made with cow, sheep, or goat whey left over from making other cheeses. However, I've found it difficult to make whey-based ricotta, as the gathered whey must be used within an hour or so after collection. Unless you make cheese every day, chances are you won't have just-made whey on hand when you want to make ricotta. This recipe solves that problem: you can make an equally tasty ricotta using milk. It is creamier than whey-based ricotta, which I happen to think is a good thing. If you want your ricotta to be drier, simply allow it to drain for an additional 20 to 30 minutes. Fresh ricotta is delectable layered in an herbaceous lasagna, baked into a ricotta cheesecake, dolloped onto pizza, or even stirred into pancakes.

Yield: *Approximately 1 pound*

YOU WILL NEED:

8	cups whole milk
1	cup heavy cream
½	cup lemon juice
¼	teaspoon calcium chloride mixed with ¼ cup cold, sterilized water*
½	teaspoon cheese salt or kosher salt

*Needed only if using homogenized, store-bought milk

TO PREPARE:

1. In a medium saucepan, stir together the milk, cream, and lemon juice with a metal spoon. Gradually warm the mixture to 170°F (77°C) directly over medium-low heat. Monitor the temperature closely with a dairy thermometer to avoid overheating. Expect this to take about 30 minutes. Stir only once or twice while heating to prevent sticking; any more and you run the risk of making the curd too small. Add the calcium chloride, if using, and stir for 1 minute to combine.

2. Increase the heat gradually until the mixture reaches 200°F (93°C). This will take anywhere from 4 to 7 minutes. Be sure to stop just before the boiling point. Your curds should resemble a creamy, custardy mass at this point.

3. Remove the pot from the heat, and allow it to rest for 20 minutes. Meanwhile, line a colander, drainer, or large sieve with butter muslin or a double layer of cheesecloth.

4. Ladle the curds into the colander, and allow them to drain for at least 20 minutes. For a firmer curd, allow the curds to drain an additional 20 to 30 minutes.

5. Transfer the curds to a medium bowl. Add the salt, and stir with a metal spoon to fully incorporate.

6. Use the ricotta immediately, or place it in a lidded container and store in the refrigerator. Use within one week.

Cottage Cheese

Prep/Cook Time: 6 to 8 hours
Draining Time: 20 minutes
Heating Method: Direct

Cottage cheese, also commonly known in some parts of the world as pot cheese or farmer's cheese, is an incredibly versatile addition to your home dairy repertoire. It's scrumptious on its own as a light snack but also works well with a variety of ingredients and flavorings. My personal favorite way of enjoying cottage cheese is grinding some fresh black pepper over it and then serving with fresh melon or tossing in a handful of sweet grape tomatoes. Delicious! Cottage cheese is also a fine stand-in for ricotta in lasagna or manicotti, takes well to fresh herbs for a veggie dip, is delectable made into pancakes, and is a welcome addition to quiches and omelets.

Yield: Approximately 1 pound

YOU WILL NEED:

1 gallon whole, low-fat, or skim milk

½ teaspoon (1 packet) direct-set mesophilic starter culture or 4 ounces fresh starter culture

¼ teaspoon calcium chloride mixed with ¼ cup cold, sterilized water*

1 tablespoon rennet solution (made from ¼ teaspoon liquid rennet dissolved in ¼ cup sterilized water)

¼ cup heavy cream

1 teaspoon cheese salt or kosher salt, optional

*Omit if using raw milk.

TO PREPARE:

1. In a medium saucepan, warm milk gently over medium heat to 72°F (22°C). Monitor the temperature closely with a dairy thermometer to avoid overheating.

2. Add the starter culture to the milk, stirring with a metal spoon to incorporate thoroughly. Add calcium chloride, if using, and stir for 1 minute to incorporate. Gently stir in the diluted rennet.

3. Remove the milk from the heat, cover, and allow to sit at room temperature (between 68 and 72°F [20 and 22°C]) for 4 to 6 hours, until the curd coagulates.

4. Once the curds have firmed to the clean break stage, cut them into ½-inch (1.3 cm) cubes (see page 204). Let the cubes rest for 20 minutes.

5. Place the pot of cubed curds over medium heat and very, very gradually, warm to 110°F (43°C). Raise the temperature only about 2 to 4 degrees every 5 minutes. After each 5-minute interval, stir the curds gently with a metal spoon. This will take about 35 minutes, or thereabouts.

6. Once you've reached 110°F (43°C), hold the temperature there for the next 25 minutes. The curds will begin to visibly firm up and lose their jellylike texture. To test for doneness, squeeze a curd. If it doesn't feel solid and instead feels a bit mushy, continue cooking a bit longer and then test again.

7. When you are sure your curds are properly cooked, allow them to rest in the pot for 10 minutes.

8. Next, transfer the curds into a colander, drainer, or large sieve lined with butter muslin or a double layer of cheesecloth. Set the colander over a large bowl to catch the whey. Let the curds drain for 10 minutes.

9. Tie the corners of your cheesecloth into a knot. Run the knotted bag under ice cold water for 2 minutes, or dip the knotted bag into a bowl of ice cold water two or three times. Give the bag a firm squeeze, and place it back into the colander to drain for an additional 10 minutes.

10. Remove the curds from the cheesecloth, and transfer them to a medium bowl. Use your hands to

break up any large pieces of curd that may have stuck together. Add heavy cream and salt, if using, and stir with a metal spoon to incorporate.

11. Either consume immediately or place your finished cottage cheese in a lidded container and store in the refrigerator. Use within one week.

Chèvre

Prep/Cook Time: 12 to 14 hours
Draining Time: 6 to 8 hours
Heating Method: Indirect

French for goat, chèvre is quite possibly one of humankind's oldest cheese varieties; variations of it are consumed all over the world. Customarily, it is made by simply allowing goat's milk to ripen and curdle over the course of several days. Goats are hearty, intrepid creatures, willing to travel to and eat what the more delicate cow can't or won't. Accordingly, the thistles, bitter herbs, or any other manner of vegetation goats consume accounts for the tangy flavor present in their milk. Chèvre is quite easy to make and can be enjoyed in relatively little time. Served up sweet with fig jam, or savory, rolled in fresh herbs or spices, chèvre is a highly versatile, always delicious cheese.

Yield: Approximately 1 pound

YOU WILL NEED:

1 gallon goat's milk

1/4 teaspoon (1 packet) direct-set chèvre starter culture*

1/4 teaspoon calcium chloride mixed with 1/4 cup cold, sterilized water**

*If you don't have any specifically chèvre starter culture on hand, substitute 1/4 teaspoon direct-set mesophilic culture, as well as 1 tablespoon rennet solution made from 1 drop liquid rennet dissolved in 5 tablespoons cold water.

**Omit if using raw milk.

TO PREPARE:

1. Warm the milk to 72°F (22°C) indirectly, using either a double boiler or a warm water bath (see page 202). Monitor the temperature of both the milk and the water bath using a dairy thermometer.

2. Add the starter culture and stir with a metal spoon to fully incorporate. If using a general mesophilic starter culture, whisk in the rennet, making certain that it is evenly distributed. Add the calcium chloride, if using, and stir for 1 minute to incorporate. Remove the pot from the heat source, cover, wrap with a kitchen towel, and allow the mixture to sit at room temperature (between 68 and 72°F [20 and 22°C]) for 12 hours.

3. The curd is ready when a clean break forms (use your finger or a long-handed knife to check). If, after 12 hours, a clean break isn't visible, allow the curds to sit for several more hours, and then check again. The consistency should resemble a thick yogurt, full of body, but not too firm.

4. Ladle the mixture into a colander, drainer, or large sieve lined with butter muslin or a double layer of cheesecloth. Tie the four corners of the cheesecloth into a knot. Either hang the bag over a sink to drain, or place a wooden spoon or chopsticks through the knot and suspend the bag over a catch bowl. Allow the curds to drain for 6 to 8 hours, or until no whey is visibly dripping from the bag. Alternatively, gently ladle the curds into cheese molds (it is not necessary to line the molds with cheesecloth). Place molds on a rack, such as a cookie cooling rack, placed over a collecting pan, such as a cookie sheet or baking pan. Allow to drain for 6 to 8 hours.

5. After draining, remove the chèvre from the cheesecloth or mold. Consume immediately, or place it in a lidded container and store in the refrigerator. Use within one week.

LOVELY AND DELICIOUS

If you'd like to impart a bit of flair to your cheeses for gift giving or a special occasion, there are a number of options for playing "dress up." Consider rolling your cheese in chopped fresh or dried herbs and crushed or ground spices. You could also festoon them with chopped dried fruits and finely chopped toasted nuts. Edible flowers are an unexpected adornment, enhancing both flavor and fragrance, while condiments such as honey, pickled vegetables, or balsamic vinegar are ideal for serving alongside your homemade cheeses. Here are a number of ideas for making your cheeses both delicious and dazzling!

Herbs: basil, chives, parsley, tarragon, mint, rosemary, cilantro, thyme, marjoram, oregano, savory, chervil, dill, herbes de Provence, sage, anise hyssop, lemon balm, fennel fronds

Spices: cumin, black pepper, juniper berries, red pepper flakes, curry powder, fennel seed, celery seed, caraway seed, coriander

Nuts and Fruits: walnuts, pecans, pistachios, almonds, tamari almonds, pine nuts, pumpkin seeds, dried cranberries, dried blueberries, crystallized ginger, currants, candied citrus peel, dried apple, dried pear, dried apricot, goji berries

Flowers (petals only): nasturtium, violet, lavender bud, rose, jasmine, chamomile, bee balm, borage, calendula, hibiscus, Johnny-jump-up, lilac, pansy, sunflower, red clover, scented geranium, marigold, dianthus, elderberry, honeysuckle, linden, tuberous begonia

Condiments: honey, olive tapenade, bee pollen, jam, marmalade, fruit butter, pickled vegetables, sea salt, truffle oil, aged balsamic vinegar (just a drizzle!)

Once you've decked out your cheese and swaddled it in flavor and beauty, you'll need to place it on a serving dish. I love using a chalkboard or a chalkboard-painted cutting board and writing the name of each cheese underneath it. A piece of slate would work just as well. A beautiful bamboo cutting board is also a lovely forum for showing your cheeses, as are handcrafted hardwood cheeseboards. Wrapping cheese in grape leaves is another way of adding some pizzazz to your cheese plate. It's also a fine way to prepare cheeses for gifting, as is using parchment or waxed paper, finished off with a bit of twine, raffia, or ribbon.

Mozzarella

Prep Time: 30 minutes
Heating Method: Direct

A favorite cheese for many, mozzarella has a long-standing reputation of winning hearts and taste buds. Making this soft, stretchy cheese at home is quite simple, permitted you have the correct type of milk. Store-bought milk that has been ultra-pasteurized at high temperatures is completely unusable for mozzarella-making. Such milk will render your curds more like ricotta than the pliant, malleable mass of curd needed for mozzarella stretching. I speak from experience on this topic, after wasting 2 gallons of organic milk before figuring out that the milk was actually the culprit. If you cannot access fresh-from-the-cow milk, look for low-pasteurized milk at your grocer or ask them to begin carrying it.

Yield: Approximately 1 pound

YOU WILL NEED:

- 1 gallon whole cow's milk (be certain that your milk has not been ultra-pasteurized)
- 2 teaspoons citric acid powder
- ¼ teaspoon calcium chloride mixed with ¼ cup cold, sterilized water*
- ½ teaspoon liquid rennet or ¼ crushed tablet
- ¼ cup cold, sterilized water
- 1 teaspoon cheese salt or kosher salt

*Omit if using raw milk.

TO PREPARE:

1. Place the milk in a large stockpot. Gently stir in the citric acid powder and the calcium chloride, if using. Warm the milk gently, directly over medium heat, to 88°F (31°C). Monitor the temperature closely with a dairy thermometer to avoid overheating.

2. In a small bowl, whisk together the rennet and the cold water. Add the rennet solution to the milk mixture. Continue stirring until the temperature reaches 104 to 106°F (40 to 41°C). Remove the pot from the heat, cover, and allow to rest for 15 to 20 minutes. The curds and whey will begin to separate during this time.

3. Using a slotted metal spoon, remove the curds and place them in a large microwavable glass or ceramic bowl. Press against the mass of curds with the slotted spoon, forcing out as much whey as possible, and pour it off into the pot of whey.

4. You can warm your curds one of two ways: with the microwave or with heated whey.

Microwave: Place the bowl of curds in the microwave and heat on "HIGH" for 1 minute. Remove the bowl from the microwave and press the curds, using either the slotted spoon or your hand (wear rubber gloves!), forcing out and pouring off any whey. The curds should begin to appear melted. If not, heat for an additional 20 seconds.

Add the salt, and begin kneading the curd mass with either your hands or a metal spoon, folding it over itself repeatedly. It will begin to become shiny and pliant, like taffy. Microwave again on "HIGH" for 1 minute. Press out any remaining whey. Knead the curd again, until it is quite elastic and begins to stretch out like a piece of chewing gum. If your curd breaks instead of stretching, put it back into the microwave for an additional 30 seconds, and then stretch.

Heated whey: Once you have separated the curds from the whey, warm the pot of whey to 170 to 175°F (77 to 79°C), just before it really gets boiling. Place about one-quarter of the curds into a medium bowl. Sprinkle some of the salt over the curds. Ladle a good amount of the hot whey over the curd mass. Wearing rubber gloves, begin to knead the curd until it begins to melt and stick together. You may need to add more hot whey to the curds to maintain the temperature. Repeat with the next quarter of curd, repeating the above steps until all of the curd has been warmed and stretched in hot whey.

5. Once ready, it will be pliant and spongy and shiny. You can consume the mozzarella immediately, or place it in a lidded container and store in the refrigerator. Use within one to two weeks.

"Bend Me, Shape Me, Anyway You Want Me": DIY Cheese Molds

Containers intended for other purposes can be cheaply and easily transformed into cheese-molding vessels.

YOGURT CONTAINERS

Commercially prepared plastic yogurt containers work quite well as inexpensive soft cheese molds. Simply clean out the container thoroughly, and then, using a hammer and nail or a drill, puncture the bottom and sides of the container with multiple small holes.

PLASTIC STORAGE CONTAINERS

Any home supply or grocery store will offer plastic storage containers for purchase. Opt for multiples of the same size, or choose a variety of sizes appropriately proportioned for containing a small amount of cheese. Puncture the sides and bottom as described at left, and you're all set to be the big cheese (maker, that is).

Stayin' Alive

After putting the effort into making homemade cheeses, you'll want to do all you can to preserve their shelf life. Temperature and humidity, location, and storage container all come into play when considering how to best store cheeses. The shelf life of cheeses is highly variable, with soft and fresh cheeses lasting considerably less time (one to two weeks) than their harder cousins, which can last for months.

TEMPERATURE & HUMIDITY

Cheese requires a precise range of temperature and humidity levels in order to keep well. Ideally, cheese should be stored between 35 and 45°F (2 and 7°C). Humidity levels should range between 65 and 75 percent.

LOCATION

In order to keep your cheese at the necessary temperature and humidity, store it in a warmer area of your refrigerator, such as a bottom vegetable crisper drawer. Don't use any storage bins on the door, as temperature fluctuations can cause cheese to deteriorate.

CONTAINERS & WRAPPING

Wrap hard cheese loosely in cheesecloth, parchment paper, or waxed paper, and place in the crisper drawer. Allow your cheese to breathe or it will dry out. Change the wrapping every three to four days. Store soft cheeses like feta and Brie in glass or plastic lidded containers. I store both homemade and purchased cheeses unwrapped in rectangular glass storage containers with plastic lids.

Folded paper towels on the bottom of the container, changed out weekly, collect moisture. Aside from strong-smelling cheeses like Gorgonzola that require individual storage containers, it's perfectly fine to place different cheeses beside one another in this method.

HELPFUL TIPS

→ If your cheese seems especially dry, smells "off," or develops slime or sludge, consider it a loss and throw it out.

→ If your cheese develops mold, simply cut it off about 1/2 inch (1.3 cm) down into the cheese block. This ensures you've removed invisible mold fibers that reach down farther.

→ Soft, fresh cheeses that are stored in a brine or in whey don't need to have their solution changed out. These cheeses are intended to be consumed within a short enough time span that the preserving liquid should remain fresh.

→ It's not advisable to freeze those cheeses that you intend to serve fresh. Freezing alters a cheese's texture and flavor. If you do elect to freeze a cheese, its best use is for cooking. Some hard cheeses should be grated before freezing, as attempting to do so afterward is a task of Sisyphean proportions. Don't freeze cheese any longer than two months, and be sure to thaw it out in the refrigerator rather than at room temperature.

Advanced Cheeses

H ard and mold- or bacteria-ripened cheeses are considerably more involved than their soft cousins. They require a greater amount of processing, will need to spend time in a cheese press, and must have very specific climatic conditions met in order to ripen properly. That said, for the inspired cheese-maker, they are the next logical step after dabbling in fresh and unaged cheeses. The following recipes present an offering of hard, Italian, and mold- and bacteria-ripened cheeses. A number of exceptionally well-written, advanced, artisan home cheese-making books are available for those desiring to make an even greater variety of cheeses.

Cheddar

Prep/Cook Time: 6 1/2 hours
Draining Time: 20 minutes
Pressing Time: 36 hours
Aging Time: Minimum of 3 months
Heating Method: Indirect

One of the most popular cheeses in both the United States and the United Kingdom, the term *cheddar* is both a noun, referring to the cheese itself, and a verb. To cheddar a cheese means to cut the curd into cubes, salt it, and then stack and repeatedly turn it prior to pressing. The intensity of a particular cheddar's flavor is reflective of its vintage, or aging period. In the following recipe, I've offered a cheddar made in the traditional manner, utilizing the cheddaring technique. It takes longer to age than a farmhouse-style cheddar (which omits the cheddaring process and is usually ready in four weeks), but produces an end product that is creamy and delicious. Try cheddar scattered over a tomato and marjoram frittata, melted over warm apple pie, or unadorned alongside fresh fruits, whole-wheat crackers, and a spicy chutney (my personal favorite).

Yield: Approximately 2 pounds

YOU WILL NEED:

2 gallons whole milk

1/2 teaspoon (1 packet) direct-set mesophilic starter culture or 4 ounces fresh starter culture

1/4 teaspoon calcium chloride mixed with 1/4 cup cold, sterilized water*

1 teaspoon liquid rennet (or 1/2 tablet, crushed)

1/4 cup cold, sterilized water

Cheese salt or kosher salt

Cheese wax

*Omit if using raw milk.

TO PREPARE:

1. Warm the milk to 86°F (30°C) indirectly by use of either a double boiler or a water bath in the sink (see page 202). Monitor the temperature of both the milk and the water bath using a dairy thermometer. Add the starter culture, and stir with a metal spoon to fully incorporate. Cover, and hold at 86°F (30°C) for one hour.

2. Add the calcium chloride, if using, and stir for 1 minute. In a small bowl, whisk together the rennet and cold water. Slowly add the rennet solution to the milk mixture, and stir gently for 1 minute to fully incorporate. Cover again, and allow the mixture to sit at 86°F (30°C) for an additional hour.

3. Check for a clean break. If curds cling to your cutting knife, allow the curds to sit and ripen for a bit longer. Once a clean break is achieved, cut the curds into 1/2-inch (1.3 cm) cubes. Allow the cut curd to sit for 10 minutes.

4. Slowly heat the curd to 100°F (38°C). Do this very gradually, increasing the temperature only 1 degree every 1 to 3 minutes. Stir frequently with a ladle, and gently cut any large pieces of curd that you may find.

5. Once you've reached 100°F (38°C), hold the temperature there for 30 minutes. Stir the curd frequently. The curds should begin to shrink and reduce significantly in size. Remove the pot from the heat source, and allow the curds to rest for 20 minutes.

6. Ladle the curds out of the pot and into a colander, drainer, or large sieve lined with a double layer of cheesecloth. Allow to drain for 20 minutes.

7. Remove the curds from the drainer and place onto a large cutting board. The curds should stick together, as one big mass. Cut the curds into slices around 3 inches (7.6 cm) long and ½ inch (1.3 cm) thick. This process is the beginning of cheddaring.

8. Fill your kitchen sink with water approximately 100 to 105°F (38 to 41°C). Place the curd slices into the pot used for warming, put the pot into the sink, and cover it with a lid. Maintain the temperature for 2 hours, turning the curd slices every 20 minutes or so. After 2 hours, the curds should feel rubbery and springy, and bounce back when pushed with your finger.

9. Take the pot out of the water and use a long-handled knife to cut the curd into smaller cubes, between ½ and ¾ inch (1.3 and 1.9 cm) square. Return the pot to the sink basin of warm water. Maintain the temperature for an additional 30 to 35 minutes. Use your fingers or a slotted metal spoon, and turn the curds gently about every 7 to 8 minutes to keep them from matting.

10. After 30 to 35 minutes, remove the pot from the sink basin. Sprinkle 2 tablespoons cheese salt over the curds, and stir in gently with a slotted spoon.

11. Ladle the curds out of the pot and into a 2-pound cheese mold lined with cheesecloth. If you are using a mold with an open bottom, place whatever you will be using as your drip pan underneath the cheese mold while you do this to provide a solid base for the mold (otherwise, once you transfer the mold to the cheese press, your curd will spill out everywhere).

12. Once the curds are all ladled into the cheese mold, fold the excess cheesecloth over the top, place

the follower in, and press the curd at 15 pounds of pressure for 10 minutes.

13. Take the cheese mold out of the press, remove the curd from the mold, and unwrap the cheesecloth. Change out the cheesecloth with a fresh, clean dressing, return the curd to the cheese mold, place the mold back into the cheese press, and press again at 40 pounds of pressure for 12 hours.

14. Repeat the process again, re-dressing the curd, and press at 50 pounds of pressure for 12 hours. Repeat the process one final time, re-dressing the curd, and press at 50 pounds of pressure for an additional 12 hours, for a total pressing time of 36 hours.

15. Next, remove the curd from the mold, and unwrap the cheesecloth. Place it on a cheeseboard or cheese mat, and air-dry for three to four days. Turn the cheese daily, and keep it dry.

16. After three days, you'll need to wax your cheese. Refer to page 208 for detailed instructions.

17. Store your cheese at 50 to 55°F (10 to 13°C) for at least three months, longer for a sharper flavor. Try to remember to turn it daily.

18. If you own a cheese trier (refer to page 173 for a detailed description of this nifty cheese-testing tool), you can test the cheese at three months to see if the flavor is to your liking. Otherwise, wait a bit longer before consuming your cheddar, as the flavors improve with aging. Once ready, store in the refrigerator and use within one month.

Swiss

Prep/Cook Time: 3 hours
Pressing Time: 15 to 16 hours
Brining Time: 12 hours
Aging Time: 3 months
Heating Method: Indirect

Long thought by young children to be the vestige of marauding mice, the holes in Swiss cheese are actually the result of bacteria—*Propionic shermanii*. This bacteria is responsible for both the flavor and physical appearance of Swiss-style cheeses. Carbon dioxide given off by the bacteria causes the cheese to swell during aging, forcing the characteristic holes into the curd. Specific types of Swiss cheese are named for the areas in Switzerland from which they hail, including Emmenthal and Gruyère. From the robustness of a Reuben to the comfort of a warm fondue, try your hand at this "holiest" of cheeses.

Yield: *Approximately 2 pounds*

YOU WILL NEED:

2	gallons whole milk
½	teaspoon (1 packet) direct-set thermophilic starter culture or 4 ounces fresh starter culture
1	teaspoon powdered *Propionic shermanii*
¼	teaspoon calcium chloride mixed with ¼ cup cold, sterilized water*
½	teaspoon liquid rennet (or ¼ tablet, crushed)
¼	cup cold, sterilized water
4	cups cheese salt or kosher salt
	*Omit if using raw milk.

TO PREPARE:

1. Warm the milk to 90°F (32°C) indirectly, using either a double boiler or a warm water bath (see page 202). Monitor the temperature of both the milk and the water bath using a dairy thermometer.

2. Add the starter culture to the milk, and stir with a metal spoon to fully incorporate. Scoop out ¼ cup of the milk, and mix with the *Propionic shermanii*. Add the mixture back to the pot, stirring well to evenly disperse the bacteria. Cover the pot and hold at 90°F (32°C) for 15 minutes.

3. Add in calcium chloride, if using, and stir for 1 minute. In a small bowl, whisk together the rennet and ¼ cup cold water. Slowly add the rennet solution to the milk mixture, and stir gently to fully incorporate. Cover the pot again and allow it to sit, maintaining 90°F (32°C), for 30 minutes.

4. Check for a clean break. If curds cling to the cutting knife, allow the curds to sit and ripen for a bit longer. Once a clean break is achieved, cut the curds into ¼-inch (6 mm) cubes.

5. After the curd has been cut, slowly stir it with a ladle for the next 45 minutes. This forces whey out of the curds gradually, before the curds are heated further. Hold the temperature at 90°F (32°C) for the entire duration. As you stir, the curd will become smaller and smaller as whey is forced from the curd. This is what you want. If you see any large chunks of curd, use the ladle to cut them into smaller pieces. This process is known as *foreworking*, which simply means to gradually warm the curd up before cooking it.

6. Slowly heat the curd to 120°F (49°C). Do this very gradually, increasing the temperature only 1 degree every 1 to 3 minutes. Once you've reached 120°F (49°C), hold the temperature there for the next 25 minutes. Test to see if your curds are ready to be pressed by removing a couple of tablespoons and

squeezing them together in the palm of your hand. If they break apart into individual pieces, you're all set. If they hold fast to each other, continue to cook a few minutes longer and then test for doneness again.

7. Ladle the hot curds out of the pot and into a 2-pound cheese mold lined with cheesecloth. Do this carefully, yet quickly, as it is essential that the curds be hot for pressing. If you are using a mold with an open bottom, place whatever you will be using as your drip pan underneath the cheese mold while you do this, so as to provide a solid base for the mold (otherwise, once you transfer the mold to the cheese press, your curd will spill out everywhere).

8. Once the curds are all ladled into the cheese mold, fold the excess cheesecloth over the top, place the follower in, and press the curd at 10 pounds of pressure for 30 minutes.

9. Take the cheese mold out of the press, remove the curd from the mold, and unwrap the cheesecloth. Change out the cheesecloth with a fresh, clean dressing, return the curd to the cheese mold, place the mold back into the cheese press, and press at 10 pounds of pressure for an additional 30 minutes.

10. Repeat the process again, re-dressing the curd, and press at 15 pounds of pressure for 2 hours. Repeat one final time, re-dressing the curd, and press at 15 pounds of pressure for 12 to 14 hours.

11. Prepare a brine by dissolving the salt in 1 gallon cold water. Use a stainless-steel, glass, plastic, or ceramic container, as aluminum could corrode. Dip a bit of cheesecloth into the brine, wring it out over the sink, and set it aside to dry out. Next, remove the curd from the mold, unwrap the cheesecloth, and submerge it in the brine. Place the container in the refrigerator, and allow the curd to soak in the brine for 12 hours.

12. Remove the curd from the brine, pat dry with the dry, salted cheesecloth, and place the cheese on a cheeseboard or cheese mat. Store it in either a basement or a ripening refrigerator (see Ripening Refrigerator on page 175 for a discussion of home-ripening) at 50 to 55°F (10 to 13°C) and 85 percent humidity for one week. Adjust the humidity, if necessary, by placing a bowl of warm water next to the cheese. Turn the cheese daily, and wipe it with a dry, salted cheesecloth.

13. After one week, transfer the cheese to a warm room with high humidity, such as a kitchen or pantry, and a temperature between 68 and 74°F (20 and 23°C). Keep it there for two to three weeks, turning it every day and continuing to wipe it with a dry, salted cheesecloth. The cheese will begin to swell during this period, as carbon dioxide is given off by the *Propionic shermanii*, causing holes to form inside the cheese.

14. Once the holes, or "eyes," are visible, transfer the cheese one last time back to your basement or ripening refrigerator. Keep at 45 to 50°F (7 to 10°C) and 85 percent humidity for three to six months. Monitor the humidity regularly, adding a bowl of warm water beside the cheese if needed. Turn and wipe the cheese with a dry, salted cheesecloth every few days.

15. Wait a minimum of three months before consuming your Swiss cheese. If you own a cheese trier, you can test the cheese at three months to see if the flavor is to your liking. Once ready, store in the refrigerator and use within three weeks.

Parmesan

Prep/Cook Time: 2 hours
Pressing Time: 15 to 17 hours
Brining Time: 24 hours
Aging Time: 6 to 10 months
Heating Method: Indirect

This hard, grainy-textured cheese originally hails from the Parma, Reggio Emilia, Modena, Bologna, and Mantova provinces of Italy. A lengthy aging period is required to produce the grittiness and flavor characteristic of true Parmesan. Although its hard texture renders it ideal for grating, it is also delicious sliced and paired with fresh fruit and nuts as an after-dinner course.

Yield: Approximately 2 pounds

YOU WILL NEED:

2	gallons skim or low-fat (2 percent) milk*
½	teaspoon (1 packet) direct-set thermophilic starter culture or 4 ounces fresh starter culture
¼	teaspoon calcium chloride mixed with ¼ cup cold, sterilized water**
½	teaspoon liquid rennet (or ¼ tablet, crushed)
¼	cup cold, sterilized water
4	cups cheese salt or kosher salt
1	gallon cold water

*You can also use 1 gallon of skim or low-fat cow's milk and 1 gallon of whole goat's milk. This will result in a sharper flavored cheese.

**Omit if using raw milk.

TO PREPARE:

1. Warm the milk to 90°F (32°C) indirectly, using either a double boiler or a warm water bath (see page 202). Monitor the temperature of both the milk and the water bath using a dairy thermometer.

2. Add the starter culture and stir with a metal spoon to fully incorporate. Cover, and hold at 90°F (32°C) for 30 minutes.

3. Add the calcium chloride, if using, and stir for 1 minute. In a small bowl, whisk together the rennet and ¼ cup cold water. Slowly add the rennet solution to the milk mixture, and stir gently for 1 minute to fully incorporate. Cover again and allow to sit, maintaining the target temperature, for 30 minutes.

4. Check for a clean break. If curds cling to the cutting knife, allow them to sit and ripen for a bit longer. Once a clean break is achieved, cut the curds into ¼-inch (6 mm) cubes. Allow the cut curd to sit for 5 minutes.

5. Slowly heat the curd to 100°F (38°C). Do this very gradually, increasing the temperature only 1°F (-17°C) every 1 to 3 minutes. Stir frequently with a ladle, and gently cut any large pieces of curd that you may find.

6. Once you've reached 100°F (38°C), raise the temperature to 124°F (51°C). Stir the curd frequently. The curds should begin to shrink and reduce significantly in size. Remove the pot from the heat source, and allow the curds to rest for 10 minutes.

7. Ladle the curds out of the pot and into a 2-pound cheese mold lined with cheesecloth. If you are using a mold with an open bottom, place whatever you will be using as your drip pan underneath the cheese mold while you do this, so as to provide a solid base for the mold (otherwise, once you transfer the mold to the cheese press, your curd will spill out everywhere).

8. Once the curds are all ladled into the cheese mold, fold the excess cheesecloth over the top, place the follower in, and press the curd at 5 pounds of pressure for 15 minutes.

9. Take the cheese mold out of the press, remove the curd from the mold, and unwrap the cheesecloth. Change out the cheesecloth with a fresh, clean dressing, return the curd to the cheese mold, place the mold back into the cheese press, and press again at 5 pounds of pressure for another 30 minutes.

10. Repeat the process again, re-dressing the curd, and press at 15 pounds of pressure for 2 hours. Repeat one final time, re-dressing the curd, and press at 20 pounds of pressure for 12 to 14 hours.

11. Prepare a brine by dissolving the salt in 1 gallon cold water. Use a stainless-steel, glass, plastic, or ceramic container, as aluminum could corrode. Next, remove the curd from the mold, unwrap the cheesecloth, and submerge the curd in the brine. Allow to brine at room temperature for 24 hours.

12. Remove the curd from the brine, and pat dry. Place on a cheeseboard or cheese mat, and store in either a basement or a ripening refrigerator (see Ripening Refrigerator on page 175 for a discussion of home-ripening) at 50 to 55°F (10 to 13°C) and 85 percent humidity. Adjust the humidity, if necessary, by placing a bowl of warm water next to the cheese. Turn the cheese daily, and wipe with a dry cheesecloth or paper towel if any mold appears.

13. Store your cheese in this environment for six to 10 months. Monitor the humidity regularly, adding a bowl of warm water beside the cheese if needed. After the first month, turn the cheese weekly, continuing to remove any mold that appears with a dry cheesecloth or paper towel.

14. After two months, rub the surface of the cheese with a thin layer of olive oil. This will help prevent the rind from becoming too dry.

15. If you own a cheese trier, you can test the cheese at three months to see if the taste is to your liking. If you can wait, though, six to 10 months of aging will produce a much more intensely flavored Parmesan. Once it's ready, store the cheese in the refrigerator and use within one month.

Gorgonzola

Prep/Cook Time: 14 hours
Ripening Time: 3 days
Aging Time: 4 months
Heating Method: Indirect

Named after the small Italian town from which it originates, Gorgonzola is one of Italy's most beloved blue-veined cheeses. Salty, tart, pungent, and creamy, this crumbly cheese is equally delicious tossed with penne, crumbled over arugula, scattered atop pizza, or baked alongside fresh pears. The telltale blue lines found in Gorgonzola are the result of the mold *Penicillium roqueforti,* responsible for both the flavor and appearance of the cheese. In this recipe, you'll make one batch of curd, leave it to drain overnight, and then make a second batch the next morning.

Yield: Approximately 2 pounds

YOU WILL NEED:

- 2 gallons whole milk (cow's milk or goat's milk)
- 1 teaspoon (2 packets) direct-set mesophilic starter culture or 4 ounces fresh starter culture
- ¼ teaspoon calcium chloride mixed with ¼ cup cold, sterilized water*
- 1 teaspoon liquid rennet (or ½ tablet, crushed)
- ½ cup cold, sterilized water
- ¼ cup cheese salt or kosher salt, plus extra for sprinkling
- ⅛ teaspoon *Penicillium roqueforti*
    *Omit if using raw milk.

TO PREPARE:

1. Warm 1 gallon of the milk to 86°F (30°C) indirectly, using either a double boiler or a warm water bath (see page 202). Monitor the temperature of both the milk and the water bath using a dairy thermometer.

2. Add ½ teaspoon or 1 packet powdered starter culture (or 2 ounces, if using fresh) to the milk, and stir with a metal spoon to fully incorporate. Cover, and hold at 86°F (30°C) for 30 minutes.

3. Add the calcium chloride, if using, and stir for 1 minute. In a small bowl, whisk together half the rennet with ¼ cup cold water. Slowly add the rennet solution to the milk mixture, and stir gently for 1 minute to fully incorporate. Cover again and allow to sit, maintaining the target temperature, for 45 minutes.

4. Check for a clean break. If curds cling to the cutting knife, allow them to sit and ripen for a bit longer. Once a clean break is achieved, cut the curds into ½-inch (1.3 cm) cubes. Allow the cut curd to sit for 15 minutes.

5. Ladle the curds out of the pot and into a colander, drainer, or large sieve lined with a double layer of cheesecloth. Tie the four corners of the cheesecloth into a knot. Either hang the bag over a sink to drain, or place a wooden spoon or chopsticks through the knot and suspend the bag over a catch bowl. Allow the curds to drain overnight or until no whey is visibly dripping from the bag.

6. The next morning, repeat steps 1 through 5 with the second gallon of milk, leaving this batch of curd to drain for just 1 hour.

7. Remove the first batch of curd from the cheesecloth, cut into 1-inch (2.5 cm) cubes, and place in a bowl. Repeat with the new batch of curd, placing it in a separate bowl. Mix together the salt and *Penicillium roqueforti* in a third bowl. Disperse this mixture evenly over both bowls of curd. Carefully stir the salt/mold mixture into both batches of curd.

8. Add half of the newest batch of curd to a sterilized 2-pound cheese mold. Place the curd on the bottom and up the sides of the mold, leaving a depression in the center. Put all of the first batch of curd into that depression, and cover with the second half of the newer curd. It's entirely possible that you may end up with an extra bit of curd left over from both batches, unable to squeeze it all into the mold, so don't be alarmed if that occurs.

9. Place a clean cheeseboard on your countertop. Put a cheese mat on top of it, and then place the cheese mold in the center of the mat. Place a second cheese mat on top of the mold, and then top with a second cheeseboard. You will be flipping your cheese frequently over the next few days, and this setup makes turning the mold considerably easier.

10. Place the cheeseboard/mat/mold combination in a 55 to 60°F (13 to 16°C) environment, such as your basement or cheese fridge (see page 175). For the next 2 hours, flip the entire setup over every 15 minutes. I've found that placing the cheeseboard/mat/mold combination on a rack positioned over a 9 x 13-inch baking pan or dish is ideal for collecting the whey as it drains from the mold.

11. After 2 hours, place the cheeseboard/mat/mold combination in the 55 to 60°F (13 to 16°C) environment, making sure the humidity is at 85 percent. Keep it there for three days, flipping the apparatus over twice daily.

12. Take the cheese out of the cheese mold. Sprinkle salt over the entire surface of the cheese. Age at 55 to 60°F (13 to 16°C), with 85 percent humidity, for the next four days. Rub the entire surface with salt every day.

13. With the end of a sterilized ice pick or the tip of your dairy thermometer poke the cheese about 30 times, making sure to pierce all the way through the curd. Return the cheese to the 55 to 60°F (13 to 16°C) environment, with 85 percent humidity, and age for 30 days. During this time, the bacteria in the cheese will begin to grow and proliferate.

14. At the end of 30 days, move the cheese to a slightly colder area, around 50°F (10°C), still at 85 percent humidity. Leave to age in this environment for three months. Check the cheese every few weeks, scraping off any mold with a clean knife.

15. At the end of three months, your Gorgonzola is now ready to eat. Taste it and see if it is to your liking. If you prefer a stronger flavor, continue aging in the same environment, scraping off mold every few weeks, for another month or so. Once it is ready, store in the refrigerator and use within three weeks.

MAKING A HOMEMADE CHEESE PRESS

While it is entirely possible to purchase a fully constructed cheese press, it's actually quite easy to simply make your own. Furthermore, making a DIY cheese press, like crafting many things yourself, is considerably less costly. With a few simple steps, you can turn two cutting boards and some pipes into a lean, mean, pressing machine! When you're ready to press, don't forget to take the weight of the top cutting board into account.

Supplies & Materials

1 piece plywood or scrap board cut to the approximate size of the cutting boards

2 wooden cutting boards, each 1 inch (2.5 cm) thick, anywhere from 9 x 13 to 12 x 16 inches (23 x 33 to 30.5 x 40.6 cm)

4 galvanized pipes, each 18 inches (45.7 cm) long, with a 1/2-inch (1.3 cm) diameter

4 galvanized floor flanges for 1/2-inch (1.3 cm) pipe

16 wood screws, 3/4 inch (1.9 cm)

4 pipe end caps, if desired (for appearances only)

1 drip pan (You can purchase a metal drip pan from a cheese-making supplier as shown, or use an aluminum pie pan in which you've cut out a pouring spout.)

An assortment of weight-lifting plates, totaling 50 pounds (23 kg) (I use four 10-pound plates (4.6 kg) and one 5-pound (2.3 kg) plate; the remaining 5 pounds (2.3 kg) come from the weight of the cutting board itself.)

Tools

2 wood clamps

Electric drill

7/8-inch (2.2 cm) Forstner drill bit

1 1/2-inch (3.8 cm) Forstner drill bit

Drilling Frame Holes

1. Begin by placing the scrap board on a few soup cans or similar objects. The cans are necessary to add elevation, in order to accommodate the wood clamp.

2. Place one of the cutting boards on top of the scrap board. Line up the edges, and clamp the cutting board and the scrap board together. This will help to keep the drilled holes from splintering.

3. Using the ⅞-inch (2.2 cm) Forstner bit, drill holes in all four corners of the cutting board, so that the edge of the hole is 1 inch (2.5 cm) from the edge on each side of the corner. Be sure to drill all the way through the cutting board, but be careful not to drill through the scrap board. Remove the drilled cutting board and the scrap board from the cans. When assembled, this cutting board will be the bottom board of the cheese press.

4. Next, place the undrilled cutting board on the cans. Put the drilled cutting board on top of the undrilled cutting board, line up the edges, and clamp the boards together with the wood clamp.

5. Use the holes in the top board as guides for drilling into the bottom board. Using the ⅞-inch (2.2 cm) Forstner bit, drill just far enough to make a guide mark with the pointy center of the bit. Separate the boards.

6. Place the scrap board on top of the cans. Next, put the cutting board with the pilot holes on top of the scrap board and line up the edges, then clamp the two boards together firmly.

7. Following your pilot holes, drill holes through the cutting board with the 1½-inch (3.8 cm) Forstner bit. When assembled, this will be the top board of the cheese press.

Attaching Pipes and Flanges
1. Attach the pipes to the flanges by turning each through the interior threads.

2. Slide the pipes through the cutting board with the ⅞-inch (2.2 cm) holes (the "bottom" board).

3. Next, attach four screws through the bottom of each flange up into the bottom of the cutting board. The flanges will serve as feet.

4. Standing upright, slide the pipes through the holes in the cutting board with the 1½-inch (3.8 cm) holes (the "top" board).

5. Screw endcaps on if desired.

Assembling the Press
1. When you're ready to press some curd, lift the top cutting board up the pipes and off of the press.

2. Place your drip pan on the lower cutting board. Situate it so that the draining spout reaches to the edge of the cutting board.

3. Position a low-sided pan underneath the spout to serve as a catch tray for draining whey.

4. Place your curd-filled cheese mold, with its follower on top, on the drip pan. You'll need to put a "pusher" on top of the follower, to aid in compressing the curd. I use a pint-sized mason jar with a plastic lid. A smaller cheese mold, fitted on top of the follower, works great, too.

5. Slide the top cutting board back over the pipes. Situate it evenly over your cheese mold/follower/pusher setup.

6. Add the amount of weight indicated in your recipe by placing the weight-lifting plates on top of the top cutting board. Be sure they are balanced squarely over the cheese mold. When calculating pressure, remember to account for the weight of the cutting board itself. The sheesham wood board used in my cheese press weighs 5 pounds (2.3 kg).

| The setup | Detail | Curd in cheesecloth | Follower on top | Pusher atop follower |

Book 4

Keeping Bees

The importance of the honeybee in relation to human food systems cannot be overstated. When you consider that over one-third of the foods eaten by humans (including foods consumed by the animals that humans rely on) depend in some part on the tireless efforts of honeybees, you begin to get a sense of just how essential their survival, and our stewardship of them, truly is. From rooftops to orchards, tiny slivers of backyards to expansive farms, beehives are becoming more and more visible and integral in modern homesteads. In this section, I'll share with you the lessons I've learned in my years as a beekeeper. We'll also examine what to consider beforehand; discuss hive hierarchy and what precisely is meant by the term "bee space"; delve into hive housing, location, and feeding requirements; explore how to obtain and install honeybees into a hive; and so much more. My hope here is that you come away with confidence and clarity on what it takes to keep a hive of honeybees.

Chapter 1

Understanding Bees

Humans have had bees in their bonnets, as it were, since the first hunter-gatherer sat beside a buzzing log and got a whiff of the ambrosial fragrance emanating from within. Honeybees are one of the few types of insects purposely kept and managed by humans (observatory ant farms or flea circuses notwithstanding). Long admired for their social organization, architectural feats, and, of course, their products, honeybees are fascinating creatures in their own right. While most beekeepers are in it for the honey, maintaining a thriving hive requires a thorough understanding of bee behaviors, preferences, quirks, and basic make-up. Fledgling beekeepers will benefit enormously from learning a bit of honeybee anatomy, social organization, communication, and life stages before lighting up the smoker or donning a bee veil.

HUMANS & HONEYBEES

Prehistoric cave paintings in Africa and western Europe, dating as far back as 15,000 B.C., depict scenes of harvesting honey and beeswax from wild bee colonies. Before the invention of specialized units for housing bees, gatherers would climb trees and fill wild beehives with smoke in order to harvest honey. Our intrepid ancestors undoubtedly subjected themselves to countless bee stings along the way, as protective bee clothing is a modern phenomenon. Until sugarcane made its way out of the tropics and around the world, honey was the primary sweetener available, so coveted that it was worth all the suffering required to obtain it.

Ancient Egyptian beekeepers were hive pioneers, housing honeybees in stacked cylinders made of clay, dung, or woven grasses. Ancient Rome and Greece engaged in beekeeping, as well, housing bees in a variety of structures, including hollowed-out logs, pottery, and straw baskets called skeps, the form that still comes to mind to many when they hear the word "beehive." Early northern Europeans first harvested honey from wild hives, using systems of ropes, slings, pickaxes, and even spiked footwear for scaling trees. They eventually moved on to use of structures similar to those used by ancient Greeks and Romans.

Unfortunately, the design flaw of these early housing units was that in order to harvest honey or beeswax—or even to take a peek inside—the housing unit had to be destroyed, along with the entire hive. With few exceptions, this remained the case until the invention of the moveable hive by Lorenzo Langstroth in 1852. A pastor from Pennsylvania, Langstroth created a boxlike hive structure composed of interchangeable, easily removable frames. Langstroth's keen understanding of *bee space*, or how much room honeybees (workers, drones, and queen) require to move about easily within a hive, was essential to the success of the design, which has survived, virtually unaltered, for more than 150 years. No small wonder then that he is often considered the father of American beekeeping.

A collection of antique bee skeps

HONEYBEE ANATOMY 101

The body parts of bees enable these versatile creatures to execute a large and varied set of tasks. Gaining a basic understanding of bee anatomy will prove beneficial not just for knowing what's going on and who's doing what, but for learning how to tell if a hive is healthy.

Exoskeleton

Unlike mammals, whose skeletons are located demurely within our epidermis, insects' skeletons are located on the outside. The honeybee's exoskeleton comprises three distinct parts: the head, thorax, and abdomen, each with its own highly specialized components.

Covering the entire surface of the exoskeleton are a multi-tude of spindly hairs. These are crucial for pollination, as pollen gathered from flowers hangs onto these hairs and holds on for the ride of a lifetime.

Head

The bee uses its head to get its bearings, orienting itself to the world around. The head is where you'll find the bee's sensory organs of taste, smell, sound, sight, and, to a lesser extent, touch.

Eyes

Honeybees have five eyes, two large ones on each side of the head, known as compound eyes, and three smaller eyes clustered in a triangle in the center of the head, called **ocelli**. The compound eyes are used for vision as we understand it, allowing bees to detect yellow, blue, and green shades in the color spectrum, along with ultraviolet light, which is not visible to humans. With the ocelli, bees detect light levels, allowing them to orient themselves inside the darkness of the hive.

Antennae

Sometimes referred to as feelers, the two antennae attached to a bee's head are its version of a nose. Capable of detecting scents at concentration levels imperceptible to humans, bees use their feelers to search out fragrant lilacs and blooming tulip poplars, nearby water sources, their hive-mates, and every other scented thing under the sun. Antennae also process touch sensations.

Mandibles

Two jawlike mandibles comprise part of a bee's mouth and are used in different ways depending on the bee's gender and caste. Tasks performed by the mandibles include molding wax into honeycomb, moving objects around the hive, gathering up pollen, and feeding larvae.

Proboscis

Used to slurp up nectar from flowering plants, the proboscis is the honeybee's version of a tongue. When a bee is not foraging, its proboscis is at rest, retracted up into the mandibles. When it's time to guzzle nectar, the proboscis unfolds into a narrow strawlike tube measuring ¼ inch (6 mm) long.

Thorax

The "core" of a honeybee's body, the thorax is the source of all locomotion. Additionally, the thorax is crucial to gathering pollen and propolis, a resinous, glue-like substance sourced from trees and plants and used by honeybees to seal any crack or tear in the hive that needs securing or repair.

Wings

Honeybees have two sets of wings. Tiny muscles attached to the wings control minute changes of position, enabling bees to dart and change direction with rapidity and ease.

Legs

If I had a honeybee's legs, I'd be able to accomplish six different things at once. The ultimate multitaskers, three sets of legs, each with their own specific abilities, work in concert to let bees complete numerous jobs simultaneously. Interior brushes on each leg are used to remove pollen bits from the body. The front pair of legs cleans the antennae. The middle pair takes up pollen and propolis, passing it back to the hind legs. The middle legs are also used in

Bee Anatomy 101

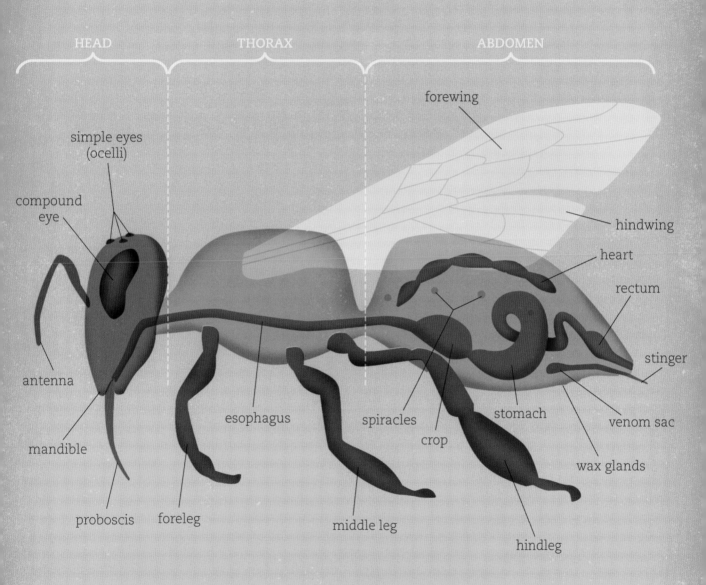

HEAD   THORAX   ABDOMEN

forewing

simple eyes
(ocelli)

compound
eye

hindwing

heart

rectum

antenna

stinger

esophagus

spiracles

stomach

mandible

crop

venom sac

proboscis

foreleg

middle leg

wax glands

hindleg

walking, grooming the wings, and, in worker bees, grabbing onto the wax secreted from their abdomens to make honey-comb. Worker bees' hind legs contain tiny devices called *corbicula*, where pollen collected during foraging flights is stored. Attached to each leg is a tiny foot, consisting of two claws and a central pad. This claw-and-pad powerhouse lets bees hang onto surfaces both smooth and rough.

Abdomen

The abdomen is where all of a honeybee's most precious bits and pieces are housed. From digestive organs to those used in respiration and reproduction, the abdomen contains parts essential to both a bee's life and its potential progeny.

Respiration Organs

Running the length of a bee's abdomen and thorax are the tiniest of holes called *spiracles*. These spiracles allow the honeybee to breathe, taking in oxygen and sending it along to trachea and air sacs. Tracheal mites, a parasite we'll study in greater detail in chapter 9, enter the trachea of honeybees through the first spiracle.

Digestive and Cardiovascular Organs

A heart, true stomach, intestines, elimination organs, and a honey stomach, or *crop*, are all found in the abdomen. The digestive systems of bees are comparable to humans'; food travels down a long esophagus and is digested in the stomach. The intestines take up all of the nutrients extracted from food and then shuttle the waste along to elimination organs. A long tubular organ, the honeybee's heart runs throughout the abdomen, moving *haemolymph* (bee blood) about its entire body instead of just into individual blood vessels, as in humans.

Reproductive Organs

Honeybees, like most creatures, are sexually divided into males and females. The queen and worker bees all possess ovaries and sperm storage areas (the queen, in her role as chief baby-maker, has considerably larger versions of both). Drones contain all of the assorted and sundry "equipment" needed for fulfilling their reproductive roles, including testes, penis, and seminal vesicles.

Wax and Scent Glands

Worker bees have several additional organs, used in communication and building. Wax glands produce liquid wax, which is squeezed out from the underside of the abdomen. When the wax firms up it hardens into scales that bees chews on with their mandibles and work into honeycomb cells. Worker bees' scent glands secrete various pheromones, chemicals that convey messages to other bees.

Stinger

Pity the poor drone! He's the only honeybee lacking a stinger. Used in defense, a stinger is attached to the backmost end of the abdomen of worker and queen bees. The bee venom housed inside the stinger delivers a payload of painful sensations to the victim of a sting. Use of the weapon exacts a price, too: once a bee deploys its stinger and flies away, the stinger tears out of its backside, resulting in its ultimate demise.

HIVE HIERARCHY

A honeybee hive is a highly orchestrated, synergistically operating entity. Each bee's distinct role contributes not just to its own well-being but to the hive's success and continued survival. Tasks and functions are divided into "castes," or social roles, determined biologically before birth. A honeybee literally does what it was born to do. It's not necessarily all honeycomb and happiness inside the hive, however. If a member fails to live up to its role or succumbs to illness or injury, the colony may decide that its continued residency in the hive is detrimental. Then the honeybee in question is promptly (and, often, forcibly) removed or even killed. Optimal function is the hive's chief objective.

The Queen Bee

While she doesn't rule the hive, per se, the queen bee certainly regulates it. Through her single-minded devotion to her task, the queen ensures the literal survival of the species. As egg-layer-in-chief, the queen spends her days positioning her rear over honeycomb cells, depositing eggs, and doing precious little else (no wonder, when you consider the energy it would take to lay up to 2,000 eggs a day!). She leaves the hive only once in her lifetime, for an airborne amorous embrace with a gaggle of pheromone-driven drones, and then returns to live in darkness and perform her duty to the hive.

In addition to making babies, the queen's presence ensures that the hive will be on its best behavior. The pheromones she releases prompt forager bees to keep gathering nectar and pollen, guard bees to stand sentry, and nurse bees to attend to the young, among many other messages. In her absence, or when she ages and begins to fail in her duties, the hive can lose its direction. When a queen dies or begins to decline (signaled by a change in pheromones), a hive will raise a new queen. If eggs or larvae less than three days old are present, worker bees will choose one to become the new queen and begin feeding her *royal jelly,* a nutritious milky-white substance secreted by nurse bees. If no eggs or young larvae are available, latent ovaries in

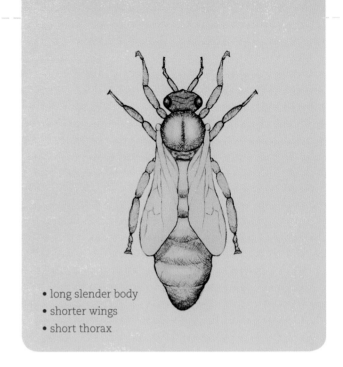

- long slender body
- shorter wings
- short thorax

worker bees—no longer set to "off" by the queen's scent—begin to develop. As workers are incapable of mating, the eggs they lay will be unfertilized, developing into drones. A hive populated almost exclusively by drones cannot survive for long.

The longest-lived member of a colony, a queen can live for two or more years, provided she continues to lay eggs regularly. A queen may succumb to old age or illness, or she may be a victim of *supersedure,* in which a new queen kills an existing queen. Pretty much as soon as the newly hatched queen emerges, the existing queen is thrown out of the colony, left to starve and die outside the hive, or stung to death and removed by undertaker worker bees.

When examining a hive during routine inspections, you'll always want to attempt to locate the queen. I say attempt because in some species of honeybee, her dark-colored body can be difficult to find. Look for her long, slender body, which distinguishes her from her royal subjects. The queen also has shorter wings than workers or drones, covering only about two-thirds of her body. You can also spot the queen by her short thorax, which is considerably smaller than that of worker bees.

Drones

Male honeybees, or drones, have one purpose in life: to mate with the queen. They do this by making periodic flights, searching for an on-the-prowl midair queen. Aside from that, they are cleaned up after, fed, and otherwise cared for by their busy little sisters. Males don't even take the time to do their "business" outdoors, leaving soiled honeycomb in their wake for others to clean up. I can only imagine all the eye-rolling that must go on in the hive.

With about a hundred female workers per drone, you might think the males of the hive have got it made. I beg to differ. Lacking stingers, drones cannot defend themselves, should the occasion call for it. Furthermore, they lack the ability to feed themselves or even seek out food. Toward the end of summer, when nectar stores are low and no food is being collected, drones that have failed to mate get kicked out of the hive. As if that weren't bad enough, a drone's passionate embrace with a virgin queen will also be his last. When the queen emerges from her coupling, the drone's genitals remain attached to her, leaving him to fall from the sky and die.

Drones, like the queen, are relatively easy to spot in the hubbub of the hive. Their bodies are longer than those of worker bees, yet smaller than the queen's. They have fat, rounded bottoms and lack stingers, pollen baskets, or wax glands. Perhaps the drone's most distinguishing physical attribute is its large compound eyes. These eyes are much larger than those of the queen or worker and meet at the top of the drone's large head.

- large compound eyes
- bodies longer then worker bees, yet smaller than queen
- fat, rounded bottoms
- lack stingers, pollen baskets, and wax glands

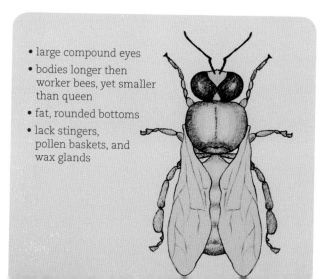

Worker Bees

Aside from reproductive activities, a worker bee is responsible for every other task required within a hive. Its roles vary throughout its short lifetime. As it ages, its sting and wax glands develop, enabling it to perform activities it was previously not physically capable of.

During its lifetime, a worker bee either works from home or heads out into the world to perform its duties. These "house" or "field" activities are determined by its age. Accordingly, when you happen upon a bee out on a foraging expedition, know that you are encountering a more senior member of the hive. Worker bees born during the summer months live only about six weeks, literally working themselves to death. Those fortunate enough to be born late in autumn, when there's less work to do, may live up to six months, providing warmth and necessary functions for wintertime survival.

- much smaller than drone and queen
- broad food glands
- scent glands
- pollen basket

It's never a challenge to locate worker bees in a hive. Open the cover and they're pretty much the first thing you see! Much smaller than the queen or drones, worker bees possess several distinguishing specialized structures. Brood food glands, scent glands, wax glands, and pollen baskets provide all of the tools these hardworking busy bees need to make the hive thrive.

WORKER BEE DUTIES

Housework

The following in-house duties are performed during the first three weeks of a worker bee's life.

NURSING

Feeding and caring for growing larvae

ATTENDING

Grooming and feeding the queen

CLEANING (HIVE)

Cleaning honeycomb cells and keeping the hive debris-free, including removing dead bees to the front of the hive

CLEANING (BEES)

Cleaning dust, pollen, and debris off other bees

UNDERTAKING

Removing dead bees from the hive

BUILDING

Secreting wax from wax glands and rendering it into honeycomb

CAPPING

Secreting wax from wax glands and capping pupae and ripened honey cells

PACKING

Taking pollen from returning foragers and putting it in cells to eat later

RIPENING

Fanning honey in cells to remove water, thereby preserving it

REPAIRING

Placing propolis over any cracks in the hive or any foreign matter too large to carry out

Fieldwork

Once its mandibles and stinger are fully formed, a worker bee is ready to take on the outside world. At three weeks of age it heads out in the wild, fully equipped for foraging duties.

**COLLECTING
(NECTAR, POLLEN, PROPOLIS, AND WATER)**

Gathering up food and water supplies and transporting them back to the hive via either honey sacks or pollen baskets located on a bee's legs

GUARDING

Stinging interlopers and releasing an "alarm" pheromone as a warning to the hive of impending danger

BECOMING ADULTS

Before a bee becomes a bee, it must pass through several developmental stages: egg, larva, and pupa. These three stages are collectively referred to as brood. Each caste goes through a similar sequence, but important distinctions in fertilization and length between stages dictate the caste a bee will be born into.

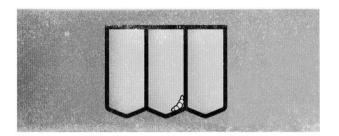

Egg

A queen is a fastidious mama. She'll only lay eggs in the most scrupulously clean cells available, prepared for her by worker bees. Once the queen finds a cell to her liking, she backs in her rear and deposits a single egg at the very back of the cell. Unfertilized eggs will become drones, while fertilized eggs become worker bees, and, on occasion (if the hive decides it needs a new one), queens. The ratio of females to males is carefully controlled in the hive by worker bees, who construct larger cells for males and smaller cells for females in very specific amounts. The queen recognizes the cell size and deposits the correct egg accordingly, usually concentrating worker eggs in the main body of the frame and drone eggs at the farther and lower ends of the frame.

Looking like the tiniest grains of white rice imaginable, the presence of eggs in honeycomb cells is a clear signal that you've got a healthy, laying queen. The eggs are incredibly small, measuring around 1.7 mm, so spotting them is no mean feat. Once you learn what to look for, locating eggs will become easier. A pair of reading glasses or magnifying goggles may help until you get more skilled at eyeballing eggs directly. Holding the frame up to the sunlight during inspection helps as well. Eggs develop for three days before moving to the larval stage.

Larva

Honeybee larvae are called grubs. At this point, they look like pearly white, glistening, curled-up semicircles. Over the next few days, the larvae are fed first royal jelly, then weaned to a blend of honey and pollen. If the hive decides to produce a new queen, she will continue to be fed royal jelly—lucky lady! The larvae grow rapidly during this period, eating like ravenous teenage boys, and shedding their skins five times. Around day six, the larvae stop eating and straighten themselves out in their cells. Ever-vigilant worker bees notice this and set about sealing them over with light brown wax, placing flat disks atop worker larvae and rounded disks atop drone larvae. Once snugly sealed up inside their temporary holding cells, the larvae spin a silken cocoon around themselves and sit tight.

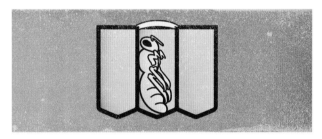

Pupa

Over the next several days, the pupae undergo a profound metamorphosis and begin to take on the appearance of adult bees. Their previously white, moist skin gains color and texture, beginning with the emergence of the black compound eyes. The pupa then chews through the wax cap, emerging as an adult bee 7, 12, or 14 days later, depending on whether a queen, worker, or drone is in development. In total, it takes a queen 16 days in her journey from egg to adult, a worker bee 21 days, and a drone 24 days.

HIVE TALKIN'

While they might not dish gossip or gripe audibly about having to feed the babies and clean up the hive *yet again*, honeybees are in constant communication. Using choreographed movements and specific scents, they keep one another in the loop about everything from where a food source has been found to where the queen is in the hive and so much more.

Pheromones

Found in a number of insects as well as plants (and possibly also in humans), pheromones are composites of chemicals that send a specific message or cause a desired response in others. The pheromone system found in honeybees is one of the most complex known to exist. At least 15 different compounds interact, resulting in either releaser or primer pheromones. Releaser pheromones are short term and change the behavior of the recipient honeybee, while primer pheromones are long term and alter physiology.

Some pheromones are universal to all honeybees, while others are exclusive to each caste. Queen-specific pheromones include the all-important *queen mandibular pheromone*, which regulates hive activities, induces swarming, and even halts the ovarian development of worker bees, among other things. Drones come equipped with a pheromone that tells other drones to meet up in the sky at a certain location to mate with a queen. Worker bees, busy little creatures that they are, come with a virtual pheromone arsenal, enabling them to do everything from sending a "we're over here" aroma into the air for returning foragers (the *Nasonov* pheromone) to an odor shouting "Help! We're under attack" (the aptly titled *Alarm* pheromone). A well-prepared smoker (see page 279) and slow and easy movements help make sure your visits to the hive won't trigger the release of this pheromone.

Dances

When a foraging bee returns from a successful food-seeking expedition, does it keep the location a guarded secret, loading up on nectar and pollen to its tiny heart's desire? To the contrary. As soon as it gets back, a foraging worker bee turns into a dancing machine, conveying detailed information about a food source's location with, while not exact, a rather good degree of precision.

The round dance says "nectar nearby," while the waggle dance conveys "you've got some distance ahead of you, friends." With each dance, the in-the-know bee dances around the hive in a circle, crisscrossing and making figure-eight patterns to provide site specifics. Just how valuable the nectar source is can be gauged by the length and intensity of the dance. Discovered by German researcher Karl von Frisch, who won the Nobel Prize in 1973 for his work, a bee's dance is always based on its orientation to the sun. Accordingly, the same site discovered by a bee at a different time of day will result in a slightly different dance on account of the sun's changing position.

Honeybees engaged in communication

Chapter 2 🐝
What to Consider:
To Bee or Not to Bee

The siren song of beekeeping can be difficult to resist. Honeybees are fascinating to observe, essential to the pollination of over one-third of foods enjoyed by humans, and produce a number of desirable items such as honey and beeswax. Although the craft is not necessarily difficult, not everyone is a good candidate for honeybee caretaking. Like any form of stewardship, beekeeping requires investments of space and time as well as money. You're reading this book, so your interest is clearly piqued. Let's examine some preliminary considerations before you get your heart set on an adorable Italian or intrepid Russian (honeybee, that is!).

ON LOCATION

Compared to other forms of animal husbandry (dairy cows come to mind), honeybees require very little space—just what is needed for a hive and a little room to work. You can keep honeybees everywhere from urban rooftops and quarter-acre backyard plots to vast, rural expanses. Honeybees are skilled foragers and will travel miles from the hive searching for nectar and pollen.

Urban bees seem to do quite well in cities where a fairly good degree of biodiversity persists. Public parks, landscaped office buildings, antiquated churches planted long ago with ambrosial roses, rooftop gardens, backyard veggie patches, potted herbs on balconies—the amount of urban flora and fauna is profuse. Packed into such dense spaces, nectar and pollen available from these sources, along with water from lakes, creeks, rivers, birdbaths, and puddles, provide ideal foraging grounds for our buzzing friends.

Honeybees are capable of surviving and thriving in a wide range of climates and terrains, albeit with a little assistance from you. You can find honeybees in rugged hillsides and flat valleys, from locales where winter means pulling out the snow shovel and layering on wool sweaters to those where flip-flops and a beach towel are all that's needed. Provided there are plants that bloom and flower, honeybees will hang their hats wherever you hang yours.

As you are considering where to place a beehive or two, keep in mind that while bees don't take up much room, the area where you locate their hives will need to key criteria. It will require some sort of windbreak, a bit of morning sunlight, and some degree of shade. You will also need access to water and room for you to navigate around the hive for examinations and extraction. We'll discuss these needs in greater detail in chapter 3 when we examine hive components and where best to situate your hive.

MONEY MATTERS

Unless your preferred pastime is cloud watching or counting raindrops, the hobbies you already engage in most likely incur a bit of expense, either at the outset or over time. So, too, with beekeeping. When you factor in the cost of the hive itself, protective gear, equipment such as a smoker (used for calming the bees), and the bees themselves, in addition to food (should you need to supply it), medications (should you opt to use them), resource materials, and vessels for holding honey, the initial expense of beekeeping can seem daunting. While I will admit that the startup costs are considerable, there are a number of ways to begin beekeeping without breaking the bank.

An assortment of beekeeping gear

A local beekeeping chapter is a great resource. Such organizations may have periodic giveaways or be recipients of donations from larger organizations looking to fund novice beekeepers. When I first began my foray into the world of *Apis mellifera*, I attended a two-weekend-long beginning beekeeping school sponsored by my regional beekeeping organization. All attendees were entered into a contest for a litany of apiary goods to be given away at the conclusion of the school. I won an expertly written book on bee-keeping, while other attendees went home with everything from smokers to full hives. Many chapters have more costly equipment, such as honey extractors, available for rent. My local chapter rents out its mechanized extractor for a mere $11—the same equipment costs hundreds to purchase.

It might be tempting to purchase secondhand beekeeping equipment or hives. While something like gently used protective clothing and gear poses no threat, used hives might harbor disease. This is where your local chapter can assist you in connecting with a reputable seller in your area. You could also contact the regional governmental representative for beekeeping concerns, such as a state or county bee inspector, to solicit advice on used bee goods. If you elect to buy new, I'd encourage you to shop around. When first buying my hives and equipment, I found a great variety in prices between suppliers. Search for deals, but don't scrimp too much. When it comes to beekeeping equipment, it pays to start with the best. Going cheap all around will only require greater investment later when bargain gear begins to break down or fall apart.

After you've got the major infrastructure in place, the ongoing expenses of beekeeping are relatively small. You'll need sugar for feeding them when nectar isn't present for foraging; additional supers (page 262) for when the honey starts coming in; new queens when the occasion merits it; jars and labels for the honey; and additional hives, if you decide to acquire more bees or split an existing hive (more on this in chapter 6). If you live in bear country, add bear fencing to the list. Overall, maintaining a hive of bees is quite affordable, especially when compared to the costs of food and veterinary care for pets such as cats and dogs.

KEEPING TIME

If you take a dog for a daily walk or clean a cat's litter box regularly, you're already devoting more time for animal maintenance than will ever be required in beekeeping. You'll spend the largest amount of time with your bees during the first year, inspecting them, looking for problems, checking that a queen is present, feeding them if necessary (we'll discuss that in greater detail in chapter 4), and other getting-to-know-you tasks. Thereafter, visits to the hive may be few.

Over the winter, you'll visit your hive only occasionally, just to check in and make sure nothing has caused any structural damage (like a predator, strong gust of wind, or fallen tree branch). As the warmer months approach, it will be necessary to stop by every week or two to check the hive's progress. When honey is available, several hours will be required for removing the supers, extracting the liquid, and cleaning the equipment when done. A bit of fall maintenance to prep your hive for the impending cold weather closes out a year's activities for the beekeeper. I'll offer more information about the best time of year to get started with bees, as well as seasonal upkeep, in chapter 8.

While there isn't a great deal of daily care involved in beekeeping at any given time, bear in mind that your bees will need to be looked after regularly. If you're the type to take lengthy vacations during the summer months, or get pulled away at work for weeks at a stretch, it would behoove you to find a beekeeping friend before setting up your hives. A reciprocal arrangement with a fellow beekeeper, whereby you offer to care for one another's hives when life calls you away from home, can be especially advantageous. A "bee-sitter" can drop in, inspect the hive, provide food if needed, and add a super or two if honey is beginning to fill up.

LAW-ABIDING CITIZEN

While many places in the world gladly welcome beekeeping, there are those that do not. In the United States, each state has its own rules on beekeeping. Within those states, variations in what is and isn't allowed exist from one municipality to the next. Before you place an order for bees, gear, or equipment, bear in mind that some cities forbid beekeeping outright, while others place restrictions on it, such as hive location or number of hives per residence. Some renegade apiarists house bees in cities that prohibit doing so while simultaneously trying to have the laws changed in their favor. These "outlaw" beekeepers accept the risks that such a practice may incur (fines, relocation of hives, and so on). Check the codes in your city—available through the Department of Agriculture, local zoning board, town hall, bee club, or governing body—to determine what is allowed.

BEING NEIGHBORLY

The popular saying "good fences make good neighbors" is especially apropos when it comes to beekeeping. If your neighbors are within your direct line of sight, I would urge you to mention your beekeeping plans beforehand. Unfounded or not, some people have fears about bees. Popular ignorance and misinformation about bees has resulted in widespread opinions that are simply not true. It's your job, then, to raise awareness, dispelling myths before they fester into false beliefs. The following tips will go far toward assuaging your neighbors' concerns about your winged, foraging friends.

→ Start with gentle bees to begin with. If you find your bees to be aggressive, consider requeening. This often calms the hive within a month or so.

→ Be inconspicuous. Place your hive in a location that doesn't put neighbors, pets, or children in a direct flight path. Returning foragers follow a routine pattern and could potentially sting anything that crosses their path. If your neighbors are quite close, plant a high hedge or install a fence at least 6 feet (1.8 m) tall to encourage bees to fly up, over, and away from anything nearby. Also, position the hives to face away from children's playgrounds, dog kennels, and neighbors' doors.

→ Many complaints from neighbors are based on thirsty bees drinking from their birdbath, swimming pool, pond, or other water source. Once bees discover a water source, it's difficult to get them out of the habit of visiting, so provide water near the hive and put a stop to this situation before it begins. I'll cover water options in greater detail in chapter 3.

→ Don't keep more than four hives on property smaller than a quarter acre. When you are working the bees, or if a colony should swarm (leave the hive in search of a new home), all those buzzing bees can make the neighbors nervous, even though *you* might know there's nothing to be worried about (a swarm is actually quite docile; they're just looking for a place to start setting up house and care for the babies).

→ Remember, as the saying goes, you can catch more flies with honey than with vinegar. Ply your neighbors with honey. Bake them sweet delicacies made with your honey or craft them some homegrown beeswax candles. Invite them over to watch as you examine the hives, showing them just how good-natured and rather indifferent to your actions the bees are. Let them know that the life of a beekeeper, their friends, and neighbors is one characterized by sweetness, in word, deed, and flavor.

Avoiding Bee Stings

While the occasional sting may happen, there are a number of precautionary steps that can be taken to minimize the risk.

→ Wear protective gear when working with your bees, including gloves, a veil, and thick, light-colored outerwear. Tuck pant legs into boots or shoes to prevent bees from sneaking in—they love to explore dark cracks and crevices.

→ Move slowly when working the bees. Quick, jerky movements make them concerned that danger is approaching.

→ Smoke the hive entrance before opening it. This will help calm the bees. Be sure your smoker is well lit before you begin your examination and that it will remain lit for the duration of your visit (I'll discuss lighting a smoker on page 279).

→ Situate your hive so that the entrance doesn't directly face children's play areas or other heavily trafficked areas. Keep in mind, though, that the best hive positioning is to face east or southeast to take advantage of morning light. Similarly, don't block the hive entrance when working with the bees. Stand to one side or at the back.

→ Avoid working your bees on inclement weather days. Also, try to avoid working the bees either too early or too late in the day. During bad weather, early mornings, or twilight hours, most of the hive will be at home. It's best to visit when a good number of the hive's residents are out foraging.

→ Try not to bang, hit, or otherwise jar the hive. Strong vibrations upset the bees. Be gentle when working the bees and they will react in kind—in fact, they'll most likely just ignore you.

PETS & CHILDREN

Pets and children share one defining trait: curiosity. When it comes to beekeeping, this is often good for children, while not so ideal for pets.

When introducing children to bees, one hopes to kindle a natural curiosity about the hive, its occupants, and its goings-on. I've seen kids as young as five who are active beekeepers, assisting Mom or Dad with hive chores, honey extractions, and the like. The lessons on pollination, synergistic workload, and hive interdependence are fantastic learning opportunities for children. Beekeeping gets the little ones outdoors and moving (albeit slowly and gently, when actively working the hives), breathing fresh air into their developing lungs, and experiencing the living world around them. Bee suppliers carry protective gear in children's sizes, and a number of books and videos written expressly for educating children about honeybees are available. If you encounter a child who harbors a fear of bee stings, do your best to explain to them all of the precautionary measures that can be taken to prevent stings from occurring, as well as the fact that honeybees really don't want to sting humans. You could also put together a "just-in-case" sting kit, with ointment and colorful bandages. Show it to your young beekeeper to assure them that help is available should they ever need it, and put it in a readily accessible location, easily reached by hands large and small alike.

As for pets, many will quickly learn that the hive is nice from a distance, but something else entirely if they move in too close. Cats and dogs might take a sniff or two, or even move toward the front of the hive, but most will back away as soon as they get a sense of what's in there. My dogs and cats have always steered clear of the hives, perhaps knowing on some level that the bees are not their friends. While they are out foraging, honeybees are of no real threat to animals. They are extremely focused when foraging, and an attack is highly unlikely. That said, if your pets exhibit too much curiosity, a barrier of some sort might be in order. Larger animals such as goats, sheep, or horses should definitely be prevented from accessing the bee area, as their movements could knock over the hive.

As I've had a close encounter with a bear on my property (see page 318), I keep my hives surrounded by electric fencing. Once, while I was outside in the chicken coop, my dog must have ventured a bit too near the fence while sniffing out some creature or other. I heard a sudden yelp, and then saw him running from the direction of the hives. He continued looking in that direction for the next few minutes with a "there's something mean over there!" look on his face. To date, he's shown no interest whatsoever in exploring the hives.

ALLERGIES

Honeybees take all the blame. Fingers get pointed at *Apis mellifera* for stings that actually came from wasps, yellow jackets, hornets, bumblebees, carpenter bees, sweat bees, and many other insects. Any sting will result in swelling and redness at the site of the wound. The subsequent pain and soreness will last anywhere from a few hours to several days. This is entirely normal.

However, for those with an allergy to bee venom, a bee sting may cause life-threatening anaphylactic shock. While this condition occurs in less than 1 percent of the general population, it is extremely dangerous. An allergist can conclusively diagnose allergies to honeybee venom. If you or a member of your family are allergic to bee venom,

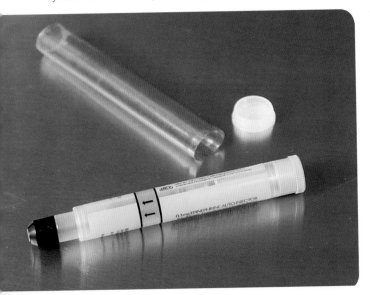

consult with your physician for the best course of action. They may suggest carrying an epinephrine auto-injector, in which sensitive individuals self-administer an antidote to bee venom. Conversely, you may choose to abstain from beekeeping altogether. There are plenty of ways to enjoy and assist honeybees without necessarily keeping them yourself. You could plant a garden with our many pollinators in mind (in an area not directly near your home, such as a community garden or church yard), attend a lecture at a bee club, or participate during the extraction of a beekeeping friend's honey.

SPECIES VARIATIONS

Next you will need to consider what species of honeybee to acquire. Having evolved in different geographic regions, different honeybee species possess different traits and characteristics. A bee hailing from a cold region, such as Russia, might manage harsh winters better than its sun-loving Italian cousin, for example. In addition to hardiness, bee species vary in terms of their aggression, resistance to pests and diseases, and their propensity for *robbing*. Robbing is a truly undesirable situation, when a stronger hive (or population of wild pollinators, such as wasps) invades a weaker hive, stealing honey.

Honeybees belong to the genus *Apis*, meaning "beelike" in Latin, of which there are eight species. *Apis mellifera*, literally "honey-bearing bee," is one of these species and is further broken down into 24 races, or subspecies. The following are some of the most popular and common races of honeybees kept by beekeepers, which are readily available from bee suppliers.

Carniolan (*A. m. carnica*)

Hailing originally from east-central Europe, the Carniolan was introduced to North America in 1883 and can now be found across the world. This variety of honeybee is dark-colored, with gray bands running across its body instead of yellow. Advantages of Carniolans include an exceptionally gentle temperament, good management of winter food stores, rapid buildup of brood (i.e., baby bees) in the spring, small robbing tendency, and a general likelihood toward surviving winter conditions (see page 309).

Caucasian (A. m. caucasica)

This race of bees is named after the Caucasus region, sandwiched between the Black and Caspian seas. These bees are visually characterized by their gray-black bodies. Advantages include a very gentle temperament, the ability to overwinter well, and the longest proboscis of all European honeybee races, which allows them to extract nectar from a wide range of plants. Disadvantages include a tendency toward swarming, liberal use of propolis (which can make examining the hive challenging to the beekeeper), and susceptibility to certain diseases such as nosema (see page 312).

German (A. m. mellifera)

German honeybees, also known as "black" or "north European" bees, were the first species imported by early American colonists to pollinate European varieties of fruits. Once the most common honeybee in North America, German bees dominated the landscape of their new environs until the introduction of Italian bees. Although hardy producers of brood and honey, Germans had a reputation for aggression, prompting American apiarists to search out a more docile bee.

Italian (A. m. ligustica)

Discovered in 1859, the gentle Italians are now one of the most popular species of honeybees kept in North America. Characterized by yellow-golden and brown bands, these honey workhorses hail from the Apennine Peninsula in the "boot" of Italy. This species all but completely replaced the German bee when introduced to the United States, as its relative lack of aggression, coupled with intense honey production, made it a fast favorite. Italians are readily available from most bee suppliers. Advantages of this species include production of a large amount of brood and honey,

buildup of large winter colonies, and low swarming tendency. Disadvantages include robbing tendency, as large winter colonies often eat through their food stores too soon, and susceptibility to certain pests and diseases (although not European Foulbrood, to which they exhibit marked resistance; see page 311 for a detailed discussion).

Russian

The U.S. Department of Agriculture, in cooperation with the Russian government, began a research project in the 1990s, looking for a species of honeybee with resistance to varroa and tracheal mites, two parasites with a reputation for incurring large losses of honeybee populations (see pages 313–315). After discovering that Russian bees had long lived with and developed resistance to the haemolymph-sucking pests, importation began in earnest. A hardy stock, this variety of bee has faired rather well in North America. Russians resemble Carniolans in a number of ways, including slowing down the buildup of brood and food consumption when nectar supplies are low, leading to smaller winter colonies. They are comparable to Italians in a heavy production of brood and honey when nectar and pollen are readily available. Russians are now available from many bee suppliers.

Africanized Honeybees (AHB)

As a beekeeper, I can think of few things as ominous sounding as a "killer bee." Given that sensationalistic moniker by the media, these bees are known to apiarists as Africanized honeybees. In the late 1950s, a group of Brazilian researchers were attempting to create a hybridized bee capable of producing plentiful honey while withstanding tropical heat and humidity. Such a bee could aid in pollination, offer export products, and provide work for the nation's poor. The notoriously aggressive African bee (already adapted for a warm climate) was imported and bred with the considerably more laid-back European honeybee. Unfortunately, in the process, 26 African queens escaped, fled into the wild jungles of Brazil, and bred with the wild European bee populations.

What resulted is a fiery-tempered honeybee, not to mention a public relations headache for the cause of AHB's quieter, more docile kin. *Apis mellifera scutellata*, as Africanized honeybees are technically known, possess a reputation for being intensely protective of their hives.

They are quick to attack, will travel far distances to pursue an "assailant," and stay annoyed for days afterward. Africanized honeybees are, understandably, quite difficult to keep. Under intense management, however, the bees are quite productive, and Brazil's beekeeping industry has thrived. Ongoing efforts there at re-domestication of the bees over the past few decades have resulted in the development of more docile stock, which in turn can serve as an entry point for breeding future generations of gentler AHBs.

The danger, however, has arisen from swarming AHBs that have moved across South and Central America, into Mexico, and, now, into a number of southern U.S. states, stretching in a band from California to Florida. Improperly managed or wild Africanized honeybees can be lethal to animals. Human deaths are extremely rare and have involved almost exclusively elderly persons unable to protect themselves from an attack.

Buckfast (hybridized)

Developed by Brother Adam, an English Benedictine monk, in the 1920s, Buckfast bees are named after the abbey in which they were first produced. By carefully crossbreeding several races, Brother Adam created a docile, highly productive bee that exhibited strong resistance to tracheal mites and overwintered well. One disadvantage of Buckfast colonies is the need to requeen annually. As members of a hybrid species, Buckfast offspring queens will not "breed true," with traits identical to their mother. Therefore, supersedure, if allowed, would result in genetic drift within the hive. Buckfast bees also have a tendency toward slow buildup of brood in the spring and are therefore not the best choice if you're looking to pollinate early spring crops (Carniolans are better suited for that purpose).

Starline (hybridized)

The world's only hybrid race of Italians, Starline honeybees were developed to produce well when used for commercial purposes. This strain of bee builds up a large amount of springtime brood, produces ample honey under the right conditions, and uses a minimal amount of propolis, allowing for easy inspections and frame removal come extraction time. On the down side, Starlines may have difficulty overwintering; as with most Italian honeybees, their large colonies can create wintertime food scarcities. Like Buckfast bees, colonies may need to be requeened annually to prevent genetic drift.

Chapter 3 🐝
Housing:
Understanding
Bee Space

A crucial component in keeping bees, housing is what separates the practice of beekeeping from wild colonies of bees. Here we'll examine the parts of the hive, details about purchasing housing equipment, and where to place your bees. After reading this chapter and acquainting yourself with bee housing essentials, you should feel considerably more informed about choosing proper lodging for your new companions.

ANATOMY OF A HIVE

Although composed of individual members (queen, workers, drones), a beehive can be thought of as a distinct, fully integrated, functioning organism. All of the residents' actions work toward the optimal well-being and survival of the entire hive. Should one or more members begin to fail in their duties, the entire hive is put at risk. Bees are inherently social creatures, rubbing elbows with their hive co-members not out of politeness, but out of necessity. They *need* each other, in the truest sense of the word.

Once they have found a suitable home, honeybees go about the business of forming vertical sheets of hexagonally shaped comb, produced from wax excreted from their bodies. The sheets of comb are suspended from the roof or top of whatever vessel they've elected to set up shop in. No matter whether that space is a tree trunk or a human-made hive, honeybees maintain a minimum distance between combs of never less than ¼ inch (6 mm) nor greater than ⅜ inch (9.5 mm). These regular intervals allow them to easily navigate around straight, evenly spaced combs. That space, with its rigidly determined parameters, is referred to as *bee space*. If the bees encounter a space larger than bee space, they build additional comb. Too-small spaces will be filled with propolis so that no smaller interloper can wiggle its way into the hive.

HIVE COMPONENTS

While several different models of beehives are found around the world, the most commonly used form is the Langstroth hive. As described on page 243, Langstroth invented the moveable hive in the mid-19th century. Prior to his invention, most hives needed to be seriously damaged or destroyed for honey extraction and beekeeping inspections. The Langstroth hive is essentially a series of stacked wooden boxes. These boxes build on the bees' natural style of honeycomb building, permitting the hive to build following the principles of bee space mentioned above.

Through attentive observation, Langstroth was able to determine the exact parameters guiding honeycomb construction. He then created housing appropriate to the honeybees' unforgiving specifications. Once comb is built, bees fill it up with brood or food, and then move on to the next available space. Adding boxes, or *supers*, on top of existing boxes permits the bees to increase both the hive's size and food supply. The stacked boxes are filled with removable vertical frames. These frames resemble flat drawers and are the surface upon which the honeybees build their comb. Beekeepers can easily inspect each frame for hive health and remove them as needed for honey and wax collection.

The components of the Langstroth hive are known as *woodenware*, as they are usually made of pine, cedar, or cypress, although a number of plastic models are also becoming available. We'll examine the function of each component below and on the following pages.

Hive Stand

The hive stand is the primary support for the entire hive. Keeping the hive off the ground is quite important, for a number of reasons. First, excess moisture can be a death knell for bees. Raising the hive off the ground prevents precipitation from pooling or condensing in the hive. Second, elevating the hive moves it out of easy access from most other insects and opportunistic predators, as well as preventing low-growing plants from blocking the entrance. Lastly, having the hive above ground level keeps the beekeeper from needing to bend and stoop over to examine the hive, feed bees, remove frames, or do any other hive-related activity.

Hive stand

While most hives come with a wooden stand consisting of three side pieces and a gently sloped landing board, many beekeepers feel the hives are not quite high enough using only those pieces of woodenware. Most prefer to raise them somewhere between 2 to 3 feet (61 to 91.4 cm) off the ground. This can easily be achieved either by constructing a wooden stand out of 2 x 4s, or resting the hive atop concrete blocks, railroad ties, or some other strong support that can withstand up to 200 pounds (91 kg) of weight (a possibility with an active colony in full honey and brood production). If you opt to use concrete blocks, as I do, you might want to place a flat board of heavy lumber between the blocks and the underside of the hive to give you a work space to rest tools or hive components during examinations.

Bottom Board

Essentially the hive's floor, the bottom board also contains the entrance to the hive. Bottom boards may be made from solid pieces of wood or from metal screening. Screened bottom boards are beneficial for providing ventilation and temperature regulation to the hive during warm summer months. They can also be used to monitor and control the population of the parasitic varroa mite. When mites are a problem, beekeepers can either allow mites to simply fall out of the hive (preventing them from crawling back in) or place a sticky mat atop the screen, which traps falling mites, and count the population to determine the rate of infestation (more on this in chapter 9).

Screened bottom board

Entrance Reducer

This small, removable piece of woodenware is a strip of wood running the length of the hive's entrance with carved notches of varying size on both sides. The different notches

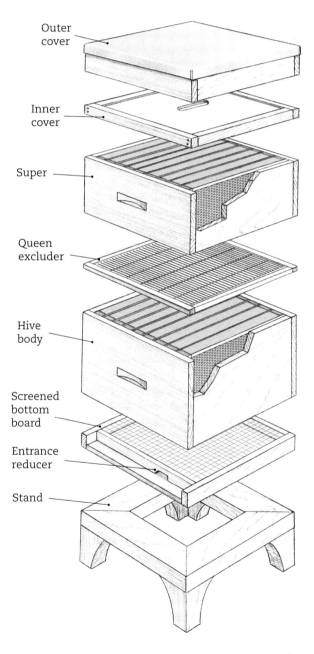

Outer cover

Inner cover

Super

Queen excluder

Hive body

Screened bottom board

Entrance reducer

Stand

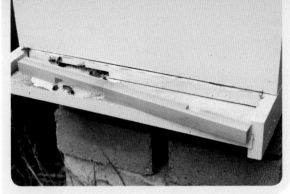

Entrance reducer

provide openings of varying size, permitting the beekeeper to regulate the degree of access to the entrance. Under ideal circumstances during warmer months, the larger entrance is used. When the weather cools, the smaller side is installed, in order to prevent chilly mice looking for a free place to couch surf from entering the hive. The smaller entrance may also be utilized if robbing should ever occur.

Hive Body

Also known as *brood chambers, brood boxes, deep hive bodies,* or simply *deeps,* hive bodies are the largest boxes in the hive. They sit directly atop the bottom board and house the queen, brood, and the food the bees eat themselves. Hive bodies are about 9½ inches (24.1 cm) tall and can hold 9 to 10 frames (more on frames on page 265). Many are made of wood, either pine or cypress, although there are plastic models available. These structures have four sides but no top or bottom, so that bees can climb from one box to the next inside the hive. They have recesses cut into their sides to allow for lifting or hoisting, should the need arise.

The decision to use one or two hive bodies is usually determined by the climate in your area. If you live in a region where harsh, extended, truly cold winters do not occur, then you should be fine with one hive body. Those living in cold-weather areas may need to use two hive bodies to provide enough space for brood and food to last all winter long. A combination of one hive body and one medium super or a collection of three medium supers will achieve the same goal. When full of honey, wax, bees, brood, nectar, and pollen, a hive body can easily weigh between 60 and 80

pounds (27 and 36 kg), a hefty burden for even the most muscular among us. Some beekeepers use a configuration of smaller supers to create both brood chambers and honey storage. Using a consistently sized super throughout your hive allows for the interchange of frames, should you need to move things around.

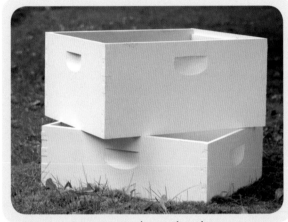

Supers come in varying sizes.

Supers

Shallow and medium supers are the boxes placed above the hive body and are used for honey storage. The honey stored in these boxes is for the beekeeper's use, while the honey and food for the bees themselves will be in lower boxes, closer to the brood. If you opt to forgo use of deep hive boxes completely, medium supers will then constitute the make-up of the hive itself, with three medium supers for housing topped by any number of shallow supers.

Medium honey supers are 6⅝ inches (16.8 cm) high. They are also occasionally referred to as *Dadant, Western, or Illinois* supers and weigh around 50 pounds (23 kg) when full. Shallow supers are 5¹⁄₁₆ to 5⅜ inches (12.9 to 13.7 cm) high and will weigh somewhere between 40 and 45 pounds (18 and 20 kg) when full. As a petite woman, I've found a combination of one deep hive body, topped with a medium super, followed by additional shallow supers, to serve me well. Select the setup that best suits your needs based on your physicality and activity level with the bees in terms of frequency of visits to the hives and opportunities for extraction (mediums will hold more honey, but will weigh more than shallows).

Frames and Foundation

Frames are the supports on which bees build their comb, "framing" out their environs. In the wild, comb would simply be built (referred to in beekeeping jargon as *drawn out*) from the top of whatever enclosure the bees choose to set up shop in. In a hive tended by a beekeeper, frames, enclosed on four sides by wooden or plastic panels, allow for easy inspection without breaking or otherwise harming the comb. Most supers hold 10 frames, although some will accommodate more. You can opt to either purchase frames fully assembled or unassembled. The cost will be somewhat less for unassembled frames, but, accordingly, time will have to be spent putting them together yourself. This isn't necessarily difficult, but if you're short on time, or not particularly adept at assembling things, I'd spring for the assembled frames.

Frames are usually a standard length of 17⅝ inches (44.8 cm). Depending on the depth of the super they are being placed in, either 9⅛-, 7¼-, 6¼-, or 5⅜-inch-deep (23.2, 18.4, 15.9, or 13.7 cm) frames are used. Standard frames consist of a top bar, two side bars, and a bottom bar. They hang inside supers on ledges called rabbets. Attached to the center of each frame is a thin sheet of either beeswax or plastic known as *foundation*. The frames provide support for the foundation, giving it structure and rigidity so it will hold up over time, particularly when subjected to the fast speeds used in centrifuges during honey extraction (see page 330 for more on extraction). Most frames have a removable top bar, so that foundation can be replaced or added as necessary.

Foundation, whether plastic or beeswax, is embossed with hexagons. The honeybees use these shapes as a guideline for drawing out the comb, producing wax cells from their bodies, and then chewing and manipulating it in place. I find the entire process stunningly beautiful, a mystical honeybee alchemy. Whether you choose to use beeswax or plastic foundation is a matter of personal preference, as each has its advantages and disadvantages. Plastic will last considerably longer, and it resists wax moths particularly well. However, bees are somewhat slower to accept and begin building on plastic foundation. Realizing this, some manufacturers have begun coating plastic foundation with a very thin sheet of natural beeswax. Natural beeswax foundation, while readily accepted by the bees, is considerably more fragile than plastic. It requires wire supports, inserted between two beeswax sheets, in order to provide it with body and structure.

Frames

Beeswax foundation

Queen Excluder

This piece of woodenware is used when honey production is in full swing. It consists of a wooden frame that encloses either a metal or plastic slatted grid. As the name suggests, it excludes the queen from certain parts of the hive. If you intend to harvest honey, a queen excluder will keep the queen from entering the supers where honey is being produced and stored. Placed on top of the hive bodies, where brood is stored, the queen excluder allows

Plastic foundation

Queen excluder

worker bees to easily pass through but prohibits the larger queen's access. Using this tool helps to keep the developing baby bees separate from the honey. Without it, you could have a great deal of brood mixed in with the honey come extraction time. Since keeping the colony growing and thriving is the beekeeper's goal, killing off brood is to be avoided. Once the honey flow comes to an end, the queen excluder should be removed.

The use of queen excluders is somewhat controversial among beekeepers. Some argue that its use actually hinders and slows honey production by limiting the bees' movement. Honeybees are highly efficient and may be reluctant to move up into higher supers to store nectar if the brood chamber still has cells available for filling. To encourage their movement, then, it is suggested that the bees be allowed to move freely between the hive body and the supers before the queen excluder is added. This way the bees will have begun to store nectar in the supers, and, again guided by efficiency, they will be encouraged to move upward and cap it for honey production.

Inner cover

Inner Cover

If you think of the hive as a house, the inner cover is the interior ceiling. Resting atop the uppermost super and underneath the outer cover, the inner cover prevents the bees from gluing the hive shut with propolis and wax. It also affords an additional layer of insulation from the harsh heat of direct sun in summer and the chill of cold, moisture-laden air in winter. Inner covers have an oblong hole cut out of the center to allow air to circulate, increasing ventilation at all times of the year.

Inner covers are made of wood, Masonite, or plastic, and are flat on one side with a raised rim on the other side. When positioning the inner cover over the top of the upper super, the flat side faces down. You'll know it's on the right way if the rimmed, traylike side is oriented skyward. Some inner covers also have a small notch carved out of one of the shorter ends. This is for additional ventilation and should be positioned at the front of the hive. Inner covers are known as *crown boards* in some parts of the world.

Outer Cover

The uppermost component of the hive, the outer cover, serves as its roof. Framed by wood, the cover itself is most often made of galvanized tin or aluminum. Its sides extend beyond those of the boxes beneath it, much like a roof extends beyond the walls of a house. This allows precipitation to drip off the sides and onto the ground, keeping the hive itself dry. The outer cover fits perfectly over the inner cover, enclosing both it and the top portion of the highest super.

Other Hive Types

While the Langstroth hive is the most commonly used model around the world, it is not the only hive type in use.

NATIONAL HIVE

The most well-known hive type in the United Kingdom, the National hive makes use of smaller frames than those found in a Langstroth hive. The top bar frames in a National hive are also longer than those in a Langstroth, allowing it to hold 11 frames. The bee space, the area in which honeybees move freely, is located at the bottom of a super in a National hive, while it can be found at the top of Langstroth hive supers.

COMMERCIAL HIVE

As its name suggests, the Commercial is the hive model most favored by commercial production beekeepers. These hives have large brood boxes and are often used interchangeably with National hive supers. Commercial beekeepers like this model because it permits a large colony of bees to live comfortably in the hive, minimizing the risk of swarming.

WBC HIVE

This attractive structure was invented by Englishman William Broughton Carr and is the more ornamental of the U.K.-designed hives. The WBC is a double-walled hive, as compared to single-walled models such as the Langstroth or National. Such hives are covered by an exterior layer of wood, with the supers and hive body nestled inside. The WBC has sloped sides and a gabled roof and must have the outer panels removed before the interior may be accessed. While gaining entry to the hive may be more challenging for the beekeeper, the exterior panels of the WBC provide additional insulation, allowing interior supers to be made with less thick wood, making them lighter and easier to lift. WBC hives hold 10 frames.

TOP BAR HIVE

Also known as the Kenya hive, this model was created as a cheaper alternative to traditional hives. Owing to their low cost, these hives are more commonly used in developing nations. Top bar hives are physically quite different from other models. While they make use of the concept of bee space and use frames, the frames only have one side, the top, hence the name. When working with such frames, the beekeeper allows the bees themselves to create honeycomb without foundation support (sometimes foundation is used, but only as a tiny piece). As opposed to stacked wooden supers used in other hives, top bar hives extend horizontally. The structure is a trapezoid shape, instead of a cube, which encourages bees to draw the comb so that it hangs down instead of attaching it to the walls of the hive cavity.

While comb from top bar hives cannot be placed in a centrifuge for honey extraction (the comb would fall apart), the repeated buildup of new honeycomb after each extraction does create a surplus of beeswax that can be sold. Honey production from top bar hives is quite a bit less than that from other modern hive types. On the plus side, bees can be encouraged to store honey separately from brood, making it less likely that bees will be killed during comb removal, as is common with more rudimentary beehives like skeps. As cute as they might be, it is worth noting that it is illegal to keep bees in skeps in both the United States and Canada.

A top bar hive uses a trapezoid shape

WHERE TO PLACE YOUR HIVE

Once you've acquired your hive components and put them together, it's time to situate the fully assembled hive somewhere on your property. Several crucial variables should factor into your location decision, including sun exposure, windbreak availability, water source, flight path, weed suppression, accessibility, and moisture prevention.

Sun Exposure

The hive needs a bit of sunshine to keep it warm and active. A southeast exposure provides morning sunshine, stimulating foraging bees to rise, shine, and get busy gathering nectar. Siting your hive in this direction also warms the hive in cooler months while shielding it from the hottest midday rays of summer. Avoid placing the hive in direct sun, as that can warm the hive too much; a too-shady spot, however, may have problems with too much moisture.

Windbreaks

Bees need a bit of protection from heavy winds. In considering where to site your hive, be sure to keep it out of the direct path of wind gusts. After you've determined your spot to be relatively wind-free, place the hives with a windbreak of some form at the rear. This can come in the form of a hedgerow, a cluster of bushes, a fence, the edge of a forest, or, as in my case, the side of a building. If you're an urban rooftop beekeeper, you might want to consider locating your hives close to a wall, beside the roof access door, or near some potted shrubs to provide added protection from bracing winds.

Water

Access to water is crucial for a bee's survival, especially for temperature regulation inside the hive during warm months. Honeybees also use water to thin out any honey that may have become too thick. If you live adjacent to a natural water source such as a creek, stream, river, or pond, you're in great shape. Otherwise, consider a garden pond, birdbath, terra-cotta pot filled with water (and small rocks, so that the bees don't drown while drinking), or chicken waterer (what I use in the event the small stream located adjacent to my hives dries up, which happens periodically during summertime droughts). If you have nearby neighbors, establishing a designated water source right from the onset is crucial. You don't want your bees quenching their thirst in an unwelcome location, like your neighbor's dog bowl or koi pond.

Flight Path

Bees are creatures of habit. Accordingly, once they've set up a flight path out of the hive, they remain pretty steadfastly dedicated to it. When placing your hives, face them in the most unobtrusive direction possible. You want to face southeast, of course, but if your southeast happens to point directly toward a sidewalk, you'll need to provide some form of barrier. If your property line is close, plant a high hedge or put in a fence at least 6 feet (1.8 m) tall. The barrier will encourage the bees to fly up and away from anything in the immediate vicinity.

Weed Suppression

If you intend to site your hives in a grassy area, it will be important to stay on top of lawn maintenance. Keep the area in front of and on the sides of the hives free of weeds and grass. This prevents uninvited critters from catching a ride on a windblown blade of tall grass and jumping inside the hive for a look-see or a snack. Low ground cover also provides a free flight path for your bees.

Accessibility

Be sure to place the hive in a location that can be easily accessed. If it's crammed up against a building, moving around and behind it can be a challenge. Conversely, if it is placed in a wide, open field, far from any roads, getting there to do regular maintenance may be a chore. Site your hive where it can be both directly accessed with ease and where a vehicle, wagon, or other means of locomotion can reach it when the time comes for honey harvesting.

Moisture Prevention

While bees need water, they don't need it inside the hive. Excess moisture can be hazardous to bees. The hive's near-constant internal temperature of 90 to 95°F (32 to 35°C) causes water vapor in the air to condense, forming drops of water on the interior ceiling, which then drip down onto the bees, chilling and possibly killing them during colder weather. When choosing a site, avoid areas that are continually shady, that have perpetually wet ground, or that are near overhead water sources, like gutters or downspouts.

To remedy an overly moist hive, begin by placing the housing in an area that does not pool damp air. Tilt the hive forward slightly by placing 1-inch (2.5 cm) blocks of wood behind the two rear corners of the hive. This way, moisture will drop off and away from the hive. For additional winter ventilation, permanently glue four very thin, flat pieces of wood (such as craft sticks) onto the four corners of the flat side of the inner cover. A bit of additional airflow between the supers and the inner cover will help prevent condensation.

SETTING UP HOUSE

Once you've established where you'll locate your hive, determined that location meets all the criteria necessary for your bees to thrive, given your neighbors a heads-up, and examined local ordinances on beekeeping, it's time to purchase housing. A wide range of reputable beekeeping suppliers can be found worldwide (I've compiled a list in the Resources section on page 341). Order a few catalogs or peruse their websites, compare pricing, and consult with established beekeepers to decide which hive model and setup will work best for your purposes. My first two hives came as new colonies in separate deep hive bodies. I purchased an additional medium super for each so that the bees would have adequate storage space for food come winter. I make apiary purchases online or through a nearby beekeeper who keeps all manner of bee equipment on hand for purchase. He's about 45 minutes from me, so we rendezvous halfway when I discover I need something.

Housing is available for purchase either assembled or unassembled. If you're handy with carpentry and have time to spare before you need the equipment, unassembled hives and frames are a low-cost option. You'll pay about 10 percent more for preassembled housing. I was in a rush to get my bees into their new digs, so I opted for assembled housing when I was getting started. Depending on your level of woodworking abilities, it may be worth your while to do the same.

In most cases, your hive components will come without any paint or coating on them. If you've purchased woodenware, you'll want to paint all outer surfaces of the housing to keep it from rotting. Apply two coats of latex or oil-based paint to ensure that all porous surfaces are covered and no moisture can creep in. Choose light-colored paint, as anything too dark can cause the hive to get quite hot during warmer months. Paint only the outside of the woodenware. Frames never need to be painted or stained, nor do any surfaces that live inside the hive, such as queen excluders, wooden feeders, or the inner cover. It is worth repeating: the interior surfaces and woodenware should never be painted or stained.

Chapter 4 🐝
Feeding Bees:
Keeping the Hive Abuzz

Flower pollen and nectar are a honeybee's preferred foods. It's no coincidence that they are also the very best foods for them. As a bee happily gobbles up these plant secretions, it transfers pollen on its fuzzy legs, pollinating the plant. This symbiotic relationship permits bees and plants to simultaneously reproduce and flourish. On occasion, bees may fall short of meeting their food needs on their own. This is when you, their conscientious steward, will be required to step in, supplying food in order to stave off starvation of the entire colony. Bees can weather a great deal, but without sufficient food they'll perish, especially during colder weather. With a bit of aid from beekeepers, hives will stay well fed all year long, allowing them to not just survive, but thrive.

THE BIRDS & THE BEES

Many species of plants rely on other life forms to help them reproduce. A plant must be fertilized before it can produce seeds; this is achieved via pollination. Male components of flowers, called *anthers*, produce brightly hued yellow pollen globules. When these bits of pollen are transferred to the plant's female parts, called *stigma*, they unite with the egg inside the plant's ovary. Germination then begins. The flower grows, then dies back, drops its petals, and produces fruit and seeds.

While some plants are pollinated by wind or water, many plants rely on what is known as *biotic* pollination, getting by with a little help from their friends. In biotic pollination, helpful organisms known as *pollinators* transfer pollen from anthers to stigma; without assistance, the plant would not fertilize itself and could not reproduce.

Many different species of organisms may serve as pollinators and assist in this alchemical exchange, including vertebrates

and invertebrates. Insects, however, shoulder the largest share of the work. The honeybee is one such pollinator among many; wasps, bumblebees, ants, beetles, birds, bats, hummingbirds, butterflies, moths, and more are vital in allowing pollination to occur. While all pollinators are critical, the anatomy of the honeybee is especially suited for the task. Tiny hairs on its body expertly gather up the sticky yellow orbs of pollen, transferring them far and wide as it buzzes about from plant to plant or moves up and down among the various parts of the same plant.

The helping hand (or rather, leg) that honeybees offer in pollination is invaluable. Up to one-third of all of the foods grown and consumed by humans are pollinated by honeybees. Bees' work in pollination is responsible for literally feeding our entire planet. Many people associate honeybees merely with honey, ignoring their indispensable work in pollinating so many of the crops consumed by humans and animals alike. Without the honeybee, the availability of many types of plant foods would be profoundly compromised.

A NEED FOR FEED

As they forage, busily pollinating along the way, honeybees gather up not just pollen but nectar, too. This transparent liquid excreted by plants is trucked back to the hive and used to make honey (we'll discuss honey production in greater detail on page 322). Honey provides the bees with carbohydrates, giving them the boost of energy they need to go about the multitude of tasks performed in their busy lives. The pollen brought back to the hive provides honeybees with fats, proteins, and vitamins. Pollen and nectar, along with water, compose the entirety of a wild honeybee's diet.

When plants are in bloom and the weather cooperates, honeybees are able to gather up all of the food they require without outside intervention. On occasion, however, a confluence of events can prevent them from acquiring nectar or pollen. Heavy rains, freak weather that kills off plants or compromises their ability to produce nectar, drought, robbing, an early, warm spring followed by a cold snap, and other situations can result in diminished honey stores for bees as they enter colder months. Without enough food to last through the winter, your colony runs the risk of starvation. In order to keep the hive alive, it may be necessary to supplementally feed your bees. The time of year determines what type of food you will provide them with. We'll examine food choices next, along with the types of feeding equipment available.

Knowing When to Feed

If you're new to beekeeping, you might wonder how exactly you'll know when supplemental feeding is required. By the end of the growing season the bees' efforts should have accumulated a honey stockpile of at least 45 to 70 pounds (20.4 to 31.8 kg). The variation in weight is based on your geographic location, with colder regions requiring larger stores of honey to overwinter your honeybees safely. If the larder is not sufficiently full, you will need to offer supplemental feed. Early spring and autumn are the two times of year when feeding may be needed.

There are two ways of assessing honey stores: *frame examination* and the *"heft" test*.

FRAME EXAMINATION

Prior to cold weather, examine each hive's frames. A shallow frame full of honey will weigh around 3 pounds (1.4 kg), a medium frame 4 pounds (1.8 kg), and a deep frame 6 to 7 pounds (2.7 to 3.2 kg). Add up the total weight to determine if your bees have enough food to last the winter.

HEFT TEST

Walk around the back of the hive and give it a lift from the bottom, checking its heft. You'll need to have a general idea of what 45 to 70 pounds (20.4 to 31.8 kg) feels like in order to perform this method of honey assessment properly. If you've ever hauled around a large bag of chicken feed, flour, or potting soil, you'll have a good idea of what such a weight feels like.

FEED OPTIONS

What you'll feed your honeybees is largely determined by the time of year. Warmer weather permits liquid feeding, while colder months call for solid food, as an excess of moisture may cause dysentery in winter. A responsible beekeeper is a prepared beekeeper, so keep supplies for making honeybee food on hand during early spring months and again as autumn approaches.

Honey

Arguably the best possible food for bees, many beekeepers keep several frames in their freezer all winter long, in the event that emergency early spring feeding is required. If you opt for this method of feeding, wait for a warm spring day to do it. Then, first scrape the *wax cappings* off of the honey-filled frame (wax cappings, more commonly known simply as beeswax, are what bees place over honey once they've filled a honeycomb cell, preserving the sweet, heady substance for future use). Bees form a tight ball (known as a cluster) during the cold months in order to trap heat. You'll want to place the uncapped frame of honey as close as possible to the cluster. If you have a strong colony, you can place the frame above the cluster in an upper super. If your colony is weak, you'll want to place the frame beside it, without actually touching or otherwise disturbing the cluster.

Only use honey frames from hives you know to be disease-free. While it may be tempting to purchase someone else's frames, it's not advised. Diseased honey could infect a hive already stressed by cold weather, resulting in avoidable deaths. Never feed your bees with store-bought honey. While purchased jars of honey are fine for you to eat, the stuff can be lethal for bees. Spores of dangerous AFB (American Foulbrood, a potentially devastating disease; see page 311) are often found in such items, especially those produced by large-scale honey-production companies.

Sugar Syrup

Lacking a frame full of honey, sugar syrup is the next best bee-feeding option. This method only works, though, when the weather allows bees to take periodic flights outside the hive. If it is still too cold, bees won't break the cluster to reach the syrup. Workers will also need to leave the hive to relieve themselves, and liquid food requires more frequent flights for doing so.

Use only granulated white cane sugar to make sugar syrup for feeding. Don't use brown sugar, raw sugar, sucanat, molasses, or sorghum, as such products can cause dysentery in bees. For spring feeding, you'll want to use a 1:1 ratio of sugar to water. For autumn feeding, increase the sugar to a 2:1 ratio. The thicker autumnal syrup creates a less moisture-laden feed, allowing the bees to render it into honey more quickly, preparing their cold-weather food supplies more expediently. To make the syrup, simply warm water before

adding sugar, stir, and then allow to cool completely. If you're warming the water on the stovetop, do not allow the sugar mixture to boil. The sugar could caramelize, forming a somewhat indigestible and, at worst, toxic substance for the bees. Bear in mind that, when they really need it, they'll likely drink the sugar syrup dry in a day or two, so you may want to make a couple of gallons and refrigerate them up to three weeks until needed. The upcoming discussion on feeders presents a variety of options for making this sugar syrup readily accessible to tiny honeybee tongues.

Dry Sugar

During the chill of colder months, emergency measures can sometimes be necessary for a colony that has all but exhausted

its honey stores. This can happen in late spring, when the queen has begun laying brood again and large amounts of honey are being fed to developing bees. Some beekeepers use dry granulated white sugar in such instances. Placed either directly around the opening of the inner cover or on a piece of paper laid atop the uppermost frames, the sugar gives honeybees access to an immediate food supply. This feeding method doesn't always work, though. Sometimes the bees gobble it up straight away, other times they'll ignore it completely, and sometimes they carry it out of the hive completely, thinking it is waste in need of removal. If you opt to feed with granulated sugar, check back to see whether it is being consumed or not while doing so as gently, quickly, and discreetly as possible.

Fondant

Also referred to as *sugar candy*, fondant is another emergency food option. Simply a stiffened mixture of sugar, corn syrup, water, and often a thickening agent such as cream of tartar, fondant is formed into patties and placed directly on top of the uppermost frames. You can make the sugar candy yourself, order it from a beekeeping supplier, or even purchase it at a bakery (bakeries often use fondant in frosting cakes).

Put a patty of fondant inside a plastic freezer bag, roll it with a rolling pin to about a 1-inch (2.5 cm) thickness, and store it in the refrigerator until needed. When the time comes, score the bag with a knife on one side in an X. Then turn the panels of the X back, and place the bag on top of the uppermost frames. Place an empty super on top of the fondant, so that the bees can have adequate space to move freely around the patty.

Homemade Sugar Fondant

Making your own fondant is quick, easy, and inexpensive. All of the ingredients, if not already in your pantry, can be found at any grocery store.

YOU WILL NEED:

1½	cups water
2	cups granulated sugar
2	tablespoons corn syrup (organic, if possible)
⅛	teaspoon cream of tartar

TO PREPARE:

1. Combine the water, sugar, corn syrup, and cream of tartar in a small stainless-steel pot, and warm over medium-high heat. Stir gently with a metal spoon until the sugar is completely dissolved.

2. Once the sugar dissolves, discontinue stirring. Clip a candy thermometer to the side of the pot, and monitor the temperature until it reaches the medium-ball stage, around 238°F (114°C).

3. Remove the pot from the heat, and transfer the mixture to a shallow plate or dish. Allow it to cool until just warm to the touch.

4. Transfer the candy to a mold, such as a loaf pan, pie pan, or cake pan, and allow it cool until firm.

5. At this point, you can cut off a slice and take it to the hive, or store in a plastic bag in the refrigerator until needed.

Pollen

Densely rich in nutrients, pollen is fed to bee larvae and young bees. If a developing bee doesn't receive adequate pollen during the first few weeks of its life, deformities can occur. There is no perfect substitute for real plant pollen, so the foragers' gathering duties are absolutely essential for the next generation to thrive.

When flowers are in bloom, bees gather up large quantities of pollen, carrying it back to the hive in pollen baskets (*corbicula*) on their legs. In the hive, worker bees take the pollen from foragers and deposit it into honeycomb cells. As they fill the combs, the bees add a bit of saliva to keep the pollen from germinating, and cover each cell with a protective layer of honey and wax. This sealed pollen is referred to as *bee bread*.

During the early spring, when the queen begins laying brood once again but before flowers are producing pollen, the risk of running out of pollen stores becomes pronounced. If the colony has run through its supply, there are serious risks to developing and fledgling bees. During fall inspections (to be discussed in detail in chapter 8), you will want to check for pollen stores. Depending on the plant it was gathered from, pollen ranges in color from bright yellows and oranges to reds,

Homemade Pollen Cakes

Provided you have pollen from your own colonies on hand, making pollen cakes is a relatively straightforward process. Soy flour can be obtained at natural food stores, as well as online through natural food purveyors.

YOU WILL NEED:

$^1/_4$ cup bee pollen*

1 $^1/_3$ cups granulated sugar

$^3/_4$ cup hot water

$^3/_4$ cup soy flour

*If you don't have pollen from your bees on hand, substitute either $^1/_2$ tablespoon brewer's yeast, 1 tablespoon powdered skim milk, or $^1/_4$ cup soy flour. With brewer's yeast or powdered skim milk, you may need to add extra soy flour until you achieve a consistency resembling peanut butter.

TO PREPARE:

1. Combine the pollen and the sugar in a small mixing bowl. Add the hot water, and stir. Add the soy flour, stirring as the mixture thickens.

2. Transfer the mixture to a sheet of waxed paper. Place another sheet of waxed paper on top, and press the mixture ½ to ¾ inch (1.3 to 1.9 cm) thick.

3. At the hive, remove one side of the waxed paper and place the exposed side of the cake directly on top of the uppermost bar, where the cluster is. Flip the inner cover over after placing the cake on, so that it accommodates the patty within the hive.

4. Check after one week, and replace with a new cake before the previous one has been completely consumed.

purples, and pale greens. Supplemental pollen can be provided by making pollen cakes or patties using pollen gathered from your own bees in summer. It is not advisable to feed your hives with pollen gathered from another hive, as there is the possibility of spreading disease.

If you don't have any pollen from your own colonies available, the next best thing is a pollen substitute. Available from beekeeping suppliers, pollen substitutes are a protein source containing all of the nutrients needed by developing bees without actually containing pollen. Once you begin supplying pollen, you will need to continue to do so until naturally available pollen appears on plants. If an interruption occurs in pollen access, it will adversely affect the rearing of brood and young bees. Similar to adding fondant, when adding pollen patties or pollen substitute to the hive you'll need to provide extra room for the bees to move around the food. Flip the inner cover over, so that the ledge on it faces down. Replace the inner cover and outer cover, and weigh down the whole thing with a heavy rock or brick to prevent the top from flying off during blustery weather.

FEEDERS

A number of different feeder models for holding sugar syrup are available to the beekeeper. Differences are largely characterized by the material the feeder is made out of and whether the feeder is inside or outside the hive. Advantages and disadvantages exist with each model.

Boardman Entrance Feeder

This feeder model is one of the least costly options available. A wooden or plastic base holds a screw-top glass or plastic jug into which syrup is added. Some beekeepers, myself included, aren't fans of this model, for a number of reasons. The Boardman hangs from the side of the main bee housing, so in order to access the syrup, the bees have to climb off of the cluster, down the frames, and out of the hive. Another problem is that, owing to their location outside the hive, Boardman feeders can cause robbing if neighboring bees get a whiff of the syrup. Additionally, most of these models only hold a quart of syrup at a time. When you have bees in serious need of feeding, refilling the feeders can become a hassle. Furthermore, this model of feeder is vulnerable to theft or abuse by predators, such as raccoons or possums, who can easily swipe it off or pull it out.

While a similar feeder, made of plastic, contains a flat base that slides into the hive, allowing the bees to access syrup from inside, it too presents the same challenges of robbing and small capacity as the Boardman.

The Boardman does have a good purpose, though. Instead of being used as holders of sugar syrup, they are perfect for holding water. When the sun is bearing down during warmer months, the entrance feeder is an ideal vessel for an immediate water source. In extreme drought, a hive can easily go through a quart of water daily. Keeping water available in such close proximity to the hive allows you to closely and easily monitor their water use, replenishing as necessary.

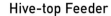
Boardman entrance feeder

Hive-top Feeder

Also known as *Miller feeders*, this model of bee feeder is made of either wood or plastic and covers the entire top of the hive. Variations exist, although the general design is the same: a shallow pan running the length of a super with screened areas in which honeybees can access sugar syrup.

I use a hive-top feeder with my bees and find it enormously convenient. It rests atop the uppermost super and underneath the outer cover (no inner cover is needed with this model), so you are never in direct contact with the bees. This format enables the beekeeper to feed the colony without disturbing it, reducing the likelihood of being stung. Hive-top feeders also have a large holding capacity. Anywhere between 1 and 4 gallons (3.8 and 15.2 L) can be added at a time, depending on the model. Less frequent feedings are therefore required—great news for a beekeeper busy with other caretaking tasks in late spring and autumn.

The disadvantage of this model is that it is awkward to remove when full. Hive inspections can become potentially quite messy, especially if you opt for a plastic model, as it can wobble and spill syrup during removal. As such, I'd suggest planning your inspections in between feedings. Wait until the feeder is empty, check on your winged friends, replace the feeder, fill 'er up with sugar syrup, replace the outer cover, and rest contentedly.

Division Board

Also known as a *frame feeder*, this feeder model resembles a trough-like frame and rests alongside other frames directly within the hive. Made of either a single unit of molded plastic or wood, it replaces one or two frames. Accordingly, it allows for placement right beside the bees. Some beekeepers opt to keep division board frames inside their hives year-round.

Disadvantages to this model include the fact that the bees will be directly exposed to the weather when refilling. Cold-weather exposure can chill the bees, while hot-weather exposure can result in a robbing when neighboring colonies get a whiff of the sugar syrup. Another disadvantage is that fewer frames will be available for honey, pollen, and brood, as one or more must be removed in order to accommodate the feeder. Lastly, the design of division board feeders, with their open bin of syrup, can result in drowning for particularly overzealous bees. Some plastic models have interior walls with rough edges for bees to gain a foothold. Otherwise, if using a wooden model, you might add a U-shaped bit of metal hardware cloth over the top of the feeder to provide a base for your bees to grasp onto. A wooden dowel added to the feeder will achieve the same goal.

Feeder Pail

A feeder pail works by the formation of a vacuum, similar to that produced in a water cooler. Either a ½- or 1-gallon (1.9 to 3.8 L) plastic pail is filled with syrup, covered with a lid perforated with six to 10 tiny holes, and placed lid-side down either directly over the uppermost frames (if the hive is weak) or over the opening in the inner cover (if the hive seems strong, but low on food supplies). Bees can access the syrup with their tongues, gathering up small beads. One of the biggest risks posed by the feeder pail model is that of leakage, an especially precarious situation if you're using this feeder in cold weather, as the dripping syrup could chill the bees. In order to assure that leakage doesn't occur, after placing on the pail's lid, turn the feeder upside down and allow it to drip either somewhere on the ground away from the hive (not directly next to it) or on the inner cover until it ceases to drip. Only then should you place it on the uppermost frames or over the inner cover opening. Place an empty deep super over the

pail, then replace the outer cover, and top off with a heavy rock or brick to prevent the cover from flying off in windy weather.

Though inexpensive and relatively easy to use, the feeder pail does have its disadvantages. Because it will be placed either directly on top of the colony or over the inner cover, you will have to smoke the bees each time you refill the feeder. Smoking will put the bees on alert, increasing the likelihood for stings (see page 279 for a discussion on using a smoker). You know that your heart is in the right place and that you're just trying to help your pollinating buddies survive, but they don't know it. One way to reduce the risk for stings, if using the feeder over the inner cover opening, is to place a bit of closely woven hardware cloth on top of the inner cover, introducing a barrier between the feeder pail and the bees. They can still access the syrup, they just can't directly access you.

Plastic Bag Feeder

By far the most inexpensive feeder available, this model is exactly what its name indicates. All you need to do is pour some sugar syrup into a resealable 1-gallon (3.8 L) plastic freezer storage bag and then lay it over the uppermost frames. Using a razor blade, score the bag with several 1- to 2-inch (2.5 to 5 cm) cuts. Give the bag a gentle squeeze once you've made your cuts, allowing a bit of syrup to ooze out and entice the bees. Then place an empty super over the bag, topped by the inner and outer covers.

Plastic bag feeders, like hive-top feeders, reduce the likelihood of robbing, as the feeding is occurring inside the hive. The downside to this model of feeder is that, once cut, the plastic bags cannot be reused and must be discarded. Additionally, because the feeder goes directly on top of the frames, the beekeeper will need to interact with the bees directly, disturbing them and risking being stung. Opening the hive during cooler weather also runs the risk of chilling the bees.

Feeder pail

Feeding Bees

Chapter 5 🐝

Essential Equipment:
Bee Prepared

Like any hobby, beekeeping has its share of accoutrements and supplies. In order to safely and successfully care for your winged charges, a bit of protective (and placating) gear is necessary. Some items, such as the smoker, are indispensable, while others serve more as handy, albeit nonessential, tools. Here we'll examine items both crucial and ancillary to the beekeeper. Each general category has multiple styles and models within it. Chat with fellow beekeepers about which makes, models, and styles they prefer, and provision yourself accordingly.

SMOKER & FUEL

The smoker is one of a beekeeper's most essential tools. Its use disorients the bees, permitting access to the hive. The technique may have been discovered when a prehistoric honey-seeker visited a wild hive by fire-lit torch one night and discovered the smoke seemed to induce a less focused (and ornery) hive. There are several reasons smoke has such a profound effect on bees.

As discussed in chapter 1, most of the communication between bees occurs via pheromones, scent-specific chemical messengers. If they perceive an attack on the hive, sentry bees emit an alarm pheromone, essentially sending out a silent, wind-borne SOS signal. The signal is picked up by other bees, who gather around their sisters in distress, scoping out the scene and stinging if the threat signal is perceived to be valid. Smoke blown into the hive interrupts pheromone communication, incapacitating the bees' ability to spread information. The bees then experience a short-lived breach in the chain of command, becoming confused. This interruption provides an opportune moment for the beekeeper to open the hive, examine it, and move out before order is restored.

In addition to disrupting pheromone communication, smoke also triggers some unusual behavior. Having evolved in the wild, dwelling in hollowed-out trees, honeybees recognize the scent of smoke as a potential threat of destruction by fire. Therefore, when smoked, a typical hive comes to a standstill. The bees gobble up honey, presumably in an effort to shore themselves with sustenance until a new home can be found. This gorging placates the bees, rendering them temporarily sluggish.

Centuries of encounters with honeybees can attest to the smoker's efficacy. While many incarnations have existed over

the years, in its current guise, a smoker is a stainless-steel or copper canister, enclosed in a cage (to prevent the smoker from burning the beekeeper), with a raised spout and a bellows attached to one side. Kindling and fuel are placed into the canister and then lit. The bellows are blown vigorously, and the fire inside is allowed to burn until it smolders and produces a cool, white smoke. This is the smoke you are looking for. If you see any sparks, or your smoke pours out hot to the touch and in a thin, gray stream, then it's much too warm to apply to your hives. Wait for it to cool down, until it produces a steady, thick, abundant white smoke that feels comfortable when puffed onto your wrist.

What should you use for fuel? Good choices include burlap, pine needles, cardboard rolled into a cylinder, bailing twine, dry leaves, and wood chips. My preferred manner of fueling my smoker is to roll a strip of cardboard up in burlap. (I source the burlap from a local coffee roaster, but it could also be found at a fabric store.) After adding a few broken sticks of dry kindling to the bottom of the canister, I tuck in some balled-up newspaper, ignite it, and then, once I see flames, add in my cardboard roll. A few good squeezes of the bellows works to bring the flames up into the roll. I give my smoker about five to 10 minutes of continuous, cool smoking before suiting up and approaching my hives.

Give a puff to the hive entrance when you first walk up. Wait a few minutes, and then lift the lid and give another puff.

Cool, white smoke is ideal.

You don't want to suffocate your bees, merely to occlude their conversational abilities. Your smoker must stay lit for the entire duration of your examination. Be sure that it is adequately fueled and smoldering before you approach the hives. The smoker, when properly fueled, should be capable of producing smoke for up to 30 minutes. If you have multiple hives to examine, check between hives to be certain that you still have enough fuel. Better to refuel in advance than run out of smoke just when it is needed most! If the bellows on your smoker should ever give out or become damaged, it's possible to order a replacement part from beekeeping equipment suppliers.

SUITS & VEILS

A close contender for the "most valuable player" in the beekeeping equipment roster would be a beekeeping suit and veil. Wearing protective clothing while working with your hives helps assuage fears of getting stung. From full-body zippered jumpsuits resembling overgrown marshmallows to half-body jackets, beekeeping clothing comes in a wide range of styles and sizes. Bee suits are available with or without attached veils and are typically made of either cotton or lightweight polyester. The veils shroud and protect your head, permitting visibility but preventing access by curious (or cantankerous) honeybees. If attached to a suit or jacket, you merely zip the veil into place. Veils sold separately from suits are secured by wrapping drawstrings attached to the veil around the waist and then tying them in the front.

The rationale for protective clothing rests more on the fact that honeybees are notoriously curious than it does on any notion of aggressiveness. It is true that bees may act defensively if they feel the hive is threatened, which could occur if you jar the hive unnecessarily or overstay your welcome with too long an inspection. In most cases, however, any bees that land on you do so because they are curious. They are examining you just as you are examining them. Be mindful of exposed wrists or ankles, as bees especially enjoy dark areas and will climb into tight spaces to explore. Full-body beekeeping suits have elastic bands around ankles and wrists, while jackets enclose only the wrists. If you opt for a jacket (which is what I use), be sure to tuck your pant legs either into tall rubber boots or down into your shoes. Some beekeepers even affix tape around their pant legs and wrists to fully block bees from gaining access. Strips of Velcro or rubber bands will work just as well.

Tuck pant legs into boots or shoes to keep bees out.

Ready for action

The zipper prohibits a bee's entry into the veil.

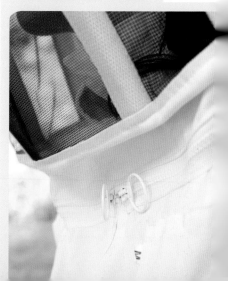

No matter what form of protective clothing you choose, be sure it is light-colored. Generations of interactions with dark-furred forest creatures such as bears, raccoons, and other darkly dressed, hive-assaulting critters have created for honeybees an aversion to darkly colored moving things. Smooth-surfaced garments in white or other light colors placate honeybees, while dark or rough textures such as wool could trip the "danger" alarm if such surfaces are mistaken for fur. Play it safe and stay on the lighter end of the color spectrum.

GLOVES

Your protective gear will also need to extend to your hands. Long gloves made of leather or canvas are available for purchase from beekeeping suppliers. Basic rubber kitchen or latex gloves (such as those used in a medical setting) also work well. Many experienced beekeepers prefer to forgo the use of gloves completely, claiming they're cumbersome and prevent getting a firm grip on frames and other bits of equipment. I'd suggest that while a no-glove policy might be perfectly acceptable for someone with years of beekeeping experience, it's not the wisest choice for the novice. You don't need to be worrying unnecessarily about the possibility of stings on your hands while you're getting acquainted with feeding or trying to find your queen on a frame filled with

thousands of bees. Take your time, use your gloves, and then, as you gain more confidence, decide if working with gloves or bare hands is the better fit for you.

HIVE TOOL

While it might look like it holds no special powers, the thin, metal hive tool is indispensable in beekeeping. As discussed in chapter 3, honeybees seal up any cracks and crevices in the hive with super-sticky propolis, blocking out bacteria, bugs, or any other hive interloper. Phenomenally viscous, propolis is no easy substance to pry apart. Enter the hive tool. Broad and flat on one end, the hive tool wedges expertly between all bits of woodenware, permitting you, the beekeeper, to gently force apart pieces that have become stuck together. A hive

Hive tools help pry open hives and frames.

tool is also helpful for scraping away wax comb the bees may have built in undesirable locations, such as between or on top of frames (this type of comb is referred to as *burr, wild,* or *brace* comb). The other end of the hive tool curves upward, enabling the beekeeper to pull up and otherwise manipulate frames. While you might be tempted to just use a putty knife or screwdriver instead, I can't recommend it. A putty knife lacks the strength of a hive tool, while a screwdriver's small head can damage woodenware.

Sturdy gloves are indispensable.

HELPFUL EXTRAS

Whereas the aforementioned bits of gear and equipment are essential to keeping bees both safely and properly, the following items, while not crucial, are quite helpful. Before rushing off to buy everything mentioned, chat with other beekeepers about some of their favorite tools. No two beekeepers are alike, and they'll undoubtedly have different opinions about what equipment is top tier. Solicit their feedback and then make an informed decision about what items you think would be best to have on hand.

Queen excluder

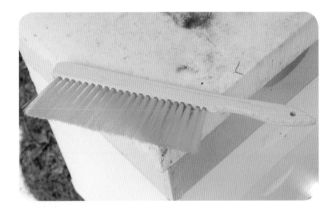

Bee Brush

This long-handled, soft-bristled brush is useful for gently coaxing bees off any surface you'd prefer they not be on. Use the brush, or a long, soft feather, instead of your hand, which could accidentally squish bees. A bee brush is perfect for the delicate removal of honeybees from clothing and frames alike.

Queen Excluder

A wooden frame covered with perforated metal or plastic, the queen excluder is basically a "no queens allowed" restraint. The slats in the queen excluder are small enough for worker bees to move through with ease while prohibiting the larger queen from gaining entry. Placed between the hive body and the supers above it, the excluder confines the queen to the lower portion of the hive so that brood and pollen are compartmentalized separately from honey. Come extraction

time, all that will be in the frames will be the sweet, sticky substance, preserving the honey's clarity while simultaneously allowing all brood to develop.

Sometimes honeybees are reluctant to crawl up through the excluder and begin storing honey above until all available space within lower frames has been filled (they're quite the models of industry and thrift). To coax them upward, first place a super filled with empty frames intended for honey atop the hive body without the queen excluder. Once you've determined your bees are storing nectar in the upper chamber, insert the excluder. After you've extracted all of the honey you plan to extract for the season, remove the queen excluder.

Frame Holder

When a frame—shallow, medium, or deep—is filled with honey, brood, propolis, pollen, and wax, it gets heavy. Really heavy. Add to that the massive amount of buzzing, active

honeybees covering it, and you've got a weighty, delicate situation on your hands, literally. Assuage any fears about dropping your precious cargo by employing a frame holder. The frame holder does exactly what it says: it holds frames so that you don't have to. Two metal clamps grip onto the side of the super, with long shelflike arms extending out from the side. You simply remove a frame from the super and place it into the waiting arms of the frame holder. To see the other side of the frame, simply turn it around and replace it on the holder.

Frame Grip

Looking a good bit like metal jaws, a frame grip allows you to easily extract a frame from the hive with one hand. The grippers on each side of the spring-hinged handle grab hold of the frame firmly and securely. It is then quite easy to pull the frame from the super without harming any bees that might be moving over the frames. You can examine the frame with one hand, or move the frame to a frame rest for safekeeping.

Notebook

A small notebook can be enormously helpful for tracking the progress of your hives. Every time you visit, make notes about what you did, what you saw, and any impressions you have of the hive's health. Keeping a dated log of your actions can prove indispensable should problems arise.

Storage

Having all of your beekeeping supplies all together in one easily transportable collection streamlines the whole endeavor. A handled bucket or basket makes a good container. Stash everything in it, including your smoker, fuel, matches, veil, gloves, hive tool, bee brush, notebook, and more.

Take some time to read up on essential equipment options well in advance of acquiring your bees. You'll be that much better prepared to care for your new additions safely and properly.

Chapter 6

Obtaining Bees

After all of your research and planning, the time has finally come to get your bees! There are a number of methods of obtaining a hive of buzzing beauties. In the following pages we'll discuss package bees, nucs, established colonies, and swarms as possible means for honeybee acquisition. Each option possesses its own set of advantages and disadvantages. When I was a "new bee," I was completely lost when it came to this part of the beekeeping process. Thankfully, I had mentors and friends to advise me. Likewise, you have me right here with you, cheering from the sidelines, providing detailed information on each option. Learn what possibilities are out there and then make an informed decision about what seems best for you.

A TIME & A PLACE

As we've discussed in previous chapters, several key considerations need to be addressed prior to acquiring your first hive of honeybees. Before you welcome honeybees into your life, you must first determine whether it is permissible to keep bees where you live, select the proper location for siting your hives, assemble all of the necessary housing and equipment, and assess whether you have the time and resources needed for keeping bees. Brush up on the subject of beekeeping by reading books on the topic (such as this one!), seeking out bee organizations in your area, and befriending or shadowing an experienced beekeeper. The beekeeping organization in my neck of the woods has been an absolutely invaluable resource. Through it, I've attended two years of bee school, connected with area suppliers of equipment and bees, participated in hands-on "field day" demonstrations, and met a woman who has become a cherished mentor.

After all of those preliminary measures have been attended to, the next step is to determine what type of bee you will keep. In chapter 2 we examined a number of the more popular species. Look over the list again, select what seems to be the best bee breed for your needs, and then begin looking for a supplier. The best time of year to get honeybees is late spring, before it becomes too hot to safely ship them. That said, you don't necessarily want to wait until then to begin your search, as most suppliers operate on a "first come, first served" ordering basis. During the quiet stretch of colder months (beginning even as early as November in North America), you can put in your order for honeybees. Then, once the warmer weather rolls around, your bees will be ready for pickup and installation into their new digs. Most suppliers begin shipping (that's right—bees can be sent in the mail!) or making bees available for pickup in mid-spring and continue on until June (in the United States, most bees are shipped from southeastern states; after June, the weather becomes too warm to permit safe shipping).

When the bees are due for arrival, be sure you've got their housing prepared to receive them. Much as you wouldn't wait until after anticipated houseguests arrive to tidy up the guest room and change out the sheets on the bed, don't wait until you've got a buzzing package of bees on your hands to order supers and a smoker. From the time they arrive, you've got about 48 hours to get them installed into the hive. Be a gracious host and greet your guests with proper hospitality.

"Going Postal"

If you opt to have your bees shipped to you (as opposed to using a local supplier and picking them up on location), it is imperative that you give your post office a heads-up in advance. They will call you as soon as your humming, buzzing shipment arrives. Be aware that post offices work through the night, and your package may very well show up at 3 a.m., so have the car keys handy! Tell the postal clerk to put them aside somewhere quiet and cool, hop in your car, and make a beeline for your new wards. You'll want to get your bees out of there pronto. Doing so not only keeps you on the good side of your postal staff, but also gets the bees out of the potentially inhospitable climatic conditions of the receiving area of the post office.

A PACKAGE DEAL (PACKAGE BEES)

Many fledgling beekeepers opt for package bees, for a number of good reasons. Package bees are exactly that: a package of bees and nothing else. Acquiring bees in this manner allows the novice to see the process of beekeeping from inception on through to care, maintenance, extraction, and beyond. If you are beginning with new woodenware, you'll witness its metamorphosis from empty foundation to drawn-out comb. Package bees are also small in number. Compared to the amount of bees present in a full hive (around 50,000 to 60,000), package bees permit the beekeeper to get a few notches in their apiary tool belt before advancing on to caring for the needs of an active, developed hive. If you're ordering package bees to place on frames with drawn-out, existing honeycomb, you can arrange to install the package in early April. Otherwise, if you will be adding bees to frames possessing only foundation, wait until it's a bit warmer to do so. Once the daytime temperature averages 56 to 58°F (13 to 14°C) (depending on where you are, late April to early May), you can then safely install your bees.

Available in 2-, 3-, and 5-pound (.9, 1.4, and 2.3 kg) packages (each pound comprises about 3,500 bees, so 3 pounds [1.4 kg] would fetch you just over 10,000 bees, perfect for starting out), package bees include a newly mated queen (cordoned off in a separate wire cage, often—but not always—with two or three attendant bees), a complement of worker bees, and sugar syrup for the bees to feed on in transit. Queens are isolated from the rest of the bees because, coming from different colonies, worker bees don't yet recognize her scent and may kill her before becoming accustomed to her pheromones. The whole package is about the size of a shoebox. Four sides are made from wood and two are covered with fine wire mesh screen for ventilation. The queen cage is approximately the size of a large book of matches. Her cage will come with a small amount of sugar candy for her and her attendants to consume while the other bees sip the sugar syrup.

You'll need to carefully examine your package as soon as you receive it. Look for a live queen and lots of moving, active bees. A bit of mortality in transit is normal, but any more than a half inch of dead bees on the bottom of the package should be reported. If your queen or large numbers of workers have died, either inform the clerk if you are collecting your bees from the post office or the individual from whom you are picking up your bees. Do so as soon as possible so that you may have your losses replaced. Package bees have undergone a good bit of stress during transit and should be housed, or *hived*, as it's referred to, as soon as possible. Most suppliers won't deliver directly to you, so it will be necessary to keep them warm (but not hot!) while transporting them to their new home. If you intend to carry the package home in the open bed of a truck, cover it up with a loose-fitting cloth so that they don't get chilled, especially if the weather is cool. Otherwise, the interior of your car (minus the heat blasting at full throttle) is perfectly fine.

Once you get home, mist the package with cool sugar syrup. Not only does this give the bees a bit of food, it wets their wings, making it difficult for them to fly away (a good thing when you're attempting to move 10,000 bees into a new home). Next, move the package somewhere dark and cool (50 to 60°F [10 to 15°C]), such as a basement or garage, for about an hour. The bees will cluster around the queen and relax a bit. Have all your woodenware assembled and in its location of choice in advance. If at all possible, install the bees late in the afternoon or during the early evening hours. This limits the likelihood that any bees will fly away and lose their way home. It will be necessary to begin feeding your bees as soon as they've been added to the hive, and continue to do so until the first nectar flow occurs. A nectar flow, also referred to as a *honey flow*, describes the time period when nectar in flowering plants and trees is available for bees to consume. The flow periods vary widely, as do the nectar-bearing plants themselves, from region to region. To learn what is flowering in your area, check with your local beekeeping chapter or look online for information regarding seasonal nectar flows.

Two packages of honeybees

INSTALLING A PACKAGE

In order to successfully install a package of bees into an empty hive, you'll need the following items:

- ▢ A package of bees
- ▢ Hive body with frames
- ▢ Protective veil and suit or jacket
- ▢ Gloves (over time, you may come to feel gloves are unnecessary; in the beginning, though, I urge you to use them)
- ▢ Spray bottle of 1:1 sugar-water solution
- ▢ Hive tool
- ▢ A sewing needle, toothpick, or small nail
- ▢ Entrance feeder, hive-top feeder, or pail feeder

2 Wearing your protective gear, mist the package of bees with the sugar-water solution. You're trying to douse them, not saturate them, so don't overdo it when spraying. This step not only wets the bees' wings, making it difficult for them to fly away, but compels them to clean and groom the syrup off of each other, giving them something to occupy their time and energy.

1 Begin by removing four or five frames from the empty hive and setting them aside (you'll add them back in once you've emptied the package). Push the remaining frames all to one side. The empty space created will house the bees once you dump them from the package.

3 Holding the package in both hands, shake it down firmly against the ground. This loosens the bees from the interior of the package, causing them to fall to the bottom. Then, using your hive tool, gently pry open the flat wooden lid on the top of the package. Set it aside, but don't move it too far out of reach, as you'll use it again soon.

6 Shake any bees off of the queen cage and then examine it. Is the queen alive? If not, you'll need to call the supplier right away and request a replacement. You can continue with the installation of the other bees, though.

4 Inside you'll see a metal canister of sugar syrup with a strip of metal attached to its side. With the edge of your hive tool, pry up a corner of the canister. As you begin removing it, place a finger or two over the attached strip of metal; this strip is connected to the queen cage. Remove both the cage and the feeding canister at the same time.

7 Queens are commonly shipped in small containers known as *Benton cages*. This style of queen cage consists of three circular sections cut out of a wooden block and covered on two sides with mesh screen. Two of the sections, or chambers, are for the queen to move around in, while the third contains a sugar paste (also known as a "candy plug"), made expressly for the queen to munch on in transit. You'll find corks on each of the shorter sides of the queen cage. Remove the cork from the candy end of the cage. Using a sewing needle, toothpick, or small nail, puncture the candy plug, taking care to not jab the queen in the process. The worker bees will use that puncture hole to begin chewing through to the queen over the next day or so. This gives them enough time to become accustomed to her scent and accept her. If introduced too quickly, before they've had time to acclimate to her, worker bees can sometimes attack and kill a queen.

5 Temporarily replace the wooden lid over the top of the box. Shake any bees from the feeding canister, and set it aside.

8 Carry the queen cage over to the empty hive body. With the candy end facing toward the sky, place the queen cage down in between the two center frames. Use the metal strip to form a hook over one of the frames, providing extra support. Some suppliers will use a short piece of plastic packing strap. In this case you will have to staple it to the top of a frame.

9 Give the package of bees another light spray of sugar water. Once again, firmly shake the package against the ground. Remove the wooden lid, and gently shake a cluster of bees over the queen cage. Next, shake the remaining bees into the area left by the removal of the frames. Place the package on the ground, beside the bottom board. Any remaining bees will vacate the package over the next 24 hours and fly into the hive.

10 Gently replace the frames, taking care to not squish any bees in the process. Given the opportunity and with gentle, slow, patient movements on your part, they'll shimmy out of the way when they feel and see the frames coming toward them.

11 Install your chosen feeding apparatus (hive-top feeder, feeder pail, or entrance feeder, see page 276) and replace the inner cover.

12 Put the outer cover on. Leave the bees to settle into their new space for about a week. When you return, check to be sure that the queen has been released from her cage. If so, remove the cage. Feed the hive continuously until an active nectar flow is occurring.

13 If the queen wasn't released from her cage, you'll need to release her directly into the hive. Remove the cage from the hive, take out the cork on the end opposite the candy plug, cover it with one of your fingers, and push the candy end of the cage—which by now should be free of candy, or close to it—into the front entrance to the hive. You're covering over one end so that she can only move out and into the hive, instead of moving toward you and flying up into the air.

A nuc of bees

(NUC)LEAR ENERGY

A nucleus of bees, more commonly referred to as a "nuc," is a miniature version of a hive. Nucs are comprised of a box containing three to five frames of bees in all stages of development. These frames will contain brood, baby bees, worker bees, food, and a laying queen. All you need to get started with a nuc is to remove the frames from their transporting box and insert them in a super.

The advantage of a nuc over a package is that the population of the colony will grow much more rapidly, as the queen's laying schedule will not be interrupted. A queen with brood, food, and a host of workers will have a wing up on the competition, so to speak. The entire hive will be that much further along the path of perpetuating itself. Bees in packages need time to draw out comb on foundation and will need up to three weeks before new bees are born. Nucs are also easier to install—simply put the frames into a super, and you're set!

As they contain more material (frames, brood, food) than packages, and are further along in colony development, nucs will cost more. That said, what is incurred in outgoing expense can usually be made up quickly. Given favorable weather conditions and consistent nectar flows, nuc colonies may have surplus honey available for extraction the first year you keep them.

One disadvantage to purchasing nucs is the potential for disease. Nucs do not have to undergo inspection or certification before being sold. As such, diseases or pests such as mites may be present. You can largely sidestep the risk of an unhealthy hive by purchasing nucs from a reputable supplier. Ask beekeepers in your community for recommendations. Local- and state-level organizations will be able to give you supplier evaluations, as well. If your nuc supplier happens to be nearby, contact a bee inspector and arrange to have the seller's hives inspected prior to purchase. You can find your local bee inspector by contacting your state or county extension agent or your local governmental agricultural agency.

SWARMING INTO ACTION

A third means of acquiring bees is through swarm collection. Swarming is a natural tendency of honeybees, serving as a means of propagation. When a hive swarms, it departs with the existing queen and about half of the colony, leaving new queen cells (these cells, which are slightly rounded and larger than those used to house worker bees, will be used to grow a replacement queen for the colony) and the remainder of the bees behind. Initially, the swarm flies around in a black cloud, eventually settling on a surface where it will temporarily rest while scout bees seek out a more suitable new dwelling. It is during this pause that you must act, if you wish to secure the swarm easily. Swarms can be an incredibly thrifty means of increasing, or establishing, your apiary. A swarm of bees contains somewhere in the neighborhood of 25,000 bees,

A swarm in action

including the queen. Compare that to the 10,000 or so bees in a package, and you've made quite the score! Of course, you'll want to make sure, to the best of your ability, that no one else has rights to the swarm. If any of your neighbors keep bees, do the neighborly thing and ask if any of their hives have recently swarmed before claiming the find.

Contrary to popular opinion, a swarm of bees is quite docile. Honeybees are protective of their homes and will act defensively to protect its contents. In the absence of an actual hive—and its attendant brood and food—bees are quite calm. Prior to swarming, bees consume about three days' worth of honey to fortify themselves until they can set up shop elsewhere, which satiates them. That said, while not difficult, capturing a swarm isn't really a job for a fledgling beekeeper. At the very least it would be helpful to have a seasoned beekeeper in tow to advise and assist you in the endeavor. An experienced beekeeper will also be able to determine if the swarm contains Africanized bees, in which case you should stay far away.

If a swarm alights in a convenient spot, such as a low tree branch or close-to-the-ground object like a picnic table, then capturing a swarm might not be too difficult. If the swarm lands in the upper reaches of a tree or other inaccessible location, however, then it might not be worth the trouble of removal. To capture a swarm from an area that can be reached safely, you'll need some kind of receptacle. Good choices include a cardboard box punctured for ventilation (poke about 20 tiny holes in each side with a barbeque skewer or ice pick), a super containing four or five frames of brood and food, or an empty nuc box. It's advised that less experienced keepers wear protective clothing for this undertaking.

If the swarm is hanging from a tree branch or bush, center the capturing box directly underneath it. Next, give the branch a quick, firm shake. This should dislodge the bees from the branch and down into the box below. Alternatively, carefully cut the branch off the tree or bush while holding it so that it doesn't fall to the ground once cut. Slowly carry the branch to the waiting box, delicately place it inside, close the top, seal it shut with tape, and then transport it quickly to its new home. If the swarm is hanging from a low-lying

An experienced keeper capturing a swarm

structure like a fence post or picnic table, place the capturing container underneath it, and then use a bee brush or your gloved hand to gently coax the bees downward. Inhibit their inclination to fly away by first wetting their wings with a light misting of water from a spray bottle.

You can hive the swarm into its new home several different ways. If you used a super with several frames of brood and food in it to capture your swarm, place the additional frames into the hive body once the swarm is in it, add a feeder and food (see page 276 for a review of feeders), and replace the outer cover. If you used a nuc or cardboard box for capture, you'll want to have a hive body with frames and foundation or drawn comb set up in advance for receiving them once you return home. You'll be feeding the bees as soon as you hive them (unless there's an active nectar flow happening), so have your feeder of choice in place, filled with sugar syrup, as well. Then, using either a bedsheet or a long sheet of plywood, create a ramp leading from the ground up into the hive entrance. Next, shake the honeybees directly onto the ramp as close to the entrance as possible. Compelled by the scent of the comb and food, coupled with pheromones emanating from their fellow hivemates and queen, the bees will begin a steady march upward into their new home. After two to three days, take a peek inside and look for the queen. If you can't find her, look for indications that she's there, such as eggs and capped brood. Absent those signs, you might have a queen-less hive, in which case you'll need to purchase and add a new queen as quickly as possible.

THE ESTABLISHED ORDER

A final option for obtaining bees is to purchase fully established colonies. This setup involves acquiring full hives of bees (supers, frames, bees) from a local beekeeper, often one who is moving, retiring, or needing to unload an abundance of bees from busy hives. While this arrangement can give you a leg up on establishing a beekeeping operation, it can be a bit daunting for the beginner. You suddenly have a thriving, buzzing, busy mass of 50,000 to 60,000 bees on your hands, possibly needing food, additional supers, and a bit of skill where their care is concerned.

As such, jumping into beekeeping in this manner is usually not recommended for first-time beekeepers. It can be daunting to encounter so many bees all at once. Additionally, some of the subtleties witnessed when starting from scratch with new woodenware will be lost, including viewing comb formation, the creation and later capping of brood and honey, and introducing a queen. Full hives of bees could potentially harbor diseases and pests, and used woodenware may be antiquated or worn-out.

That said, when I got started with bees, I elected to dive right into the deep end, purchasing not just one, but *two* full hives. I'd devoured a mountain of books on beekeeping, attended two weekends' worth of bee school, and secured a host of mentors. A tip from a fellow beekeeper about a 30-year beekeeping veteran wanting to sell off some of his many hives

for a bargain sealed the deal for me. My bee buddy Jenny and I grabbed our gear, her truck, and an intrepid spirit and headed two counties over to secure my hives. We waited until most of the bees had come home for the night, sealed them up, and then moved them, slowly, to the back of Jenny's truck. Arriving at my house past dark, we carefully, steadily moved them to their new location in my fledgling bee yard.

Admittedly, it *was* daunting opening the hives the first time. Fortunately, Jenny came back around to assist with adding supers, and another local beekeeper came by for a full hive inspection. I'm a quick learner, and I always love a challenge, so my decision to start with established hives worked well for me. Only you can decide what feels comfortable to you. Assess all of the ways of obtaining bees carefully, and make the decision that best suits your needs and concerns.

SUPPLY & DEMAND

So, you've considered all of your procurement options, selected the breed of bee you want, checked in with the neighbors and the local authorities, gotten all of your woodenware and gear together, and are now primed and ready to take on bee stewardship. Where to find all of those packages and nucs and established colonies? Depending on where you live, it may be possible to source bees from a nearby supplier. Check with your local beekeeping organizations for referrals. Your local newspaper may have classified ads offering bees for sale, as well. If you're dealing with an individual, as opposed to an established company, have the government-appointed bee inspector for your area check the prospective hives for diseases and pests before purchasing. Otherwise, seek out reputable suppliers who will ship bees or make pickup arrangements with you. You can find many by simply conducting an online search. There are also a number of fantastic periodicals advertising trustworthy companies (see Resources on page 341 for periodical and supplier listings). As with any business, some honeybee suppliers will offer better customer service and "product" care than others. Ask your fellow beekeepers and local organizations for suggestions about who to trust.

Chapter 7

A Look Inside

You've acquired your bees and situated them safely inside the hive. Now it's time to open it up and take a peek. Much like any house visit, a bit of etiquette will go far in engendering goodwill toward your hosts. You want to get invited back, don't you? Here we'll cover the proper way to visit your hives, as well as what to be on the lookout for during inspections.

BEING A GOOD HOUSEGUEST

It's important to keep in mind that bees have schedules just like we do. They also have preferences when it comes to being called upon. As such, there are a number of do's and don'ts when it comes to visiting your hives. Knowing when it's time to say "howdy do" and when to say "perhaps another time" are essentials in being a good houseguest to your bees.

Do's

- ▶ Choose a warm, sunny day.
- ▶ Visit during the hours of 10 a.m. to 6 p.m., when a large proportion of the colony will be out foraging.
- ▶ Check in once every two weeks in early spring and mid- to late autumn.
- ▶ Move gently and quietly; fast, brusque movements put the hive on alert.
- ▶ Practice good personal hygiene around the bees; heavy sweat or body odors are not appreciated in the bee yard.
- ▶ Wear your veil. Even if it's the only protective garment you decide to use, always use it.
- ▶ Wear gloves or, if going gloveless, take off your rings, in the event that your hand gets stung and you're unable to remove them.

Don'ts

- ▶ Come by on rainy, windy, or cold days.
- ▶ Overdo it with the smoker; a gentle puff is enough to give the hive a sense of what's going on.
- ▶ Inspect excessively or unnecessarily.
- ▶ Linger; the bees will be fine with a short visit, but overstay your welcome and they'll be less than pleased.
- ▶ Drench yourself with perfume or cologne before visiting the hive; the scents can attract bees, which you don't want (you're trying to remain as inconspicuous as possible, remember).
- ▶ Breathe heavily on the hive; it's apt to make them ornery. Whatever you do, don't eat a banana and then breathe on the hive; bananas smell like the bees' own alarm pheromone, and you might inadvertently sound the "danger" call.

INSPECTOR GENERAL

In order to perform seasonal inspections and attend to your hives properly, you'll need to know what exactly it is that you're looking for each time you open the hive. Bees neither like nor benefit from unnecessary visits, so being prepped on what to look for benefits you both. Here are step-by-step instructions for how to open the hive, how to remove a frame, what to look for on those frames, and how to replace the frames and put the hive back together.

OPENING THE HIVE

1 Put on your protective gear. Ignite your smoker (see page 279 for instructions), and be sure it is well-lit and producing cool smoke.

2 Approach the hive from the side or the rear, never from the front (doing so will interfere with the bees' flight path, which could irritate them). Stand to the side of the hive's entrance and gently direct two or three long, full puffs of smoke at it. Wait three to four minutes for the smoke to take effect.

3 Move to the rear of the hive. Lift one corner of the outer cover, and direct two or three puffs of smoke inside. Wait a few seconds for the smoke to take effect.

4 Set your smoker on the ground or use the curved end of it to hook it to the super's edge. Remove the hive's outer cover, exposing the inner cover or hive-top feeder, if you are using one. Turn the outer cover upside down, and place it either on the ground or on a raised object directly adjacent to the hive. You will be stacking other woodenware on top of the outer cover.

5 If you are using a hive-top feeder, give a puff of smoke to its outer edges, where the bees gather to feed at the screened areas (only remove a hive-top feeder when it is empty, or you could end up with a big mess on your hands). Otherwise, you'll be removing the inner cover. Using your hive tool, gently wedge it under one corner of the inner cover and the super below.

6 Give another puff of smoke under the inner cover. Moving slowly and carefully, pry off the remaining corners of the inner cover. Lift up the inner cover, and look to see if the queen is there. If you see her, gently brush her back down into the supers below. If no queen is present, using two hands, remove the inner cover, bees and all. Place it diagonally toward the entrance, so that the bees still clinging to it can walk back inside.

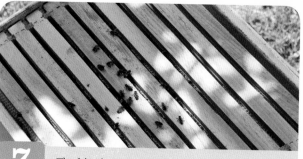

7 The hive is now open for business. Give a few, long, full puffs of smoke into the super, across the bees. You'll see them start to move down into the lower supers. Time to start removing frames and determining what's going on inside the hive!

REMOVING FRAMES

1 You'll be inspecting frames from one end to the other side. Always work in a clear, chronological order. The bees arrange things very specifically on the frames, and you need to be mindful of that.

2 Using the curved end of your hive tool, gently wedge it between the first and second frames. If any bees are in the way, a gentle nudge with the hive tool is all that's needed to get them moving.

3 Move the hive tool slowly from side to side, loosening the first and second frames from each other. Do the same thing on the opposite end of the same two frames.

4 The frame should now be loosened. If you find any burr comb between the frames, use the flat end of your hive tool to scrape it off. I bring a glass wide-mouth canning jar with me on my inspections and scrape any burr comb I come across into it for later use in beeswax-making projects. Using both hands and making certain you have a firm grip and that no bees are under your fingers, lift the frame up and out of the super.

5 Gently rest the frame vertically on the ground beside the hive, inside of the overturned outer cover. It will most likely have bees on it, and that's perfectly fine. Again, mind the bees, taking care not to crush any as you put the frame down. Alternatively, if you've got a frame rest, you can mount the first frame on there.

6 You've now created an open area, which will enable you to access and inspect the remaining frames with greater ease. Remove the second frame in the same manner as the first, only this time don't put it on the ground or right into the frame rest.

7 With the sun behind you, examine the frame on both sides, turning it vertically (end-over-end) as you do so, remembering to hold it firmly. Again, if you're using a frame rest, you can simply put the frame in the frame rest, examine it on one side, remove it, turn it vertically end-over-end, and place in the frame rest to examine the opposite side. Once you've examined the second frame, either leave it in the frame rest, if using, or place it beside the first frame, similarly resting vertically on its side on the ground. If you have chosen to use a Top Bar Hive (see page 267) that does not use frames, you will need to keep the comb hanging vertically during your inspection or it may snap right off the top bar.

8 Continue moving through all of the frames in this manner, working thoroughly but quickly. As you move closer into the cluster of bees in the center, be careful that you don't allow your queen to fall to the ground. Hold each frame over the hive opening when you are inspecting those frames, so that any bee falling off will fall right back down inside.

9 You'll most likely need to give a few more puffs from your smoker midway through your inspection, which is why you want to be certain your smoker is going strong right from the onset.

10 Ideally, your entire inspection should take no more than 10 to 15 minutes total. If it takes you a bit more than that in the beginning, don't worry. You'll get the hang of it over time, and the hive will let you know when they've had enough of you for the day by an increased pitch in buzzing.

WHAT TO LOOK FOR

So, then, what exactly is it that you'll be looking for? Essentially, everything you're concerned about relates to the queen. What she is or is not doing will be evident via a trail of visible indicators. Those are what you're after.

1 Begin by looking on a frame for the queen herself. She will most likely not be on any outer frames, but you never know! If you don't find her, start looking for her "signs."

2 With the sun to your back, look on a frame for the presence of eggs. These resemble tiny grains of rice and should be placed one per cell. Their presence means the queen is alive, or at the very least that she was there as recently as two days ago. Ideally you want to find eggs every time you inspect. While egg-laying will taper off and ramp up at different times of the year, eggs should generally always be visible when you're inspecting (laying ceases during colder months, but then, you shouldn't be inside the hive inspecting it to find that out!).

3 As the eggs grow, they move through various stages of physical development (see page 251). During the larval stage, you'll see white grubs in the cells. Once they mature into the pupae stage, the grubs will be capped over by nurse bees. Referred to as "capped brood," this stage is evidenced by the appearance of dark, tan-colored wax.

4 The pattern that the capped brood appears in is quite telling. Ideally, it should be in a "rainbow pattern," meaning that the middle of the frame should hold capped and uncapped brood, with each cell filled, followed above it by foodstuff, including pollen, royal jelly, and both capped and uncapped honey. The colors should all progress in a gradient fashion, much like a rainbow. If the brood pattern is spotty, spread out, and missing in lots of holes, you might have a problem on your hands. Furthermore, the cappings on the brood should be smooth, glossy, and curling slightly outward. If they are curling inward or otherwise look ragged, this could be another indication that your hive's queen may be ill or simply failing from old age. We'll discuss several means of handling this situation, should it present itself, ahead in Requeening (see page 306).

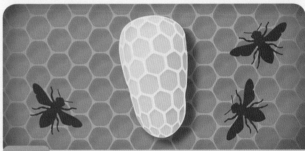

5 During spring inspections, and to a lesser extent in summer, you'll also be looking on frames for indications of the presence of queen cells. These will show up either as swarm or supersedure cells, or both. Both cells look an awful lot like peanuts—bulbous and slightly elongated. *Swarm cells*, usually visible on the bottom bar of frames (although sometimes simply in the lower half of the frame itself), indicate that the hive has become too crowded or that it is too stuffy inside in order for it to function as it should. *Supersedure cells* indicate that the colony has decided, for one reason or another (including old age, disease, or injury), that their queen needs replacing. These cells will most often be situated on the upper portion of a frame. The presence of either type of queen cell usually calls for a response on your part. We'll examine dealing with both situations on pages 305–306, under spring management practices for your hives.

REPLACING FRAMES

1 Push the frames back together in the order you first encountered them. Make sure they are also facing the same direction as they were when you first removed them. If you turned them over end-to-end vertically, move then back through the same movement sequence until they face their original positioning.

2 Push the frames together as a single unit, instead of pushing each one back into place individually. You're much less likely to accidentally squish and kill any bees this way.

3 Return the first frame last. If any bees remain on it, give one edge of it a sharp rap onto the inner cover resting in front of the entrance.

4 Make sure all the frames are placed both equidistant from each other (the rabbets on their ends will do this bit, provided you've pushed them together snugly) and from the outer walls of the super on both ends. This is very important. If you leave unequal distances, the bees will gladly fill it up with burr comb, making expedient access to the interior of the hive less likely during your next inspection.

5 Once the frames are replaced, it's time to close up the hive completely.

CLOSING THE HIVE

2 Grab hold of the outer cover and gently slide it into position over the inner cover, making sure you don't cover up the ventilation notch. This is easily achieved by pushing the outer cover, once atop the inner cover, all the way forward.

3 That's a wrap. Everyone and everything is as it should be!

1 Once you've returned all of the frames, return the hive-top feeder, if you're using one, and refill it. Firmly knock any last bees off of the inner cover by giving it a firm rap on the ground. Slide the inner cover on, taking care to move slowly from rear to front so that any bees can move out of the cover's way. If your inner cover has a ventilation notch cut out, it should be facing upward.

Chapter 8
A Year of Bees

The needs of your bees change with the seasons. Some periods will be full of activity, both for the hive and for you, the beekeeper. Others will be characterized by dormancy and rest. This chapter offers detailed checklists for what care the hive needs during different times of the year. Being prepared for meeting the bees' needs will go far toward ensuring the success of your hive.

SPRING

Early spring is characterized by fluctuations between warm and cold weather. In the same week, there could be a series of sunny days and blooming flowers followed by a burst of snow. This extreme weather variation occurs when the hive is at its most vulnerable. The warm periods and longer days prompt the queen to begin laying eggs again. If brood production occurs quickly, the colony may eat through its food stores before new nectar sources are available or consistent in supply. Your job during the spring months, as the hive's steward, is to watch carefully for starvation, swarming, or external threats such as robbing or predation. Under your supervision, if your hive was strong going into the winter and was provided with adequate food, your winged friends should make it through spring without a hitch. On the following pages you'll see some important spring-specific tasks you'll want to consider addressing with your bees. Find complete seasonal checklists for the entire year on page 337.

Checklist

Early/Mid-Spring

☐ Look inside only on warm, sunny days.

☐ Check for eggs, uncapped and capped brood, and general indication of a queen.

☐ Begin supplemental feeding if food stores are low; continue until an active nectar flow occurs (remember, nectar flows will vary from one geographic location to the next; if in doubt, try to connect with other beekeepers in your area to learn when nectar flows occur).

☐ Remove mouse guard and entrance reducers.

☐ Install queen excluder, if using, over brood box.

☐ Add supers as soon as brood box is full of bees.

☐ Continue adding supers as each new one fills with honey or bees.

☐ Begin weekly inspections in mid-spring, checking for swarm cells. See page 305 for measures to take for swarm prevention.

☐ Remove old frames and replace with new frames and foundation if equipment looks worn.

☐ Make splits as needed (see page 303).

☐ Requeen or allow natural supersedure as necessary (see page 306).

Mid-/Late Spring

☐ Reverse hive bodies (see page 303), as this may act as a deterrent against swarming.

☐ Determine what swarm-capturing method you will use, in the event that one should occur.

☐ If an intense nectar flow happens, a late-spring honey extraction may be necessary.

☐ Plant honeybee-loving plants near your hive and around your property (see page 320 for some suggestions).

☐ Examine varroa mite population and treat as desired (see page 313 for a discussion of varroa mites).

Reversing Hive Bodies

Reversing hive bodies is exactly what its name indicates: switching the positions of the hive bodies, moving the one on top to the bottom. This is done to prevent swarming, as bees congested up near the top of an upper hive body (where they snuggled together to cluster for the winter) are unlikely to move back down below. Wait until a clear, warm day to do this. Reversing hive bodies when the weather is too cold could result in brood becoming chilled in the lower hive body as the queen and worker bees move upward into the upper hive body to being laying more eggs. Of course, if you wait too long, the hive could swarm. The timing of reversing hive bodies, is, admittedly, a tricky dance, but you should have no problem if you follow these steps.

1. Don your protective gear and light your smoker.

2. Lift the outer cover and give the hive a gentle smoking. Place the outer cover on the ground.

3. Using your hive tool, pry open all four corners of the upper hive body. With the inner cover in place on top of it, gently place the hive body on top of the outer cover.

4. Remove the lower hive body. It should be mostly empty of bees. Place it across the first hive body you removed, facing the opposite direction.

5. Take this opportunity to clean off your bottom board. Use the flat end of your hive tool and scrape out any wax or dead bees that may have accumulated. Be sure to hang on to the debris, though, as leaving it on the ground may entice predators to come snooping.

6. Now, take the hive body that is mostly empty (the one resting on top of the two hive bodies on the ground) and place it temporarily on the ground. If you have an empty hive stand or a level object like a cement block available, place the hive body on top of it.

7. Place the second hive body, the one that was formerly on top and is full of bees, in position over the bottom board.

8. Give the new lower hive body (the one full of bees) a gentle smoking, and use your hive tool to pry off the inner cover.

9. Take the hive body you have placed to the side (the mostly empty one) and put it on top.

10. Replace the inner and outer covers. All finished!

NOTE: If you are using a configuration of woodenware other than double-stacked hive bodies (I'm thinking here of a friend who uses all medium supers), reversing hive bodies is performed in the same manner as just described. Simply switch out the uppermost super with the lower one, following all of the steps as detailed.

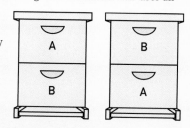

Making Splits and Nucs

Although essentially the same thing, in bee parlance, *splits* or *making a split* are terms used to describe dividing a hive for one's personal use, whereas *nucs* refer to divisions of bees one intends to sell. Making splits or nucs are both means of reducing the size of a hive that has become too congested and may be exhibiting signs of an intention to swarm. Divisions should only be performed on strong, thriving hives.

In your first year of beekeeping, it is highly unlikely that the size of your hive will increase to the extent that making splits or nucs is necessary. However, in subsequent years, such measures may need to be taken. If you are nervous about making splits or nucs on your own, I'd encourage you to either shadow an experienced beekeeper as they make divisions in their own hives, or ask them to accompany you in your bee yard. The best time to make a division of any sort is in early spring, once it warms a bit but around a month or so before the first nectar flow. Here's how to do it:

1. Once you've determined that you have a strong enough colony to merit division, put in an order with your preferred beekeeping equipment supplier for all of the makings of a new hive: bottom board, hive body, supers, frames with foundation, feeder, and so on. If you're making a nuc, you'll need the woodenware for a nuc box.

2. Next, place an order for a queen. Alternatively, if swarm or supersedure cells are present, you can allow the hive to produce its own queen (see page 306).

3. Once your queen arrives or you find capped-over queen cells, it's time to make a division. Position your new woodenware where the new hive will be situated. It needs to be at least 3 feet (91.4 cm) from the original hive.

4. Light your smoker, lift the outer cover, and give the hive a gentle smoking. Place the outer cover on the ground.

5. Look through the occupied hive body and find a frame with some honey and pollen on it. Place this frame in the empty hive body or empty nuc box if you're making a nuc.

6. Locate the frame containing the queen. Move this frame into the empty hive body or nuc box. If you see any other queen cells on this frame, remove them.

7. Look for two additional frames containing pollen, honey, and brood in all stages of development (eggs, plus capped and uncapped brood). Place these frames into the empty hive body or nuc box, along with all of the bees on them.

8. Fill up the remaining spaces in the new hive body with empty frames. Fill your feeder of choice with sugar syrup, put it in place, and put on the outer cover.

9. Return to the original hive. It will contain queen cells but no queen. You can now do one of two things: introduce the new queen you've ordered, or allow for a virgin queen to emerge from a supersedure cell.

For natural supersedure, remove any capped or just-about-to-be-capped queen cells (these are bulbous, rounded cells with openings at their bottoms or sides, typically located at the upper portion of a frame) from the original hive, leaving several that have visible larvae in them. Push the remaining frames together, fill the empty spaces with new frames, install your feeder, and put on the outer cover.

If you will be introducing a new queen, push the remaining frames almost together, leaving enough room in between the two innermost frames to hold onto a queen cage. Review the steps outlined on page 288 for installing a package, and position the queen cage between the frames with the candy end facing upward. Fill the remaining spaces with empty frames, install your feeder, and put on the outer cover.

10. Whichever method of generating a new queen you choose, return after one week. If using a purchased queen, check to be sure that she has been freed from her cage. Remove the empty queen cage and continue feeding until the first nectar flow. If allowing for natural supersedure, remove all but one of the now-capped queen cells (it's smart to leave the first capped cell you find and move on looking for others; it might just turn out to be the only one in the hive, and you'd hate to have destroyed what would be your only available queen!). Close up the hive and leave it for one month, continuing to provide sugar syrup as needed.

11. You've now successfully created two hives from one! Either monitor the new hive, providing sugar syrup and supers as needed, or sell your nuc box to another beekeeper.

Preventing Swarming

Sometimes, no matter how hard you work to prevent it, your hive will swarm. It's the bees' genetic tendency—they're literally doing what nature tells them to do. That said, the following measures will go far toward thwarting swarming. Again, they're not foolproof, but if swarming is something that you absolutely want to prevent (some beekeepers feel more strongly about preventing swarming than others), then taking these steps adds an extra bit of insurance to your goal of keeping the bees right where they are.

→ Add supers as needed. Be attentive to how much space the bees have. If they feel crowded, they're more inclined to secure new digs. Beat them to the punch and give them the extra space they need before it's too late.

→ Add a queen excluder. Do this in early spring, before nectar flows might prompt swarming.

→ Reverse hive bodies. Bees like to move upward. If they're gathered in a cluster in the upper portion of the hive body and the queen resumes egg-laying, they might soon run out of room, even if a lower hive body has plenty of vacant space. By reversing hive bodies, moving what's on top beneath and vice versa, you provide "upstairs" rooms for storing food, brood, and more. Do this in early spring, before the first nectar flow. See page 303 for details on how to reverse hive bodies.

→ Provide proper ventilation. If the hive feels too hot to the bees, they'll feel inclined to search for somewhere a bit more hospitable. Keep air circulating and the bees will regulate the interior climate to just the right temperature. Make sure the ventilation hole on the inner cover is turned upward and is open. For more details on providing additional ventilation, see Moisture Prevention on page 269.

→ Provide access to water. Bees need water to dilute honey and provide natural "air conditioning" to the hive. In early spring, natural water sources may still be frozen. Providing fresh, unfrozen water, situated in a sunny location, keeps the bees from looking elsewhere for a water source.

→ Remove swarm cells. If, during your inspections, you come across swarm cells, you'll need to decide what to do with them. Should increasing your apiary size be an attractive option to you, then you'll want to make a split, which is the noun used to describe "splitting" up one hive into additional hives (see page 303). Alternatively, you can simply remove and discard any swarm cells you come across. You'll need to be extremely fastidious in your removal, as leaving even one swarm cell behind may induce the hive to continue on with its plans to swarm. If you take them all out, the colony won't swarm; in the interest of self-perpetuation, it won't leave a colony without a queen to go form a new one. That said, once you find swarm cells, even if you completely remove them all, it's likely that the colony will make more pretty soon.

→ Make splits as needed. Splitting up colonies with swarm cells present on frames is one way to both prevent swarming and increase the amount of hives you have in your apiary. Alternatively you can make nucs to sell to other beekeepers.

Requeening

Sometimes the colony decides it wants to replace its queen. As discussed on page 293 in A Look Inside, when the hive makes that decision (which is promoted by a change in pheromones produced by an aging or diseased queen), it begins creating supersedure cells. During your inspections, if you should discover supersedure cells (which are usually located on the upper portion of a frame, as opposed to swarm cells, which are found on the bottom), you have two options: 1) *requeen*, meaning that you will physically remove and kill one queen and replace it with a new one that you purchase, or 2) allow natural supersedure to occur. There are strong advocates for both approaches. If the colony is allowed to supersede naturally, some time will be lost as the new, virgin queen must first mate with drones before she will begin laying eggs. That process takes about a month. Requeening is done with an already-mated queen, allowing for no interruption in egg-laying.

Personally, I prefer supersedure. I'm an overall "let nature take its course" sort of gal anyway, so this personal philosophy extends to my beekeeping practices. If I miss out on a bit of honey-production time, I'm not bothered. If I were in the business of making money from my honey, however, I might feel differently. In natural supersedure, the first virgin queen to emerge from her cell usually kills off any other queen cells right away. She may or may not then also kill her mother. Sometimes, both new and old queen will continue laying eggs until the elder queen dies or the hive kills her off (often by forming a ball around her, which kills the queen through heat exhaustion). On occasion, the first queen to emerge will swarm, taking half of the hive with her, when the other virgin queens emerge. This is called a cast swarm, and it can continue happening with each subsequent queen's birth. If that happens, unless you can recapture the swarm, you will eventually lose your entire colony. There is really no way to know which avenue the virgin queen will take: divide and conquer (killing off the competition) or moving on (throwing a cast swarm). Some beekeepers elect to remove all but one supersedure cell to prevent this from occurring. They do this only after discovering an opened queen cell, meaning the virgin queen is present in the hive. Confident in the knowledge that at least one new queen has emerged and is alive, they will then remove any other supersedure cells.

There is some concern over limited genetic diversity in beekeepers' hives, prompting some to make the decision to requeen instead of allowing for supersedure. If many of the beekeepers in your area are ordering their bees from the same source, genetic diversity may become reduced. This could impair the queens' reproductive capabilities and the quality of eggs over time. However, if you know the bees in your area have been sourced from a variety of bee suppliers, this may not be an issue. The only way to know this, of course, is to get to know your fellow beekeepers. I cannot stress enough the importance of making the acquaintance of beekeepers in your area for reasons just such as this, in addition to the incredible wealth of information and assistance they may provide the novice beekeeper.

If you decide to requeen, the process is usually performed every two years. A queen is purchased from a respected queen supplier (and a local one, if at all possible) and introduced into the hive in her queen cage in the same manner as that performed when installing a package of bees (see page 288). On occasion, a colony will suddenly go *queenless*, meaning the queen perished without the colony having any time to prepare for it by building up swarm and supersedure cells. When this occurs, you can either purchase a new queen straightaway, or allow the hive to rear into a queen one of the youngest eggs the queen laid before perishing (this process is known as *emergency supersedure*). If the queen perishes with no young eggs present, however, then one of the workers will take over the responsibilities of laying. This is a no-win situation, however, as laying workers have never mated and will only produce drones. To attempt to prevent this situation from ever happening in the first place, move slowly and carefully while inspecting your hive so that you don't accidentally kill the queen and induce this panic situation. Staying on top of inspections and performing them regularly will also go far toward finding your colony queenless too far into the process.

SUMMER

As the heat of summer sets in, the hive is working at full steam. Colony numbers are at their peak, and nectar flows are abundant. All the bees are active, diligently toiling away at their individual roles, making all the necessary preparations for the colder months to come. The beekeeper's primary task in the warmest months is extraction. Other than that, the work tapers off during summer, unless a drought or heavy rains hinder the bees' access to nectar. In such cases, supplemental feeding will be necessary. Pay attention to weather forecasts in your area, check in on the hive periodically, make plans for extraction, and otherwise let the bees get on with the business of being bees.

Checklist

☐ Inspect the hive every week, monitoring the queen's activities, honey production, and presence of any swarm cells. Look for eggs, larvae, and other indications of active laying.

☐ Add supers as needed, for honey as well as for brood. Consider adding a second brood box if your hive seems to be "boiling over" with bees, an indication that the queen may need more room.

☐ Offer sugar syrup if your area experiences atypical weather, such as a drought, unseasonably cool temperatures, or excessive rainfall, as such situations may affect the bees' access to nectar sources.

☐ Install an entrance reducer if there is evidence of robbing or wasps or yellow jackets attempt to gain entry to the hive.

☐ Examine the varroa mite population and treat as desired (see page 313 for a discussion of varroa mites).

☐ Be prepared to extract, most likely in late summer (sometimes, an extraction in late spring or early summer is also possible). Have extracting equipment on hand, or reserve it in advance. Keep empty bottles and lids available. When you extract, be sure to leave adequate stores for the bees to get through winter (see page 309 for more information).

AUTUMN

As autumn arrives, the queen begins tapering off her egg-laying. Nectar flows and pollen sources begin to dry up while the still-busy bees fastidiously fill nooks and crannies securely with propolis, give the boot to any lingering drones, and start hunkering down for the winter. With a decrease in egg production comes a reduction in the colony's overall population. The preparations you make now will largely impact whether your hive makes it unscathed through the winter. Take the time to shore up your bees now, so that, come springtime, you'll all be basking in the sun's rays and reveling in the sprouting crocuses and apple blossoms.

Housed bees are much more likely to make it through the colder winter months than are wild colonies such as this one.

Checklist

☐ Check in on the hive every two weeks. Stop inspections completely once the temperature drops below 50 to 55°F (10 to 13°C) during the day.

☐ Confirm the presence of a queen. Look for eggs, capped and uncapped brood, and a good laying pattern.

☐ Assess capped honey stores. If they are low, you will need to feed supplementally (see page 272 for how to calculate how much honey is in a frame). Begin supplemental feeding in early autumn, around September, so that the bees will have enough time to convert your provided food to honey before the weather becomes too cold.

☐ Consider planting some winter-blooming bulbs such as snowdrops, hellebores, and crocuses to offer your colony a winter pollen source.

☐ Tilt the hive slightly forward to allow rain and snow to run off.

☐ Ventilate the inner cover (see page 269).

☐ Remove the queen excluder, if using.

☐ Stop all feeding by late autumn. Remove your hive-top feeder, if using, and replace the inner cover.

☐ Install a mouse guard.

☐ Install an entrance reducer, if not already using.

☐ Secure the hive with either a large, heavy rock atop the outer cover or a strap running the circumference of the hive (from side to side, not from entrance to rear).

☐ If you live in an area that experiences severe winters, insulate the hive by wrapping it with black roofing tar paper (see Wrap It Up on page 309 for more information).

☐ Store empty honey supers in a secure location, away from inclement weather, bears, and wax moths (see page 333).

❄ WINTER

There won't be much for you, the beekeeper, to work on during the winter. That said, late winter and early spring are when the bees are at their most vulnerable. Hive losses

occur more at this time than at any other. Preparations made during autumn really come into play now. The bees will gather together inside in a football-shaped cluster to keep warm, periodically changing positions to access food stores. Total population numbers will have diminished considerably, balancing out somewhere around 10,000. Egg-laying, which tapers off in autumn, will resume again in mid- to late winter. Strong hives, offered plenty of their own food and given proper ventilation, should make it through winter unscathed.

Checklist

- Check the bee yard regularly for damage caused by storms or animals.

- Gently tap on the side of the hive. If you hear buzzing, the colony is alive. No need to open the hive, as you wouldn't want to expose them to the cold.

- Check that mouse guards are still in place.

- Check food stores by lifting the hive to determine weight (see page 272). Consider supplemental feeding if necessary (see page 273 for discussion of dry sugar and fondant feeding).

- If no unfrozen water source is available nearby (such as a creek or river), provide water; be sure to place it in a sunny location.

- Order more frames and supers, or other equipment, as needed.

- Continue reading and learning about honeybees.

Wrap It Up

In climates with severely harsh winters, where temperatures remain below freezing for months, wrapping hives with tar paper can be the difference between hives that perish and those that thrive. Tar paper, which is really quite inexpensive and readily available at most building supply stores, absorbs the sun's rays, warming the hive and melting any snow that may fall on it. As a consequence, the bees are able to break out of their wintertime cluster and move to honey stores. I've heard of bees dying of starvation with honey nearby, but just far enough away that they weren't able to break away from the cluster. Tar paper acts as a mini solar cooker, giving the hive just the right amount of warmth. Simply measure your hives and cut the tar paper with a craft knife. Wrap the tar paper around the supers and the outer cover, leaving the entrance open, and secure it in place with a stapler.

Body Count

If you should come to check on your hives one winter day and discover a number of dead bee bodies lying about, don't be alarmed. Casualties occurring during winter are normal, the natural passing of the hive's more senior members. House bees wait until a moderately warm and sunny day to remove the bodies. At other times, bees will leave the hive on winter days for "cleansing flights" (bathroom breaks, essentially), only to alight upon snowy ground, become chilled, and perish. This breaks my heart, but there is very little that can be done about it. The one consolation I find in it is that it is at least an indication that the hive is still alive, with its members strong enough to take flight.

Chapter 9
Health & Wellness

Like all other living things, honeybees can get sick, they can get attacked, and they can get injured. They are just as fragile as humans, if not more so. Your job, as their steward, is to take action to keep them as healthy and happy as possible. If you're like me, you practice preventive care for yourself and your family and keep a vigilant watch for any sign of potential health problems, addressing them before they have the opportunity to advance into full-blown crises. You will need to exercise the same proactive approach with your bees. In this chapter we'll examine the most common diseases, parasites, and pests that threaten the health and well-being of your hives. Knowing what to look for during routine inspections will go far toward keeping trouble out of the hive while promoting health within.

DISEASES

American Foulbrood (AFB)

If "foulbrood" sounds awful, it's because it is. It's foul, vile, and ultimately, quite sad. Foulbrood, as its name suggests, is a disease attacking brood. Caused by the bacterium *Paenibacillus larvae* ssp. *larvae*, American Foulbrood is possibly the most devastating of all bee diseases. It is highly contagious, both within a hive and among neighboring hives. If AFB is detected, there is no remedy; the only treatment is to destroy the hive completely by fire. The entrance must be covered and the entire hive burned in a shallow pit, frames and all. The ashes should then be covered over by dirt so that no robbing can occur. AFB spores can live for many, many decades, so burning and burying infected hives is the only safe treatment solution.

AFB Characteristics

- ▶ Brood die capped
- ▶ Brood cappings sink inward and look punctured or perforated
- ▶ Brood pattern is spotty instead of compact
- ▶ Brood change color from a pearly white to a milk- to dark-chocolate brown
- ▶ Brood emits a sharp, sulfurous, foul stench
- ▶ Brood cells possess a "ropy," stringy, stretchy texture if punctured with a small stick

There are two antibiotics used to prevent AFB, Terramycin and tylosin. Deciding on whether or not to use them is largely a matter of your overall approach to beekeeping. Like many beekeepers, I am opposed to routine antibiotic use, on the grounds that repeated applications of antibiotics eventually result in both antibiotic-resistant bacteria and toxic residues in honey and honeycomb. Instead, I advocate hygiene as the best form of prevention. If you have more than one hive, consider heat-sterilizing your hive tool between hives using a blowtorch, lighter, or lit match. Don't feed your bees any food from other hives that may possess AFB spores (if you use outside honey or pollen stores, confirm the supplier's hives are AFB-free). Don't purchase used equipment unless, as with food, the supplier is known and trustworthy. Lastly,

if you are ever faced with the need to purchase a queen, consider hygienic queens. Reared with the genetic ability to both detect and remove perceived hygiene threats (including a number of bee diseases and hive pests), *hygienic* queens rear generations of bees possessed with the same self-maintaining qualities. These approaches would be considered Integrated Pest Management practices, or IPM. They exemplify the manner of beekeeping that I espouse and will be looked at more fully on page 314.

European Foulbrood (EFB)

Similar to American Foulbrood, European Foulbrood is a brood-attacking disease caused by the bacterium *Melissococcus plutonius*. EFB is harmful, but not nearly as devastating as AFB. European Foulbrood spores don't persist in the environment as AFB spores do; accordingly, if the disease manifests in your hives, such extreme measures as burning and burial are not necessary. Strong hives can often stave off the disease on their own, while weak hives may need your assistance. Frames containing uncapped, healthy larvae from strong colonies may be added to EFB-infected hives, allowing healthy larvae to attract attention from nurse bees to themselves, and away from diseased larvae.

Being able to distinguish between the two forms of foulbrood enables you, the beekeeper, to determine which course of action to take in handling the disease. I advocate the use of integrated pest management practices to prevent EFB.

EFB Characteristics

- ▶ Brood die uncapped, making them clearly visible to the beekeeper
- ▶ Brood pattern is spotty and random
- ▶ Brood cappings sink inward and look punctured or perforated
- ▶ Brood color changes from pearly white to an off-white or yellow-brown
- ▶ Brood often appear as though they have "melted" in their cells
- ▶ Brood emits a sour smell, but not nearly as bad as that produced by AFB
- ▶ Brood cells will not possess the "ropy," stringy, stretchy texture associated with AFB

Chalkbrood

Appearing most commonly during spring months when temperatures fluctuate between cool and warm extremes, Chalkbrood is another disease affecting brood. Caused by the fungus *Ascopsphaera apis*, Chalkbrood may occur when brood become chilled, allowing fungal spores to germinate and spread, moving into the larvae's gut and competing there with it for nutrients. The larvae may then die, permitting the fungus to invade and overtake the entire larval mass, rendering it into a white, hard, mummified body resembling a piece of chalk. The hardened masses are easy to remove from honeycomb cells, which undertaker bees do at their first fair-weather opportunity.

The first indication that your brood might have a Chalkbrood issue will be the appearance of their chalk-white bodies on the entrance board or on the ground in front of the hive. Chalkbrood isn't a devastating disease in the manner of AFB or EFB. For the most part, utilizing the IPM practices outlined for AFB will work to prevent Chalkbrood from ever appearing in your hives. Additionally, remember to consider the recommendations for hive siting suggested on page 268. Keeping hives out of damp, dank, low-lying locations, as well as providing good overall ventilation, will go far toward preventing Chalkbrood spores from finding a hospitable environment in the first place. Furthermore, some beekeepers suggest periodically culling old frames. Depending on their condition, completely replacing frames every two to five years eliminates any accumulated pathogens or toxins that may have built up on honeycomb cells. Finally, should your hive go queenless or you decide you'd like to requeen with purchased stock, consider a hygienic queen. Her offspring will be inclined toward culling any Chalkbrood-infested cells from the hive.

Sacbrood

Caused by a virus, this condition is considered somewhat rare. The Sacbrood virus infects brood during the prepupal stage. You will know it is present by the appearance of watery, limp, yellow-brown larvae. Sacbrood is somewhat analogous to the common cold. If supplied with good-quality food (like nectar and honey) and predisposed of a robust constitution, the hive should recover fully on its own. As suggested with Chalkbrood, culling and replacing old, worn frames with new frames periodically will also go far toward keeping Sacbrood in check. You may remove the Sacbrood-afflicted larvae from cells with tweezers or leave that task to the bees.

Nosema

Whereas the previously mentioned diseases are threats specific to brood, nosema is a condition affecting adult bees. Also known as dysentery, nosema is the most serious of all adult bee diseases. Caused by a single-celled protozoan, *Nosema apis*, the virus attacks the bees' digestive system. It most often appears in early spring, when bees have been cooped up due to cold or inclement weather and are subsequently unable to take "cleansing" flights to relieve themselves.

As worker bees go about the business of keeping the hive clean, they busily bite and lick surfaces within. In so doing, they may ingest *Nosema apis* spores.

Once consumed, the protozoan can seriously impair the bee's ability to digest food, resulting in reduced honey consumption and reduced colony buildup. In addition to a diminished post-winter colony buildup, visible characteristics of nosema include bees that appear to be disoriented, stumbling about the entrance of the hive. Also, nosema may evidence through streaking or spotting, evidenced by dark yellow-brown dots and streaks around the front of the hive and sometimes on frames. The disease may or may not kill bees. It will certainly weaken them.

Ways that you can prevent nosema include proper ventilation; siting the hive in sunny, dry, and draft-free locations; periodically culling frames (to remove spores that may live on in bee feces); and providing plenty of honey going into colder months. Some beekeepers treat preventively for nosema with the antibiotic fungicide fumagillin (Fumidil B) during autumn. As a beekeeper employing organic beekeeping practices with my hives, after careful reading and consideration on the topic, I have elected not to use this treatment. The decision to use or not use antibiotics with your bees is entirely up to you. Read up on the topic and make the choice that best suits your beekeeping approach.

PARASITES

While you're doing all you can to bolster and fortify your bees, a number of organisms, both large and small, are working in the opposite direction. All that the honeybee offers, from brood to pollen, honey, and a warm, cozy home, are terribly attractive to a wide variety of living things.

Varroa Mites

Perhaps the most serious condition affecting both bees and beekeepers alike, the ravages incurred by the *Varroa destructor* mite have become an international problem. Tiny red or brown-colored parasites resembling miniature ticks, female varroa seal themselves away in brood cells just before they are capped. Once inside, they suck haemolymph (bee blood) from developing bees, resulting in deformities including chewed, deformed wings, transmission of viruses, and crippled, sickly bees that are essentially useless in the hive. Many larvae simply die in their cells, too crippled by varroa to emerge alive. As the queen's laying tapers off in late autumn and into winter, varroa populations decline, as there are fewer brood cells within which to feed and reproduce. Instead, the mite populations that remain huddle into the wintertime bee cluster, feeding off the haemolymph of adult bees.

If varroa mite infestation is left untreated, entire colonies may eventually disappear. The first line of treatment, then, is monitoring. By keeping a watchful eye over varroa populations, the parasite can be maintained at a level that will not harm the colony. Attemping to fight off infestation is often futile, as almost every beehive on the planet will have some level of varroa present. Complete removal of the parasites is less the goal than developing a manageable coexistence.

During routine inspections, you can detect the presence of varroa one of three ways: by seeing the mites on the bees themselves, by witnessing them on uncapped larvae, or by the presence of deformed wings on adult bees. If any of these signs are visible, employ one of the following methods to check varroa population numbers: powdered sugar shake,

opening drone brood cells with an uncapping fork, and utilizing sticky mats on screened bottom boards.

Powdered Sugar Shake

You'll need to gather up a quart-sized mason jar or other jar with screw-top threads, a canning screw ring to fit the jar's opening, and hardware cloth cut into the circumference of the opening and fitted into the screw band. You'll also need a sheet of plain white paper. Add ¼ cup of sifted, lump-free powdered sugar to the jar.

Don your protective gear, light your smoker, and open your hive, moving through supers until you reach the brood nest. Once there, scoop a large amount of bees (you're hoping to gather up around 300 bees) from off of the brood frames into your jar. Secure the jar lid and close the hive back up.

Place one hand over the screened lid and shake the jar repeatedly, until the sugar completely coats the bees. This doesn't injure them in the slightest, and their sisters will lick them clean once they return to the hive.

Remove your hand, and shake the sugar through the screening and onto the sheet of white paper. Uncap the jar and let the bees fly out (be sure you're wearing your protective gear, as they will be less than thrilled by your presence at this point).

Shake any remaining sugar onto the sheet of paper, and count the number of mites in the powdered sugar. If you count more than 10 mites, you've got a serious infestation on your hands. We'll discuss treatment options ahead.

Opening Drone Brood Cells

Varroa are especially fond of laying eggs inside drone cells. By checking a sample, you can assess the level of mite infestation in your hive. Here's how:

Don your protective gear, light your smoker, and open your hive, moving through supers until you reach the brood nest. Remove a brood frame and look for capped drone brood (these protrude out farther than their sisters).

Integrated Pest Management

During inspections of varroa populations, if you should discover problematic infestation levels, you'll need to take action. The methods that I like to employ are collectively referred to as *Integrated Pest Management* or IPM. These strategies work to manage pest populations. They don't eradicate them completely, but ideally they keep intruders at a level that the hive can handle themselves. With IPM, regular inspections and prevention are preferred to acute treatment. Optimally, IPM approaches will reduce or omit entirely the use of hard chemical applications. So-called soft treatments, which generally involve subtle hive and hive component manipulation, are employed with the goal of supporting the hive to naturally defend and heal itself from within.

Use the following techniques to support an IPM-based approach to managing varroa populations:

- Insert a screened bottom board so mites will fall through and populations may be monitored.

- Remove drone brood cells.

- Maintain strong colonies through routine inspections, providing proper ventilation, leaving the hive with proper food stores in winter, siting the hive in a sunny location, preventing robbing, and so on.

- Purchase bees known for varroa resistance. Some bee suppliers advertise varroa-resistant bee strains, and hygienic queens are beneficial for removing infected larvae.

- Reduce robbing, as this can spread varroa between colonies.

- Treat hives in spring and autumn with an essential oil-based supplement such as the much-touted *Honey B-Healthy*. Research indicates the product, while not killing mites, instead fortifies honeybee constitutions, thereby enabling them to fight off any parasitic attacks; treatment must be done when honey supers are not on, as the honey could take on the flavor of the essential oils; accordingly, it is usually administered before the spring honey flow and after the last autumn honey flow.

- Shake organic, sifted, cornstarch-free powdered sugar over the bees. Do this only if you are using a screened bottom board. Use either an empty powder bottle or any other sort of container with a sifter top, and shake a light dusting of the sugar over all of the bees on each frame. If this low-fi approach works as planned, mites will lose their footing on the honeybees, dropping down to the screened bottom board and out of the hive. Repeat weekly for the first few weeks of early spring, once the bees have broken cluster, and again in autumn.

Using either a bee brush or a firm shake, remove the bees on the frame (do this over the open brood nest in the event that the queen should be on the frame; you want her to go back into the brood nest and not fall onto the ground).

Move to the side or rear of the hive, turn your back to it, and, with the aid of an uncapping fork, open approximately a quarter to a third of a cluster of drone brood. Pierce the larvae and pull them out.

If you see more than two mites on a single larvae, you've got a serious infestation on your hands. Counting only a few mites in your sample indicates the presence of a small varroa population.

Sticky Screened Bottom Boards

In order to utilize this method, you will need to have screened bottom boards in place. Screened bottom boards are a good idea in any case; under normal circumstances mites fall through, leaving the hive, never to return. With a solid bottom board, mites that fall to the bottom of the hive simply hitch a ride on the next adult bee to fly by.

Most of the year, the screened bottom board is open, permitting optimal ventilation inside the hive. During inspection times, the removable plastic insert that comes with screened bottom boards is inserted. Before you insert the plastic board, coat it with a sticky substance such as vegetable oil. Now, mites that fall off of bees will collect on the bottom board and be stuck.

After three days, remove the bottom board and count the number of mites gathered. Divide the total number by three, which will give you a rough daily mite fall number. Between 20 and 50 mites total is tolerable. If you count more than 50 or so mites, you have an infestation and will need to do something about it.

Tracheal Mites

Considerably smaller than their varroa cousins, tracheal mites are undetectable to the naked eye. Accordingly, their presence cannot be monitored via inspections. As their name indicates, these pesky creatures live in the thoracic trachea of honeybees, where they reproduce. Tracheal mites bite into the tracheal (breathing) tube and suck on the bee's haemolymph. Eventually, tracheal mites so fully congest the breathing tube that the bee is unable to get enough oxygen to fly.

Absent a microscope for performing thoracic inspections of deceased bees, it's almost impossible to detect the presence of tracheal mites. Subtle clues can give you a heads-up that there might be a problem, however. If you notice bees stumbling on the ground in front of the hive or trying unsuccessfully to fly, you might have a tracheal issue. Grease patties infused with essential oils can help prevent or treat tracheal mite infestation. Once consumed by honeybees, the oils in the patties cause the resident mites to become confused in their search for a host. Grease patties have the added benefit of reducing varroa mites, as the grease prevents mites from securing a strong hold on the bees. Accordingly, they fall to the bottom where, if screen bottomed boards are in place, they will then fall completely out of the hive.

Grease Patties

1. Mix 2 parts granulated sugar to 1 part saturated fat, such as all-natural vegetable shortening or coconut oil. The exact amount doesn't matter so long as you adhere to the 2:1 sugar-to-fat ratio.

2. To this mixture, add ¼ to ½ cup honey as needed to make a soft-but-not-runny consistency. Stir 5 to 10 drops of wintergreen, spearmint, or peppermint pure essential oil into the mixture. The finished product should be quite stiff.

3. Using an ice cream scoop, scoop uniformly sized lumps and press the mixture into patties with your hands. Repeat until all of the mixture has been formed into flattened patties.

4. Place one patty directly onto the top bars of the brood chamber. Allow the bees to consume the grease, and replace with a new patty as needed. Store additional patties between sheets of waxed paper in a sealable bag or lidded container in the freezer until needed.

PESTS

Small Hive Beetle (SHB)

Technically known as *Aethina tumida*, the small hive beetle was introduced to European honeybees via Africa. Easily handled in their native environment, this exotic insect has the potential to wreak havoc on small, weak colonies. Dark brown to black in appearance once mature and slightly larger than a tick, female small hive beetles lay eggs inside the hive. Their larvae go on to eat pretty much everything inside the hive except for the honeybees themselves—pollen, larvae, honey, wax, eggs, the works. As if that weren't bad enough, they then leave an oozy trail of excrement, which, should it pollute uncapped honey stores, causes fermentation and a subsequent bubbling mess in the hive. Small hive beetle larvae slowly work their way down and out of the hive, heading toward soil where they will burrow and pupate, "sliming" the entire hive on their way out.

As a tropical pest, small hive beetles are of smaller concern to beekeepers in northerly climates, although northern hives should not be considered immune. The best measure of defense against small hive beetles is to keep colonies strong by following IPM practices such as providing appropriate ventilation, adequate food stores, and proper hive siting, and using genetically resistant bee stock. Consider the use of beetle traps if you have a problem.

The most readily available models of small hive beetle traps are the Hood trap and the West trap. The Hood trap is designed to capture adult hive beetles and consists of a small plastic tank or reservoir that is attached to the interior bottom edge of a frame. The tank is filled with a mixture of vinegar and oil to attract and trap the beetles. The West trap is designed to trap larvae on their exit route. Attached to the bottom board, this model of trap contains a tank running the length of the hive (much like a hive-top feeder). The tank is filled with oil, into which the larvae will fall and become

trapped. A grip running the entire length of the tank prevents bees from falling in as well. Both types of small hive beetle traps can be sourced from many beekeeping suppliers.

Wax Moths

The greater wax moth, *Galleria mellonella*, is often merely a nuisance. If allowed to flourish, however, this scavenger can destroy a hive. Once female wax moths have penetrated the hive, they lay eggs in the brood box. Their young then tunnel through brood comb, leaving silvery, threadlike webbing and feces everywhere. During warmer weather, they can ravage entire frames of comb in as short as two weeks. Strong hives will often manage wax moths themselves, while small or stressed hives are more susceptible to infiltration.

The best line of defense against wax moths is to practice proper storage of empty honey supers (refer to Cold Storage on page 333 for storage suggestions). Also, you want to be sure to add honey supers only when the supers below are almost completely filled. Doing so minimizes the spaces in the hive that are absent of bees; sufficient, strong numbers of bees in a hive can patrol, defend, and ward off interlopers in empty cells. After extraction, replace the extracted supers back onto the hive, taking them back off again after the first hard frost; this allows bees time to remove any residual honey.

It's possible to also practice preventive treatment against wax moths (however, this method won't work after an infestation is present). An annual spray of diluted Bt (*Bacillus thuringiensis*) over the wax comb on each frame has proven almost 100 percent effective at deterring wax moths. Bt is a so-called "soft" treatment consistent with integrated pest management and is considered an alternative to paradichlorobenzene, a synthetic, aromatic compound similar to that found in moth balls. This chemical is not permitted in organic beekeeping practices.

Ants

More of a nuisance than a serious problem, a few ants in the hive are fine, but too many can make a hive head for more hospitable environs, especially one that is small or weak. To keep ants from becoming a major issue, elevate your hives on a wooden hive stand or cinder blocks. If your hive is situated in an area where grass grows, remain vigilant about keeping the grass trimmed in the bee yard.

If ants are moving into the hive en masse, put the hive stand's legs in containers of water or oil. The water or oil moat will prevent ants from gaining entry by creating a rather insurmountable barricade.

Mice

Come cooler weather, mice will start searching for warm, toasty housing in which they can overwinter. You don't want to give them any opportunity to decide that your hives will make ideal lodging. If allowed entry (which they will do at night, as the colony begins to form its cold-weather cluster), they will eat pollen, chew through the woodenware, bring in grass and leaves, and generally make a mess of the place. Mice aren't a problem during warmer weather, as an active hive will thwart their entry with multiple stinging attacks. Once the bees are clustered, though, the mice can sail past the entrance unnoticed. While they pose no direct threat to the bees themselves, they can destroy precious food stores and equipment.

To stop a mouse or any other rodent (you definitely don't want rats in your hive, *ever*) problem from developing, install mouse guards over the hive's entrance when the weather begins to cool in late summer or early autumn.

Galvanized strips of metal (usually zinc) perforated with multiple bee-sized holes, mouse guards will keep mice out while allowing both air and bees to circulate within. Remove the mouse guard in the spring when the cluster begins to break and activity inside the hive resumes.

Skunks, Raccoons, and Opossums

For the most part mere pests, these nocturnal foragers can cripple weak colonies, as well as strong colonies left open to repeated assault. A skunk's calling card will be the presence of scratch marks at the hive's entrance. Guard bees come out to check on the disturbance, only to be gobbled up (skunks seem to be immune to stings on their paws, mouth, or throat). They'll repeat this process a number of times, returning the next night for another free meal. If you detect scratch marks or muddy paw prints on the hive entrance or landing board, or torn up sod or mulch on the ground in front of the hive, you might have a skunk problem on your hands. Opossums operate in a similar manner, only minus the presence of scratch marks. Another surefire sign that your hives are under nighttime attack will be an aggressive disposition. Agitated, angry bees can be a hallmark of a hive on extreme alert.

If you sense you might have a skunk or opossum issue, there are three lines of defense you can pursue. First, elevate your hives off the ground. Skunks or opossums would then have to expose their vulnerable (and, thankfully, sensitive) underbellies in order to access the bees. The stings will turn them off of their pursuit in short order. Secondly, you could hammer tacks or nails through a piece of plywood and situate the board on the ground in front of the hive. Just don't forget that it's there when you approach the hive, or you'll get the rude awakening intended for your thieving intruders! Lastly, you can cordon off the area in front of the hive by either placing a large roll of metal fencing in front of the entrance, secured down with a brick, cement block, or heavy rock, or stake metal rods into the ground and thread chicken wire fencing around them as a protective barricade.

Raccoons are less interested in the bees themselves, preferring instead the bees' pollen, honey, propolis, and wax. Marauding raccoons will remove the outer and inner covers of a hive and pull out frames. They'll then take the frames over to a corner of the bee yard and greedily munch away. Securing the lid of the hive with a heavy rock or brick can easily prevent this entire debacle. Because the scent of wax or other bee products can serve as an attractant to raccoons, avoid discarding any hive by-products onto the ground of your bee yard. When performing hive inspections, gather up any debris in a lidded jar and remove it from the area.

Bears

Honeybees have a long, storied, and rather controversial history with bears. Bears love to eat honey and brood—it's almost as simple as that. Bears are also big and strong, and not particularly bothered by bee stings. Accordingly, if allowed entry to your bee yard (often at night), they will not only decimate almost every hive in sight, they will remember their tasty exploits, returning again and again. As such, the best defense is advance precautions.

If you live in an area known to possess bears (as I do), make every attempt to keep your bee yard free of any equipment or hive debris, including empty supers, wax, drone cells, and so on. For greater security, consider installing electric fencing. In order for electric bear fencing to be effective, it needs to be well grounded, properly charged at all times, and the area around it needs to be regularly maintained (grass and weeds need to be trimmed, branches must be kept off the fence, etc.). Don't choose a location adjacent to trees, as

branches may fall and disarm the charge; determined bears might also climb the tree, dropping down directly into the bee yard. The voltage will need to be checked periodically with a handheld portable device called a voltmeter. Fences can be either permanent or temporary, but should consist of wires 8 to 10 inches (20.3 to 25.4 cm) apart. The bottom wire should be 8 inches (20.3 cm) from the ground, and the fence itself needn't be any higher than 3 to 4 feet (.9 to 1.2 m). Batteries for electric fencing may be either electric or solar and need to support at least 12 volts. Whichever option you select, the battery must be reliable and continually charged.

Beekeepers refer to the heartbreaking act of a bear destroying one's hives as having been "Yogi-ed," a reference to the cartoon character known for his robust appetite for honey. Should you suffer the devastating ravages of a bear assault, compensation for your losses may be possible. If you live in an area determined to be a known bear habitat, register your bees with your local wildlife or conservation agency. "Bear" in mind, however, this will need to be done well in advance of an actual attack.

A bee yard utilizing bear fencing

Colony Collapse Disorder (CCD)

It's not just honey-obsessed bears or opportunistic diseases that pose risks to our winged friends. Entire populations of honeybee colonies have begun disappearing completely. Poof. Gone. It would be all good and well to joke about alien abductions or other fantastical notions were the issue not of such grave concern. In 2006, beekeepers in the United States, upon performing routine inspections, began finding a good number of their hives to be totally empty of bees. Losses began to mount, with beekeepers reporting greater and greater numbers of completely empty beehives. Dubbed Colony Collapse Disorder, the mysterious syndrome has since spread, appearing internationally and affecting commercial and hobbyist beekeepers alike.

The jury is still out on what is behind CCD. It may stem from a single source or could very well be multicausal. An international cadre of scientists is working with feverish dedication toward identifying the culprit. No consensus currently exists, and no definitive causes have yet been determined. Some of the more widely espoused potential causes include:

→ Varroa mites

→ Nosema

→ Environmental change-related stresses such as drought and climate change

→ Malnutrition, possibly from securing nectar exclusively from one source (more common in commercial-scale beekeeping)

→ Pesticides

→ Insecticides such as neonicotinoids

→ Migratory beekeeping and the stress it could be causing honeybees

→ Cell phone radiation

→ Genetically modified (GM) crops

What then characterizes Colony Collapse Disorder? While there is some variation between hives, CCD-affected colonies largely evidence the following traits:

→ A complete absence of bees, with no or little dead bee buildup near the hives

→ The presence of capped brood

→ The presence of honey and pollen food stores

→ The queen is present

→ The overall workforce at the time of collapse consists largely of young bees

→ The workforce is reduced in overall numbers

→ Other potential hive robbers, such as wasps or other honeybees, avoid the hive, even though it is unguarded and full of food

The greatest threat posed by CCD to humans concerns our food supply. Honeybees are responsible for the pollination of over 30 percent of the foods that many people regularly consume. As we all have to eat to survive, the threat holds potentially devastating consequences. Furthermore, many livestock animals rely on honeybees to pollinate the crops they consume. Absent honeybees, many crops would require hand pollination, a highly labor intensive endeavor. The diligent work of these pollinators saves an enormous amount of money for the producers of agricultural products, averaging somewhere around $15 billion annually. Other native pollinators such as wasps, bumblebees, and butterflies cannot be managed or transported in the same manner as *Apis mellifera*. While an identifiable cause of CCD and corresponding cure are being researched, many agriculturists are making efforts to encourage alternative native pollinators to their crops. Until we know more about its causes, I feel a beekeeper's best defense against CCD is practicing integrated pest management techniques.

A BEE GARDEN

An indispensable way to promote the well-being of honeybees—both wild populations and those in your care—is to provide them with abundant sources of nectar and pollen. Four seasons' worth of offerings will help keep our winged beauties in food supplies year-round, creating safe and nurturing habitats. The end result is that we get to enjoy expertly pollinated, fragrant, eye-pleasing, and delicious plants while the honeybees delight in readily accessible food stores.

When selecting plants and trees for both you and the bees, consider heirloom varieties, which are more likely to contain the greatest quantities of pollen and nectar. I'd also highly encourage the use of organic, pesticide- and insecticide-free gardening practices. If you're new to those techniques and uncertain how to proceed, a great number of books are available on the topic. Check around your area to find organic gardening and IPM classes.

The following list highlights a number of flowering trees and plants known to attract honeybees. Though far from exhaustive, it presents a broad base of varieties and offers something for every season. Feed your bees throughout the year and they'll work valiantly toward feeding you in return!

FLOWERING TREES

- → Apple
- → Basswood
- → Cherry
- → Linden
- → Maple
- → Orange
- → Pear
- → Plum
- → Sourwood
- → Tulip poplar
- → Willow

FLOWERING PLANTS

- → Angelica
- → Anise hyssop
- → Aster
- → Basil
- → Bee balm
- → Black choosy
- → Borage
- → Butterfly Bush
- → Calendula
- → Catmint
- → Catnip
- → Clover
- → Coneflower
- → Crocus
- → Daffodil
- → Daisy
- → Dandelion
- → Flowering quince
- → Goldenrod
- → Heather
- → Honeysuckle
- → Hyacinth
- → Lavender
- → Lemon balm
- → Marigold
- → Meadowsweet
- → Mullein
- → Nasturtium
- → Nettle
- → Peppermint
- → Poppy
- → Rosemary
- → Sage
- → Snowdrop
- → Spearmint
- → Stonecrop
- → Sunflowers
- → Sweet pea
- → Thyme
- → Winter aconite
- → Wintergreen
- → Witch hazel

Chapter 10

Honey

A popular reason for getting into beekeeping in the first place, honey is the sweetest reward for your labor of love. Locally sourced, backyard (or rooftop!) collected honey far surpasses its processed, grocery store kin in both flavor and overall quality. Modern beekeeping practices result in the production of a surplus of honey, benefiting bee and beekeeper alike. Here we'll examine all the crucial details relating to how the liquid gold is created, extracted, stored, and sold.

MAKING MAGIC

From plant to capped comb, the manufacture of honey is a multistep, labor-intensive, fascinating process. The sweet substance we, and the bees, crave begins as a plant secretion known as nectar. Found on a wide range of vegetation, these tiny beads of sugary liquid consist of mostly water (around 80 percent) and several complex sugars. As described in chapter 4 (see page 270), as honeybees gather up nectar from plants, they also gather pollen, transferring it across the plant's reproductive organs and enabling pollination in the process. The plants get a helping hand in propagating themselves while the bees get a food source. Everyone wins.

To access nectar, a honeybee uses its skinny, hairy, tube-like tongue, known as the proboscis. While foraging, the bee stores the lapped-up nectar in its honey stomach for safekeeping until it returns to the hive. Honeybees have two stomachs, one of which is expressly dedicated to holding nectar. This honey stomach holds almost 70 milligrams of nectar and, when full, will weigh almost as much as the bee herself. In order to gather enough nectar to fill its honey stomach, a bee will visit anywhere from 150 to 1,500 flowering plants daily.

Foraging bees generally travel up to 2 miles (3.2 km) to gather nectar. If nectar offerings in that range are paltry, they will occasionally fly as far as 5 miles (8 km) to secure a source. The nectar not only provides the raw material for what will become honey, but it also provides fuel for the long-haul flights foragers make searching for it and food for growing larvae.

Upon returning to the hive, the foraging bee will regurgitate the contents of its honey stomach. A house bee then puts a drop of nectar on its proboscis and sort of "chews" it over for 20 to 30 minutes. As the bee chews on the nectar, exposing it to air, its digestive enzymes begin converting the nectar from a complex to a simple sugar. This step reduces the water content in the nectar, which in turn works toward preserving the honey against opportunistic, moisture-loving bacteria once it is stored. After the house bee has chewed on the nectar, it deposits each tiny bead into a honeycomb cell, repeating the process until a cell is filled. The nectar will still have a rather high proportion of water at this point; if left in its present state, this moisture could induce the inherent, wild yeasts within it to ferment the simple sugars. Bees intuitively know this and get busy fanning the stored nectar furiously with their wings to further reduce the moisture content. As the moisture in the nectar diminishes, the sugars become more concentrated and thicken, thereby inhibiting fermentation.

Honeybees will continue fanning the stored nectar until, mysteriously (and, in my humble estimation, miraculously), they determine it has reached a moisture content right around 18 percent. Once this occurs, they will then cap the cell over with a thin layer of beeswax. The honey will be stored therein for use as a winter and early spring food supply. Depending on its size, a hive can produce between 120 and 250 pounds (54 and 114 kg) of honey annually.

Beekeeping practices, which utilize supers or other vessels to house colonies and supplement feeding when necessary, encourage a surplus production of bee products. A greater amount of honey is stored in a hive maintained by a beekeeper than would ever be found in a wild colony. Accordingly, beekeepers can safely take off excess honey stores without endangering the hive. Provided beekeepers are mindful of leaving enough honey for the hive to survive on during colder months when nectar sources are scarce, taking off honey from the hive doesn't really "rob" them, as honey removal is sometimes referred to.

THE HONEY HOUSE

You may have noticed—honey's sticky. Really sticky. Stick-to-every-surface sticky. It's also, unsurprisingly enough, really attractive to bees. As such, you should plan your extraction location mindfully, creating your "honey house" with care and attention. By definition, a honey house is simply a building used for extracting honey and storing beekeeping and extracting equipment. While I love the idea of a building devoted exclusively to the bees and all of their needs, I'm going to guess that many of you, like myself, lack the luxury (or space) of fashioning such a dedicated structure. Unless you have a business based around honey or other bee products (beeswax, propolis, pollen), more than likely you'll be extracting only once or twice a year. In that case, any indoor area such as a garage, basement, outbuilding, barn, or kitchen will suffice as an occasional honey house.

Wherever you choose to extract, the single most important concern is that it can be fully sealed off from bees or other curious, honey-loving, winged creatures, like wasps. Not only is there the risk of being stung (less from the honeybees than the wasps, as bees are generally disinclined to sting when away from the hive), but also, if permitted to gain access to the honey, the bees will make short order of carting it drop-by-drop back to the hive. So, find a sealed, fully enclosed area to work in. If at all possible, stage your extraction in an area with a floor that can be mopped. Either way, lay down a good amount of newspaper and have extra on hand for inevitable spills or messes. A water source is also extremely handy. Otherwise, keep several buckets of warm water on hand for rinsing off hands, knives, and other equipment. This is also not the time to have your dog or cat wandering around, full of curiosity, not to mention loose hairs. We all love our pets, but ultimately, no one loves finding animal hair in their honey.

THE HARVEST

Honey harvest time is one where a sticky situation offers a much-loved reward. Let's examine what's involved in knowing when, as well as how, to take off honey, and beeswax, from your hives.

Timing Is Key

Knowing when to harvest is key. If you remove honey too soon, you run the risk of collecting honey that still possesses a high degree of moisture, which could, in turn, cause fermentation once bottled. On the other hand, if you harvest too late, you might be dealing with honey that the bees have already begun eating or honey that is too firm and solid in the honeycomb cells to extract. Late removal of honey supers can also incite robbing. The perfect time to harvest is basically when the bees give you the go-ahead to do so. That signal is indicated by the presence of white, sealed or "capped" honeycomb covering 90 to 95 percent of the frame. For the most part, honey that is not yet capped contains a moisture level greater than that pivotal 18 percent. When the bees cap over the honey, they are telling you that the moisture level is just where it needs to be to prevent the natural yeasts in the nectar from fermenting over time.

Fermented honey isn't really palatable by either humans or honeybees, so bide your time, let the bees do their thing, and extract when the proper time arrives.

In addition to determining when the honey is ready, you'll want to make sure your calendar is clear come extraction time. Depending on the method of removal you use, it's possible for the entire process to take several days. Some options, such as bee escapes (see page 327), require 36 to 48 hours to work. After you clear the supers of bees, you'll then need to schlep them to the extraction site (which should be all ready and primed for action in advance), extract the honey, bottle it, and then clean up the whole sticky mess. I say give yourself a weekend, or some similar two- to three-day stretch of time. You don't want to rush this, nor can you, really. Good things (of the sweet, sticky, oozy, delicious kind) come to those who wait.

Some for You, Some for Me

In addition to knowing *when* to extract, it's of equal importance, if not more, to be aware of just *how much* you can extract. The bees make honey for themselves. Yes, human intervention in the form of modern-day beekeeping permits them to make a surplus. However, they still need some if they are to survive during colder

months. It is necessary to leave the bees 60 to 70 pounds (27 to 32 kg) of honey for hives situated in colder climates, and 20 to 30 pounds (9 to 14 kg) for those in warmer locales. Two methods of assessing honey stores are described on page 272. When full of honey, a shallow frame should weigh roughly 3 pounds (1.4 kg), a medium frame 4 pounds (1.8 kg), and a deep frame 6 to 7 pounds (2.7 to 3.2 kg). So, let's say your honey is stored in shallow supers. Let's also say that you have 10 frames full of honey in those shallow supers. Finally, we'll add that you live in a location with cold winters. In order ensure that your bees will have adequate stores to get them through the winter, you'll need to be certain to have at least two full shallow supers (totaling 20 frames of honey) on top of the hive body. Or, say you have a medium super, also with 10 frames full of honey. That's 40 pounds (18 kg) of honey, meaning the bees will need another super with 20 to 30 pounds (9 to 14 kg) of honey in it to get through the winter. Make sense? Anything after that is gravy and is perfectly fine for you to extract.

A Helping Hand

Although it is entirely possible to extract honey with one person, an extra set of hands is invaluable. If you have a good number of supers you'll be extracting, having another person around to help you haul them to the extracting site will streamline the entire process. It also expedites things to have one person uncap frames while another works the extractor. Finally, clean up and bottling is always easier with four hands instead of two. Come extraction time, ask around. You'd be surprised at just how many people are curious about honey extraction, especially if there's an offer of a jar or two of honey in exchange for their labors. A young child or even a non-beekeeping buddy may be willing to pitch in and process the liquid gold.

Fully Equipped

Several tools are necessary in order to extract honey. Depending on the size of your operation, you'll need to decide whether or not it's worth the expense of purchasing your own equipment. For many, extraction is an endeavor done once, possibly twice, annually. If you are a hobbyist beekeeper, with fewer than 10 or so hives, it might not be worth purchasing equipment solely for personal use. Many beekeeping organizations rent out extracting gear for a very nominal fee (as mentioned previously, mine rents for a really quite reasonable fee). If you don't have a beekeeping organization in your area, but find the cost of purchasing equipment prohibitive, try to connect with other area beekeepers and see if they might be willing to loan it out to you. Offer to pay, cook them a nice dinner, babysit, pet sit, or some other skill you possess in exchange.

Uncapping Knife

Essential to your first step in extraction, an uncapping knife removes the wax caps on honeycomb cells. An electric knife provides its own heat, much like an iron. If you don't have an electric model, a simple serrated bread knife will do the trick, as long as you dip it in hot water between uses (be sure to thoroughly wipe off the water before touching the comb, though, as you don't want to introduce any outside moisture to the honey).

Uncapping Comb

Sometimes uncapping knives miss several, or many, sealed cells. You don't want to miss out on any of the honey tucked into the honeycomb. That's where an uncapping comb, also known as a scratcher or fork, comes into play. Very much resembling a long-tined hair pick, the uncapping comb is used to rake, or scratch, down the length of the frame, releasing any trapped honey. Some beekeepers prefer the uncapping comb to the knife and use it exclusively. Try both until you can determine what works best for you.

Wax Cappings Basin

As you scrape off the wax seals, you'll need somewhere to keep them. They contain an awful lot of honey, so using a wax cappings basin with a built-in strainer is ideal. The wax cappings fall off the comb as you cut them and into a tub lined with a strainer, grate, grid, colander, or similarly perforated panel. While they rest there, the honey on them drips down, collecting in the lower basin. Ideally, this tub will have a spigot, allowing for easy removal of the honey collected at the bottom of the tub when you're finished uncapping frames.

Extractor

A device using centrifugal force to draw honey out of uncapped comb, an extractor is the best, and fastest, means of honey removal. There are as many models of extractors as there are types of beekeepers. Inexpensive, albeit less durable, extractors are usually made of plastic and are manually operated (meaning you, with your arm muscles, will be providing the centrifugal force). More rugged outfits are made of stainless steel, available with or without electric motors. Again, assess your needs, finances (the more powerful, mechanized models can cost hundreds of dollars), and resources communally available, and select the extractor that best suits your purposes.

Bottling Bucket/Dispenser

During extraction, honey will flow out of a spigot on the extractor and into a collection vessel. Ideally, this container will have a spigot itself, so that, come bottling time, dispensing honey into jars can be handled with ease. Your collection vessel should be either food-grade plastic or stainless steel. Available for purchase from beekeeping suppliers, 5-gallon (19 L) lidded bottling buckets will hold around 60 pounds (27 kg) of honey. After extraction, be sure to place a lid over your collected honey. Its inherent hygroscopic properties can pull ambient moisture from the atmosphere, possibly resulting in fermentation.

Filter/Strainer

Before you can bottle up your sticky sweet abundance, you'll need to filter it, removing any extraneous debris. Beeswax, bits of wood from the frames, even, sadly, bee parts can all potentially wind up in the honey. A fine mesh filter does this job expertly. Available from beekeeping suppliers, filters intended expressly for honey fit over the top of honey bottling buckets. It's also possible to use other sorts of meshed sieves, provided they are large enough (plastic paint strainers available from paint stores work well). Honey flows pretty fast when it's coming out of the bottling dispenser. Use too small a filter and you may end up with a sticky mess of honey overflow.

so wear protective gear, too, from head to toe. You'll also need a bee-tight receptacle to store the frames or supers as you collect them. If you're extracting from just a few frames, large, plastic tubs or containers with tight-fitting lids will work. If you're removing full supers, you'll need bee-tight covers on both the top and bottom of the super. Use either two pieces of plywood, plywood on the bottom and a heavy cloth on top, or painter's plastic above and below. Whatever you choose, just be sure it's sturdy enough to securely keep bees out.

Shaking or Brushing

A bee brush or your gloved hands are all you need for this low-tech means of removing bees from the hive. Hold a frame by the ends of the top bar, and then gently shake or brush bees off of each individual frame in front of the hive entrance. Then place the cleared frames in an empty, waiting super, and cover with a bee-tight top and bottom. Repeat the process until you've gone through each frame bound for extraction. This means of removal works fine if you've only got a hive or two. Bigger bee yards necessitate other evacuation plans, as shaking or brushing is a time-consuming endeavor. If you opt to remove bees using a bee brush, be sure to start at the bottom of each frame and move upward. Stroking the brush in a downward motion can injure or even kill bees working inside cells due to the inherent downward slant of honeycomb cells.

Escape Plan

When harvesting time comes, you'll need to remove the bees from the supers you intend to extract. You've got a number of different evacuation options. Read them over and see what seems like the best fit for your situation. Ask fellow beekeepers their preferred method, as well—most will be all too willing to opine. Whichever you choose, fire up your smoker first and give the hive a gentle smoking (not too much, or you may affect the flavor of the honey). The bees aren't especially pleased when honey is removed,

If removing bees with a brush, be sure to brush upward.

Blowing

Using either a specialized bee blower (available for purchase from beekeeping suppliers) or a basic backyard leaf blower, this means of removal essentially blasts the bees out of the hive. Remove the supers intended for extraction, and move them, bees and all, about 20 feet (6 m) from the entrance to the hive. Place the supers sideways on or directly beside whatever you intend to use for transport, be that a car, wheelbarrow, wagon, or what have you. Then engage the blower and point it directly toward the supers, where it will forcibly blow the bees out and away. Bees don't like this, mind you. Should our situations find themselves reversed, I don't imagine I'd like being blasted away from my home either. That said, blowing as a means of removal can be highly efficacious if you've got a load of supers to attend to. Remember to cover the supers with bee-proof tops and bottoms once cleared of bees, and then place them in whatever you'll be transporting them in straightaway.

Bee Escape

Another means of clearing bees out of supers bound for extraction, bee escapes are devices added to the hive. They allow bees to head down and out of the hive, but not back in the same way, at least, not right away. It takes about 36 to 48 hours for bee escapes to successfully vacate a super. However, it takes right around that same time frame for bees, clever creatures that they are, to figure out how the escape works and return. So, if you intend to use a bee escape, know in advance that you'll be making two trips out to your bee yard—first to install the bee escape, and then another, a few days later, to remove it.

Though beekeepers have utilized bee escapes of varying styles for years, two models are the most frequently used in modern beekeeping: the Porter bee escape and the triangular escape. Porter escapes, made of either plastic or metal, are placed over the inner cover opening. The inner cover, with the Porter escape in place, is then situated between the supers bound for extraction and those that will remain in place. Triangular escapes consist of a wooden cover with two, interlocking sets of triangles in the center, which are covered over with wire mesh. Like the Porter escape, it is situated in between supers with honey to be extracted and those that will be left with the bees. Both models work in the manner detailed above, permitting bees to move down to lower supers and out of the hive, but not back up into the honey supers. Porter escapes cost less than their triangular cousins; however, their design, which enables only one bee at a time to exit, can cause clogging, making evacuation of the super more drawn out.

If any brood is present in the frames, a good number of the bees will not leave. You can prevent the queen from

Triangular bee escape

laying brood in honey supers by installing queen excluders in those hives for which you intend to use bee escapes come extraction time. When using bee escapes, make sure all upper entrances to hives, such as those found on the side panels of inner covers, are closed off and that the outer cover is firmly in place. Over the course of several days, opportunistic bees from other colonies can rob supers full of honey while you are waiting for your bee escape to take full effect. When you return to the hive to gather up the honey supers, simply brush off any bees still clinging to the frames. Remove the full super, cover the top and bottom with a bee-tight cover, place it on whatever means of transport you will be employing, and proceed until finished. Remove the bee escape, replace the inner cover to the hive, and top off with the outer cover.

Bee escapes are most effective when evenings are still somewhat cool, which entices bees to move down to the brood box to keep warm. If you find you need to harvest honey while nights are still warm, bee escapes may not be the best means of getting the bees to evacuate. Bees in upper supers have no real incentive to move down then. On those occasions, you want to look into other means of evacuating supers.

Fume Board

A final option for removing bees from supers intended for extraction is the use of a fume board. These boards employ the use of an airborne repellent to move bees off of supers. They resemble outer covers, with the exception that their interior is lined with an absorbent material, such as flannel. To use a fume board, begin by smoking the hive gently. Remove the outer and inner cover. Sprinkle about 1 tablespoon (you needn't measure this, just be judicious and eyeball the amount you dispense) of your repellent of choice (more about repellent options ahead) evenly over the absorbent side of the fume board. Place it atop the topmost honey super, and leave it in position for three to four minutes. This is usually all it takes for the bees to move down into the next super. Take off the fume board,

Fume board

and confirm that the bees have left the super. Remove the super, seal it on the top and bottom with a bee-proof cover, and move it to whatever means of transport you will be using. Move on to the next super, repeating the process until complete. A sunny day is ideal for this operation, as the sun's warmth enhances the repellent's abilities.

There was a time when the only repellent options were highly noxious, hazardous to the bees and environment at large, and, well, just plain smelly. Included in this category are repellents such as benzaldehyde and butric anhydride (in the form of "Bee Go"). Not only do the bees loathe the smell of these chemicals, so will you. If you get a drop on any of your protective gear, consider them history. You'll never want to smell them again. Fortunately, a new repellent utilizes natural oils and herbs with results just as good as its toxic forebears. Known as Bee Quick, this natural repellent safely evacuates bees (who find its scent distasteful, but not harmful), while smelling pleasantly of almonds to human noses.

Comb honey

Chunk honey

Extracted honey

Whipped honey

STYLES OF HONEY

Most commonly found in its runny, liquid incarnation, there are actually several styles of the beloved sweet stuff. For the beekeeper just getting started, you'll probably want extracted honey, as navigating both the equipment and the technique used in harvesting comb honey are concepts better grasped once the more rudimentary aspects of beekeeping are learned. I recommend saving comb honey extraction for your second year.

Comb Honey

This style of honey is extracted exactly as the bees made it, comb and all. To collect the comb, beekeepers may either simply cut the entire portion out of a frame and then section it up (remember to remove the foundation wire), or use special frames intended for the formation of individualized sections of comb and honey. If you are using a top bar hive, comb honey is your only option. Carefully remove the capped honeycomb, cut it free of the top bar and move on to your packaging options.

Chunk Honey

A little bit of both, chunk honey combines comb and extracted honey. A sizable bit of comb is added to a jar and then topped off with liquid honey. Chunk honey offers something for every honey-loving palate.

Extracted Honey

Perhaps the best known form of honey, extracted honey is the liquid portion removed from uncapped frames. By far the most economical means of production, extracted honey allows for comb-filled frames to be returned to the hive after extraction, saving the bees the work of fashioning it again.

Whipped Honey

Honey is a completely saturated solution, meaning that it contains more dissolved sugar than can normally remain in solution form. Accordingly, this solution is quite unstable and, in time, looks to rebalance itself. Over time, the excess glucose in honey separates out, forming granulated crystals. Whipped honey is simply a method of controlling this crystallization, rendering a smooth, spreadable substance out of the granules. If you have honey that has crystallized, becoming a thick, solid, grainy substance, mix one part of it with nine parts liquid honey to create homemade whipped honey.

Extraction Action

2 · Position a frame over the wax cappings basin.

Most of these basins will have the point of a small nail sticking out from a strip of wood running the length of the tub. Holding a frame from the one end of the top bar, place the opposite end onto this nail point. The nail helps to hold the frame in place as you slice off the wax. It also helps you swing the frame back and forth, accessing both sides with ease. Lacking this, simply position your frame over whatever you are using to cap wax cappings, and hold the frame as steady as possible.

Once you've determined an appropriate extraction location, gathered up all the necessary equipment (and extra sets of hands, if at all possible!), and evacuated the bees from the hive, now it's time to get down to business. The amount of time the entire endeavor will take depends completely on the number of frames you'll be extracting from. Plan on at least several hours from first frame uncapped to cleanup completion.

3 · Working from top to bottom, remove the white cappings with your uncapping knife.

Use a gentle back-and-forth sawing motion, holding the knife against the wax comb as you run it the entire length of the frame. Repeat on the other side. Hold the frame at such an angle that the wax cappings fall down into the tub below.

1 · Begin by preheating your uncapping knife.

If you are using an unheated knife, remember to dip it in hot water between uses and wipe off any water remaining on the blade. Position a bottling bucket/dispenser topped with a filter/strainer beneath the spigot of the extractor.

4 If, after using the knife, any cells of honeycomb remain uncapped, **use the uncapping comb to break them open.**

5 **Place the uncapped frame vertically into the extractor.**

Repeat with the remaining frames until you've used them all or the extractor is filled. Depending on your model, your extractor might hold only two to four frames, or many, many more. Some models are also reversible, wherein baskets inside the extractor pivot the frames, extracting from both sides; with nonreversible models you'll need to manually lift and flip around the frames in order to remove honey from the opposite side. Finally, your model may be hand-cranked or electric. Based on the specifics of the model you are using, fill your extractor evenly (much like a washing machine, if the frames aren't evenly distributed, the extractor will become unbalanced and wobble), spacing frames across from each other to spread out the weight.

6 **Slowly begin to extract, gradually increasing the speed.**

The centrifugal force will begin literally flinging the honey out of the comb and onto the extractor walls. From there, it will drip down and out of the spigot into the bottling bucket/dispenser positioned below. If you are using a nonreversible model, you will need to flip the frames halfway through the process, extract on the other side, and then repeat again on the other side. If you are using a hand-cranked model, you will need to stop at some point and drain off some of the honey into the bottling bucket and filter below; otherwise, it will pool in the bottom, blocking the extractor's ability to spin with ease. Don't wait too long in a two-frame extractor to reverse the frames. The weight of the inner side can cause the emptying side to crack in half. You may have to do the reversing process several times.

7

When the spinning becomes audibly lighter and no more honey seems to be coming out of the frames, stop the extractor.

Remove the frames from the extractor, put them back into an empty super, and place the super outside for the bees to clean.

8

Place a lid over the filtered honey bucket to prevent moisture, dust, or other ambient debris from entering, and leave the newly extracted honey to settle for around 24 hours or so.

This gives time for any air bubbles inside the honey to rise to the top of the bottling bucket, keeping them out of jars once bottled.

9

Clean your extracting equipment thoroughly with hot water and dish soap.

If you borrowed or rented the equipment, you'll want to be sure to return it just as clean as you received it. Once the frames are emptied of honey, put them back into empty supers and return the supers to the hive. Place them on top of an inner cover that has a hole in the center. Put the outer cover on and leave on for three to four days, then remove the cleaned and dried-out supers. The bees will slurp up any remaining droplets.

10

Bottle and label your honey.

Labels are available through beekeeping equipment suppliers, or you can use those found in craft stores or online, through sites such as Etsy.

A variety of honey containers

THE HONEY LARDER

Honey quality changes over time. The temperature at which it is stored, along with how long it is kept, can help to extend its integrity. Ideally, unprocessed, raw honey should be kept below 57°F (14°C). At higher temperatures, honey stored for any lengthy period of time will begin to granulate. While certainly not harmful, granulation can make honey somewhat less attractive, which is really only an issue if you intend to sell it. Light, either natural or artificial, can also compromise honey taste and texture, so store in a darkened area. A basement would be ideal. Lacking that, store it in the coolest area in your home.

A wealth of containers are available for bottling honey. From simple mason jars to small hexagonally shaped glass vessels to plastic honey bears and beyond, come jarring time you won't suffer from a lack of options. If you intend to offer your honey only to yourself, your friends, and your family, then repurposing any clean, crack-free glass container is fine (plastic will work too, provided it contains absolutely no residual smells or residues, as plastic containers sometimes can; give it a thorough cleaning in a dishwasher first). Be certain to use clean, odor-free lids; this is not the place for pickle jar tops, as the scent will permeate the honey.

If you'd like to sell your honey to the general public, you'll need to use newly purchased, sterilized jars. Beekeeping suppliers carry a range of bottle varieties for purchase. You can also find a treasure trove of options from companies

Cold Storage

Once you have finished extraction for the year, you'll need to store your honey supers in a cold, safe, secure area, far from the reaches of bacteria, fungi, and wax moths. These moths, which we discussed in detail in chapter 9, can seriously wreak havoc in a hive. How to safely store the supers, then?

If you've used a queen excluder, never allowing the queen to lay brood in your honey supers, the moths don't seem to really be a problem. When the season is over, store the extracted honey supers on a flat surface. This can be done either indoors or outdoors; whichever you choose, the environment needs to be cold and exposed to air. To store, stack the empty supers at 90° angles, one atop the other. If storing outdoors, make sure the supers are in a location with an overhead cover, keeping them protected from rain or snow.

Should mice be of concern in your storage area, once you've found a level surface, stack the hives directly on top of each other and cover with an outer cover. The cover keeps out mice while the cold temperatures keep bacteria, fungi, or wax moth larvae (should they have managed to access your supers) from growing. Storing the supers with the frames in transparent trash bags (also in an unheated area) would also work well, as the wax moths don't like light.

selling glass bottles online. One of my favorites is the Muth jar, named after its creator, Charles Muth of Cincinnati, Ohio. Square vessels with cork tops and skep scenes embossed onto their fronts, Muth jars harken back to the 1800s, imparting a bit of nostalgia, whimsy, and beauty to modern honey.

No matter what style of bottle you use, remember to let your honey rest for at least 24 hours after extraction. This step allows air bubbles to rise to the surface, preventing them from flowing into the jars and rising to the top, producing foam. Although not in the least bit harmful, the presence of foam could incur a bit of unfounded worry in your customer. Be sure to place lids onto the honey-filled bottles just as soon as you finish adding the honey to them. You want to limit the honey's exposure to air, which could introduce undesirable moisture.

HONEY MONEY

If you plan on selling your honey, keep in mind that honey is a food. As such, it falls under the same regulations governing other foods sold to the public at large. Standards on what is or isn't required will vary widely by locality, so check with your governing food regulatory agency (such as the Department of Agriculture in the United States, which has individual state outposts) to learn what rules govern your area. For the most part, though, labels must contain the following information:

- The word "Honey" must be very visible.
- The weight needs to be indicated.
- The method of processing, or lack thereof, should be detailed (this includes designations such as "pasteurized," "unheated," "untreated," "raw," "natural," or "unfiltered").
- Your name and address need to be listed.

When it comes time to start selling, cast your net wide. From Web-based food and craft sites to natural food stores and farmers' markets, many opportunities exist for finding an audience for your precious honey. In my area, a good number of restaurants feature locally produced honey in their dishes. You could even pair up with cottage businesses making homemade honey-based body care products as a supplier. Small boutiques selling food, home, and gift items would be worth contacting, as well. See if you can sell some at your children's school. The options for selling your honey are limited only by your imagination.

WHAT'S IN A NAME

Organic? Orange Blossom? Lavender? In order to call your honey any of these things, or any other highly specific designation, you'll have to prove it—which isn't always easy to do. If you intend to market your honey as coming from a certain flower, you might need to have a pollen analysis performed. It might be obvious that your honey

Properly labeled honey for sale

Lavender honey

was sourced from heather if the hive happens to be sited within a large tract of land planted with heather. Bear in mind, however, that bees travel quite far in their quest for nectar. If you're uncertain what flowers they paid a visit to, then simply calling it "wildflower honey" may be the best option.

Organic certification is even more difficult than varietal designation. Certified organic honey must come from crops that have not been treated with pesticides. Even if you're growing organically, it's entirely possible that your neighbor isn't. Unless you own all of the area within a bee's foraging radius (about 5 miles [8 km]), there's no way to be sure the bees haven't gathered nectar from treated plants. Regulations overseeing organic certification vary widely from one locality to the next. Check with your governing food regulatory agency to determine what is required in your area.

SWEET REWARDS

While honey presents its own tasty appeal, several other treasures can also be gathered from a thriving hive. Beeswax, pollen, propolis, and royal jelly benefit both honeybees and humans alike. Beeswax can be endered into a multitude of useful items, while the other hive products offer numerous health benefits.

Beeswax is another valuable hive by-product.

Wound Care

In addition to being both delicious and nutritious, honey has a number of beneficial medicinal properties. As part of its chemical composition, honey contains hydrogen peroxide, as well as a number of antibacterial phytochemicals. Furthermore, the fact that it is such a supersaturated solution creates a high degree of osmolality, meaning that water cannot freely move into an area where honey is present, thereby preventing the spread of microorganisms potentially present in water. These natural antimicrobial properties make honey an ideal candidate for use in wound care.

A dab of honey, added to a dressing, can then be applied directly over a wound. The amount of honey to be applied depends largely on how intensely the wound is weeping fluid; the greater the weeping, the greater the amount of honey necessary. Honey is also quite beneficial when applied to minor burns. Of course, those infected wounds or those of extreme severity should be examined by a physician.

HEALTH FROM THE HIVE

We all know that honey tastes good—really good. What's even better is how good it is for us. Honey, as well as other products from the beehive, are nutrient powerhouses, chock-full of goodness. Here's a look at some of the vitamins, minerals, and other nutritional offerings available from consuming honey, pollen, propolis, and royal jelly.

Honey
Vitamins A, C, D, E, K, beta-carotene, B-complex vitamins (all of them), calcium, chlorine, copper, iodine, iron, magnesium, manganese, phosphorus, potassium, sodium, sulfur, and zinc

Pollen
All essential amino acids, vitamins C and E, beta-carotene, B-complex vitamins (all of them), calcium, copper, iron, magnesium, manganese, phosphorus, potassium, zinc, trace minerals, rutin, lecithin, and lycopene

Propolis
Vitamin A, biotin, calcium, cobalt, copper, iron, magnesium, manganese, niacin, potassium, phosphorus, riboflavin, silica, thiamine, and zinc

Royal Jelly
Vitamins A, C, D, and E, adenine, biotin, cobalamin, folic acid, inositol, calcium, chromium, iron, magnesium, niacin, phosphorus, potassium, pyridoxine, riboflavin, silicon, sulfur, thiamine, and zinc

Notes

BEE CARE CHECKLIST

Care for honeybees is largely influenced by the changing seasons. Knowing what to do and when is essential for proper stewardship of your buzzing beauties. Here I've provided a seasonal listing of tasks, duties, activities, and such. I'd suggest making a copy, placing it in a plastic sleeve, and attaching that sleeve to the underside of your hive's outer cover for safekeeping and easy reading.

Spring

EARLY

- Look inside only on warm, sunny days.
- Check for eggs, uncapped and capped brood, and the presence of a queen.
- Begin supplemental feeding if food stores are low; continue until an active nectar flow occurs.
- Remove mouse guard and entrance reducers.
- Install queen excluder, if using, over brood box.
- Add supers as soon as brood box is full of bees.
- Continue adding supers as each new one fills with honey or bees.
- Begin weekly inspections in mid-spring, checking for swarm cells.
- Remove and replace old frames and foundation.
- Make splits as needed.
- Requeen or allow natural supersedure as necessary.

LATE

- Reverse hive bodies.
- Determine what swarm-capturing method you will use, in the event that it should occur.
- If an intense nectar flow happens, a late spring honey extraction may be necessary.
- Plant honeybee-loving plants near your hive and around your property.
- Examine varroa mite population and treat as desired.

Summer

- Inspect the hive every week, monitoring the queen's activities, honey production, and presence of any swarm cells. Look for eggs, larvae, and other indications of active laying.
- Continue adding supers as needed, both for honey as well as for brood.
- Be prepared to extract, most likely in late summer.
- Be prepared to offer sugar syrup should your area experience atypical weather, such as a drought, unseasonably cool temperatures, or excessive rainfall, as such situations may affect the bees' access to nectar sources.
- Install the entrance reducer if robbing evidences or wasps or yellow jackets attempt to gain entry.
- Examine varroa mite population and treat as desired.

Autumn

- Check in on the hive every two weeks. Stop inspections completely once the temperature drops below 50 to 55°F (10 to 13°C) during the day.
- Check for the presence of a queen. Look for eggs, capped and uncapped brood, and a good laying pattern.
- Check on capped honey stores. If they are low, you will need to feed supplementally. Stop all feeding by late autumn.
- Tilt hives slightly forward to allow rain and snow to run off.
- Ventilate inner cover.
- Remove queen excluder, if using.
- Remove hive-top feeder, if using, and replace inner cover.
- Install a mouse guard.
- Install entrance reducer, if not already using.
- Secure hives with either a large, heavy rock atop the outer cover or a strap running the circumference of the hive (from side to side, not from entrance to rear).
- Wrap hives with black roofing tar paper if you live in an area experiencing severe winters, where temperatures remain below freezing for months.
- Store empty honey supers in a secure location.

Winter

- Check the bee yard regularly for damage caused by storms or predator animals.
- Check that mouse guards are still in place.
- Check food stores by lifting hive to determine weight. Consider supplemental feeding if necessary.
- If no water source is available nearby (such as a creek or river), provide unfrozen water; be sure to place it in a sunny location.
- Gently tap on the side of the hive to hear buzzing (an indication that the hive is alive).
- Order more frames and supers, or other equipment, as needed.
- Continue reading and learning about honeybees.

Metric Conversion Charts

Metric Conversion Chart by Volume (for Liquids)

U.S.	Metric (milliliters/liters)
¼ teaspoon	1.25 mL
½ teaspoon	2.5 mL
1 teaspoon	5 mL
1 tablespoon	15 mL
¼ cup	60 mL
½ cup	120 mL
¾ cup	180 mL
1 cup	240 mL
2 cups (1 pint)	480 mL
4 cups (1 quart)	960 mL
4 quarts (1 gallon)	3.8 L

Cooking Measurement Equivalents

3 teaspoons = 1 tablespoon

2 tablespoons = 1 fluid ounce

4 tablespoons = ¼ cup

5 tablespoons + 1 teaspoon = ⅓ cup

8 tablespoons = ½ cup

10 tablespoons + 2 teaspoons = ⅔ cup

12 tablespoons = ¾ cup

16 tablespoons = 1 cup

48 teaspoons = 1 cup

1 cup = 8 fluid ounces

2 cups = 1 pint

2 pints = 1 quart

4 quarts = 1 gallon

Temperature Conversion

Fahrenheit	Celsius
32°	0°
212°	100°
250°	121°
275°	135°
300°	149°
350°	177°
375°	191°
400°	204°
425°	218°

Metric Conversion Chart by Weight (for Dry Ingredients)

U.S.	Metric (grams/kilograms)
¼ teaspoon	1 g
½ teaspoon	2 g
1 teaspoon	5 g
1 tablespoon	15 g
16 ounces (1 pound)	450 g
2 pounds	900 g
3 pounds	1.4 kg
4 pounds	1.8 kg
5 pounds	2.3 kg
6 pounds	2.7 kg

Altitude Adjustment Chart

Altitude Variations for Boiling Water Bath Processing

Altitude in Feet (Meters)	Processing Time
0–1,000 (0–300 m)	Time in recipe
1,001–3,000 (301–900 m)	Add 5 minutes
3,001–6,000 (901–1,800 m)	Add 10 minutes
6,001–8,000 (1,801–2,400 m)	Add 15 minutes
8,001–10,000 (2,401–3,000 m)	Add 20 minutes

Altitude Variations for Pressure Canning Processing

Altitude in Feet (Meters)	Weighted Gauge	Dial Gauge
0–1,000 (0–301 m)	10	11
1,001–2,000 (301–600 m)	15	11
2,001–4,000 (601–1,200 m)	15	12
4,001–6,000 (1,201–1,800 m)	15	13
6,001–8,000 (1,801–2,400 m)	15	14
8,001–10,000 (2,401–3,000 m)	15	15

Resources

KEEPING CHICKENS

POULTRY AND SUSTAINABLE LIVING MAGAZINES

Backyard Poultry
http://countrysidenetwork.com
/category/daily/poultry/

Fancy Fowl (UK)
http://www.fancyfowl.com

Grit
www.grit.com

Hobby Farms
www.hobbyfarms.com

Living the Country Life
www.livingthecountrylife.com

Mother Earth News
www.motherearthnews.com

Poultry Press
www.poultrypress.com

Practical Poultry (UK)
http://www.practicalpoultry.com

POULTRY INFORMATION WEBSITES

BackyardChickens.com
www.backyardchickens.com

An extremely comprehensive site, with information for the novice and the experienced flock owner alike

ThePoultrySite.com
www.thepoultrysite.com

A website dedicated to information regarding poultry health

TheCityChicken.com
http://thecitychicken.com

A site for all things related to urban chicken enthusiasts

FeatherSite
www.feathersite.com

Comprehensive website with information on various types of poultry, with videos, photographs, and extensive zoological information

Poultry One
poultryone.com

This site contains articles, research, and a wealth of information for poultry enthusiasts.

Chicken Feed
lionsgrip.com/chickens.html

A highly informative site all about chicken feed, with information ranging from how to make your own feed to antiquated and traditional modes of feeding poultry. Also contains a state-by-state listing of organic feed producers.

HATCHERIES AND SUPPLIERS

Belt Hatchery
7272 S. West Avenue
Fresno, CA 93706
559-264-2090
www.belthatchery.com

Cackle Hatchery
P.O. Box 529
Lebanon, MO 65536
417-532-4581
www.cacklehatchery.com

Decorah Hatchery
406 W. Water Street
Decorah, IA 52101
563-382-4103
www.decorahhatchery.com

Double R Supply
5156 Minton Road Northwest
Palm Bay, FL 32907
dblrsupply.pinnaclecart.com

Egganic Industries
3900 Milton Highway
Ringgold, VA 24586
800-783-6344
www.henspa.com

Eggcartons.com
9 Main Street, Suite 1F
P.O. Box 302
Manchaug, MA 01526-0302
888-852-5340
Containers for selling and marketing eggs

Eglu
646-434-1104
www.omlet.us
Home of the Eglu housing unit

Estes Hatchery
805 N. Meteor Avenue
P.O. Box 5776
Springfield, MO 65802
800-345-1420
www.esteshatchery.com

Hoover's Hatchery
205 Chickasaw Street
Rudd, IA 50471-5025
800-247-7014
www.hoovershatchery.com

Meyer Hatchery
626 State Route 89
Polk, OH 44866
888-568-9755
www.meyerhatchery.com

My Pet Chicken
501 Westport Avenue #311
Norwalk, CT 06851
888-460-1529
www.mypetchicken.com

Nasco Farm & Ranch
901 Janesville Avenue
P.O. Box 901
Fort Atkinson, WI 53538-0901
800-558-9595
www.enasco.com/farmandranch/

Privett Hatchery
P.O. Box 176
Portales, NM 88130
877-PRIVETT
www.privetthatchery.com

Sand Hill Preservation Center
1878 230th Street
Calamus, IA 52729
563-246-2299
www.sandhillpreservation.com
Purveyors of endangered and heirloom breeds

Welp Hatchery
P.O. Box 77
Bancroft, IA 50517
800-458-4473
www.welphatchery.com

Canning & Preserving

JARS, LIDS, WATER BATH CANNERS, PRESSURE CANNERS, FOOD MILLS, STRAINERS, AND TOOLS

Canning Pantry
800-285-9044
www.canningpantry.com

Jarden Home Brands/Bernardin Ltd.
800-240-3340
www.freshpreserving.com or
www.homecanning.com/can (Canada)

Kitchen Krafts
800-298-5389
www.kitchenkrafts.com

Lehman's
877-438-5346
www.lehmans.com

Leifheit Jars
www.householdessential.com

Weck Jars
www.weckjars.com

Spices and Herbs

Frontier
www.frontiercoop.com

Mountain Rose Herbs
www.mountainroseherbs.com

Penzeys
www.penzeys.com

Simply Organic
www.simplyorganicfoods.com

Vinegar

Bragg Health Products
www.bragg.com

Eden Organic
www.edenfoods.com

Spectrum
www.spectrumorganics.com

Sugar

Florida Crystals
www.floridacrystals.com

Wholesome Sweeteners
www.wholesomesweeteners.com

Pectin

Pomona's Universal Pectin
www.pomonapectin.com

Pickling and Kosher Salt

Morton Canning and Pickling Salt
www.mortonsalt.com

Mrs. Wages Canning and Pickling Salt
www.mrswages.com

FARMERS' MARKETS AND U-PICK

Local Harvest
www.localharvest.org

A comprehensive U.S. listing of farmers' markets

Pick Your Own
www.pickyourown.org

U.S. and international listings of U-pick farms

PERIODICALS

The following publications often contain useful information on home preserving:

Grit
www.grit.com

Hobby Farms Home
www.hobbyfarms.com

Mother Earth News
www.motherearthnews.com

Home Dairy

CHEESE MOLDS, CHEESE PRESSES, CULTURES, MOLD POWDERS, LIPASE, RENNET, AND BEYOND

CANADA

Glengarry Cheesemaking and Dairy Supply Ltd.
888-816-0903
www.glengarrycheesemaking.on.ca

UNITED KINGDOM

Ascott Smallholding Supplies, Ltd.
0845-130-6285
http://www.ascott-dairy.co.uk

Moorlands Cheesemakers
0174-985-0108
www.cheesemaking.co.uk

UNITED STATES

Caprine Supply
913-585-1191
www.caprinesupply.com

Hoegger Supply Company
800-221-4628
http://hoeggerfarmyard.com

Leeners
800-543-3697
www.leeners.com

Lehman's
888-438-5346
www.lehmans.com

New England Cheesemaking Supply Company
413-628-3808
www.cheesemaking.com

The Beverage People
800-544-1867
www.thebeveragepeople.com

The Cheesemaker
414-745-5483
www.thecheesemaker.com

Live Kefir Grains

Cultures for Health
800-962-1959
www.culturesforhealth.com

Happy Herbalist
888-425-8827
www.happyherbalist.com

Organic Cultures
231-269-3261
www.organic-cultures.com

Raw Milk

A Campaign for Real Milk
202-363-4394
http://www.realmilk.com/real-milk-finder

Spices and Herbs

Frontier Natural Products Co-op
800-669-3275
www.frontiercoop.com

Mountain Rose Herbs
800-879-3337
www.mountainroseherbs.com

Penzeys Spices
800-741-7787
www.penzeys.com

Simply Organic
800-437-3301
www.simplyorganicfoods.com

Vinegar

Bragg Health Products
800-446-1990
www.bragg.com

Eden Organic
888-424-3336
www.edenfoods.com

Spectrum
800-434-4246
www.spectrumorganics.com

PERIODICALS

The following publications often contain useful information on home dairy-making:

Culture
www.culturecheesemag.com

Grit
www.grit.com

Hobby Farms Home
www.hobbyfarms.com/hobby-farm-home-portal.aspx

Mother Earth News
www.motherearthnews.com

Urban Farming
www.hobbyfarms.com

Keeping Bees

SUPPLIERS

Bee Commerce
11 Lilac Lane
Weston, CT 06883
www.bee-commerce.com

Betterbee
8 Meader Road
Greenwich, NY 12834
800-632-3379
www.betterbee.com

Brushy Mountain Bee Farm
610 Bethany Church Road
Moravian Falls, NC 28654
800-233-7929
www.brushymountainbeefarm.com

Dadant and Sons
51 South 2nd
Hamilton, IL 62341
888-922-1293
www.dadant.com

Long Lane Honey Bee Farms
14556 N. 1020 E. Road
Fairmount, IL 61841
www.honeybeesonline.com

Mann Lake
510 S. 1st Street
Hackensack, MN 56452-2589
800-880-7694
www.mannlakeltd.com

Miller Bee Supply
496 Yellow Banks Road
North Wilkesboro, NC 28659
888-848-5184
www.millerbeesupply.com

Rossman Apiaries
P.O. Box 909
Moultrie, GA 31776-0909
800-333-7677
www.gabees.com

The Walker T. Kelley Company
P.O. Box 240
807 W. Main Street
Clarkson, KY 42726
800-233-2899
www.kelleybees.com

Western Bee Supplies
P.O. Box 190
5 9th Avenue East
Polson, MT 59860
800-548-8440
www.westernbee.com

National Bee Supplies
Merrivale Road
Exeter Road Industrial Estate
Okehampton, Devon EX20 1UD
United Kingdom
+44 (0) 1837 54084
www.beekeeping.co.uk

E. H. Thorne Beehive Works
Wragby
Market Rasen LN8 5LA
United Kingdom
+44 (0)1 673-858-555
www.thorne.co.uk

HoneyBee Australis
P.O. Box 298
Ipswich, Queensland 4305
Australia
(07) 3495 7095
www.honeybee.com.au

Pender Beekeeping Supplies
28 Munibung Road
Cardiff, NSW 2285
Australia
(02) 4956 6166
www.penders.net.au

PERIODICALS

American Bee Journal
www.americanbeejournal.com

Bee Craft **(UK)**
www.bee-craft.com

Bee Culture
www.beeculture.com

Beekeepers Quarterly **(UK)**
http://beekeepers.peacockmagazines.com

ORGANIZATIONS

**American Association of
Professional Apiculturists**
http://aapa.cyberbee.net

American Beekeeping Federation
www.ABFnet.org

**International Federation of
Beekeepers' Associations**
http://www.apimondia.com/en

**African Beekeeping Resource
Centre (Kenya)**
www.apiconsult.com

**Canadian Association of Professional
Apiculturists**
www.capabees.com

British Beekeepers' Association
http://www.bbka.org.uk

**International Bee Research
Association (UK)**
http://www.ibrabee.org.uk

Apiculture New Zealand
http://apinz.org.nz

WEBSITES

Bee Source
www.beesource.com
Forums and international
supplier listings

Honeybee News
www.honeybee-news.com
International news, interviews,
and helpful links

**Harry H. Laidlaw Jr. Honey
Bee Research Facility**
beebiology.ucdavis.edu
Research facility at the University
of California at Davis

**Texas A&M University
Honey Bee Information**
honeybee.tamu.edu
Links to state beekeepers'
associations

Glossary

Acidify. The process of using vinegar or other sour ingredients to raise the level of acid in foods; this allows foods with an otherwise low acid level to be safely processed in a boiling water bath.

Acidity. Introduced via starter culture or an acidifying agent (such as vinegar), acidity refers to the percentage of lactic acid present in a dairy product at varying stages in its production. Acidity levels differ between milk, whey, and curd as a product ages. Also refers to the amount of tartness or sourness in a dairy product.

Africanized Honeybee. A race of honeybee, originating in Africa, that crossbred with feral bee populations in Brazil during the 1950s and has since crossed into North America. These bees are very defensive and known for their aggressive behavior.

Aging. Also known as "ripening," aging is used to develop flavor and texture in cheese-making. Refers to the length of time cheese is held at a specific temperature and humidity level. Fresh cheeses are, by definition, not aged.

Air sac. An airspace found inside the rounded end of a fertilized egg; it helps in retaining moisture, assisting in embryo development.

Albumen. The transparent protein surrounding an egg yolk, otherwise known as an egg white

Altitude Adjustment. The process of modifying processing times to account for variations in altitude; standard processing amounts are based on conditions at sea level or up to 1,000 feet (300 m) in elevation. As elevation increases, water boils at increasingly lower temperatures. In order to ensure that harmful bacteria are killed, processing times must be increased.

Annatto. Produced from the reddish-tinted pulp that surrounds seeds of achiote tree fruit, annatto is used to color everything from cheese to margarine and even lipstick. It mimics the yellow that would otherwise be found in the milk of grass-fed cows.

Apiary. Known also as a "bee yard," the apiary is the specific physical site of one or more beehives.

Ascorbic Acid. More commonly known as vitamin C, a water-soluble vitamin available in tablet or powdered form; ascorbic acid is used in canning to prevent discoloration of certain fruits during preparation.

Ash. Derived from dried salt and vegetables, ash creates a hospitable environment for surface mold growth, desirable in certain cheeses. Adding ash, an alkaline substance, works to neutralize the acidity found in cheese, which might otherwise slow down ripening and, consequently, flavor development.

Bantam. A small breed of chicken, whose size is roughly one-quarter that of a standard-size chicken; while most bantams are merely scaled-down versions of their larger counterparts, several breeds have no larger version and are referred to as "true" bantam breeds.

Bedding. The absorbent material used to line coop floors and nesting boxes, also referred to as "litter"

Bee Brush. A long-handled tool with gentle bristles used for delicately removing bees from a surface

Bee Escape. A device inserted between honey supers and brood chambers to remove bees from those supers bound for honey extraction

Bee Space. The area around a hive that bees naturally maintain and move between; used in determining where comb will be built. Bee space measures at least ⅜ inch (9.5 mm).

Bee Yard. Also referred to as an "apiary," the bee yard is the specific physical site of one or more beehives.

Beeswax. The product excreted by honeybees via glands in their abdomen. Used in building comb that will house brood and food.

Blanch. To drop fruits or vegetables into rapidly boiling water for a very brief time; this is done to deactivate enzymatic actions that would otherwise cause browning. Blanching also loosens peels, making them easier to remove. Blanched produce items are submerged into an ice-water bath immediately after boiling.

Bloom. The protective coating on a freshly laid egg that seals its pores, thereby keeping bacteria from getting in and moisture from escaping

Boiling Water Bath. One of the two processing methods for home canning; a boiling water bath can be used to preserve high-acid foods, including foods that have been acidified. In this method, water is brought to a boil in a large kettle or stockpot, filled mason jars with two-piece closures are submerged, and the jars are left to boil for a specific period of time. This processing method destroys yeasts, some types of bacteria, and mold, in addition to deactivating enzymes.

Bottom Board. The lowest part of a hive, essentially its "floor"

Botulism. An odorless, colorless, and potentially lethal type of food poisoning caused by the spores of *Clostridium botulinum*; they are found primarily on low-acid foods, which must be processed in a pressure canner, as this is the only way to ensure they have been destroyed. Killing botulism spores requires a higher temperature than that which can be achieved in a boiling water bath.

Breed. A group of chickens with related physical attributes, such as comb, shape, and plumage; also used as a verb to describe the act of mating between a hen and a rooster to create fertilized eggs

Brevibacterium linens. A red mold, used to create orange and yellow coloration on cheese surfaces. Often referred to as "red cultures," it develops quickly, assisting with ripening. The sulphurous aromas produced by the mold are characteristic of brick, Limburger, and Muenster cheeses.

Brine. A solution of salt and water used in making pickles; sugar and herbs are sometimes added as well.

Brining. The process of submerging cheese in a solution of salt and water. In cheese-making, brining helps flavor to develop, rinds to form, and bacterial growth to be curtailed.

Broiler. A young bird intended for table to be served in parts; also referred to as a "fryer"

Brood Box. Also referred to as a "brood chamber," "hive body," or simply a "deep," the brood box is where the queen lives, developing bees are raised, and a large part of the hive's activity takes place.

Brood. Used as a verb to describe the act of a hen sitting on eggs, attempting to hatch them, a brood is also used as a noun to describe the hatched chicks themselves. A hen either sitting or displaying characteristics of a desire

to sit is referred to as a "broody" hen. The heated enclosure used to keep chicks warm in lieu of a hen is a "brooder." Also, the term used to collectively describe all phases of immature, developing bees: eggs, larvae, and pupae.

Burr Comb. Known also as "brace" comb, this type of comb is built between frames or between frames of the hive's woodenware. Burr comb must be removed by the beekeeper before frames may be removed and manipulated.

Calcium Chloride. A liquid solution used in cheese-making when working with pasteurized and homogenized milk. Such processes impair the ability of rennet to properly coagulate when making cheese. Calcium chloride permits the formation of a firmer curd. Not necessary when working with raw milk.

Candle. A technique used to examine the contents of an egg, performed by shining bright light through it; the device used in producing light is called a "candler."

Canner. One of two pieces of equipment used in home canning; for boiling water bath processing, a kettle or large stockpot is used. For pressure canning, either a dial-gauge or weighted-gauge pressure canner is used.

Cannibalism. In relation to chickens, the acts of pecking one another's feathers, body parts, or eggs

Casein. The primary protein found in milk. Casein coagulates not via heat, but through its interaction with rennet and acids. Its presence in milk is responsible for importing structure to cheeses.

Cheddaring. A style of cheese-making, named after the village of Cheddar in Somerset County, England, from which the cheese originated. The process of

cheddaring refers to kneading curd with salt after heating and draining off whey. The curds are then cut into blocks, which are stacked onto one another and turned repeatedly until any remaining moisture is pressed out and a firm curd results.

Cheese Mat. Similar in use to cheese-boards, cheese, or "drying," mats are made of bamboo or food-grade plastic. These mats are necessary for draining cheeses such as Brie, Camembert, and Coulommiers, and also aid in the aging and air-drying process following pressing.

Cheese Molds. Used for forming curds into specific shapes, cheese molds are utilized in the final stages of cheese-making and determine the ultimate shape of a cheese. From rounds to pyramids, columns to hearts, molds come in a variety of shapes and sizes. Commercially purchased cheese molds are made from wood, stainless steel, ceramic, and food-grade plastic.

Cheese Press. Necessary when making hard cheeses, cheese presses work by applying continued pressure onto curds that have been placed into a mold. The pressure squeezes whey from the curds, forming them into a solid mass.

Cheese Salt. Flake, or cheese-making, salt is a coarse, non-iodized salt that completely dissolves in water, leaving behind no grit, grains, or residue of any kind. Iodine can kill off important cheese cultures, as well as slow down the aging process. Cheese salt is available from cheese-making suppliers; you can also use kosher or canning salt with equal success.

Cheese Trier. A tool used by cheese-makers to sample a bit of cheese from the center of a wheel to test for ripeness. Made of stainless steel and used only when making hard cheeses, the trier lets a cheese-maker check on where their cheese is at in its aging process without having to cut a wedge out of the wheel itself.

Cheese Wax. Assists in preventing hard cheeses from drying out during aging. This type of wax is made especially for use in cheese-making and is deliberately soft and pliant. In addition to preventing dryness and brittleness, wax also keeps harmful bacteria out of cheese while it is ripening.

Cheesecloth. A fine, thin woven cloth used in a number of cooking techniques; in home canning, cheese-cloth can be used for straining jelly or as a pouch for holding herbs and spices during cooking. As its name implies, cheesecloth was originally used to wrap cheeses for preserving. While still used for this purpose, depending on the cheese being made, it is more routinely used to drain whey from curds and for lining cheese molds intended for hard cheeses.

Clean Break. This refers to the state of curds when they are ready to be cut. When the curds reach the correct stage, they will break cleanly and evenly when either a thermometer, curd knife, or finger is inserted into them.

Cleansing Flight. A flight taken during warm breaks in otherwise cold weather conditions wherein honeybees relieve themselves of accumulated bodily excrement after an extended period of confinement

Cloaca. A chamber inside a chicken where the urinary, digestive, and reproductive systems meet and open to the vent

Cluster. A round, football-shaped formation that honeybees fashion around the queen during cold-weather months. Used to generate and maintain heat inside the hive.

Clutch. A group of eggs that are hatched together

Coagulation. This is the process by which milk becomes thickened, firm, and custard-like. Coagulation occurs due to interaction between milk and either rennet or an acid. Necessary for the development of curd.

Cock. A male chicken at least one year of age or older; more commonly referred to as a "rooster"

Cockerel. A male chicken less than one year old

Comb. The red, fleshy protrusion topping a chicken's head

Coop. The enclosed area in which a flock of chickens live; both indoor and outdoor quarters are often collectively referred to as the "run."

Crest. The outcropping of feathers adorning the heads of some breeds of chickens, such as Polish, Crèvecœur, Houdan, and Silkie; also called a "topknot"

Crop. A pouch inside a chicken's esophagus where food is stored and softened before moving on to the rest of the digestive system; often visible as a bulge in a chicken's chest at the end of the day

Crossbreed. A chicken whose parents are of two different breeds

Cull. The act of removing a chicken from your flock, either through butchering or relocation to another home

Cultured. Cultured dairy products are, by definition, those that have undergone fermentation. *See* Fermentation.

Curd. The solid, coagulated mass formed in milk through the interaction of rennet and bacterial cultures. Curd is largely comprised of milk protein and fat.

Dial-gauge Pressure Canner. A type of pressure canner equipped with a pressure regulator and a gauge that gives exact numeric readings of the pressure inside the canner; if the pressure is too low or too high, raising or lowering the heat level of the burner adjusts it. Dial-gauge pressure canners must be checked annually for accuracy.

Drawn comb. Comb with cells built by honeybees onto sheets of wax foundation

Drone. A male honeybee

Droppings. Chicken poop

Drying. A process used to form rind on some cheeses. Drying, or "air-drying," aids in protecting the interior of cheeses during the sometimes lengthy aging process.

Dual-purpose Breed. A type of chicken kept for both eggs and meat

Dust Bath. An area of dry, sandy soil in which a chicken will root around, spread dirt over herself, and rest; assists in killing mites and lice

DVI/Direct Set Cultures. Laboratory-born cultures containing all of the important characteristics found in traditionally made cultures without the need to first be cultured. Available in powdered form and stored in the freezer until needed, direct-set cultures are simply added to warmed milk. Many come in single-use packages, intended to work in 2 gallons (7.6 L) of milk.

Egg. The first stage in a bee's three-phase development

Embryo. An unhatched fertile egg

Entrance Reducer. A device inserted into the hive's entrance to prevent cold weather, robbing bees, or pests from gaining entry into the hive, thereby making the hive easier to defend

Exhausting. Also known as "venting," this is a necessary step in pressure canning that forces all the air inside of the canner out. Air is allowed to escape from the vent on the lid of a pressure canner for no less than 10 minutes. Failure to vent adequately could alter temperatures inside the canner and result in improperly sealed food. Exhausting must be done every time a pressure canner is used.

Extractor. A device, either manual or electric, used to remove liquid honey from wax cells

Feeder. Any of a number of devices used for providing sugar syrup to bees

Fermentation. When applied to foods, fermentation refers to the transformation of carbohydrates into alcohols and carbon dioxide (as well as other organic acids), on account of the presence of yeast and bacteria. During dairy fermentation, bacteria found in milk and air interact, turning milk sugar (or "lactose") into lactic acid. The bacteria responsible for this conversion can include *Streptococcus*, *Lactobacillus*, *Lactococcus*, and *Leuconostoc*.

Fingertip-tight. This is the tension that should be applied to screw bands when attaching them to jars. Tighten the screw band until resistance is met, then apply slightly more pressure until the band is attached only as firmly as your fingertips could easily remove it.

Flock. A group of chickens who inhabit the same living quarters

Fondant. A solid emergency food for bees made of sugar, water, corn syrup, and a thickening agent

Food Mill. A hand-cranked sieve used in cooking to purée foods; the seeds and skins of foods are collected in the top part of the sieve, while the purée accumulates in the bottom half.

Foulbrood (AFB & EFB). Bacterial diseases affecting brood. Can be life-threatening to entire hive if left unchecked. AFB is highly contagious, and any affected equipment must be burned to contain spread of the disease.

Foundation. A sheet, made of either beeswax or plastic, embossed with hexagonal cells that is positioned between the sides of a frame. Bees will build wax cells onto the hexagonal imprints, developing "drawn comb."

Frame. A rectangular structure made of either wood or plastic, which hangs from the interior of a super, upon which comb is built. An integral component of a Langstroth hive.

Free-range. Chickens permitted to forage and pasture without confinement

Fume Board. A device used to quickly remove bees from supers bound for honey extraction

Gel Stage. The point reached in the production of jams, jellies, marmalades, and butters where soft spreads gel and hold their shape; this occurs when the pectin in the mixture solidifies, usually around 220°F (104°C).

Geotrichum candidum. Used in conjunction with other molds, *Geotrichum candidum* contributes to both flavor and physical integrity during the ripening process of cheeses such as Brie and Camembert. It is also used in ripening for some goat cheeses. The mold aids in creating a neutral environment in which *Penicillium candidum* and *Brevibacterium linens* can flourish.

Gizzard. The part of a chicken's digestive system where grit is stored and food is ground down

Grease Patty. A mix of vegetable shortening and granulated sugar, often including essential oils, fed to honeybees to control tracheal mite populations

Grit. Small pebbles, sand, or other stony material eaten by chickens and used to grind up food in the gizzard

Hatch. The act of live chicks emerging from their shells

Headspace. This is the space between the top of the food in the jar and the underside of the lid. Generally, whole fruits and any pickled and acidified foods such as chutneys, relishes, pickles, condiments, and tomatoes require ½-inch (1.3 cm) headspace, while fruit spreads and juices need ¼-inch (6 mm) headspace. Providing accurate headspace is vital to creating a proper seal, as well as for keeping a jar's contents inside where they belong.

Heavy Cream. Defined in the United States as cream with a fat content between 30 and 40 percent. Also called whipping cream or heavy whipping cream.

Hen. A female chicken at least one year old

High-acid Food. Refers to foods that have enough acid, either naturally or as an added ingredient, to achieve a pH level of 4.6 or lower; many fruits are naturally high-acid; fruit juices, jams, jellies, tomatoes, and other types of soft spreads are normally high-acid as well. Most vegetables are low-acid and can only become high-acid through the addition of an acidifying agent such as vinegar or lemon juice.

Hive Body. Also referred to as a "brood box," "brood chamber," or simply a "deep," the hive body is where the queen lives, developing bees are raised, and a large part of the hive's activity takes place.

Hive Tool. A device that is flat on one end and curved on the opposite, used in opening and manipulating supers and frames

Homogenization. The process used to combine two insoluble substances into an emulsion. Homogenization punctures the butterfat particles in milk. These particles are then made small enough to no longer separate from the water found in milk, creating a uniformly distributed product.

Honey Flow. The seasonal and regional-specific periods of time when flowering plants are producing abundant amounts of nectar. This period influences the behavior of both bees and beekeeper alike.

Honey. The by-product resulting from the dehydration and enzymatic alteration by honeybees of plant nectar. A food source for both honeybees and humans.

Hot Pack. A canning method that involves cooking ingredients before placing them into jars; the hot pack method forces trapped air out of fruit or vegetable tissues before they are jarred, helping to form a tighter vacuum seal. It also prevents items from floating.

Hybrid. Chickens bred from two different breeds to produce desired characteristics, such as egg-laying ability or meat production

Incubate. The act of creating favorable atmospheric conditions for successfully hatching eggs

Inner cover. A wooden component of the hive, separating the outer cover, or uppermost portion, of the hive from the supers below

Integrated Pest Management (IPM). A style of pest control encouraging the use of non-chemical practices and preventative care to optimize hive health

Lactic Acid. An acid formed during dairy fermentation. Bacteria present in the milk and air consume milk sugar (or "lactose"), transforming it into lactic acid.

Lactose. The naturally occurring sugar found in milk. Lactose comprises anywhere between 2 and 8 percent of milk's total weight, varying between species and individuals.

Langstroth Hive. The most commonly used model of beehive. Composed of removable frames and wooden boxes.

Larva. The second stage in a bee's development. Larvae are white, shiny, grub-like organisms.

Layer. A chicken kept for purposes of egg production

Lid. One part of the two-piece closures used for topping jars in home canning; the flat lids are fashioned from tin-plated steel that has been covered in a food-grade coating. Running the circumference of the underside of the lid is a rubber compound, specially formulated for vacuum-sealing foods canned at home. Lids should be used only once.

Lipase. A type of enzyme made by certain animals (including humans) that breaks down dietary fats during digestion. In the home dairy, the role of lipase is to impart certain types of

cheeses with their characteristic strong flavors. Coupled with ripening time, lipase provides the nuanced flavors that distinguish certain cheeses.

Litter. The absorbent material used to line coop floors and nesting boxes, also referred to as "bedding"

Low-acid Food. Foods that are low in naturally occurring acid; vegetables, meats, seafood, and dairy products are low-acid and must be processed in a pressure canner in order to be safe for use in home canning. If low-acid foods are made more acidic through an acidifying agent, they can be safely canned using the boiling water bath method.

Mason Jar. A generic term now used to describe the model of jar developed by John Mason during the mid-19th century; the jars are made of tempered glass that is safe for use in either a boiling water bath or a pressure canner. Two-piece lids, which screw on to threaded rings at the neck, create a vacuum seal during processing. The jars are available in regular or wide-mouth varieties and range in size from 4 ounces to 1 gallon (120 mL to 3.8 L). So long as they remain crack-free, mason jars may be reused indefinitely.

Meal. Coarsely ground grains given as food to chickens, often with added supplements; also referred to as "ration"

Mesophilic Starter. This form of starter culture is considered "non-heat loving," meaning it doesn't do well if heated beyond 103°F (39°C). Mesophilic cultures are used to make cheeses preferring low milk and curd temperatures, such as Gouda, cheddar, and feta.

Milling. A step in the cheese-making process. Curds are broken or torn up into smaller, irregular pieces before being placed into a mold and pressed.

Mold-ripened Cheese. A type of cheese to which a specific mold has been added and encouraged to proliferate. Molds are added either internally, as in the case of blue molds, or externally, for white mold cheeses such as Brie and Camembert.

Molt. The annual shedding and renewing of feathers; done twice during a chicken's first year of life

Mouse Guard. A metal device with perforated openings installed over a hive's entrance during cooler months to keep mice out while allowing bees to come and go

Nectar. The sweet, sugar-rich liquid secreted by certain plants to attract insects for pollination; gathered by honeybees for transforming into honey

Nesting Box. The location in which a chicken lays eggs; ideally, it should be situated in the darkest, quietest part of the henhouse.

Nosema. A digestive disorder of adult honeybees caused by the protozoan *Nosema apis*

Nuc. An abbreviation for "nucleus," a small hive consisting of a queen, brood, and worker bees used for beginning new colonies

Outer Cover. The uppermost portion of a hive. Often referred to as a "telescoping" outer cover, the edges of this covering extend beyond the supers beneath it, permitting rain and snow to fall out and away from the hive.

Oviduct. A tube-shaped reproductive organ inside a hen through which eggs pass en route to the vent

Package Bees. A mesh-screen shipping container of several pounds of bees, including a mated queen and a feeder can. Used for creating new colonies.

Pasteurization. Named after French chemist and biologist Louis Pasteur, pasteurization is a process that greatly slows the growth of microbes in food. First performed in 1862, pasteurization curtails the number of pathogens likely to cause disease in foods, permitting that a product, once pasteurized, is refrigerated and consumed in an expedient manner. The process kills all bacteria in milk, which is why it is necessary to add starter culture to milk that has undergone pasteurization.

Pasting/Pasty Butt. A life-threatening condition most often affecting chicks in which the vent becomes crusted over with droppings

Pecking Order. The hierarchy naturally established within a flock of chickens

Pectin. A naturally occurring, water-soluble type of carbohydrate that is found in the tissue, skin, and seeds of all fruits; pectin reacts with sugar and acid to create a gel, or bond. Depending on whether the fruit you are using is naturally high or low in pectin, the addition of commercially prepared pectin may be necessary to achieve a gel.

Penicillium camemberti. This white mold is quite similar to *Penicillium candidum*, producing many parallels in characteristic flavor and appearance. *Penicillium camemberti*, however, is used more often in producing goat's milk (as opposed to cow's milk) soft cheeses.

Penicillium candidum. A white mold used to ripen Brie, Camembert (made with cow's milk), Coulommiers, Sainte-Maure, and some French-style goat cheeses. After it is sprayed onto the surface of the curd, it spreads and grows incredibly quickly, keeping other molds from developing in the process. It is then allowed to age, during which time its characteristic white bloomy rind forms.

Also contributes to the development of flavor during the ripening stage.

Penicillium roqueforti. A type of blue mold. Found in Stilton, Roquefort, Gorgonzola, Danablu, and other blue cheeses, the mold imparts the characteristic blue-green ripple typical of such cheeses, along with a smooth, creamy, spreadable texture. Enzymes found in *Penicillium roqueforti* are responsible for producing the pleasingly pungent flavor and aroma associated with blue cheeses. These enzymes cause the mold to grow inside of the curds, breaking down complex molecules into simple ones, changing the fibrous chemical structure into a smoother one, and imbuing it with piquant flavor and smell.

Perch. The ledge or pole on which a chicken sleeps, also called a "roost"; may also refer to the act of standing on a roost

pH. Literally the "potential of hydrogen," this measuring system is used by chemists to determine a solution's acidity or alkalinity. High pH values are low-acid, while low pH values indicate high acidity. In home canning, a food's pH value determines whether it needs to be processed in a boiling water bath or a pressure canner. Foods with a pH of 4.6 or lower are generally considered safe to can using the boiling water bath method.

Pheromone. An air- or contact-borne hormonal chemical excreted by bees to arouse certain behaviors in other bees. The "alarm" pheromone, indicating danger, "queen substance" pheromone, indicating the queen's presence in the hive, and "Nasonov gland" pheromone, indicating where a hive is located, are three examples of the numerous pheromones used by honeybees to exchange information and influence behavior.

Pickling. This is a form of food preservation in which fruits or vegetables are submerged in a high-acid solution, such as brine or vinegar, and allowed to cure, or develop flavor, over time. Often herbs and spices are added, as well as sugar.

Pickling Salt. Salt specifically indicated for home-canning use; listed in stores as either "pickling" or "kosher," these salts are free of iodine and anticaking additives and are very fine-grained, allowing them to dissolve easily.

Plumage. The feathers covering a bird's body

Point of Lay. The time at which a young female could begin laying eggs, usually around 18 weeks of age

Pollen. The dusty, powdery substance produced by the male reproductive cells of flowers and used by honeybees as a source of protein

Pollination. The act of moving pollen from a plant's anthers (pollen-producing part of a plant) to its stigma (pollen-receiving part of a plant). Honeybees, due to their physiology, are remarkably adept at pollination.

Pressing. A step in cheese-making in which pressure is applied to curds that have been added to cheesecloth-lined molds. Pressing allows any excess whey to be removed from the curds. It also causes the curds to meld into one another, producing one continuous mass. Variations in applied pressure are based on curd size and intended texture.

Pressure Canner. A tall metal pot equipped with a locking lid containing a pressure-regulating gauge; this type of canner creates steam inside the pot, allowing temperatures of 240 to 250°F (115 to 121°C) to be reached. If you intend to can any low-acid foods, then a pressure canner is absolutely essential.

Process. The term used to describe the act of preserving foods in a boiling water bath or pressure canner; heated jars are filled with foods and subjected to high temperatures for specific periods of time in order to kill off harmful molds, yeasts, bacteria, and enzymes. Processing allows foods to be safely preserved at home.

Propolis. The sticky, resinous fluid excreted by plants and gathered by honeybees; used to seal up any cracks, crevices, or openings within the hive to keep drafts and pathogens out of the hive

Proprionic shermanii. A white mold responsible for putting the holes (or "eyes"), smell, and taste into Swiss, Emmentaler, and Gruyère cheeses.

Pullet. A female chicken less than one year old

Pupa. The third and final stage of development in a honeybee's metamorphosis from egg to adult bee

Purebred. A breed that has not been crossed with any other breed; a chicken whose parents are the same breed

Queen Cage. A small, screened box used to house a queen while in transit, as well as to introduce her gradually to a colony

Queen Cell. An elongated, peanut-shaped cell, often found on the side of a frame, housing a future queen

Queen Excluder. A mesh screen used to prohibit upward movement by a queen into honey supers while permitting access to worker bees. Used to keep brood and honey separate.

Queen. A sexually developed female bee that lays eggs. Her presence, or lack thereof, regulates activity within the hive.

Ration. Coarsely ground grains given as food to chickens, often with added supplements; also referred to as "meal"

Raw Milk. Milk that has not been subjected to any processing whatsoever. Raw milk possesses a number of qualities that are otherwise destroyed or reduced during pasteurization and Homogenization, including beneficial bacteria (such as lactic acids), heat-sensitive enzymes (including lactase, lipase, and phosphatase), and vitamins A, B_6, and C (all heat-sensitive nutrients).

Raw Pack. Sometimes referred to as the "cold pack" method, raw pack involves packing jars with raw, uncooked ingredients, and then processing them. While this method is certainly faster than heat packing, it often results in foods shrinking and floating once jarred.

Rennet. A collection of naturally occurring enzymes, rennet is found in the stomach of any mammal, and is used in digesting mother's milk. One proteolytic (protein-digesting) enzyme in particular, chymosin (or rennin), coagulates milk, separating curds, or solids, from whey, the liquid portion of milk. Helpful in mammals for digestion, the role of rennet is equally important in cheese-making.

Requeen. The process of artificially introducing a new queen to a colony, wherein the former queen is replaced

Rind. The outermost layer of a cheese. Cheese rind is formed as the surface dries during aging. Harder than the interior, the rind works to seal in both moisture and flavor. While many rinds are edible, consuming them is often a matter of personal preference.

Ripening. Also known as "aging," ripening is used to develop flavor and texture in cheese-making. Refers to the length of time cheese is held at a specific temperature and humidity level. Fresh cheeses are, by definition, not ripened.

Roaster. Chickens raised for the table to be served whole

Robbing. The act of one hive stealing food from a neighboring hive. Other insects such as wasps can also perform robbing.

Roost. The ledge or pole on which a chicken sleeps, also called a "perch"; may also refer to the act of standing on a roost

Rooster. A male chicken at least one year of age or older; also referred to as a "cock"

Royal Jelly. A highly nutritious substance secreted by worker bees and fed to future queens.

Salting. A step in cheese-making in which non-iodized flake salt is added to curd. This is often done at the time of milling, before molding or pressing. Salt is also sometimes added to the surface of finished cheeses.

Scratch. Whole cereal grains fed to chickens

Screened Bottom Board. A mesh screen used in lieu of a solid bottom board for management of varroa mite populations within a hive

Screw Band. One part of the two-piece closures used for topping jars in home canning; these threaded metal bands fit atop the lids, securing them in place over the neck of the glass jar. During processing, the screw bands hold down the lids, allowing the sealing compound to secure the lid to the jar.

Sexed Chicks. Newly hatched chickens whose sex is determined prior to purchase

Shank. The lower part of a chicken's leg, located between the thigh and the foot

Shelf Life. The length of time a processed food remains good to eat; foods are their freshest and most tasty when consumed within their shelf life. In home canning, foods should ideally be eaten within one year of preparation.

Small Hive Beetle. A scavenging, small beetle that feeds on brood and food within a hive. Can be of grave concern if not managed properly.

Smoker. A device used during beekeeping inspections and frame removal to transfer cool smoke into the hive, thereby masking the alarm pheromone otherwise given off and calming the bees

Spice Bag. A fabric pouch fashioned out of either cheesecloth or muslin into which whole spices and herbs are placed; the spice bag is then placed in with the ingredients during cooking and removed before the jars are filled. Using a spice bag allows flavors to be imparted into a product without the added risk of discoloration or too strong a taste that might occur should the spices remain in the mixture once jarred.

Spur. The sharp, pointy protrusions found on the backside of a rooster's shank

Standard. A chicken meeting the ideal characteristics for its breed; also used to refer to those characteristics as described in the Standard of Perfection

Starter Culture. Bacterial cultures that consume lactose, or milk sugar, giving off lactic acid as a by-product. Lactic acid, in turn, helps to curdle milk, enabling the creation of cheese, yogurt, and a number of other home dairy items.

Sterlize. The process of killing any living organisms; in home canning, this is achieved before processing by submerging jars in boiling water for 10 minutes as well as during processing itself by placing filled jars into either a boiling water bath or a pressure canner for a specified length of time.

Straight Run. A group of newly hatched chicks whose sex is undetermined at purchase

Sugar Syrup. A fully saturated sugar and hot water mixture fed to honeybees during periods of nectar dearth or initial colony buildup

Super. The general term describing the wooden boxes used to hold frames and house colonies of bees. The combination of various supers forms a hive. Available in deep (9½-inch [24 cm]), medium (6⅝-inch [16.8 cm]), and shallow (5⅜-inch [13.7 cm]) sizes.

Supersedure. The natural formation of a new queen by worker bees; performed in order to replace an existing queen, usually due to illness, old age, or death

Swarm. A mass of unhived bees. A genetic trait of honeybees, performed for purposes of reproduction and species expansion. Swarming is an activity many beekeepers work fastidiously to prevent, so as to curtail honey production losses.

Thermophilic Starter. This form of starter culture is considered "heat loving." Thermophilic cultures can withstand temperatures of up to 132°F (56°C), making them ideal for making hard Italian cheeses, such as Parmesan and Romano, and Swiss-type cheeses.

Tracheal Mite. A microscopic parasitic mite that lives in the breathing tubes (trachea) of adult bees

Uncapping Fork. A pronged tool used in honey extraction to puncture wax cappings

Uncapping Knife. A heated, sharpened tool used to slice off sealed wax cappings from frames in order to extract the liquid honey contained inside

Vacuum Seal. The absence of normal air pressure and atmospheric conditions that happens when filled jars are heat processed; as the jars' contents are heated, they expand, forcing air out. Once cooled, the contents shrink, creating a vacuum. The rubber compound surrounding the underside of canning lids reinforces this vacuum and aids in preventing air from getting back into the jar. Vacuum sealing prevents spoilage and keeps harmful pathogens out of preserved foods.

Varroa Mite. A small parasitic mite that feeds on the haemolymph (bee blood) of both brood cells and adult bees. Potentially devastating to a hive if populations are not managed.

Veil. A protective netting covering placed over a beekeeper's head and worn during hive inspections. Permits good ventilation and vision while keeping the face safe from potential stings.

Vent. The opening at the rear of a chicken, through which eggs and excrement are eliminated

Wattles. The two red flaps of flesh dangling from either side of a chicken's chin

Weighted-gauge Pressure Canner. A type of pressure canner that is fitted with a weighted pressure adjustment; these models allow small quantities of steam to escape from the lid every time the gauge whistles or rocks back and forth during processing. Altitude adjustments must be made on weighted-gauge pressure canners, as their accuracy is affected by changes in elevation.

Worker. A sexually immature (unmated) female bee, comprising the bulk of a hive's occupants. Worker bees move through a series of duties during their lifetimes, performing all of the hive's nonreproductive functions.

Index

Note: Page numbers in *italics* indicate recipes.